THE INSIDERS' GUIDE TO

Boise
& SUN VALLEY

THE INSIDERS'® GUIDE

TO

Boise

& SUN VALLEY

by
Peter Rose
and
John Gottberg Anderson

Insiders' Publishing
105 Budleigh St.
P.O. Box 2057
Manteo, NC 27954
(252) 473-6100
www.insiders.com

Sales and Marketing:
Falcon Publishing, Inc.
P.O. Box 1718
Helena, MT 59624
(800) 582-2665
www.falconguide.com

•

FIRST EDITION
1st printing

•

Copyright ©1998
by Falcon Publishing, Inc.

•

Printed in the United States
of America

•

Publications from The Insiders' Guide®
series are available at special discounts for
bulk purchases for sales promotions,
premiums or fundraisings. Special editions,
including personalized covers, can be
created in large quantities for special
needs. For more information, please write
to Karen Bachman, Insiders' Publishing,
P.O. Box 2057, Manteo, NC 27954, or call
(800) 765-2665 Ext. 241.

ISBN 1-57380-057-0

Insiders' Publishing

Publisher/Editor-in-Chief
Beth P. Storie

Vice President/New
Business Development
Michael McOwen

Creative Services Director
Deborah Carlen

Art Director
David Haynes

Managing Editor
Dave McCarter

Regional Sales Manager
Greg Swanson

Market Manager
Nadine Buscher

Project Editor
Amy Baynard

Project Artist
Carolyn McClees

Insiders' Publishing
An imprint of Falcon Publishing Inc.
A Landmark Communications company.

Preface

You've probably heard the term sleeper: It usually refers to an underperforming racehorse that has the ability to win but is denied victory because of disposition, effort, training or extenuating circumstances. Boise is a sleeper whose time has come quite suddenly, with the turn into the last decade and its gallop into respectability, wider awareness and even envy. Part of its supremacy in an elite circle of best small American cities has to do with the desperate struggle across the country to lead a quality existence. Crowded, dirty, unsafe and lacking of job, recreational, cultural and educational opportunities — none of these applies in '90s Boise as it often does in other besieged and battered mainstream areas that grew faster and are better known.

We authors came here in recent years searching for an alternative that was farther away and unspoiled. We wanted to leave behind the soiled concrete claws of a high-price freeway existence and the madness of the melting heat of a low-desert metropolis that expands forever into scrap-iron mountains and dry rivers. The oasis effect of an overlooked green and fertile territory at the end of a barren and prickly sagebrush rainbow seduced us, as it has others. But once here, in place, we were snowed. As a visiting Midwestern football player conjectured, raising his head from the blue artificial turf at Boise State University, "There must be people up there in the white hills, skiing and sledding, and families up there with their dogs and kids, and people taking pictures, enjoying the views, and the trees and the mountains." He said this with the wonder of the deprived flatlander who could never have imagined such a panorama so near. A similar reflection came from a visiting professional ordering brewpub drinks for family and friends, shaking his head, his eyes bright and hard, his voice too loud as everything else was forgotten — "If only we could figure out a way to live here."

Boise offers the newcomer a friendly embrace, an easiness of participation in a broad range of community activities, events and programs as well as a wrap of wilderness and parklands that points to odyssey, frolic and toasted frankfurter buns. Its business circles, social cliques and governing bodies, on the other hand, are harder going. It's a kind of mirage, because one is so easy and the other may catch you in an undertow.

Familiarity and roots are as vital and enduring here as they are in the hills of West Virginia or a New England town square. A degree from Boise State University or the ownership of a farm in Burley are of far more value than graduating cum laude from Harvard or performing rare agricultural feats in Madagascar. The governor is a feisty onion farmer, the state's richest man actually does live on a towering green hill beneath a huge American flag that elicits sharp snaps like cannon shots while flapping in the wind, and an ultraconservative woman senator has inspired the bumper sticker "Can Helen Not Salmon" for her insensitivity to the environment. It's that kind of place. It's easy but rigid at the same time. The territory is wide-open in so many respects and as closed as an alligator's jaws on a poodle in others. But that is changing too, at least in outlook and intelligence that guides the public will. The ascendance of two of the best liked and most respected senators in Congress, Idahoans Kempthorne and Crapo, are good bets to guide the state's future course with the same excellent vision, care and perseverance as its past champions Andrus, Borah and Church.

So if you are moving here, expect an excellent, varied lifestyle; fantastically easy getaways to the mountains, fields, forests and streams; an enticing Old West downtown that is sprinkled more each year with shiny modern architecture; a pleasant mall; a spread of old, historic neighborhoods and new subdivisions on the outskirts; tolerable traffic and air quality; relatively crime-free streets; good food and specialty shops; and a generally positive outlook from most inhabitants.

If you are visiting you'll be surprised by the ease of partaking in a grand and diverse scale of high-quality events and activities, whether they be sports and recreation, arts or history, wildlife or science, festivals or celebrations, or merely going to restaurants and attending concerts. The Treasure Valley lives up to its name — it is a different and exciting space that you won't mistake for anywhere else. It has its old and new and wacky slant on things; its quota of refined culture and bursts of spontaneous enthusiasm; and perhaps most of all, most of the time, it has a good mood.

About the Authors

Peter Rose

Peter Rose has worked as a reporter, columnist, photographer, editor and publisher for publications in five western states.

At the *Arizona Republic*, the daily newspaper in Phoenix, Rose had writing assignments throughout the United States and in 88 foreign countries. His feature stories and "Travel Detective" columns were widely distributed by Associated Press. He won the national Harold Hirsch Ski Writer of the Year award and state press association honors.

Previously, Rose was sports editor at the *Nevada Appeal* in Carson City, Nevada; covered news, business, and entertainment for the *Gazette-Telegraph* in Colorado Springs; and at the *Republic* enjoyed meeting and writing about well-known figures in a number of fields — writers Ray Bradbury, John D. Macdonald, Paul Theroux, Elmore Leonard and Peter Jenkins; mountaineers Lou Whittaker, Lute Jerstad and Michael Covington; movie luminaries Jaclyn Smith, Chevy Chase and Bob Zemickis; ski filmmaker Warren Miller; ice skater Dorothy Hamill; archaeologist Johan Reinhard; and Arizona Gov. Bruce Babbitt (now Interior Secretary).

In Boise, Rose was on the staff of the largest Idaho daily newspaper, *The Idaho Statesman*, and the weekly *Idaho Business Review*. He published and edited a monthly publication, *Going Places*, that circulated in southern Idaho and was boarded on United Airlines flights. He also served as public information officer for Idaho at the state Capitol.

Rose has also written movie screenplays and treatments in conjunction with Los Angeles directors and producers; book manuscripts; and magazine stories.

He graduated with a journalism degree from the University of North Carolina, where he wrote for *The Daily Tar Heel* and played third base on the baseball team. Of the same age and playing the same position as his namesake, Pete Rose, he says "Obviously, I was a much better hitter." After college Rose went through two years of Army training to earn a Green Beret and served with the 10th Special Forces Group in the Bavarian Alps.

Rose's wife Natascha is an orthopaedic nurse at St. Alphonsus Regional Medical Center in Boise, where she won nurse of the year honors two of the last three years. His daughter, Sabina, is a California teacher and son, Roland, is a firefighter and ski supervisor in Oregon.

John Gottberg Anderson

Wanderlust has taken John Gottberg Anderson many times around the world, from Quito to Kyoto, Canberra to Katmandu. He has been a chef in Australia, a ski instructor in France, a musician in New Zealand, a carpenter in Sweden, a bartender in The Netherlands. But apart from those jobs, he has always been a writer. And when he moved to Boise in 1994, he found the home base he had always searched for.

Born in northern Wisconsin, the second-generation descendant of Swedish immigrants, Anderson has called the Pacific Northwest home since his family relocated to Oregon before his 10th birthday. Educated at the universities of Oregon and Washington, he worked for daily newspapers in Honolulu and Seattle before and between his peregrinations. In the wake of a fellowship in Asian studies at the University of Hawaii, Anderson became the editorial director for Apa Publications' Singapore-based series of Insight Guides (no relation to Insiders' Guides). He later returned to the United States to freelance from the Seattle area but was lured away to the bright lights of southern California, where he spent several years as the news and graphics editor for *The Los Angeles Times* travel section.

He eventually moved to Boise to resume his freelance career. Anderson is the author or coauthor of 18 other travel books, two of them on the state of Idaho, and the primary editor of another 17 books. His many magazine credits include *Travel & Leisure*, *Islands* and numerous in-flight publications. He also is a contributing editor to *International Living* magazine.

Anderson has a 13-year-old son, Erik, with whom he shared as many of his foreign and domestic travels as possible. He lives with a 2-year-old chocolate labrador, Baloo, and a 7-year-old Myers parrot, Emilie. Whenever he's home in Boise, Anderson spends as much of his free time as possible enjoying outdoor activities, especially skiing in winter, backpacking and whitewater rafting in summer. And as restaurant critic for *The Idaho Statesman*, the city's daily newspaper, he dines out regularly … although, as readers will avow, he's met many a meal he didn't like.

Photo: William H. Mullins

For a birds-eye view of Boise, fly with one of the hot air balloon companies in the area.

Get Connected

with Micron Internet Services

To get ahead in the information age, you need connections. We're not talking about any old connection: it's the Internet, the World Wide Web, the Information Superhighway.

In Boise and the Intermountain West, Micron Internet Services is the clear choice for quality Internet connections. We offer a range of services from personal and business dial-up plans to high speed connectivity and Web hosting.

Call **1(800)336-8892** to connect with Micron Internet Services.

www.micron.net

MICRON
INTERNET SERVICES

Table of Contents

Directory of Maps

Boise and
Surrounding Areas

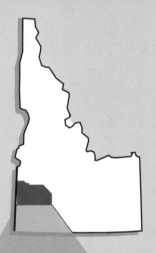

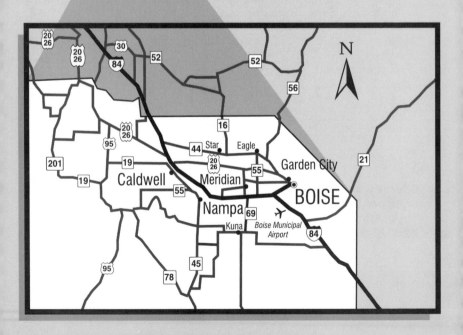

Downtown Boise

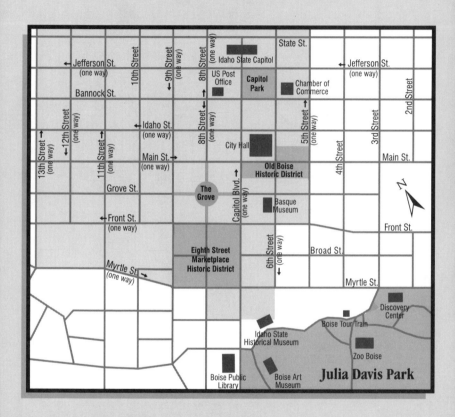

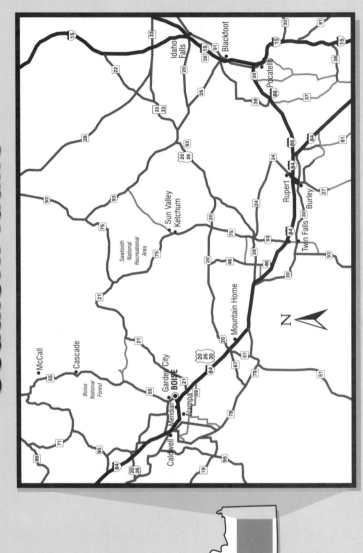

Southern Idaho

How to Use This Book

These pages present more than Boise lying on a tabletop or stacked in a shelf. Between the front and back covers, Boise is under a magnifying glass, with 21 chapters examining everything from history to nightlife, worship to spectator sports, kidstuff to retirement. But Boise, as isolated as it may be in a state that some distant, uninformed sophisticates may still consider feral, is not a castle with its moat drawn up. It is part of the aptly named Treasure Valley, which includes the cities of Nampa and Caldwell to the west, where population and business growth are rapidly rising.

Boise is the Paris of Idaho — the state capital, financial and education center and cultural and sports magnet — and by almost any measure, one of the best small cities in the country to live. But despite Boise's numerous attributes and accolades, for many people outside Idaho and around the world the state is recognizable not for its capital city but first and foremost as the location of Sun Valley. So how could we write about Boise and leave out that fantastic resort location, only 150 miles east, where the ski lift was invented, Hemingway wrote and died, celebrities and top business people reside, and tourists pour in by the plane-, bus- and carload? Such an act of dismissal would be more than the frivolity of cake without frosting, unlaced shoes, uncombed hair and warm brew. Plain and simple, it would be unpardonable.

So yes, Nampa, Caldwell, smaller Treasure Valley communities, and Sun Valley, too, are included between the covers of this indepth guidebook. Although Boise, at the center, is by far the main attraction, as its size, intelligence, influence, power and prosperity

Photo: William H. Mullins

The Boise River is an angler's paradise.

deserve. In each chapter, where appropriate, the assets of Nampa and Caldwell, and sometimes those of smaller places such as Meridian and even Kuna, are included with what Boise has to offer. Some chapters, such as Annual Events and Festivals, Kidstuff and Retirement and Senior Services, do not split up Treasure Valley cities, but look at the compact area as a whole rather than setting it apart by location. Others, for reasons that should by their titles be clear, such as Accommodations and Neighborhoods and Real Estate, present Boise, Nampa and Caldwell as separate entities. Where Boise, Nampa and Caldwell are treated separately, expect to find businesses in the cities of Meridian, Kuna, Garden City, Star and Eagle under the "Boise" subhead.

Sun Valley, across mountain ranges and valleys, is quite removed from the Treasure Valley mix; it's even thought of by some people as a separate region of its own that just happens to fall within the borders of Idaho. Because of its distance and difference, Sun Valley gets its very own section, virtually a book within a book.

We've provided independent chapters for quick-and-easy access to everyday, practical information. If you're hungry, fork open the Restaurants chapter; if you have a plane to catch, zoom in on Getting Here, Getting Around; if professional baseball or college basketball is your thing, kick into Spectator Sports. Our headings and concise reports are loaded with the most important information and details that should provide you with a clear and thorough understanding of the subject on your agenda. In this sense the book is bits and pieces, an encyclopedic wealth of matter that at any moment can help you find or know about the media, or healthcare, or where to shop, setting you up for the progression of your own needs, tastes and designs. With this in mind, keep the book handy. It's not made for dust or spiderwebs. More than a resource, it's a friend that doesn't gossip, bore or tell lies (if you can imagine such a thing) and consistently and faithfully enhances your knowledge of Boise and Sun Valley.

Looked at in another, all-encompassing light, as a whole that examines the skeleton, brain, muscle, tissue, fiber, bone and skin — the inside and out — of its locations, the book may serve as a scouting or intelligence report that can be used smartly for considering a family or business move, for increased perception by people who already live here or for the complete enjoyment of a visit. Much of its information can be gathered here or there, piece-by-piece, from libraries, agencies, publications, the Internet, motel lobbies, street stands, mailings and ads; we have pulled it all together in a logical lump and added, as only involved residents and professional communicators can, our own sensibilities.

If not an entertainment vehicle, the book does include imagery, insights and references that may cause you to crack a smile or slide into philosophic reverie. Chapter prefaces have been crafted to condense in a revealing, appealing and even profound and enlightening fashion the subheaded nitty-gritty that follows. Our Close-ups of the top, most fascinating personalities and community situations provide intellectual and artistic relief from the vital life necessities of who,

what, where, when and how. Tips sprinkled throughout the chapter may send you racing on a new course or be stored in your gray matter, where they wiggle about for future use.

A word here is appropriate about the phone system in Idaho. Everything is within the 208 area code. When dialing in the Treasure Valley, where Boise is located, or Wood River Valley, where Sun Valley is located, no 208 prefix is necessary; when dialing outside those immediate vicinities to other places in the state, it is necessary to dial 1-208 before the number, as it is for callers to Idaho from elsewhere.

We've gone to great lengths to provide as accurate and thorough a book as possible. Inevitably, some mistakes are made or information slips inadvertently through the fingers. We hope they are small mistakes and far between. If you find mistakes in our book, if you disagree, if you'd like to see additions or changes in future editions, or even if you love the guide and just want to give us a pat on the back, we would appreciate your taking the time to write us at

The Insiders' Guide® to Boise & Sun Valley
P.O. Box 2057
Manteo, NC 27954
or contact us at www.insiders.com.

Dress for Success

(A) Upon joining the Idaho Air National Guard, you'll wear a U.S. Air Force uniform for a selected 39 days throughout the year. You'll receive great pay for your part-time commitment and excellent job training. You'll also be building a most impressive resume at the sametime.

(B) You'll be able to attend college full time as the Idaho Air National Guard will pay a major part of your expenses. Study whatever you like. If you choose to work full time you can still earn college credits and even an associates degree from the Community College of the Air Force at no expense to you.

(C) Hundreds of men and women have become a part of the Idaho Air National Guard to help get themselves through college and on to a promising career in an area that best suits them.

(D) With experience and education behind you, you'll have a great start on life and take advantage of the things you like best. Call your representative today to learn more about the opportunities available for you to dress for success.

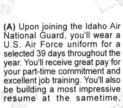

IDAHO
AIR
NATIONAL GUARD

1-800-621-3909

History

Boise's isolation was at once the bane and the saving grace of its historical development. The first Fort Boise was established in 1834 as a trading post. It later became a way stop for Western emigrants on the Oregon Trail who rolled through in their wagons and in the blink of an eyelash continued to greener West Coast locations and ocean ports.

Gold and silver strikes to the north, south and east, the construction of a new Fort Boise by the U.S. Army for regional protection against the Indians, and cropland that fed the miners, soldiers and through traffic all eventually led to Boise's settlement. On July 7, 1863, Boise held its first town meeting and the next day platted 10 city blocks between the river and foothills. The settlement, which was a result of powerful natural forces that happened to transect its location, became, within decades, a neat, shady refuge of civilization, made possible by a river and irrigation ditches spanning in all directions. Boise's remoteness finally became a virtue — the population hordes that would have trampled its fragile environmental assets never showed up.

Tradition brought from elsewhere molded the outpost: broad city streets, a magnificent Capitol square, stately buildings, a blaze of electric lights. The former trading post was even compared to conventional New England.

But the excitement and overnight growth of the 1860s gold rush era became a long wait for railroads that shunned the sagebrush maverick. A burst of city building, after the turn of the century, became the malaise of "What's next?" As elsewhere, Boise suffered during the Depression, but unlike other locations, it didn't change much during World Wars I and II, when city leaders sought and failed to secure industries that served the war effort. The difference was its geographical location — it was too far off and too small to matter. But World War II did lead to the construction of Gowen Field for B-24 bombers, and the De-pression brought on the New Deal and the leap ahead for construction, food processing, lumber, mining and agricultural concerns. Postwar Boise was a haven for stability, opportunity and peace for returning service people. But downtown Boise became old and vacant in the 1960s, and with the long delay of a regional mall that was supposed to go in, a recession hit.

The 1980s were a boom everywhere else but dismal for Boise, tucked away on a high desert shelf at the western edge of a dominating mountain range. People left to find work elsewhere. Companies struggled to survive. With the construction of a mall west of the city, the revitalization of downtown and the shift from a resource-based economy to computer chips and laser printers, the doldrums of the '80s were followed by a '90s high-tech takeoff. Boise went from a remote, stumbled-upon, out-of-the-way place to a star on the map. Space and distance that made things difficult before are now celebrated for their preserving aspect.

This is a city of self-made titans who made it economically bigger than its boots. Harry Morrison built dams around the world; Joe Albertson's supermarkets sprout like mushrooms in distant states; J.R. Simplot's frozen French fries are gobbled everywhere; Micron's computer chips are an industry staple. And other talented individuals, successful companies and families looking for a better place to live are moving in.

Boise, discovered! After all these years.

Before Gold

About 225 million years ago, the granite ridge that became Boise's bedrock was created as an upwelling of molten rock, just as California's Sierra Nevada was rising farther west. Cracks filled with veins of precious minerals as the molten rock cooled. Rivers drained westward, creating the bed of the Snake River. About 200 million years later, successive flows of lava spread a sheet of basalt across the Snake River Plain before giving way to huge Lake Idaho, which covered most of what is now southwestern Idaho for some 7 million years. Its subtropical shoreline became one of ancient North America's most prolific ecosystems for such early mammals as mammoths, camels, sloths, giant bison and the ancestors of modern horses.

During the Second Ice Age, Lake Bonneville formed. This enormous inland sea, which covered most of adjacent western Utah, burst its banks about 15,000 years ago, draining in a torrent whose dimension has been estimated at three times the modern flow of the Amazon. The Bonneville Flood, as it has come to be known, scoured the modern Snake River Canyon and left the Boise area with the sedimentary floodplain now so vital to the region's agricultural economy. Volcanic activity continued until only about 2,000 years ago, creating the tables of pressurized water that even now bubble to the surface as hot springs.

The earliest permanent residents were American Indians of the Shoshone, Paiute and Nez Perce tribes. They were seminomadic hunters and gatherers who found the forests rich in deer and elk, the rivers and streams abundant in salmon and trout and the meadows flush with camas, bitterroot and other vegetables. The 16th-century introduction of the horse, a legacy of Spanish conquistadors in the Southwest, greatly expanded the world of these Native Americans, suddenly allowing their hunters to cross the Rockies to hunt buffalo. Meanwhile, Plains Indians ventured west and bartered for Idaho salmon. Indians from a large geographical area gathered for summer trade fairs that took place primarily in the shadow of the Wyoming Rockies, but also northwest of Boise near present-day Weiser, Idaho.

The 1804-06 Lewis and Clark Expedition never got closer to Boise than the Clearwater River, about 250 miles north, but its impact was felt far and wide. Meriwether Lewis, an Army officer and private secretary to President Thomas Jefferson, and William Clark, a soldier and frontiersman, were the first white men to pass through the region. Sacagawea, a Lemhi Shoshone Indian of what is today Idaho, played a key role in their successful journey from St. Louis to the Pacific Ocean and back by easing tensions with potentially hostile tribes. Journals and maps from the expedition went a long way toward educating the young nation about the topography, native peoples and animal and plant life of the American West. Of most immediate impact, they sparked a rush of fur trappers attracted by the prospect of valuable pelts from beavers, otters and other mountain creatures.

In 1811, members of John Jacob Astor's Pacific Fur Company explored what would become Boise, igniting a vigorous competition for beaver and other fur throughout the Snake River plain. Not long thereafter, French Canadian trappers name the area, shouting "Les Bois!" "Les Bois!" after crossing the desert in 1836 and catching sight of this green, river oasis. "Boise" is French for wooded; hence, Boise's current motto "City of Trees."

Beginning in the 1840s, Oregon Trail pioneers traveled along the Boise River, past the site of the modern city, but didn't stop until they reached Fort Boise at what is today the town of Parma. The fort was built in 1834 by Hudson's Bay Company near the confluence of the Boise and Snake rivers to store surplus trade goods. Few pioneers considered settling in Idaho's high-desert country until September 30, 1860. That was the day Elias Davidson Pierce struck gold in northern Idaho. Suddenly Idaho was more than just a wasteland to hurry through.

From Way Stop to Capital City

Congress established the Idaho Territory in 1863, making Idaho City, 21 miles northeast of Boise, the Pacific Northwest's largest city. It had 6,275 residents; the total of nearby

Photo: William H. Mullins

Wagon wheel ruts can still be seen in the Oregon Trail at Bonneville Point outside of Boise.

Placerville, Pioneer and Centerville topped 8,000. This was a boom town, mining circle that found $250 million worth of gold in only a few years. However, gold was of more benefit to those who supported the zealous, wide-eyed adventurers than to the miners themselves. Boise farmers and merchants established long-term futures by supplying these flash-in-the-pan locations.

Southerners escaping the ravages of the Civil War gravitated to the gold fields, farms and businesses of Boise and the surrounding area. Chinese immigrants were also attracted by the gold. Basques began coming from Spain and France as early as the 1860s. They herded sheep, started businesses, farmed and today in Boise number 20,000, forming the largest concentration of Basques outside the Pyrenees Mountains in southern Europe.

The construction of a regional military fort to protect frontier roads and settlements from the Shoshone and other Indians led to the founding of Boise on July 7, 1863. Boise made sure of its advancement from a regional supply center by fighting off bids by Lewiston and Virginia City to become territorial capital in 1864. By 1868 Boise had 400 buildings, including two churches, four elementary schools and 20 saloons — like the rest of the West, it was a thirsty place. A telegraph line reached the city in 1875, but Boise had no railroad, which was the genie for commercial and population growth.

The Union Pacific contemplated for many years building a railroad, to be known as the Oregon Short Line, along the Snake River. It would blaze the way for steam locomotives over the footprints of pioneers who had moved west over the Oregon Trail. The people of Idaho watched the westward push of the Union Pacific with great hope. When in 1866 it crossed Nebraska and mail from the Eastern seaboard reached Idaho two to four days faster than before, the excitement grew. In 1867 Glenville Dodge, chief engineer for Union Pacific construction, reported to his employers the feasibility of a railroad along the Snake River. Dodge estimated that with rail service available Idaho should produce $25 million a year in mineral and agricultural products. But without a federal government subsidy, the Union Pacific would not move into Idaho.

The railroad finally came to Boise in 1886, but then only in the form of a branch line and only after many disappointments. In 1884 the Oregon Short Line completed a track across southern Idaho from Montpelier on the east to Weiser on the west, but it traveled through Kuna, 20 miles away, instead of Boise. The 600-foot drop into the Boise Valley, which would have necessitated the use of helper engines, was the reason for the diversion.

Though it essentially eluded Boise, rail transportation throughout the state transformed Idaho into an active region and propelled it toward statehood. Boise's population was 2,311 when Idaho was admitted to the union in 1890. Irrigation ditchdiggers swelled the population to 4,026; 300,000 to 500,000 acres south of Boise were to receive Snake River water.

Like the railroad, water was an obsession. A valley orchard grower like Tom Davis could divert Boise River water to his trees, but farmers and ranchers on higher, "Bench" ground were without access and saw their profits drift down the river. Projected canal systems raised hopes but were never completed. Engineering problems defeated the efforts of men equipped with no more than shovels, teams of horses and initiative. Arthur Foote put together a system of irrigation canals across southern Idaho, sank a fortune into it, and never got a drop when Eastern investors withdrew their support because of a national financial panic. Outside financing that demanded immediate profits, poor canal construction and lack of cooperation among canal companies and irrigation districts continued to plague Boise's high-desert watering efforts. But a 25-mile irrigation canal system was not realized until 1899.

The 1894 Congressional passage of the Carey Act offered as many as a million acres of federal land to any state that could irrigate and farm the acreage within a decade and encouraged farmers and ranchers to homestead in Boise and elsewhere in Idaho. It was followed by the Reclamation Act of 1902, which brought federal funds to southern Idaho and allowed the dry uplands to bloom through irrigation projects.

Hot springs as well as irrigation ditches played a part in Boise's development. In 1890, the year that Idaho became a state, Boise became the first city in North America — perhaps the first in the world since the last days of Pompeii — to have many of its offices and residences geothermally heated. The Boise Hot and Cold Artesian Water Co. tapped a 172-degree hot spring at the east end of town. Today, 750,000 gallons of water are still piped every day to eight government buildings, including the Capitol, and 400 homes in the adjacent Warm Springs district.

With water and rail firmly in hand, Boise began, in the late 19th and early 20th centuries, to make itself a city. Impressive buildings constructed during this time that still stand today include the U.S. Assay Office on Main Street; the Territorial Penitentiary and Bishop's House at the Old Penitentiary grounds; and St. Michael's Episcopal and St. John's Roman Catholic cathedrals. The Idanha Hotel, built in elegant French chateau style in 1900, was joined in serving the public by the Owyhee Hotel in 1910, and the Capitol dome was completed in 1912.

Streetcars were in the works. Church and privately sponsored schools, libraries, theaters and hospitals flourished. By the turn of the century, Boise's population was 8,000 of Ada County's 10,000 total. Of that total, 1,500 were from other countries, including Japanese, Germans, British and Chinese and to a lesser extent Canadians, Irish and Swedes.

Gaining Prominence

Boise made its first foray onto the national scene in 1907 when renowned Chicago attorney Clarence Darrow came to town to defend labor leader William Haywood, who was charged with conspiracy in the assassination of former Idaho Gov. Frank Steunenberg. "Big Bill" Haywood had helped to spearhead a series of violent uprisings by silver miners in Idaho's northern Panhandle at the turn of the century, demonstrations that had been quashed by federal troops at Steunenberg's behest. Darrow won Haywood's acquittal, but the trial had other significant corollaries: It illuminated labor strife as a volatile ingredient of industrial growth throughout the country, and it brought the prosecuting attorney, William Borah, into the national limelight. Republican Borah, then a freshman U.S. senator, was a leading force in Congress until his death in 1940. Idaho's highest mountain, 12,662-foot Mount Borah, just north of Mackay in the center of the state, is named after the senator.

Boise was too isolated to attract heavy industry, so it depended on government, industrial management, regional wholesale and re-

J.R. Simplot — Enjoying the View

J.R. Simplot is King of the Hill and appears to be enjoying every minute of it.

In its 1997 list of the 400 richest people in the United States, *Forbes* magazine pegs the Boise billionaire 36th richest, up from 61st the year before.

J.R. lives in a Mediterranean-style villa at the top of a bright green 75-acre hill that can  be seen from almost anywhere in Boise. If you miss it, you might notice the 150-foot flagpole next to the house with an American flag so big that neighbors complained its snapping in the wind kept them up all night.

"Aw, shucks," says the 89-year-old extrovert and man about town, "It's just a shack on a knob. It's no big deal."

Much of what the feisty, friendly, quick-to-grin J.R. sees from his exalted command post wears his own stamp.

His J.R. Simplot Co., which has annual revenues of $2.8 billion, employs 13,000 people in 20 states and nine foreign countries. The company's growth mirrored, and in many ways influenced, the postwar development of resources in Idaho and the Pacific Northwest. Irrigated farming, livestock, mining and the development of transportation systems were essential elements to the company's success. Today cattle, potatoes, fertilizer and construction generate its big numbers.

J.R. is probably best known as the inventor of the frozen french fry and supplier of 60 percent of the fries served by McDonald's.

But everywhere you look in Boise, and everywhere he looks from his princely knob, J.R. seems to be involved.

He bankrolled Micron Technology, Boise's largest employer, when the computer chip-maker went through hard times, and owns 13 percent of its stock. He slipped into real estate development with his 2,000-home Columbia Village and purchase of the Eighth Street Marketplace and 14 adjoining acres downtown — part of the 8,000 acres he owns in Ada County. He opened the Boise Factory Outlet mall in southeast Boise. He also contributed money for the construction of the new $32 million Grove Hotel downtown.

Photo: Courtesy of J.R. Simplot Co.

J.R. is one of Idaho's biggest donors, having given tens of millions of dollars to higher education, the arts, human services and youth. The Morrison Center for the Performing Arts at Boise State University, the new YMCA complex in West Boise, and the Esther Simplot Performing Arts Academy were made possible by his support.

Despite a tough early family life, J.R. always seemed to know how to make friends and especially money. He was imaginative, took risks, surrounded himself with the best people and kept moving up.

— continued on next page

J. R. Simplot

Born on January 4, 1909, in Dubuque, Iowa, he soon moved west with his family to Sunnyside, Washington; Bend, Oregon; and finally the newly organized town of Declo, Idaho, in the Snake River Valley.

His youth was filled with hard work, a natural curiosity about how things worked and the adventures of hunting, swimming, skating and riding horses. At 14, frustrated by the overbearing manner of his father, he dropped out of school and left home. He took up lodging at Declo's Enyeart Hotel, where many of his fellow boarders were public school teachers who received their wages in the form of interest-bearing scrip. Simplot bought the scrip from the teachers at 50¢ on the dollar and subsequently secured a bank loan with the scrip he accumulated.

With cash in hand, he built a makeshift cooker to feed horse meat and potatoes to the 600 hogs he had purchased. When the price of the hogs jumped, he sold the lot for $7,500 — a dazzling sum in those days. With the proceeds he leased a team of horses and farm acreage, learned how to raise potatoes from one of the area's big farmers, Lindsay Maggart, and with Maggart purchased an electric potato sorter that was shipped by railcar to Declo. Their sorting operation spread to neighboring farms, but a dispute with Maggart led Simplot to suggest that they flip a coin to determine who owned the sorter. Simplot won and was in the potato business to stay.

At 89 years of age, J.R. exudes remarkable health. At the groundbreaking for The Grove Hotel, he helped navigate a bulldozer. He remains an avid skier, despite two hip surgeries. "He can out-ski 90 percent of the guys on the hill," says a Boise friend. At his son Don's 60th birthday, J.R. danced well into the night with his second wife, Esther, 26 years his junior and an occasional opera performer who sang "The Star Spangled Banner" before a nationally televised football game.

As for the high green hill J.R. lives on, it takes four seasonal workers and a groundskeeper to maintain it with a tractor-pulled mower, power hand mowers, an automated sprinkler system connected to a well, and 5½-day workweeks. You, too, can ascend the hill. Whenever it snows, sledders carve its white, smooth flanks. In warm weather teenagers merrily ride ice blocks down its green expanse, and couples and families picnic there.

---

tail distribution, farming and lumber to move ahead. Federal agencies have always been important to Boise's economy. In 1912 Bureau of Reclamation engineers built Arrowrock Dam, on the Boise River east of the city, into the highest structure of its kind in the world, a distinction that lasted until the construction of Hoover Dam in Nevada 20 years later. Arrowrock assured a full season of irrigation and gave high-desert Boise a surplus of water. Expanded Boise Valley farming came at a time of rising demand for agricultural products due to the outbreak of war in Europe. But a postwar collapse brought ruin to primarily agricultural Idaho, and even during 1920s prosperity, Idaho farmers continued to battle for survival.

In 1925 the Union Pacific constructed a main passenger line to a new Boise depot, setting off a big celebration for the half-century that went into this achievement. Air expansion came much easier than rail. United Airlines began as Varney Air Lines in Boise in 1926, and Charles Lindbergh landed in 1927 on a national tour after his celebrated flight to Paris. A rail trip to New York that took a week could be made by air in 30 hours. Automobiles, radios and other modern conveniences became important in Boise as in other local economies. It was during this period that Boise indulged itself by constructing the marvelous Egyptian theater, now on the National Historic Register. The architecture reflects the national fascination with the discovery in Egypt of King Tut's tomb. The theater showed old classic silent movies before it was renovated for sound.

The Big Bounce

Dismantled mills, failed banks, widespread unemployment — the Depression walloped Boise. It started in agriculture 10 years earlier than in other industries because World War I inflated farm prices, and after the war they took a dive. Boise leaders decided to use Franklin D. Roosevelt's New Deal initiatives to bring money into communities by building beautiful buildings and structures such as the Boise Hotel, Idaho First National Bank and the Capitol Bridge. The buildings were constructed with private money, the bridge with public money, and they left an elegant heritage. The New Deal construction of a city hall, courthouse, art gallery and museum also breathed life into the city.

Two enterprises begun during the Depression and World War II greatly benefit Boise today. Boise State University began as an Episcopal Church junior college in 1932 and was moved to the grounds of the Boise airfield across the river from Julia Davis Park in 1939. Since then it has become Idaho's largest university. The next year, Gowen Field was built south of the city with 1.5-mile runways to accommodate B-24 bombers. The Idaho Air National Guard flew the famous P-51 Mustang out of Gowen Field starting in 1946. It later became a permanent airport, Boise Air Terminal, capable of handling the largest commercial planes. Idaho Air National Guard aircrews, sharing local runways with commercial and general aviation, flew 1,000 combat missions between 1991 and 1993 to enforce "no-fly" zones over Iraq and to protect Kurdish refugees.

Morrison-Knudsen, which started with a not particularly successful effort — a pumping station on the Snake River in 1912 — expanded greatly by 1930 through major construction projects around the country and world. In 1954

Harry Morrison's portrait made the cover of *Time* magazine as "the man who has done more than anyone else to tame rivers, move mountains and change the face of the earth."

During World War II, Japanese Americans entered Idaho against their will, forced into housing at Hunt Internment camp near Twin Falls. After the war, some of those same Japanese families decided to stay and settled in the west end of the Treasure Valley, where most worked in agriculture. Also new to the agricultural scene were Mexican laborers who supported their families back home with local crop work. Most Hispanic families settled in Caldwell and Nampa, and some have become business owners, farmers and educators. Today Hispanics, with 7 percent of the state's population, and South Pacific/Asians, with 1.6 percent, are Idaho's two largest minority groups.

Industry, Agriculture and Conservation

After the war ended in 1945, Boise enjoyed industrial growth, expanded its school system and built subdivisions outside the city. Morrison-Knudsen and Boise-Payette, a large lumber producing and marketing firm, moved full-speed ahead. J.R. Simplot's potato processing, dairy, fertilizer, mining and lumber empire was flexing its muscles and would eventually make Simplot one of the country's richest people. Joe Albertson started a supermarket in 1939 that was grossing a million dollars only two years later. It's become the country's fourth largest and most profitable supermarket chain. A 1949 *Saturday Evening Post* story said, "Boise is the richest city of its size in the United States," and added that the city's pleasant climate and attractive outdoor environment made it slumless and racket-free.

Encouraged by this statement and not

wanting to become another Reno, Boise outlawed slot machines in 1949. To evade the restriction, slot machine operators incorporated an adjacent village, which they called Garden City because of earlier Chinese gardens in the area, and continued with their one-armed bandits until they were outlawed by the state Legislature in 1954.

Ever faithful to its agricultural roots but with an eye toward the future, Boise began dealing in high-value specialty crops, such as hybrid corn seed. Orchards, seed crops, alfalfa, sugar beets, potatoes and onions lit up cash registers. Expanded hydroelectric power from Snake River dams made Idaho Power a big player. Boise-Payette and Cascade Lumber of Yakima, Washington, merged in 1957, built a modern, stilted Boise headquarters and, as Boise Cascade, became one of the world's largest forest products companies, known for its office paper. Trus-Joist was founded in 1960 and, as Trus-Joist MacMillan, is today the largest engineered-wood manufacturer.

But wood and water cried out for conservation measures. Idaho couldn't have asked for a better champion than Boisean Frank Church, who during his four terms as a U.S. senator (1956-1980) stood behind legislation that gave Idaho more federally protected wilderness than any other state after much larger Alaska and California. The environmental ethic continued with Cecil Andrus, a longtime governor (1971-1977 and 1987-1995) and federal Secretary of the Interior in the Carter administration (1977-1981).

Boise River Greenbelt improvement surged ahead in 1969. And in an effort to protect natural areas on a grander scale, Boise established the $4 million Interagency Fire Center, which coordinates firefighting activities throughout the country when blazes cannot be controlled by local, state and regional firefighting groups, in 1970.

Dealing with Downtown

Downtown Boise was in serious decline in the 1960s. Older buildings were vacant and in a state of disrepair, and the Capital City Development Corporation, in charge of such matters, leveled whole city blocks, wiping out some of the city's most beautiful and irreplaceable architecture. The idea was to bring in a regional mall, but uncertain financing in the midst of a recession scared away anchor stores that could have made this possible. The 1980s express train economy that moved through most of the country with an extravagant, powerful, risk-taking energy bypassed Idaho's languishing capital city — just as the transcontinental railroad did a century before.

Dirk Kempthorne, now completing his first six-year term in the U.S. Senate and a candidate for the governor's position that is being vacated by Phil Batt, was elected Boise mayor in 1985 with a new city council willing to rethink the downtown development plan. An expert at forging consensus, he is well-remembered for a closed-door meeting with members of the Boise City Council, Ada County Commission, Ada County Highway District, Auditorium District and downtown development board, in which he demanded a solution for downtown reconstruction that would be agreed upon by everybody before anyone stepped out the door.

In 1987 the construction of Boise Towne Square, a pleasant and well-designed shopping mall, with The Bon Marche, Mervyn's California Department Store, JCPenney and Sears, Roebuck and Co. as anchors and 180 other permanent stores, was built west of the city center next to Interstate 84. This marked the beginning of a city comeback that continues through today and a partial shift west of Boise's economic center. Within five years of the mall opening, a revitalized downtown core emerged with economic and government institutions providing employment and a flourish of new businesses, specialty shops, restaurants, theaters, art galleries and coffeehouses moving in. The "Old Boise" historic section of the city was renovated and spruced up, and a formerly dismal and abandoned territory became the place to eat, drink and be merry as well as a source of civic pride.

Approaching the Next Millennium

In the past decade, Boise has seen a number of improvements to its existing institutions and has added several necessities and luxuries to modernize its landscape.

At the urging of Boise's first Catholic Bishop

Photo: William H. Mullins

The Idaho State Capitol is constructed of native sandstone
in the classical style of the nation's Capitol.

Alphonse Glorieux, the Sisters of the Holy Cross came to serve the healthcare needs of the young Boise community in 1894. They raised $3,000 and opened Saint Alphonsus, Boise's first hospital. A century later, in 1994, Saint Alphonsus had evolved into a 269-bed regional medical center that was staffed by 1,800 individuals. It is still expanding, while providing diagnostic and treatment services in trauma care, medicine, neurosciences, orthopedics, cardiology, oncology, ophthalmology, surgery, psychiatry and rehabilitation.

Meanwhile, in 1995, Boise's St. Luke's Regional Medical Center became one of just seven hospitals to earn The HCIA Mercer Report "Top 100 Hospital" ranking for three consecutive years. Since 1968 St. Luke's Heart Institute has been providing cardiac care for patients throughout the state and parts of Oregon, Utah and Nevada. The hospital is also well-known for its treatment of cancer patients. Like Saint Alphonsus, St. Luke's continues to expand its facility in Boise, and it has built a new medical center in Meridian and is establishing medical partnerships in other communities.

Growth, expansion and moving ahead in a

faster, more sophisticated manner are typical of what is happening not only in the medical community of the area, but also throughout the Treasure Valley. The most visual aspect is new downtown construction. While old blocks have been brought back and improved, new buildings and spaces are going in too. The Grove, a $1 million outdoor plaza, was built in 1986 for special activities, events and casual relaxation in the heart of the city. This was the first project realized by Boise Mayor Dirk Kempthorne and his new city council, elected to office a year earlier. The Grove became an especially convenient apron and passageway for the $10.5 million Boise Centre on the Grove, the city's convention center, which opened in 1990. Unlike stark concrete-and-steel centers found in some other cities, The Grove's hallways are richly carpeted, fabric and glossy tile cover the walls, and there is a comfortable, crisp, contemporary atmosphere maintained throughout the structure. The main exhibit hall offers 25,000 feet of space, and a 322-seat auditorium is ideal for meetings and presentations.

A well-designed, modern 5,000-seat sports arena, the Bank of America Centre, was completed on the other side of the Grove in 1997 and is popular for its professional ice hockey, figure skating, tennis and boxing events. But the Centre is just part of the 250-room, 17-story hotel, The Grove, which opened at the end of 1997. Across from city hall and just down from the Capitol is another new, striking white building with a wavy surface — the 11-story Washington Mutual Plaza, which has retail, office and residential space.

The engine for new construction is a healthy economy, and in the last decade, Boise's has been robust. Hewlett Packard Co., known around the world for its computer products, came to town in 1973 and employed 30 people. Three years later, it had 400 people, and it is now Boise's second largest employer with 4,000 employees. The company's multimillion dollar campus and one of the largest HP facilities in the world is located on 120 acres at the city's western border. The HP LaserJet printer was created there, and by 1995 it was the bestselling printer worldwide. HP DeskJets are made there now. Actually, HP makes more than 23,000 products that range from computers, printers, scanners and disk drives to medical electronic equipment to calculators. Its strengths lie in measurement, computing and communications — the elements driving the Information Age.

Homegrown Micron Technology is the largest Boise company, with 7,000 employees who work around the clock at its complex of white buildings on flats beside Interstate 84. It sold more silicon computer chips in its size category than any other company in 1997. Its subsidiary, Micron Electronics, in Nampa, makes personal computers.

Micron started in 1978 as a small contract firm designing semiconductors. The founders set out to make a smaller version of the 64K DRAM computer chip, a memory chip capable of holding 64,000 bits of information. They succeeded beyond anyone's wildest expectations, and by 1995 Micron posted a net income of $844 million based on net sales of more than $2.9 billion. Micron is now recognized as an industry leader in low-cost, high-volume semiconductor manufacturing. The company has been a big moneymaker and community supporter: Between 1985 and 1995 it donated more than $8 million in funds and equipment to Idaho schools, and in 1996 offered a $6 million chal-

lenge grant to Boise State University for the construction of a new engineering facility.

Albertson's Inc., the fourth largest and most profitable U.S. supermarket chain, has 2,628 employees, making it the third largest Boise company. Boise Cascade, the wood and paper manufacturing company, and Morrison-Knudsen, the construction company, are also in the top 10. Other well-known Boise companies include J.R. Simplot, which processes more than 2 billion pounds of frozen potatoes, 600 million pounds of meat and 100 million pounds of cheese annually and has more than 13,000 employees working in 20 states and nine foreign countries; Ore-Ida Foods, the nation's No. 1 retail frozen potato company and a national leader in frozen appetizers, frozen onions and frozen filled pasta; and TJ International, which controls about 65 percent of the engineered-lumber market and whose products are used in the construction of about 200,000 new houses every year.

In 1986 Boise unemployment was 8.7 percent and more people were moving out than moving in. But with the subsequent success and growth of its big companies and scores of others that have supported the giants or are spin-offs (for instance, Extended Systems, a software maker founded by former Boise HP people, employs 250 people and continues to grow like crazy) — not to mention companies that moved in because of affordable land and a good environment as well as companies that grew here and prospered — those times seem far away. In Ada County, where Boise is located, the number of nonfarm jobs rose from 86,668 in 1987 to 136,210 in 1994, a 57 percent increase. Today state unemployment is 5 percent, and Boise ranks No. 12 in the country for creating manufacturing jobs.

From 1975 to 1996, Ada County's population almost doubled, from 134,653 to 260,057. Over the same period, the population of Canyon County — where Nampa and Caldwell are located, in the western part of the Treasure Valley — jumped from 72,172 to 112,530. Too much rapid growth can cause problems when the infrastructure is not able to keep up with it. Traffic, rising housing costs, congestion at favorite fishing holes and frequent bond elections to ease classroom crowding took their toll. A 1993 Boise Future

Foundation survey found that 87 percent of 501 Ada County respondents wanted population growth of 2 percent or less. Thirty percent wanted none at all.

In response to these numbers, Hewlett Packard slowed its hiring, and Micron elected to build a new computer plant in Utah rather than expand in Boise: Both companies were concerned about their impact on schools, roads and other services. But the valley continues to be a magnet for newcomers drawn by job opportunities, outdoor recreation and small-town friendliness.

Nampa

Twenty miles west of Boise, farther from foothills that rise above the Treasure Valley and closer to the state's dominant waterway, the Snake River, Nampa was homesteaded in 1885 by Alexander Duffes at a place that was nothing but sagebrush and a railway line. He was a man with vision, for within a year, on September 8, 1886, the town was incorporated, and the first train of the Idaho Central Line rolled from Nampa to Boise, behind a construction train that was laying track.

The railway lines led to the construction of some of Nampa's most impressive buildings — the Oregon Short Line Depot and the Dewey Palace Hotel. The town's most spectacular lasting building, the Oregon Short Line Depot, was built for $30,000 in 1902, when at least 10 daily passenger trains departed from its platform. It served the train line for 24 years before it was transformed for office use and later abandoned in 1972. Now on the National Historic Register, the building is a historical museum. Brick and angular, with white trim, turrets, cylindrical rooms and a sweeping chateau-style roof, it is a vision of past splendor, beyond hardwood trees and against the sky on the north end of 12th Avenue in the historic district.

Also in 1902, Col. W.H. Dewey built the quarter-million dollar Dewey Palace Hotel, which was considered by transcontinental train

Strong Basque Presence in Boise Goes Back to 19th Century

Fiercely independent and speaking an unknown language, Basques began arriving in Boise in the late 1880s, where they found work as sheep herders because that didn't require English or prior experience. Boise's hilly, high-desert terrain and river-fed valley provided escape from the political and economic oppression of their verdant home enclave, located in southern Europe where the Pyrenees Mountains dip into the Bay of Biscay, that was ruled by Spain and France. Although their canvas-backed sheep herding wagons fitted with every practical appliance remain a Basque symbol, within several  decades of their appearance here they found work in many trades and professions, and today their estimated Treasure Valley count of 20,000 is their largest population group in the United States.

Idaho Basques are descendants of an ancient people who have maintained their identity for thousands of years. Their language is unrelated to any spoken in the world today. Their origin has been debated by scholars for centuries, even including the notion that they are survivors of the legendary lost kingdom of Atlantis that sank into the ocean.

Currently there is general support for the theory that Basques evolved from Stone Age Cro-Magnon peoples who lived in what is now southern France and northern Spain more than 10,000 years ago. Prehistoric Basques inhabited this area when Iberians and

— continued on next page

Photo: Basque Museum & Cultural Center

Red sashes and berets are the traditional garb of male Basque dancers.

Celts, ancestors of the Spanish and Portuguese, existed around 3000 BC. The first historic reference to Basques was made in Roman times when Strabo, the Greek geographer and historian, spoke of "those ferocious tribes who speak a strange language" and referred to their great personal courage and aggressive qualities as warriors.

A visit to Boise is a great opportunity to explore and experience the Basque culture firsthand.

The Basque culture takes center stage the last weekend in July when the Boise Basque Festival presents music, dancing, sports events, exhibitions, food and speakers. The Basques are known for their games and dancing. Strongmen hoisting granite balls and pulling wagons are staples of Basque celebrations. Pelota, hardball played with a harder ball, and pala, played with a heavy hardwood bat, are Basque sports. As is jai lai, performed by acrobatic athletes who throw and catch a ball with a basket in a walled enclosure that presents a complexity of angles and space. Jai lai is popular in Latin America and several American cities.

Basque dancing in America was about to become extinct when Juanita Hormaechea of Boise organized Basque dancers for a performance in the 1948 Boise Music Festival. That led to the formation of the Oinkari Basque Dancers by Al Erquiaga and Diana Urresti, a lively, traditional and colorful group whose men wear white outfits with red sashes and berets, and women white blouses beneath black tops and red skirts. They have danced in many locations including Euskadi, their grassy homeland in southern Europe that kisses the Bay of Biscay.

For a bite of Basque cuisine, head over to Gernika, a neat stone bar that's set off by itself at 202 S. Capitol Boulevard. Gernika is the ancient capital of Viskaya, "the spiritual home of the Basques," where many of Idaho's Basque people originated. Menu items include solomo, pork sandwiches spiced with pimentos and garlic, and beef tongue. Gernika is just down the block from the Basque Museum & Cultural Center at 611 Grove Street, housed in Boise's oldest brick building. (See our Attractions chapter for more about the museum.)

travelers the plushest hotel between Omaha, Nebraska, and Portland, Oregon. It had an elegant dining area, bowling alleys, a sweet shop and other amenities.

But Nampa was more than a stop along the rails. Water reached the town through irrigation canals in 1892, making farming possible and leading to an increase in population. By the turn of the century, Nampa had 799 people, a population that grew to 4,205 a decade later, after completion of the New York Canal from the Snake River to Deer Flat Reservoir. The town's 800 farms in 1900 grew to 2,900 in 1910 because of the increased irrigation. During this same period, the first sugar beet factory was built in 1905, and the town opened its own brewery in 1907. The factory only lasted until 1910, but the smokestacks of the Amalgamated Sugar Co., just north of Interstate 84, are a prominent town feature.

The brewery, on the other hand, was a sign of a change in attitudes. When Alexander Duffes homesteaded the area in 1885, he had refused to sell lots for saloons, earning Nampa the nickname "New Jerusalem." Now Nampa had its own brewery, and when prohibition came up for a nationwide vote in 1909 and 1911, Nampa opposed it.

In the next decade, higher education found a home in Nampa. Northwest Nazarene College, a small, highly rated school, was built in 1913. The next major shaping influence came in the early 1960s when The Holly Shopping Center was built. Karcher Mall became the region's shopping center until Boise Towne Square was built in 1987. Nampa residents literally built their own golf course, Centennial, with dozer, shovel and great volunteer spirit. More recently, the go-go town constructed a new city hall, civic center and recreation center.

Although agriculture is still important to Nampa, job diversity for Nampa's fast-climbing population of 35,333 has been provided by J.R. Simplot processed-food operations, computer-maker Micron Electronics, chip-maker Zilog, Mercy Medical Center and Pacific Press Publishers, a Seventh-Day Adventist religious group that moved from California. Because of its less expensive properties, Nampa is home to many Boise commuters.

Caldwell

As with adjacent Nampa, Caldwell, 40 miles west of Boise, began with the railroad. It became more than sagebrush, volcanic soil, deer and jackrabbit when a town site was platted in August 1883 by the Idaho and Oregon Land Improvement Company. By January 1884 the company had, overnight, persuaded more than 600 people to live in a community that had 150 structures.

Despite a major fire in 1884, with an estimated loss of $20,000 to businesses and property, expansion continued. Orchards and farmland did well, and Carrie Leach, the first schoolteacher, had 30 students attending her classes. In 1887 a new schoolhouse, a Presbyterian church and wooden sidewalks appeared. Six hundred trees were planted that year, and the Caldwell Building and Loan Association was organized.

In 1891 Canyon County, separate from Ada County and Boise, was created, with Caldwell chosen as the county seat.

Caldwell is home to an Ivy League-like liberal arts college, Albertson College of Idaho, renamed in recent years for its chief benefactor, the deceased supermarket king, Joe Albertson, and his wife Kathryn, who continues to pour money into the school.

The town is a classic county seat with a population of 20,000, surrounded by some of the world's finest agricultural land. Seventy-five percent of the Midwest's Cornbelt seed comes from Canyon County, where long, hot days, low humidity and cool nights make seed production ideal. The county is rated 47th out of approximately 3,000 counties in the country in agricultural production.

Local businesses include creameries, dairies, poultry plants and cattle, fruit, grain and seed dealers. Caxton Printers Ltd., a book publisher known throughout the country, is the Idaho State Textbook Depository. Like Nampa, with its cheaper land and housing prices, Caldwell is attracting workers who commute to Boise.

Interstate 84 is the primary route serving Boise, directly tying it with Portland, Oregon, and Salt Lake City, Utah.

Getting Here, Getting Around

As the largest city for more than 300 miles in any direction, Boise has become a hub of transportation not only for southwestern Idaho but for eastern Oregon and northern Nevada as well. Although Amtrak no longer stops in Boise — the national passenger-rail system ceased service on its Portland-Boise-Salt Lake City route in spring 1997 — Boise has a rapidly expanding airport and a busy network of interstate, U.S. and state highways.

Rapid population growth in the Boise area, however, threatens to overburden the existing transportation system unless steps are taken in anticipation of potential problems. Even with a projected 2.5 percent annual growth rate — significantly less than the 4 percent rate of 1990 through 1996 — the population of Ada County, dominated by Boise, will increase by more than 100,000 (to 360,000) in the next two decades.

Much of the increased traffic volume generated by this population boom will be borne by the region's sole interstate highway, Interstate 84. Because the stretches between Boise and Nampa will experience especially heavy growth, priorities will be to increase the number of freeway lanes and add more interchanges. A new bypass route could be built to transport through-traffic around the metropolitan area. Engineers also are considering the conversion of a pair of U.S. highways into limited-access expressways.

Boise's municipal airport, served by six national and regional airlines, is expanding concurrently with the highway system. And public transportation also faces an overhaul, with a European-produced light-rail system getting a close look from regional planning authorities.

In this chapter we cover all the modes of transportation for getting to and around Boise, from your own set of wheels (be they white-walled or spoked) to flying the friendly skies.

By Car

Highways

Interstate 84 is the primary route serving Boise, directly tying it with Portland, Oregon (428 miles northwest) and Salt Lake City, Utah (349 miles southeast). A four-mile spur route, Interstate 184, known locally as "The Connector," feeds Boise's city center from an intersection with I-84 on the west side of the city. Below we've listed some of the principal highways in and around Boise.

• **U.S. Highway 20** runs east-west between Boston and the Oregon coast and provides Boise's main link with Sun Valley, to the east.

• **U.S. Highway 26** runs east-west between Nebraska and the Oregon coast.

• **U.S. Highway 30** runs east-west between Atlantic City, New Jersey, and coastal Oregon; I-84 now covers most of its route through Idaho but stretches of U.S. 30 branch through Twin Falls and other communities.

• **U.S. Highway 95** runs north-south between the Canadian border north of Bonners Ferry, Idaho, and the Mexican border south of Yuma, Arizona, via the western fringe of the Treasure Valley.

• **Idaho Highway 21** links Boise with the mountain recreation center of Stanley, 136 miles northeast.

• **Idaho Highway 44** runs west on State

Street from downtown Boise, through Eagle and Middleton, to join U.S. 95 near Parma.

• **Idaho Highway 55** connects Boise to U.S. 95 at New Meadows, 132 miles north, via the lakeside resort town of McCall.

Surface Streets

Boise

Boise's geographic boundaries generally dictate the street layout. The Boise River runs in a northwesterly direction through the city; most streets to the north of the river, including the downtown area, run southeast-northwest and southwest-northeast. (Residents, however, perceive the northeasterly, foothills-oriented direction to be generally north, and this book adopts that orientation when providing directions.) On the south side of the river, atop the geological "bench" that overlooks the stream, arterials and other streets are laid out by compass in a direct north-south and east-west grid pattern.

Here's a quick guide to the main streets of Boise:

Where The Connector empties into downtown, it becomes eastbound Myrtle Street and westbound Front Street. Two blocks north of Front Street, eastbound Main Street and westbound Idaho Street are the main drags of downtown Boise. On Friday and Saturday nights, these two thoroughfares between 5th and 16th streets are often bumper-to-bumper with high-school and college students "cruising" with their car radios turned to top volume; other residents do their best to avoid this route.

Three blocks north of Idaho Street, two-way State Street passes the state Capitol and bisects the government district; this is north Boise's principal highway (Idaho 44), extending west to suburban Eagle, where it meets Idaho 55.

The main north-south street of downtown Boise is Capitol Boulevard, which begins in front of the state Capitol, at Jefferson Street, and runs directly south, bisecting two major city parks, Julia Davis Park and Ann Morrison Park. After passing the campus of Boise State

University, it curves around the former Union Pacific Depot, a city landmark, and continues south on Vista Avenue to the city airport. On the north side of the Boise River, Capitol Boulevard is one-way northbound; its southbound counterpart is 9th Street.

Broadway Avenue bounds the east side of downtown; it meets Main Street (and its eastern extension, Warm Springs Avenue) opposite St. Luke's Hospital and runs due south past BSU's Bronco Stadium to join I-84 east of the airport. East of Broadway, Boise Avenue and Parkcenter Boulevard provide primary access to southeast Boise residential districts.

Numbered north-south streets begin with short 1st Street, two blocks west of the Broadway-and-Main intersection, and march westward as far as 36th Street in north Boise, 52nd Street in Garden City. Sixteenth Street is the approximate west end of downtown Boise; across State Street, it joins Harrison Boulevard, the central corridor of the city's North End. Beyond Hill Road, Harrison becomes Bogus Basin Road, which runs uphill 16 miles to Boise's nearest ski area.

Paralleling State Street on the south side of the Boise River is Chinden Boulevard, westbound U.S. 20/26. Chinden, in fact, is not in Boise at all but in Garden City, an enclave almost entirely surrounded by the state capital but with its own civic government. At the west end of Garden City, Chinden intersects Glenwood Street, which passes the Western Idaho Fairgrounds and other recreation centers en route to joining State Street.

South of the river, east-west arterials run a mile apart. From north to south — beginning with Ustick Road, which starts at Chinden and 44th and continues west all the way to the city of Caldwell — they are Fairview Avenue, Franklin Road, Overland Road and Victory Road.

North-south arterials also usually run a mile apart, although it's only a half-mile from Orchard Street west to Curtis Road. A mile west of Curtis is Cole Road; then come Maple Grove Road, Five Mile Road and Cloverdale Road.

I-184 skirts the southeastern corner of the

Photo: John Gottberg

Downtown Boise is nestled between the Boise River
Greenbelt and the foothills of the Rocky Mountains.

square mile flanked by Cole and Maple Grove roads, Franklin Road and Fairview Avenue. This area is especially significant as Boise's principal shopping center, focused around the Boise Towne Square regional mall. The square mile is bisected north-south by Milwaukee Street and east-west by Emerald Street.

Nampa and Caldwell

Both downtown Nampa and downtown Caldwell are south of I-84, respectively 19 and 27 miles west of downtown Boise.

The easternmost Nampa exit provides access to the new Idaho Center and a developing commercial area via Can-Ada Road to the north. Garrity Boulevard breaks to the southwest here and extends via 11th Avenue to downtown Nampa.

Across 3rd Street, the main thoroughfare of downtown, Idaho Highway 45 extends south on 12th Avenue toward the Snake River and

Owyhee County. To the west, 3rd Street continues via Caldwell Boulevard and past the Karcher Mall shopping center to its sister city.

All of downtown Nampa's roadways are numbered; streets run east-west, while avenues run north-south. Street numbering begins at the Union Pacific railroad tracks, beginning with 1st Street S. and continuing to 14th Street S.; north of the tracks, streets run from 1st Street North through 10th Street North.

Avenues run from 1st through 24th, beginning at the Idaho Highway 55 junction with Caldwell Boulevard, south of the west Nampa freeway interchange, and running east through downtown.

By the time Caldwell Boulevard enters Caldwell from the southeast, it is known as Cleveland Boulevard. At the east end of downtown, Cleveland forks into a pair of one-way streets. Cleveland, which skirts the Albertson College of Idaho campus, becomes solely eastbound; its westbound counterpart is Blaine Street. Tenth Avenue, which extends north across the railroad tracks to its interchange with I-84 and south through the city to cross Ustick Road, bisects both Blaine and Cleveland in the heart of downtown Caldwell.

Rules of the Road

A person must obtain an Idaho driver's license within three months of moving to the area. In Boise you'll need to get in line at the offices of the Ada County Sheriff, near Boise Towne Square mall at 7200 Barrister Drive, (208) 377-6658. This is also where you must go to register motor vehicles; call (208) 377-6520.

In Nampa and Caldwell, go to the Canyon County Sheriff, 120 9th Avenue S. in Nampa; 1115 Albany Street in Caldwell. For a driver's licenses, call (208) 466-0420 in Nampa or (208) 454-7487 in Caldwell; for vehicle registration, phone (208) 466-2275 in Nampa, (208) 454-7452 in Caldwell.

Because traffic laws may vary from state to state, be sure to study a current edition of the *Idaho Driver's Manual* before you test for your license. Some of the more important regulations are these:

• The driver and anyone else riding in the front seat of a vehicle must wear a seat belt. Children younger than 4 and weighing less than 40 pounds must be buckled into an approved child safety seat.

• Unless otherwise posted, you may turn right at a red light after stopping, and left into a one-way street after stopping and giving way to any cross traffic.

• Your headlights must be on from sunset to sunrise, as well as when conditions such as rain, snow, fog, dust or smoke impair visibility.

• On a two-lane road, you must stop when approaching (from either direction) a school bus with its stop sign out and its lights flashing. On a highway of more than two lanes, oncoming traffic need not stop.

• You must pull to the right and stop to yield to any official vehicle answering an emergency call. Police cars have flashing blue lights; ambulances and fire trucks have red lights.

• You must yield to pedestrians at intersections and stop signs whether or not there are marked crosswalks or traffic lights, unless they are crossing against a light. You also must yield when you are turning and when you are entering a street from a driveway or alley. You must always yield when the pedestrian is a blind person with a white cane or seeing-eye dog.

• The maximum speed limit on city streets in Idaho is 35 mph, although local jurisdictions often post a 25 mph maximum speed. Outside of urban areas, the speed limit on U.S. and state highways is 65 mph, unless otherwise posted. Interstate limits are 75 mph, except through urban areas, when they fall to 65 mph.

• Drivers are considered drunk in Idaho when their blood alcohol concentration exceeds .08 percent. For an average-sized man, that's four drinks; for an average-sized woman, it's three. Penalties are severe: Even a first conviction will result in a driver's license suspension of at least 90 days, with a hefty fine and jail time possibilities. Drivers younger than 21 can be convicted if they've had more than a single drink (.02 percent).

• If you are involved in an accident, state law requires that you stop as near as possible to the scene without creating an additional traffic hazard. Give any help you can if someone is injured, and call for police and medical help as soon as possible. Exchange your name, address, phone number, driver's license number and insurance information with others involved.

Winter Driving

Boise normally is hit between late November and March by two or three snowstorms that may leave as much as a foot of snow behind. For a few days thereafter, driving becomes more perilous than usual, especially if temperatures warm sufficiently to melt the snow during the day and then freeze again at night.

Many Treasure Valley residents mount studded snow tires on their vehicles during the winter months; they're permitted only between October 1 and April 15. When driving conditions are particularly hazardous, use tire chains.

Driving on snowy or icy roads calls for slower speeds, more gradual stops and turns and longer following distances. When you start driving, don't peel out, or your wheels will spin; instead, accelerate gradually. When you stop, unless your vehicle has anti-lock brakes, pump the brakes gently and avoid turning your steering wheel suddenly.

Carry a window scraper and *use it* to clear your windshield before starting out, especially early in the morning. Make sure your wipers and defroster are operating properly.

Bridges, overpasses and other raised roadways often remain slick when other streets and highways are clear of snow and ice. Exercise special caution when crossing them.

Parking

Plenty of metered street parking can be found in downtown Boise between 5th and 12th, Front and State streets. Meters — timed at 30 minutes, one hour or two hours — will take your nickels, dimes and quarters. Normally, meter parking will cost you about 50¢ an hour.

Several parking garages in downtown Boise typically charge 50¢ per half-hour. They are at Capitol Boulevard and Main Street, 9th and Main streets, 9th and Bannock streets, 9th and Grove streets and 10th and Grove streets. The AMPCO System and Diamond Parking operate several smaller parking lots. Outside of the downtown core, free street parking may be limited to an hour or two, as posted on signs.

Parking in downtown Nampa and Caldwell is primarily metered street parking.

Riding the Rails Aboard the Boise Tour Train

The engineer opens the steam horn, rings the bell, and the *Tootin' Tater*, the little engine that could, sets out on another tour of downtown Boise, as it has done more than 250 times a year for more than two decades.

That's more than 5,000 circuits, but the *Tater* and her partner, *Big Mike*, never falter. Motorized, 1890s replica locomotives, they pull a pair of trolley cars on a one-hour circuit that leads from Julia Davis Park through the Warm Springs and Capitol neighborhoods and the central business district. Locals smile and wave at the passing "train," which they delight in riding themselves when they have out-of-town visitors.

The engineers are more than drivers: They're also narrators, well-versed in the lore of the city that they share with 60 or more passengers at a time. They'll take you past Boise's first log cabin, built in 1863 by soldier John O'Farrell for his 17-year-old bride. They'll point out the world headquarters of the Morrison-Knudsen Co., a giant engineering firm whose successes have included Hoover Dam, the Trans-Alaska Pipeline and the Cape Canaveral launch towers. They'll show you the sights of the downtown core, so you'll know what to look for when you later return on foot.

When you ride the Tour Train, you'll get more than just a tour. You'll be subjected to a running volley of that highest form of humor: the pun.

When the *Tater* rambles down Warm Springs Avenue, for instance, the engineer-guide may note that when C.W. Moore built a new house here in 1892 and piped in

— continued on next page

water from nearby hot springs to make it the first geothermally heated home in the United States, his family was really steamed.

Big Mike and the *Tootin' Tater* have their home depot next to Pioneer Village in Julia Davis Park, within sight of the historical museum, art museum and rose garden. During the peak summer season (June 1 through Labor Day), they run five times between 10 AM and 3 PM daily except Sunday, when there are four departures. In September, trains depart once daily from Wednesday to Friday, four times on Saturday and three times Sunday afternoon. In May and October there are three trips a day on Saturdays, Sundays and holidays.

Adults pay $6.50 for the tour. Seniors pay $6, children 4 through 12 pay $3.50, and children 3 and younger ride free. For information, call the Boise Tour Train at (208) 342-4796.

Photo: John Gottberg

Touring Downtown on the Boise Tour Train is a great way to brush up on local lore.

By Air

Boise Air Terminal
3201 Airport Way, Boise
• **(208) 383-3110**

It's a little-known fact that United Airlines got its start in Boise. The transportation giant's direct predecessor, Varney Air Lines, operated its first postal flights between Boise, Pasco (Washington) and Elko (Nevada) in 1926, when the Boise airport stretched along the Boise River where Boise State University now stands.

A new runway, known as Gowen Field, was built in 1940 on the edge of the desert four miles south of downtown Boise. Today, just off I-84 and connected to the central city by Vista Avenue, it's an integral part of the urban area. Six airlines, United among them, serve the Boise Air Terminal, which now ranks as the 85th busiest airport in the world. An average of 75 flights per day — that's 27,500 departures per year — carry 1.25 million out-

bound passengers, a number that doubled between 1992 and 1996.

To handle increased traffic, the airport has two parallel, two-mile-long runways and two concourses; one runway and one concourse were extended in 1996.

Current airport facilities are in the Duane W. Beeson Terminal Building, named for a World War II ace from Boise. Ticketing is on the west side of the ground floor, baggage claim on the east side. Also on this level are a cafeteria and a gift shop/newsstand, as well as public phones, ATM machines, a video arcade and an automated postal center.

Stairs, escalators and an elevator to assist travelers with disabilities rise to an upper floor. At the top of the stairs, to the left, is Reflections, a full-service restaurant and lounge; to the right is the airport's business center, with facilities to assist business travelers. To the rear of the stairs are the airport's administrative offices.

In January 2000, airport officials expect to begin construction on a new, multistory main terminal building with ticketing on the second floor, baggage claim on the ground floor and expanded retail and food-and-beverage outlets. It will take about two years to complete.

For now travelers enter the A and B concourses through a security checkpoint. This is not much different from the screening area at any other airport, except that laptop computers must still be opened and turned on for security officers here; most other airports no longer follow this procedure.

United, Northwest and Delta airlines and Delta's commuter partner, SkyWest, use Concourse A. Southwest and Horizon airlines use Concourse B. A snack shop nestles where the concourses branch, and there are espresso stands midway up each of the two concourses — welcome stops for early-morning travelers.

Smoking is not permitted beyond the security checkpoint. There are only two smoking areas in the airport: One is near the top of the escalators, between the restaurant and concourses; the other is at the far (western) end of the ticketing area.

A new, four-story, covered parking structure, completed in November 1997, alleviates many parking problems at the airport. It accommodates 1,341 vehicles; rates are 75¢ per half-hour or a maximum of $7.50 per day. The airport also has a long-term economy lot as well as curbside valet parking.

For general airport information, call the previously listed number.

Rental Cars, Taxis and Shuttles

Five rental-car firms have agencies in the baggage-claim area at the Boise Air Terminal. They are Avis Rent A Car, (800) 452-1506; Budget Rent A Car, (800) 527-0700; Dollar Rent-A-Car, (800) 800-4000; Hertz Rent A Car, (800) 654-3131; and National Car Rental Interrent, (800) 227-7368.

Persons with disabilities may want to make advance arrangements for a special rental through Access Vans, 11175 W. Emerald Street, (208) 385-7647. Vans rent for $69 a day or $400 for seven days. They have wheelchair lifts, tie-downs and seat belts. The vans can also be fitted for hand controls for functions usually performed by the feet when driving — gas, throttle and brakes.

Taxicabs await newly arrived passengers in a taxi lane opposite baggage claim: This is perhaps the only place in the Treasure Valley where you will always find a cab waiting. Expect to pay about $12 for a one-way trip between the airport and downtown Boise. Some cab company numbers are ABC Taxi, (208) 344-4444; Airport Yellow Cab, (208) 345-5555; Boise City Taxi, (208) 377-3333; and Koala Cab, (208) 385-7600.

Several hotels also offer free airport shuttle service to their guests.

In addition, Boise's city bus line makes a stop at the airport, opposite the air-traffic control tower (see The BUS later in this chapter). The route runs directly down Vista Avenue and Capitol Boulevard to City Hall and costs about 75¢. You may find it inconvenient, however, as The BUS stops at the airport only half-hourly during peak morning and late-afternoon hours, hourly the rest of the day.

General Aviation Services

On the west side of the Boise Air Terminal is the general aviation area, from which several charter companies operate small planes to small airstrips and back-country destinations. They include Access Air, (208) 387-4984; Boise Air Service, (208) 383-3300; Pinnacle Air, (208) 383-9070; and Western Airways, (208) 389-4632.

Nampa Municipal Airport
101 Municipal Dr., Nampa
• (208) 466-0529

Nampa Municipal Airport, on the east side of that city, is a general aviation facility just off Garrity Boulevard. It is home to Rocky Mountain Air, (208) 466-0529, and the Snake River Flight Training Club, (208) 467-5676. The general aviation airport has a 5,000-foot runway. There are no landing fees. Planes that fuel there will receive free tie-downs for two or three days. Renting a tie-down for a month costs $20; for a shade hangar, $66; for an enclosed hangar, $101. Three different companies provide maintenance work. Lessons to earn a private pilot's license cost $3,000. They are given in Piper Cub and Cessna 150 planes. The Unicom frequency is 122.7.

Caldwell Industrial Airport
4061 Aviation Way, Caldwell
• **(208) 459-9779**

This airport, perhaps best-known for its Warhawk Air Museum, is just north of I-84. Avjet Aviation, (208) 459-9455, and Hinkle Aviation, (208) 455-0384, both charter carriers, fly from the airstrip. The runway for this general aviation airport is 5,500 feet. Its Unicom frequency is 122.8, but it will change to 122.7, the same frequency as Nampa Municipal Airport, in late summer or early fall of 1998. There is no landing fee. Tie-downs cost $15 per month; hangar space runs from $165 to $300. Fuel and maintenance are available. Lessons leading to a pilot's license cost $2,000 to $3,000.

(For information about the Warhawk Air Museum, see the Attractions chapter.)

By Mass Transit

The BUS

Boise Urban Stages — better known by their simple acronym, "The BUS" — have an extensive system of over two dozen routes that blanket the city of Boise. Routes operate between 5:15 AM and 7:15 PM weekdays, and there is Saturday service on a handful of more important routes from 7:45 AM to 6:10 PM.

The following is a list of the most frequently traveled routes.

Routes 3 and 13 run between downtown Boise and the airport via Capitol Boulevard and Vista Avenue.

Route 5 runs between downtown and Towne Square Mall.

Route 19 serves Boise State University.

Fares run 75¢ for adults, 50¢ for youth (ages 6 through 18), 35¢ for seniors (60 and older) and for everyone on Saturdays. Children younger than 6 ride free. Monthly passes, which must be presented when boarding, cost $27 for adults, $18 for youth and $13.50 for seniors. You may purchase them at locations throughout the city, including all Albertsons supermarkets. Call (208) 336-1010 for more information.

In Nampa, **Treasure Valley Transit**, (208) 465-6411, runs a single hourly route through the city from 8 AM to 5 PM weekdays, linking downtown businesses with Nampa Recreation

Center to the south and with Karcher Mall and Boise State University's Canyon County Center to the northwest. Fares are 50¢ for adults, 25¢ for youth and seniors.

Commuters-Bus, Inc., (208) 455-4287, runs once-a-day shuttles between Nampa/Caldwell and downtown Boise, leaving Canyon County before 7 AM weekdays and departing Boise State University and downtown Boise between 5 and 5:15 PM. Tickets cost $4 one-way, $6 round-trip, $25 per week or $69.50 per month. The shuttle, a Greyhound bus, leaves Caldwell at 6:50 AM from the United Old Bulk Plant near Franklin Road and Chicago Street. It leaves Nampa at the Jackson Truck Stop, I-84 Exit 36, at 7 AM. In Boise it stops at the Capitol, St. Luke's Regional Medical Center, Morrison-Knudsen and Boise Air Terminal. Tickets are purchased as you board the bus.

Bus Lines

Greyhound Bus Lines operate three eastbound (to Salt Lake City) and three westbound (to Portland) buses daily, with morning, afternoon and evening departures. Call (800) 231-2222 for route and fare information.

In addition to Greyhound, the locally owned **Boise-Winnemucca/Northwestern Stage Lines** operate through Boise with four departures each day. Northbound buses travel to Spokane via McCall and Lewiston; southbound buses head for Reno via Nampa, Caldwell and Winnemucca, Nevada. For route and fare information, call (208) 336-3302.

Boise's intercity bus depot is downtown at 1212 W. Bannock Street. Its direct line is (208) 343-3681. The Nampa terminal is at 315 12th Avenue S., (208) 467-5122, while the Caldwell depot is at 1017 Arthur Street, (208) 459-2816. Greyhound and Boise-Winnemucca/Northwestern Stage Lines depart from all three depots.

Sun Valley Stages operates regular charter service between the Sun Valley resort community and Boise, including airport transfers. It's headquartered in Boise at 815 Ann Morrison Park Drive; call (208) 336-4038 or (800) 821-9064 to reserve a seat. A one-way fare is $49; round-trip, $89.

Mile High Shuttle & Tour, (208) 634-3495, provides a charter van service for trips from the Boise Air Terminal to anywhere in the state. For a trip from Boise to McCall, the van costs $95, and each person costs $10.

By Train

When Amtrak halted passenger rail service through Boise in 1997, the city was left with a historic depot and a good track but nothing to run on it. It didn't take long for a consortium of local government agencies to begin discussions about launching a valley-wide commuter-rail system.

During a two-week trial run in October 1997, the European-built, diesel-powered *Sprinter* impressed Idahoans with its speed and accessibility. The 174-passenger vehicle, which included wheelchair tie-downs and interior bicycle racks, ran between the Boise depot and the Idaho Center northeast of Nampa, with a spur to Micron Industries in southeast Boise.

Although the *Sprinter* was well-received, it would be overly optimistic to expect it to be in place before 2003, if at all. A regional public transportation authority must first be formed; its earliest obligations would include the purchase of the Union Pacific track corridor and the undertaking of a thorough cost and feasibility study.

Alternative Transportation

Bicycles

Most of Boise, including the downtown area, is relatively flat. This makes it an ideal city for bicycling. Two-wheelers are used not only for recreation (see that chapter title) but also as commuter vehicles by many Boiseans. Many city streets, including Bannock, Front, 10th, 15th and 16th downtown, already have bike lanes, and a much more extensive network is part of the regional transportation plan.

State laws require bicyclists to observe most of the same regulations as drivers, although full stops aren't required at signed intersections unless necessary for safety. Bicyclists must keep as far as possible to the right-hand side of the street (either side on a one-way street), and must have headlights and reflectors when riding at night. Safety helmets, while not required by law, should be worn.

The Boise Mayor's Office maintains a Bicycle Advisory Committee, (208) 384-4422. The committee advises the city on bicycle lanes and programs that encourage more bicycle riding, such as working with companies to promote commuting by two wheels instead of four.

Carriages

During special events or by charter for special occasions, Capital Coach & Carriage offers rides in horse-drawn carriages through the streets of downtown Boise, between Julia Davis and Fort Boise parks. The company has four carriages, a large one that carries 12 people and three that carry four people. For a party of two, a 30-minute ride costs $50; for four, $60. Call (208) 343-2866 for information or to make reservations.

General Information

Boise Convention & Visitors Bureau, 168 N. 9th Street, Boise, (208) 344-7777 or (800) 635-5240

Boise Chamber of Commerce, 300 N. 6th Street, Boise, (208) 344-5515

Downtown Boise Association, 300 N. 6th Street, Boise, (208) 336-2631

Caldwell Chamber of Commerce, 300 Frontage Road, Caldwell, (208) 459-7493

Meridian Chamber of Commerce, 215 E. Franklin Road, Meridian, (208) 888-2817

Nampa Chamber of Commerce, 1305 3rd Street S., Nampa, (208) 466-4641

The Idaho Travel Council, 700 W. State Street, Boise, (208) 334-2470 or (800) 847-4843

Accommodations

It is said that when Will Rogers visited Boise in the early 1930s, the famed humorist commented, "Whenever I'm in Idaho-ho-ho, I never know whether to stay at the Idanha-ha-ha or the Owyhee-hee-hee."

The Hotel Idanha and the Owyhee Plaza Hotel remain prominent fixtures in downtown Boise. But they have been joined by dozens of other hotels, motels, bed-and-breakfast homes and other accommodations to the tune of nearly 5,000 rooms in the Boise area. Today, Boise offers a very wide range of lodging choices, from downtown's beautiful new 17-story Grove Hotel to a profusion of national franchise properties.

In the listing that follows, hotels and motels are arranged by area: Boise, Nampa and Caldwell. Remember that the smaller towns of Kuna, Meridian and Garden City that are close to the city of Boise are included under the Boise subhead. We'll include the town name in our address line so you'll know when a property is not in Boise proper. Please note, too, that a separate bed and breakfast chapter follows this one.

When a lodging has a toll-free reservation number, it is included in the listing, along with its local number. Unless otherwise noted, all accommodations accept major credit cards; include private baths, heating and air-conditioning; and provide telephones and cable or satellite television in every room.

Pricing information was provided by the hotels and is presented as a guide to help you approximate likely costs. Rates may be higher during the tourist-heavy summer season. On weekends and during holiday periods, when business travel slows down, even the best hotels may cut their rates dramatically: It pays to shop around. Be sure to ask for discounts — corporate if you're on business, government or military if they apply, senior if you're beyond baby-boomer age, automobile association if you're a member — to cut costs further.

In Boise, there is an 11 percent tax on all lodging, which includes a 4 percent bed tax to support the convention center and convention and visitors bureau. Outside Boise, hotel rooms are subject to the 5 percent state sales tax and a 2 percent state bed tax, for a total tax of 7 percent.

Price-Code Key

Each listing includes a symbol indicating a price range for a one-night stay, midweek, double-occupancy.

$	Less than $40
$$	$40 to $65
$$$	$65 to $90
$$$$	$90 to $115
$$$$$	$115 and more

Boise

Ameritel Inn
$$$ • 7965 W. Emerald St.
• (208) 378-7000, (800) 600-6001

Once you get past its fortress-like exterior, you'll find this four-story hotel adjacent to Boise Towne Square quite appealing. The 124 rooms include executive and kitchen suites; all have working desks with dual-line speaker phones and computer data ports. A deluxe continental breakfast, morning paper and evening snack are included in the rate. Facilities include a large indoor pool, open 24 hours, a Jacuzzi tub, fitness center and guest laundry.

Best Rest Inn
$$ • 8002 Overland Rd. • (208) 322-4404, (800) 733-1418

Thanks to freeway rerouting, you'll have to

make a bit of a detour to reach this 86-room property: either through the Wal-Mart parking lot or through the Flying J Travel Plaza truck stop. Once here, however, you'll find a pleasant, renovated two-story property that includes a continental breakfast in its rates. All rooms have VCRs, with movies available for rent in the lobby. There's also a swimming pool, hot tub and guest laundry, and pets are accepted.

Best Western Airport Motor Inn
$$$ • 2660 Airport Way • (208) 384-5000, (800) 727-5004

The less fancy of two airport-area Best Westerns, this two-story motel has 50 rooms with king-size or two queen-size beds. Refrigerators are available on request, and the inn has an outdoor swimming pool (open seasonally) and a guest laundry. Courtesy coffee is always brewing in the lobby, and a continental breakfast is included in the room rate.

Best Western Rama Inn
$$$ • 1019 S. Progress Ave., Meridian • (208) 887-7888, (800) 528-1234

A handsome two-story motor inn adjacent to the main Meridian freeway exit, the Rama has 62 spacious modern rooms, many of which feature separate living and sleeping areas. All have microwave ovens and refrigerators. Facilities include an indoor swimming pool, hot tub and sauna, weight room and coin-op guest Laundromat. Daily newspapers are available with a free continental breakfast each morning.

Best Western Safari Motor Inn
$$$ • 1070 Grove St. • (208) 344-6556, (800) 541-6556

A pleasant two-story, downtown motel with

covered parking, the Safari has 104 spacious rooms with refrigerators and coffee makers. Facilities include a swimming pool, sauna, hot tub and fitness room, and a free continental breakfast is served each morning. The motel is two blocks' walk from Boise Centre on the Grove.

Best Western Vista Inn
$$ • 2645 Airport Way • (208) 336-8100, (800) 727-5006

One of the more luxurious of the airport-area motels, the Vista Inn boasts 87 modern guest rooms built on two levels around a central interior courtyard. Rooms have executive desks for business travelers with computer data ports. Morning newspapers are delivered with continental breakfasts. Facilities include an exercise room, a hot tub, sauna and outdoor pool. There are also extensive meeting rooms. Soundproofing keeps the sound of jet air traffic to a minimum.

Boise Park Suite Hotel
$$$$ • 424 E. Parkcenter Blvd. • (208) 342-1044, (800) 342-1044

People who like to be pampered will be pleased at this all-suite property. Each of its 238 units has kitchen facilities, including a microwave oven, refrigerator, coffee maker, toaster and utensils, and continental breakfast is delivered to guests' rooms with the daily newspaper each morning. The living rooms have sofa sleepers (for additional guests) and TVs with VCRs, and phones include one with a modem attachment. Facilities include a fitness center with a pool and hot tub, a guest laundry and a business center with secretarial services and computer rental.

www.insiders.com
See this and many other **Insiders' Guide®** destinations online — in their entirety.
Visit us today!

INSIDERS' TIP

You're pulling a recreational vehicle through Idaho, and you don't know where to stop? No problem. There are plenty of RV parks in the greater Boise area, and the Idaho RV Campgrounds Association, P.O. Box 7841, Boise, ID 83707, (208) 345-6009 or (800) RV-IDAHO, will be glad to give you further information.

Boise River Inn
$$ • 1140 Colorado Ave.
• (208) 344-9988

Another all-suite hotel is this property on wooded Logger Creek, an offshoot of the Boise River just east of the university. Ducks, squirrels and a variety of other wildlife can be easily viewed through the windows of the inn's 88 cozy guest rooms — all of which have kitchenettes with stoves and refrigerators. There's a swimming pool (open summers) and a guest laundry; a light continental breakfast is served in the lobby.

The Boisean Motel
$$ • 1300 S. Capitol Blvd.
• (208) 343-3645, (800) 365-3645

Spreading across more than a full city block adjacent to Boise State University, this motel has 136 comfortable rooms, some of them with kitchenettes. King-size beds and fire-

place suites are also available. Motel facilities include an outdoor swimming pool, exercise room and whirlpool, a guest laundry and a business center.

Budget Inn
$ • 2600 Fairview Ave. • (208) 344-8617

There's no parking problem at the Budget Inn, which spreads around a parking area west of downtown adjacent to The Capri restaurant. Most of the 44 cozy rooms have queen-size beds and coffee makers. Near the Greenbelt, the motel offers VCR rentals, a hot tub and a sauna.

Cabana Inn
$$ • 1600 W. Main St. • (208) 343-6000

This is a two-story hacienda-style motel situated downtown where Main and Fairview join. Fifty somewhat cavernous rooms have king- or queen-size beds. Although the Ca-

INSIDERS' TIP

Boise has a half-dozen options for RV accommodations: Americana Overnight Kampground, 3600 Americana Terrace, (208) 344-5733; Boise KOA Kampgrounds, 7300 S. Federal Way, (208) 345-7673; Fiesta RV Park, 11101 Fairview Avenue, (208) 375-8207; Hi-Valley RV Park, 10555 Idaho Highway 55, (208) 939-8080; Mountain View RV Park, 2040 Airport Way, (208) 345-4141; and On the River RV Park, 6000 Glenwood Street, (208) 375-7432 or (800) 375-7432.

bana is an older property, it's clean and convenient. Courtesy coffee is always available in the lobby.

Club Hotel by Doubletree
$$$ • 475 W. Parkcenter Blvd.
• (208) 345-2002, (800) 222-8733

A six-story hotel in the Parkcenter office district, this Doubletree caters to business travelers on weekdays. But it becomes a bargain for all travelers on weekends, when its rates are cut by half! The 158 rooms are nicely appointed, and a continental breakfast and late-night snacks are included in the room rate. A first-floor cafe serves meals. The hotel also has a large outdoor swimming pool and a workout room with adjoining spa.

Comfort Inn
$$ • 2526 Airport Way • (208) 336-0077, (800) 228-5150

The Comfort Inn doesn't scrimp on bed sizes: Each of the 60 guest rooms here has either king or queen mattresses. Just as you'd expect at this very affordable national chain, the rooms and amenities are basic but sufficient for the price. The motel has an indoor swimming pool and hot tub; a continental breakfast is served each morning.

Courtyard by Marriott
$$$$ • 222 S. Broadway Ave.
• (208) 331-2700, (800) 321-2211

One of Boise's newest motels, the Courtyard opened in 1997 between the downtown core and the Parkcenter business district. Its 162 rooms cater to business travelers, with working desks and computer data ports, free weekday morning newspapers, ironing boards and coffee makers. Facilities include an indoor pool and hot tub, a fitness room and a guest laundry. Breakfast is served daily in the Courtyard Cafe, and cocktails are offered nightly. Room service for dinner is available

Photo: William H. Mullins

With all of Boise's growth, it's easy to forget that the city was once just an area to pass through on the way West.

from the adjacent Perkins restaurant. Meeting rooms seat up to 40.

Doubletree Downtown Hotel
$$$ • 1800 Fairview Ave.
• (208) 344-7691, (800) 547-8010

The Doubletree group purchased this hotel and the nearby former Red Lion-Riverside in early 1997. The seven-story hotel, popular with airline crews and visiting sports teams, has 182 spacious rooms with modern amenities, including data ports, coffee makers and ironing boards. On the premises are a coffee shop and sports bar, a fitness room and a small outdoor swimming pool.

Doubletree Riverside Hotel
$$$$ • 2900 Chinden Blvd.
• (208) 343-1870, (800) 547-8010

Boise's largest hotel sprawls along the south bank of the Boise River 1.5 miles west of downtown. The expansive lobby area offers access to a coffee shop and lively lounge, a conference center and a gift shop. Beyond, beside the city-long Greenbelt, is a large fitness center with an outdoor swimming pool and Jacuzzi.

The 304 guest rooms and suites, all of them spacious and brightly decorated, have coffee makers and computer data ports as well as double vanities and oversized tubs in the bathrooms.

Econo Lodge
$$ • 2155 N. Garden St.
• (208) 344-4030, (800) 553-2666

A big white building between Main Street and Fairview Avenue at the Connector on- and off-ramps, the 52-room Econo Lodge offers comfortable basic lodging. Coffee makers and VCR rentals are available in all rooms. A continental breakfast is included in the rates, and there's a Japanese teppanyaki-style restaurant adjacent.

Extended Stay America
$$ • 2500 S. Vista Ave. • (208) 363-9040, (800) 398-7829

The founders of this national chain of efficiency studios designed their units specifically "for the long-term, value-conscious business traveler." The 107 modern rooms at this Boise location feature fully equipped kitchens including coffee makers, microwave ovens and refrigerators; computer data ports; and weekly rates that begin at less than $200! There's also a guest laundry.

Fairfield Inn
$$ • 3300 S. Shoshone St.
• (208) 331-5656, (800) 228-2800

The modern three-story Fairfield Inn is the more economy-oriented of two Marriott-owned motels that sit side-by-side just north of the airport, two blocks west of Vista Avenue. Business travelers appreciate the working desks in its 63 spacious rooms. There's an indoor spa and swimming pool, and a continental breakfast is served each morning.

The Grove Hotel
$$$$$ • 245 S. Capitol Blvd.
• (208) 333-8000, (800) 426-0670

Boise's first modern luxury hotel, a member of the WestCoast Hotels group, opened at the end of 1997 right on The Grove in the heart of downtown. Incorporating the 5,000-seat Bank of America Centre (home of sports events and concerts), the 17-story hotel has 225 rooms and 25 suites, topped by four floors of private condominiums. All rooms have cherry veneer furnishings with marble-floored baths, full entertainment centers, mini-bars, two phones with data ports, in-room coffee and ironing boards. Concierge, secretarial, laundry and valet parking services are available, along with 24-hour room service.

Emilio's, a restaurant inside the hotel, serves Northern Italian restaurant as well as a breakfast buffet (see the Restaurants chapter for more information). The hotel also has a lobby lounge and a trilevel sports bar and grill (under construction) overlooking the ice arena. One full floor of the hotel is a 15,000-square-foot athletic club with a full-size lap pool, sauna, Jacuzzi, steam bath and more weights and exercise equipment than you might imagine possible. There's also an executive business center and meeting facilities for up to 750.

Hampton Inn
$$$ • 3270 S. Shoshone St.
• (208) 331-5600, (800) 426-7866

The upscale Hampton shares the Fairfield's parking lot, but other facilities are its own, including an indoor swimming pool and whirlpool. Guests in its 64 rooms are served an excellent continental breakfast. Efficiency suites are available for just $10 more than standard rooms.

Holiday Inn Boise
$$$$ • 3300 Vista Ave. • (208) 344-8365, (800) 465-4329

With the completion of its new, high-tech Holidome indoor recreation center in early 1998, the 265-room Holiday Inn has established itself among Boise's leading hostelries. Laser-light shows and two-story-high video presentations are highlights of the Holidome, which also includes a swimming pool, hot tub and saunas, workout area, miniature golf course, state-of-the-art interactive arcade and children's playground. An additional outdoor pool is open in summer.

Pastel-hued rooms cater to business travelers, with desks or large tables, two telephones with voice mail and computer data ports; more than 12,000 square feet of conference and catering space is available. You can get a room refrigerator on request; pay-per-view movies may be viewed on TV. The hotel's restaurant, The Simmering Pot, specializes in American and Italian dishes (see Restaurants for more information). A poolside deli and a sports bar round out the dining and entertainment options. Best of all for families, children younger than 18 stay and eat free when traveling with their parents. A guest Laundromat is on the premises.

Holiday Inn Express
$$$ • 2613 Vista Ave. • (208) 388-0800, (800) 465-4329

VCR and movie rentals are a special feature of this three-story inn. The 63 spacious rooms — all of which have hair dryers — include king suites with kitchenettes. Free newspapers and continental breakfasts are served each morning in the lobby, where coffee is always waiting for the caffeine-charged. There's also an indoor swimming pool and hot tub, open year-round.

Hotel Idanha
$$ • 928 W. Main St. • (208) 342-3611

The six-story Idanha (pronounce the name with the accent on the *I*) is one of the most striking historical buildings in downtown Boise. Its corner turrets, bay windows, crenulated rooftop, striped window shades and awnings, and dramatic entranceways catch everybody's eye. Presidents Theodore Roosevelt and William Howard Taft, along with attorney Clarence Darrow, were among those who slept in the Idanha soon after it opened in 1901.

The hotel's 45 rooms have TV and telephones, and suites and kitchenettes are available. The corner rooms offer desks or reading

rooms in the turret towers. Amenities include a complimentary breakfast and airport transportation. One of the best-known gourmet restaurants in Boise, Peter Schott's, is located on the main floor (see our Restaurants chapter). There is a casual bar in the basement.

Inn America — A Budget Motel
$$ • 2275 Airport Way • (208) 389-9800, (800) 469-4667

The imposing, Colonial-style Inn America has 73 spacious rooms, many of them with king-size beds and working desks (with modem hookups). Access to all lodging, including family suites, is by key card. Facilities include a heated outdoor swimming pool, a 24-hour guest laundry and a gourmet snack and coffee vending area.

Motel 6
$ • 2323 Airport Way • (208) 344-3506, (800) 466-8356

This is perhaps the nicest of Boise's bottom-of-the-cost-barrel lodgings. Recently renovated, the motel's 91 rooms have little more than the traveler's essentials — but the property does offer a swimming pool (open seasonally) and free morning coffee, and pets generally are welcomed.

Mr. Sandman Motel
$$ • 1575 S. Meridian Rd., Meridian • (208) 887-2062, (800) 959-2230

With 85 rooms in three buildings just south of I-84 at Overland Road, Mr. Sandman is a comfortable oasis 8 miles west of downtown Boise. Guests have access to a guest laundry (no charge), hot tub and swimming pool (open seasonally), and to free continental breakfasts. JB's Restaurant is across the parking lot. Suites with kitchenettes and sofa sleepers are available at additional cost.

Owyhee Plaza Hotel
$$$ • 1109 W. Main St. • (208) 343-4611, (800) 233-4611

An expansion is planned for this venerable but fully renovated 100-room hotel, noted by many locals for its fine Gamekeeper restaurant and large piano lounge. While the cozy standard rooms are pleasant enough, the third-floor executive-level rooms are much more spacious and carry a price tag only nominally higher. Rates include a continental breakfast and access to a swimming pool and workout room. The Owyhee also has meeting and banquet facilities. Numerous offices, including those of a leading radio station, are on the upper stories.

The Pioneer Inn at Bogus Basin
$$$ • 2405 Bogus Basin Rd. • (208) 332-5224, (800) 367-4397

This condominium village's 70 rooms are open for lodging year-round, but they're especially popular between Thanksgiving and Easter, when they offer ski-in, ski-out accommodation to winter-sports lovers at the Bogus Basin Ski Area. All units have kitchens for those who prefer to prepare their own meals, but the inn also has a restaurant and cocktail lounge. Other facilities include a sauna and Jacuzzi, a guest laundry, a game room and a nursery where young children can play while their parents ski.

Plaza Suite Hotel
$$$ • 409 S. Cole Rd. • (208) 375-7666, (800) 376-3608

The 38 handsome guest rooms at this four-story hotel may be the largest standard units in Boise. All include one king- or two queen-size beds, a working desk with computer data port, in-room coffee, ironing facilities and more. A continental breakfast is served each morning beneath a skylight, beside the indoor swimming pool.

Quality Inn Airport Suites
$$ • 2717 Vista Ave. • (208) 343-7505, (800) 228-5151

Offering economy for the business traveler, the Quality Inn's 79 rooms separate bedrooms from living areas. Microwave ovens, refrigerators and in-room coffee service complement the continental breakfast served each morning. Other facilities include a heated swimming pool and exercise room, a business center and meeting areas.

Residence Inn by Marriott
$$$$ • 1401 Lusk Ave. • (208) 344-1200, (800) 331-3131

An all-suite hotel in a village of 14 buildings between Capitol Boulevard and Ann

Morrison Park, the Residence Inn is perfect for travelers seeking something with the flavor of home. Most of the 104 units (studios and one- and two-bedroom suites) have fireplaces, and all have fully equipped kitchens. You'll get a daily newspaper served with your continental breakfast each morning, and when you want to play, there's an outdoor swimming pool and Jacuzzi as well as a tennis/basketball court. The hotel also has a guest Laundromat.

Rodeway Inn of Boise
$$$ • 1115 N. Curtis Rd.
• (208) 376-2700, (800) 228-2000
This 98-room hotel is a popular stop for folks visiting nearby St. Alphonsus medical center, but it is often overlooked by others despite its convenient location at the Curtis Road exit from the Connector. The hotel has a popular and innovative restaurant and a lounge that features live music, and a full breakfast is served to full-paying guests. An indoor/outdoor swimming pool is open year-round. There's also a guest laundry, and coffee makers are provided in each room.

Sands Motel
$ • 1111 W. State St. • (208) 343-2533
Just four blocks west of the State Capitol is this lowest-priced lodging in the downtown area. Though modest, the two-story motel is clean and comfortable. Eighteen rooms have all essential amenities. Rooms with king-size beds are available on request.

7K Motel
$ • 3633 Chinden Blvd., Garden City
• (208) 343-7723
A cheerful brick building with its guest-room doors brightly painted, the 7K offers 23 basic — but clean and well-maintained — rooms. All have in-room coffee and refrigerators; you can request a full kitchenette. There's

a small outdoor swimming pool, and a three-bedroom family unit is available.

Shilo Inn — Boise Airport
$$ • 4111 Broadway Ave.
• (208) 343-7662, (800) 222-2244
An excellent value, the Shilo Inn — a short distance east of the airport at the Broadway Avenue exit from I-84 — has 79 newly remodeled mini-suites whose kitchenettes include refrigerators and microwave ovens. The inn offers an in-house cafe, where a free continental breakfast is served each morning; an outdoor swimming pool and hot tub; an indoor fitness center adjoined by a sauna and steam room; a free morning paper; and VCR and movie rentals.

Shilo Inn — Boise Riverside
$$ • 3031 W. Main St. • (208) 344-3521, (800) 222-2244
With its back to the Greenbelt, this is one of Boise's better motel bargains. The tasteful three-story inn has 112 rooms with refrigerators and microwave ovens, VCRs and free daily newspapers, and continental breakfasts are included in rates. Facilities include an indoor swimming pool and spa, a sauna and steam bath, a full fitness center and a guest Laundromat. A steakhouse and lounge are next door.

Sleep Inn
$$ • 2799 Airport Way • (208) 336-7377, (800) 321-4661
There's no lodging nearer the Boise Air Terminal than this pleasant motel, whose 69 ample rooms offer in-room refrigerators and coffee makers on request as well as oversize showers for washing away that long flight. Rooms have spacious desks with computer data ports for business travelers. VCR movie rentals are available from the lobby, which also has a coffee bar where breakfast snacks and morning newspapers are available.

INSIDERS' TIP

You'll find one RV park each in Meridian, Nampa and Caldwell: The Playground RV Park, 1780 E. Overland Road, Meridian, (208) 887-1022; Mason Creek RV Park, 807 Franklin Boulevard, Nampa, (208) 465-7199; and Caldwell Campground & RV Park, Exit 26, I-84, Caldwell, (208) 454-0279.

Statehouse Inn
$$$ • 981 Grove St. • (208) 342-4622, (800) 243-6622

Directly across 9th Street from the Boise Centre on the Grove, this well-maintained six-story hotel is convenient for convention goers, who pay nothing extra to use its large covered parking lot. Facilities in the 88 nicely decorated guest rooms include entertainment units with VCRs and computer data ports. Room service is available from the Skylight Patio Restaurant and Lounge. The hotel also has a fitness center and spa plus meeting and banquet facilities.

Super 8 Lodge — Boise
$$ • 2773 Elder St. • (208) 344-8871, (800) 800-8000

If you generally are familiar with the Super 8 national chain, this one will fit right in step: two-story mock-Tudor architecture; clean and comfortable rooms. This motel, at the corner of Vista Avenue, has 110 rooms, an indoor swimming pool and — for breakfast — a toast bar. Waterbed rooms are popular.

University Inn
$$ • 2360 University Dr.
• (208) 345-7170, (800) 345-7170

This two-story motor inn is by the BSU campus at the corner of Capitol Boulevard. Its 80 cozy rooms are pretty much standard issue, but your room charge includes a continental breakfast. Motel facilities include a large swimming pool and hot tub, a casual restaurant and the Iron Gate cocktail lounge.

Ustick Inn Residence Hotel
$ • 8050 Ustick Rd. • (208) 322-6277

This country farmhouse is nearly a century old, and Boise has long since expanded beyond its former fields. But for budget-minded solo visitors staying a week or longer, there may be no cheaper place to stay than this inn, 5 miles west of downtown. Twenty-six private rooms and small dormitories offer 42 bunks for men and women travelers, who otherwise share washrooms and showers, a library and a pair of TV lounges. The only phones are pay phones, but management will take messages for you.

Westriver Inn
$ • 3525 Chinden Blvd., Garden City
• (208) 338-1155

This property is the best value of Garden City's several budget-priced "strip" motels. Painted stucco and with a shingled roof, it has 21 clean and comfortable units with queen-size beds and all the basics. The management is friendly, and coffee is always on in the lobby.

Nampa

Budget Inn
$ • 908 3rd St. • (208) 466-3594

Forty-three small but comfortable rooms in downtown Nampa comprise the Budget Inn, which has the advantage of an authentic Mexican restaurant — El Rodeo — on the premises. Rooms have queen-size beds and coffee makers; VCR and movie rentals are available in the lobby. A handful of kitchenette apartments are popular with guests staying a week or longer.

Inn America — A Budget Motel
$$ • 130 Shannon Dr. • (208) 442-0800, (800) 469-4667

The Colonial-style facade of this handsome new motor hotel harbors several dozen spacious rooms, many of them with king-size beds and working desks (with computer data ports). There's also a heated outdoor swimming pool, a 24-hour guest laundry and a gourmet snack vending area.

Nampa Super 8 Motel
$$ • 624 Nampa Blvd. • (208) 467-2888, (800) 800-8000

Just the basics, ma'am — that's what you'll get at the Super 8. The two-story motel is indeed comfortable, its 62 rooms on the smaller side but spotless. Facilities include an indoor swimming pool and a toast bar where a continental breakfast is available.

Shilo Inn — Nampa Suites Hotel
$$$$ • 1401 Shilo Dr. • (208) 465-3250, (800) 222-2244

Nampa's most-appointed accommodation is this four-story, 83-unit motor inn just off the central Nampa exit from I-84. As the name implies, every room at this Shilo Inn is a suite.

Photo: John Gottberg

Hotel Idanha has been a downtown landmark since 1901.

There are refrigerators, microwave ovens and wet bars in every room, and eight units have full efficiency kitchens. Every room also gets a free morning paper delivered; VCR and movie rentals are available.

The hotel has a full-service restaurant (24-hour room service is offered), a deli counter and a lounge. Workout facilities include a fitness center and small indoor swimming pool, a hot tub, sauna and steam room. Meeting rooms seat up to 200 people.

Shilo Inn Motel
$$$ • 617 Nampa Blvd. • (208) 466-8993, (800) 222-2244

Nearer to downtown is this two-story cousin of the Nampa Suites. It has 61 rooms with microwaves and refrigerators as well as morning newspaper delivery. There's a small outdoor swimming pool, an indoor Jacuzzi, a sauna and steam room plus a coin-op laundry. A continental breakfast is included, and VCRs (and movies) can be rented in the lobby.

Sleep Inn
$$ • 1315 Industrial Rd.
• (208) 463-6300, (800) 321-4661

Sleep Inns ask you to pay a little to get a lot, and this one is no different. Its 81 rooms all have VCRs to play movies available from the front desk, and a deluxe continental breakfast is included each morning. The motel also has a coin-op laundry. An indoor swimming pool and hot tub as well as guest membership at a nearby athletic club are complimentary.

Caldwell

Comfort Inn
$$ • 901 Specht St. • (208) 454-2222, (800) 228-5150

Get a room on the upper floor of this three-story motel, and you're guaranteed some exercise: There's no elevator. The 65 pleasant units, however, have beds that are either king- or queen-size. Coffee makers and refrigerators are available; there are three kitchen units and three others with double Jacuzzis. A continental breakfast is served each morning, coffee and cookies in the evening. Facilities include a coin-op laundry, small indoor pool, wading pool, sauna, hot tub and exercise room — all of them open 24 hours.

Full breakfasts are served at every bed and breakfast in the Treasure Valley. No continental meals here!

Bed and Breakfasts

It's only in recent years that the Boise area has jumped on the bed and breakfast bandwagon. But it hasn't taken long for these inns to catch on, and not just with travelers. Local residents find bed and breakfasts great places to lodge out-of-town visitors or ideal getaways for themselves when a break from the usual routine of home and hearth is in order.

Each bed and breakfast inn has a character of its own. Some are historic homes, such as the Idaho Heritage Inn, a former governor's mansion, or The Maples, a 19th-century country farmhouse. Others have been custom-built specifically as bed and breakfasts; a case in point is The Inn at Shadow Valley, on a hilltop overlooking the Treasure Valley. Still others are private homes that have been reshaped into bed and breakfasts, like BJ's Secret Garden, which has become one of the area's most popular locations for weddings and receptions.

There are some things to take for granted when you stay at a bed and breakfast in the Boise area; other things you'll want to ask about.

Most Boise-area bed-and-breakfast rooms have private baths. In rare cases, two rooms share a bath, and you should expect prices for these rooms to be lower.

Full breakfasts are served at every bed and breakfast in the Treasure Valley: no continental meals here! Some inns may also serve wine and cheese or other snacks in the late afternoon or cookies and hot chocolate at bedtime.

Every bed and breakfast inn prohibits smoking indoors, both to protect its often-antique furnishings and to satisfy strict insurance requirements. Guests who must smoke are asked to step outside — onto the porch, for instance, or into the yard. Pets are usually not allowed; however, we've noted a couple of bed and breakfasts that may permit small pets in carriers.

Most inns do not encourage young children to stay, instead gearing their accommodations to adult couples and business travelers. At least one inn here, however, accepts children 12 and older, and a couple of others will take well-behaved children of any age.

Price-Code Key

Each listing that follows includes a symbol indicating an average price range for a one-night stay, double-occupancy. Bear in mind that most bed and breakfasts have a range of rooms available at different price levels. Pricing information was provided by the inns themselves and is presented as a guide to help you approximate likely costs. Unless otherwise noted, these inns accept major credit cards.

$	**Less than $40**
$$	**$40 to $60**
$$$	**$60 to $80**
$$$$	**$80 to $100**
$$$$$	**$100 and more**

In Boise, there is an 11 percent tax on all lodging, which includes a 4 percent bed tax to support the convention center and convention and visitors bureau. Outside of Boise, hotel rooms are subject to the 5 percent state sales tax and a 2 percent state bed tax, for a total tax of 7 percent.

If having a room phone or television is important to you, be sure to inquire ahead. About a third of the Boise area's bed and breakfasts assume you can do without one, offering instead a common television room for those guests who can't miss their favorite show. Another third of the bed and breakfasts take televisions to the opposite extreme, including a VCR with the set and offering free movies to go with it.

The situation is similar with telephones. Two bed and breakfasts are ideally set up for business travelers with modem links attached to their room phone lines. Two others have room phones, but without modem connections. Two inns have hookups available for phones; three have no phones in the rooms whatsoever.

When a bed and breakfast has a toll-free reservation number, it is included in the listing along with its local number.

Boise

Bed and Breakfast at Victoria's White House
$$$$ • 10325 W. Victory Rd. • (208) 362-0507

From busy Victory Road, this modern home on an acre of land in suburban southwest Boise indeed looks like a miniature of the White House in Washington, D.C. Jeannette and Pablo Tan-Baldazo bought the inn in 1985 and added antique touches to the two spacious guest rooms. One chamber has a fireplace and full entertainment center; the other boasts a private deck and small refrigerator. Breakfast is served in the formal dining room. Unlike many inns, this one welcomes children; in fact, there are two sandy play lots in the yard.

BJ's in a Secret Garden
$$$ • 2021 Kootenai St. • (208) 342-4455

Owner Bev Beumeier is a florist, a designer and a caterer, so it comes as no surprise that her wonderfully landscaped "secret garden" is popular for weddings and receptions. And it's only natural that the bride and groom spend the first night of their honeymoon in BJ's bridal suite. Overlooking the garden itself, the suite has a full entertainment center and a deck accessed through French doors. There are two other smaller rooms. Breakfast is served in the bright garden room or the formal dining room. Guests may gather before the fireplace for late-afternoon snacks or retire to the television room if there's a show that just can't be missed.

Idaho Heritage Inn Bed and Breakfast
$$$ • 109 W. Idaho St. • (208) 342-8066

Once the home of Governor Chase Clark (1941-43) and Senator Frank Church (1957-81), this 1904 mansion is listed on the National Register of Historic Places. An interesting aspect for many guests is that it's heated by a geothermal steam. A six-bedroom bed and breakfast since 1987, Boise's first, it perpetuates the atmosphere of its heyday with antique furnishings and a wide range of political memorabilia. Each room, including a Carriage House with an efficiency kitchen, has a two-line phone; two rooms have televisions. Owner Phyllis Lupher prepares a gourmet breakfast for guests each morning and serves it, in summer, on an outdoor patio.

www.insiders.com

See this and many other **Insiders' Guide®** destinations online — in their entirety.

Visit us today!

J.J. Shaw House Bed and Breakfast
$$$$ • 1411 W. Franklin St. • (208) 344-8899

A three-story, Queen Anne-style, brick-and-sandstone manor, Michael and Ruthie White's 1907 J.J. Shaw House is only a short walk from downtown Boise. Its decor is highlighted by a sitting room with a player piano, a parlor with a fireplace, and original leaded glass and bay windows throughout. All five guest rooms have coffee service and phones with modem links, catering to business travelers. A delightful attic suite is popular with honeymooners. Breakfast is often served in the sun room. Children are not encouraged.

INSIDERS' TIP

The hosts and other guests at a bed and breakfast can be a wealth of information about what to do in the area. A few moments of conversation can provide you with a full day's itinerary of must-sees and off-the-beaten-path favorites.

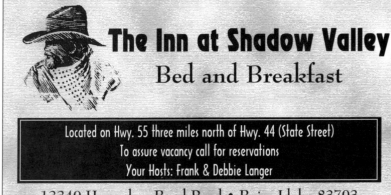

Robin's Nest Bed and Breakfast
$$$$ • 2389 W. Boise Ave.
• (208) 336-9551

A hillside stream trickles down a steep slope beside the Robin's Nest, an 1892 home moved here from the Warm Springs district in 1991 and placed on a new foundation. The four guest rooms, all with phones and televisions, feature such classic fixtures in their bathrooms as pedestal sinks and claw-foot tubs. The Claire Monde bridal suite boasts a four-poster canopy bed and a step-up Jacuzzi. Hardwood floors, Oriental carpets and vintage furniture are features of the entire house. The inn accepts no children younger than 12.

The Inn at Shadow Valley
$$$$$ • 13340 Horseshoe Bend Rd.,
Eagle • (208) 939-0585, (888) 290-5296

Built on a hilltop off Idaho Highway 55 several miles west of downtown Boise, the inn differs from others in the Treasure Valley in that it was custom-designed to become a bed and breakfast. Opened in 1995 by Frank Langer and his wife, Debbie, its open, spacious feel extends from the great room, with its cathedral ceiling and wall of windows facing a wraparound deck, to its four guest rooms, each decorated with a traditional Western motif. All rooms have phone hookups and televisions with VCRs. Debbie, a former cooking instructor, prepares a gourmet breakfast each

morning. Children are welcome in the family suite. Though the Inn does not encourage pets, small animals with carriers may be permitted. Call ahead to make sure you won't have to leave your furry friend in the car overnight.

The Maples Bed and Breakfast
$$$ • 10600 Idaho Hwy. 44, Star
• (208) 286-7419

A country farmhouse believed to have been built in 1888, now lovingly restored and remodeled, is the home of The Maples. Owners Mary and Don Wertman are teachers who brought furnishings and handmade quilts from their original home in Lancaster County, Pennsylvania, to decorate the three guest rooms. All of them have phones and televisions. Family heirlooms throughout the house include an 18th-century dining table at which breakfast is served each morning. Children are generally accepted here.

Nampa

The Pink Tudor Bed and Breakfast
$$ • 1315 12th Ave. S. • (208) 465-3615,
(800) 266-3759

A beautiful grand piano dominates the living room of this small home in south Nampa. The two guest rooms, both with a television and VCR and phone hookups, are simple but

Photo: William H. Mullins

Don't stay cooped up in your hotel room. Get out and explore the area's waterways.

pleasant. They're spotless because, says owner Marilyn Fleming, "I love to clean." Neither smoking nor alcohol are permitted, but kids are welcome to stay.

Caldwell

Harvey House Bed and Breakfast
$$$$ • 13466 Idaho Hwy. 44
• (208) 454-9874

Two miles east of I-84 Exit 25, near the village of Middleton, Angela and Bill Cyr's country home sits on three acres of land amidst fields of flowers. Three upstairs guest rooms — one king suite with a private bath, two smaller rooms that share a large bath — are built around a common room with a library, refrigerator and full entertainment center. A hot tub occupies a corner of the outer courtyard. Breakfast is served on china each morning, while Angela delights in preparing prix fixe dinners for guests by reservation. Small pets in carriers may be allowed here, but you must call ahead and clear it with the owners first.

DINING DECISIONS

*Your complete restaurant guide
to the Boise Area*

*•Easy reference charts • Area maps • Wine section
• Boise's Brewpubs • Entertainment • A complete
listing of area restaurants • And much more!*

DINING

YOUR COMPLETE RESTAURANT GUIDE TO THE BOISE AREA. *decisions*

*For information on how to get your FREE copy
Call P.V. Quinn & Company
at 385-0338
or write to:
1520 W. Washington Street
Boise, Idaho 83702*

Restaurants

What was a steak-and-potatoes redoubt has changed overnight into a far-flung, multi-faceted restaurant garden. Asians, Egyptians, Mexicans and people from other distant and overseas locations have parachuted into the Treasure Valley with food on their minds and the imagination, ability and persistence to set up and maintain their own tents. Fast-food and franchises are big here, but with the growth of a professional, educated and more worldly population, they are not nearly as automatic choices as they used to be.

Downtown's 8th Street corridor south of the Capitol to Myrtle Street is a 15-minute stroll past a score of many-striped eateries that are aided and abetted by cafes, wine bars, snackeries, benches, flowers, public art and amusements regularly promoted by the Downtown Boise Association. The 60-block downtown area shot up from 48 restaurants in 1990 to 85 in 1997, so if you don't trip over a lasagna or bratwurst, it could be a halibut, baba ghanouj or duck a l'orange.

West Boise, especially near Boise Towne Square mall, has in recent years attracted well-known nationally franchised restaurants that particularly appeal to shoppers and families with children that live in that area. Because the franchises are known throughout the country, we don't include them, although we do have a close-up in this chapter that addresses their powerful and lucrative emergence here.

Not only downtown Boise, but also various city pockets and satellite Ada and Canyon County towns are picking up restaurant speed and diversity. We include ethnic and unusual local eateries throughout the Treasure Valley with reports on some of the best bites in American, Asian, International, Italian, Mexican and Steak-and-Seafood categories.

Brewpubs and sports bars have become important to the knife-and-fork scene with food that is sometimes as good and plentiful as that found in conventional restaurants. We've included several here as well as a number of coffeehouses that have burst into the valley with aroma, style and flavor that makes it seem like they've always been here — though it's only been a few short years.

Credit cards and local checks are accepted by virtually all of these eateries. Restaurants are categorized first by type of cuisine, then by geographic region — Boise, Nampa and Caldwell. Remember that the towns of Meridian, Eagle, Garden City, Kuna and Star are included under Boise. Along with phone numbers, operating schedules, atmosphere, menu highlights, insights, notes, observations and the following price guide, this chapter should get you to an appropriate location before you die of hunger and thirst.

Price-Code Key

The price-key symbol in each restaurant listing gives the range for the likely cost of a dinner for two, not including cocktails, beer or wine, appetizer or dessert, tax or tip. Your own bill at a given restaurant may be higher or lower, depending on what you order and given fluctuating restaurant prices.

$	Less than $20
$$	$20 to $30
$$$	$30 to $40
$$$$	$40 and more

INSIDERS' TIP

Boise has restaurant chefs from a number of foreign lands, including Iran, Vietnam, Austria, Taiwan, Siam, Mexico and Egypt.

American

Boise

Big City Coffee & Café
$ • 5517 W. State St. • (208) 853-9161

You can get off your bicycle and carbo-load here in the company of old bikes, frames and tools, photographs and posters, and racing jerseys autographed by Greg Lemond and Ann Wilson. Owner Scott Cunningham, a former bicycle racer himself, heaps on the Belgian waffles, the yogurt-laced "Famers" waffles and the "Otis" waffles that are topped with fresh strawberries, kiwi fruit and bananas and sprinkled with lemon juice and powdered sugar. Soups, salads, sandwiches and pizzas attract the lunch and casual dinner crowd. Big City has its own bakery and makes its own breads, cakes and pastries. It's open for breakfast, lunch and dinner Monday through Saturday and for breakfast and lunch on Sunday.

Bittercreek Alehouse
$ • 246 N. 8th St. • (208) 345-1813

This woody, high-ceiling, big mirror and window place has a long polished bar as well as green awnings and umbrellas out front above a dozen tables. Although owned by a German named Dave Krick, it has an Irish following that favors its Guinness Stout. Appetizers include dumplings, wings, squid and drunken shellfish. The Greek Salad is made with feta, kalamata olives, tomato wedges, pepperoncinis and sweet bell peppers with a dressing of sun-dried tomatoes, olive oil, vinegar and herbs. Special dishes include teriyaki salmon, tavern finger steaks and fish and chips. A wide range of cigars is available here as is nitrogen-charged ale and specialty bottled beers such as Chimay Red Label and Hair of the Dog "Adam." Bittercreek is open daily for lunch and dinner.

The Capri
$ • 2520 Fairview Ave. • (208) 342-1442

This bright, clean and comfortable diner next to a Budget Inn is known for its breakfasts and lunches. Specials include the likes of corn chowder and marion berry waffles. The large Denver omelets, the scrambled eggs with diced ham and cheese sauce served over an English muffin, the blueberry pancakes and biscuits with gravy ring the bell. Meat loaf, cheese-and-cauliflower soup and the ham-and-cheese super burger are among the lunch items. The Capri is open daily for breakfast and lunch.

Cedar Inn
$ • 4410 E. Franklin Rd. • (208) 888-7999

The meat-and-potatoes crowd will dig a menu that features top sirloin, 10-ounce marbled rib eye and chicken-fried steak at this homestyle restaurant. Cows used to escape from a field across the street and wander around in the parking lot, but now they're gone, and crab legs, butterfly prawns and creative house salads have moseyed onto the menu. The veggies maintain their identity here, not always so at a homestyle retreat. The restaurant opens into a tavern that serves beer and wine and has a large dance floor. Cedar Inn is open for breakfast and lunch Monday through Thursday, for breakfast, lunch and dinner on Friday and for dinner on Saturday.

www.insiders.com

See this and many other Insiders' Guide® destinations online — in their entirety.

Visit us today!

INSIDERS' TIP

"Bite of Boise" usually takes place at the Boise Centre on the Grove during the Boise River Festival. It's an opportunity to sample the food of a number of Boise restaurants in small portions at a low cost. See our Annual Events and Festivals chapter for details, and call the Boise Chamber of Commerce, (208) 344-5513, for specific dates.

Chef's Hut
$ • 164 S. Cole Rd. • (208) 376-3125

This is an old-style, Western hole-in-the-wall that is friendly, direct and inexpensive — nothing on the menu costs more than $5. Five daily specials and soups are posted. Chicken grinders, chorizo omelets, eggs Benedict and giant burgers that cost the same as franchised fast-food but are tended to individually with love and care are offered by chef and owner Corky Brown, who has been going strong here since 1984. The restaurant is open for breakfast and lunch Monday through Saturday.

Danskin Station
$$ • 10.5 miles east of Garden City post office on Lowman Rd. • (208) 462-3884

Danskin Station is a 24-seat roadside restaurant with gourmet food and a delicious rural envelope that people in the Treasure Valley drive 62 miles to reach. Reservations before making the trip are recommended. Located on the South Fork of the Payette River where elk, mule deer, hummingbirds, finches and river rafters hang out, it is the home of mesquite-fired butterflied filet mignon, Memphis pork and tuna prepared with lemon juice, capers and rosemary. Raw Hood Canal oysters are served in shot glasses with cocktail sauce and lemon wedges. Bananas Foster, French vanilla ice cream topped with warm caramel sauce spiked with brandy, makes for a pleasant wrap-up. Chef Deb Conlin, her cabinet-

maker husband, son and dog live downhill between a bluff and the river. This is an unusual homespun getaway that makes the most of its surroundings. The restaurant is open for lunch and dinner Friday through Sunday.

Desert Sage
$$$ • 750 W. Idaho St. • (208) 333-8400

Restaurant owner-chef David Root, whose recipes are inspired by 19th-century cookbooks, has attracted national attention through the care and imagination he has bestowed on dishes with flavors that complement each other. Appetizers include "Idaho potato and fresh Maine lobster enchilada" and "Minnesota grilled chicken and wild rice soup." Pan-roasted duck gumbo, charbroiled Angus beef tender enough to cut with a butter knife, Southern-style grilled lamb chops served with "hoppin' John" (an old plantation dish of black-eyed peas with salt pork and rice) are among the entrees. A modern and minimalist decor contrasts the restaurant's location in Boise's old Union Block Building. Desert Sage is open for lunch and dinner Monday through Friday, for jazz brunch and dinner on Saturday and for jazz brunch on Sunday.

Dudley's Waterfront
$$$ • 3250 N. Lakeharbor Ln.
• (208) 343-0234

This is a pleasant, peaceful location set on an artificial lake where a breeze and the quack of mallards complement the light jazz music. Dudley, by the way, is a carved wooden pelican who has moved over from the Oregon coast. The Cobb salad, made with chunks of chicken breast, bacon, hard-boiled egg, chopped tomato, sliced avocado, black olives and chives on a bed of romaine and iceberg lettuces, sprinkled with Parmesan cheese, is a winner. The butterflied tiger prawns treat your taste buds. The filet mignon is served in a Burgundy wine and mushroom sauce. Dudley's is open Monday and Tuesday for breakfast and lunch, Wednesday through Saturday for breakfast, lunch and dinner and Sunday for brunch.

Grape Escape Wine Bar
$ • 800 W. Idaho St. • (208) 368-0200

Lunch and appetizers carry the menu here, and the latter are good enough to stake an evening appetite not looking for a big meal while exploring wine accompaniment. It's a classy, European-like, indoor and outdoor location with a little bar, tables, a display case stocked with wines and desserts, and sidewalk umbrellas for those who like fresh air. Sandwiches come with soup and green or pasta salad. Selections include smoked salmon with cia batten Pinzimonio, which are garden vegetables tossed with olive oils, lemon juice, fresh basil and fresh ground pepper, and the Sante Fe Tortilla Wrap, which is chicken, black beans, green chiles, corn, peppers and onions layered with gourmet cheese and wrapped in a chip and chile tortilla. A half-dozen sandwiches and salads may be ordered. Appetizers are tapas, such as the sun-dried tomatoes, mild cherry peppers, grape and seed oil and gorgonzola served hot with a Zeppole (local bakery) crouton. Another tapa is Cambuzda with roasted garlic and fresh rosemary accompanied by Zeppole bread. Six red wines and six white wines are always available for tasting. A bottle of wine can be purchased here at retail price and sipped here for a corkage fee. The Grape Escape is open for lunch and evening snacks every day.

Hyde Park Depot
$ • 1501 N. 13th St. • (208) 331-7020

The owner doesn't know what's happening here, but the customers do. "The menu is eclectic, the decor is a mishmash — we have fun doing it," allows owner Ginger Fields. This popular North End restaurant is especially known for its rosemary pot roast and shrimp salad. The tender roast comes with roast carrots, mashed potatoes and gravy. The Cajun-style shrimp salad is cooked in cayenne and other spices and is presented on a bed of mixed greens with tomato, cucumber, red cabbage, green pepper and cantaloupe. The menu also includes traditional American, Southern-style, Southwestern and Italian dishes. An extensive selection of salads and sandwiches is offered throughout the day in a spacious location that used to house an espresso shop. The restaurant is open daily for lunch and dinner and has blues and jazz music on Friday and Saturday nights.

Interlude Bar & Grill
$ • 213 N. 8th St. • (208) 342-9593

This dark and cozy neighborhood bar going back to the 1940s has a renovated kitchen that allows cooks to experiment with daily specials, a list of which is faxed to customers. The specials may be spaghetti with meatballs, chicken chimichanga, cold salmon pasta salad, Mexicali casserole and tropical chicken salad. Made-to-order pizzas and eight varieties of hamburgers fill out the menu. In warm weather a patio delivers you to the sidewalk zoo of colorful and sometimes fashionable downtown Boise. The Interlude is open for lunch and dinner Tuesday through Saturday.

Moon's Kitchen
$ • 815 W. Bannock St. • (208) 385-0472

For old-time luncheonette atmosphere, Moon's goes back to 1955 and doesn't get a day older. Ceiling fans, linoleum counter and tabletops, old Coca-Cola ads that reach back to Babe Ruth spread across a wall, the plastic mustard and ketchup containers and aluminum napkin dispensers that charmed Archie Andrews and Jughead, John Wayne grimacing down from beside a round clock — what a trip! "Home of World Famous Milkshakes" is the motto on the sidewalk sign, and people, including Idaho governors and legislators from across the street, haunt the place for its 15 kinds of shakes that include fresh strawberry and fresh banana. Another motto: "We never

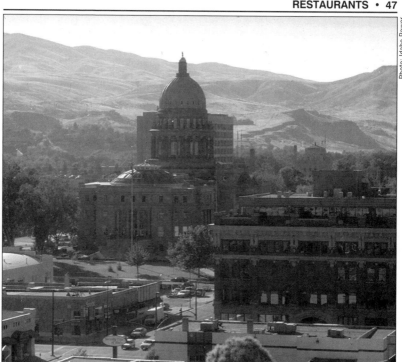

Photo: Idaho Power

A 20-square-block area containing more than 200 specialty shops and 89 restaurants is just south of the Capitol building.

met a calorie we didn't like." Breakfast visitors who indulge in the omelets — "three egg monsters!!" — French toast and hot cakes and lunch patrons who gobble the big burgers and sandwiches obviously agree. To get to Moon's you must traipse through a gift and greeting card shop, which used to be a tackle and cutlery shop and other things before, which adds to the adventure of this step back in time. Moon's is open Monday through Saturday for breakfast and lunch.

The Radio Room
$$$ • Hoff Building, 802 W. Bannock St. • (208) 345-1551

The 12th floor is as high as you go for a restaurant view of Boise that is shared by contemporary dance and disco music played by a DJ. Antique radio and movie posters portray the radio era of the 1930s at a place that works hard to be hip and casual. A grill-style menu

of chicken, steak and pasta offers soup and salad with the entrees. The nightclub atmosphere is particularly enjoyed by a young crowd that lingers for drinks and socializing when the dishes are cleared. The restaurant is open Tuesday through Saturday for dinner.

River City Grille
$$ • 750 W. Main St. • (208) 344-2808

Fresh ingredients flavored with creative sauces are prepared here by former San Francisco chefs Mitchell and Andrea Maricich. Gold-framed mirrors, classical paintings, green trees, linen and candlelight provide a relaxed atmosphere. Roast pork, leg of lamb, yellow-eyed snapper in a portobello mushroom asparagus ragout, and prime rib are among the menu choices. The presentations are simple, and the food is cooked well. River City is open for lunch on Monday, lunch and dinner Tuesday through Friday and dinner on Saturday.

R.J.'s Diner
$ • 3095 N. Lakeharbor Ln.
• (208) 853-9800

Built to resemble a chrome-colored railway dining car, this restaurant offers the tone and the dishes of the 1950s. Film posters, record jackets, sports memorabilia and photographs go back to the Marilyn Monroe-Joe DiMaggio era while people munch American Bandstand sandwiches, thick-cut French toast, chef's salads and eggs with hash browns. The diner's black-and-white interior decor, with chrome and red trim, reminds you of the bell voice of Patsy Cline, the defiance of James Dean and the swagger of Marlon Brando. Elvis croons on the counter. Yes, he does. R.J.'s is open daily for breakfast, lunch and dinner.

Sidewinder BBQ
$$ • Main Street Bistro, 607 W. Main St.
• (208) 345-9515

"Hey pardner, how 'bout that smoke rising above that courtyard in downtown Boise? How 'bout them bales of hay, Western paintings and corral? Smells like pork ribs sloppy with barbecue sauce, killer black, kidney and navy beans, grilled chicken, beef ribs and plenty of other cowboy fixin's. Giddeup Trigger. Shucks, we gotta leave the hound behind."

The Sidewinder is open for lunch and dinner Monday through Saturday.

State Court Café
$ • 2907 W. State St. • (208) 367-0751

This is quite an intriguing look back in time, a no-nonsense place just off a heavily-trafficked street that is friendly, nourishing, inexpensive, plain and simple "like the places my grandfather hauled me to," according to owner Sam Carlson. Formica tabletops, vinyl chairs, biscuits and gravy, huge bacon cheeseburgers and omelets that kick like a rodeo are familiar favorites here. The café is open daily for breakfast and lunch.

Thad's Restaurant
$ • Flying J Travel Plaza, 8000 Overland Rd. • (208) 376-0831

Gotta hit the truck stop every now and then, don'tcha, Big Wheels? You just eat up that kicked-back, baseball-cap atmosphere and suspendered flannel nonchalance, don'tcha? This here place has a pretty fair buffet and a salad bar with 18 ingredients and four dressings that will drown your boots. Their beef ribs are oversized, tender, fatty and tangy as all get-out. Jello and bread pudding with a mouth-watering rum flavor await those who get past the Southern fried chicken, baked fish, macaroni, barley-vegetable soup and chowder. Thad's is open 24 hours daily.

Vista Deli
$ • 930 Vista Ave. • (208) 344-4846

Vista offers on- and off-premise catering for weddings, open houses and business meetings. It also rustles up party platters and box lunches. But that's only part of its show. The deli is open for breakfast and lunch Monday through Saturday where it serves hot, cold, pita and specialty sandwiches, burgers, a dozen different salads and desserts that include carrot cake, baked cheesecake and a double fudge brownie. This is a pleasant and popular location with a simple yet relaxing atmosphere and fast, good food.

Nampa

O'Callahan's
$$ • 1401 Shilo Dr. at Franklin Blvd.
• (208) 465-5908

This is a family restaurant with an inventive kitchen that turns out the likes of hazelnut chicken, apple-cranberry pork and peppery, homemade New England clam chowder that is rich in potatoes, onions, celery and baked ham as well as clams. The restaurant's crab cakes blend Dungeness crab with egg breading, green onion and herbs. O'Callahan's is open daily for breakfast, lunch and dinner. A Smokehouse Buffet that features smoked prime rib, pork loin and salmon is offered on Saturday nights, and there is an extensive Sunday brunch.

Asian

Boise

Bien Hoa
$ • 1098 N. Orchard St. • (208) 388-1710

Bien Hoa is not fancy; it just serves good food. A traditional Vietnamese dining spot that is attached to an Asian market, it sports orange vinyl booths, Ansel Adams and Corona beer art, and moc-chu chicken, rice-flour crepes, bo axe sato ("spicy hot pepper beef"), bok choyu barbecue pork and a special noodle dish. Restaurant owner David Nguyen knows his noodles, having emigrated from Bien Hoa, Vietnam. Bien Hoa is open daily for breakfast, lunch and dinner.

Oriental Express
$ • 110 N. 11th St. • (208) 345-8868

You can go chopsticks or fork and spoon at this Asian, fast-food restaurant that offers four dozen dishes that are stir-fried in woks. Paper and plastic serving dishes and utensils keep the prices low for a mainly northern Chinese menu that offers kung pao chicken, volcano beef with hot sauce, shrimp lo mein and Tsingtao beers from China. All ingredients are fresh, and meals are made-to-order. Owner Jimmy Yuan enjoys catering to vegetarians. Customers especially like General Tso's chicken that is crispy-fried and adorned with spicy plum sauce. Oriental Express is open daily for lunch and dinner.

Siam Café
$ • 2710 W. Boise Ave. • (208) 383-9032

Siam shines with its traditional Thai dishes such as pineapple red curry shrimp, noodle dishes with a choice of chicken, shrimp or beef, and Pad kra pao, a spicy beef dish with fried hot green and red chiles, bamboo shoots, carrots and green onions. Seven vegetarian dishes are offered. Simple tables and booths are dressed with Asian paintings, fans and silk plants. Wine is served by the glass, and Chinese, Thai and Japanese beers are available. Owner Mone Bounyavong is from Siam. The restaurant is open Monday through Saturday for lunch and dinner and for dinner only on Sunday.

Teriyaki Palace
$ • 501 W. Main St. • (208) 345-3366
$ • 523 12th Ave. Rd., Nampa
• (208) 468-7768

Teriyaki chicken, beef and kabob, as the restaurant name suggests, are big at these locations that feature Hawaiian-Japanese cuisine. Owners Juliana and Donny Tsai cook the sauce twice a week for their Boise and Nampa restaurants. It is made with chicken broth, ginger, apples, onions, brown sugar, soy sauce and Japanese wine, a recipe borrowed from a former chef at the Benihana restaurant chain. Lunch is a choice of combination meals pictured on a menu board. Popular Chinese dishes such as sweet-and-sour chicken, Mandarin spicy chicken, fried rice and chow mein are also offered. Dinner has a family-style menu, and sushi is best at dinnertime when it is made-to-order. The restaurant offers a free delivery service for nearby customers on orders of $15 or more. Teriyaki Palace is open Monday through Saturday for lunch and dinner.

Vien Dong Vietnamese Restaurant
$ • 8616 Fairview Ave. • (208) 376-9881

If you like variety and choices, here's a menu with more than 125 dishes. Shrimp, fish, pork and beef light up the simple and austere setting, but the Vietnamese soups, noodle dishes and appetizers are the sizzlers. Deep-fried Cha Gio appetizer, very popular in Vietnam, is made from bean thread noodles, pork and vegetables cradled in rice paper. You wrap the rolls in iceberg lettuce and dip them into a sauce of red vinegar, chile and fish sauce. The Goi Cuon appetizer, made with rice noodles, bean sprouts, shrimp and pork that are wrapped with lettuce and rolled in rice-flour crepes, beg for a bath in thick peanut sauce. Vien Dong is open daily for lunch and dinner.

Yen Ching
$$ • 305 N. 9th St. • (208) 384-0384

The hearty and filling Mandarin food of northern China are enjoyed at this downtown location near the Capitol. Diners indulge in steamed bao dumplings, hot-and-sour soup, spicy beef fried with garlic and ginger and served in a gravy with peas, carrots and onions, pork chow mein and Peking duck. Onions, garlic and soy sauces are used in many dishes. The garden atmosphere and service are friendly. This is a casual but smart place that knows its stuff. Yen Ching is open daily for lunch and dinner.

Zen Bento
$ • 101 N. 10th St. at Main St.
• (208) 388-8808

Take the skewered chicken or beef from the sidewalk hibachi man and run. That's how they do it in Japan, and this deluxe box-lunch style of eating is offered in downtown Boise during lunch Monday through Friday. Grilled meats and steamed veggies come on a bed of rice, and a choice of five sauces season the fare at this open-air eatery without chairs or walls.

Nampa

China Garden
$ • 113 13th Ave. S. • (208) 467-4157

Mark S. Lin, the owner and chef of China Garden, doesn't speak much English, but he sure knows his rice soup, orange chicken, Mongolian Beef, ma pao bean curd and dry cooked string beans. He is also fluent in shrimp toast and Mandarin Fish — slices of fish that are fried and then boiled. Lin left his native Taiwan in the late '70s, has been a chef in restaurants from California to Texas and comes to life with dishes from nearly every Chinese province. China Garden is open Tuesday through Sunday for lunch and dinner.

International

Boise

Café Fresco
$ • 3000 N. Lake Harbor Ln.
• (208) 853-5575

Lakeside umbrellas, wandering ducks and a range of international dishes — Greek, Italian, Mexican, Cajun, Basque and Lebanese — await visitors at this pine wood, large-windowed, deceptively spacious location that opens onto a deck. Pesto-roasted mussels; Mediterranean salad, which features artichoke hearts, sun-dried tomatoes, sweet red peppers, green and black olives and feta cheese on a bed of mixed greens; and bow-tie pasta tossed with sauteed chicken, carrots and green onions and bathed in a spicy Oriental barbecue sauce zoom out the kitchen door. At weekend brunches champagne mimosas, cheese blintzes and expertly doctored egg dishes are served. Light jazz and other easy-listening music accompany the meals. Café Fresco is open for breakfast, lunch and dinner Monday

through Saturday and for breakfast and lunch on Sunday.

Cazba
$$ • 211 N. 8th St. • (208) 381-0222
$$ • 9 S. Orchard St. • (208) 338-9400

Three Iranian men, Max, Ali and Medhi Mohammadi, present restaurants with style, grace and friendliness that offer excellent Greek, Turkish and Lebanese food. The specially designed 8th Street location's columns, arches and clouds recreate a Greek palace from the days of myth. There's a balcony, main floor and outdoor seating. Appetizers include toasted pita bread served with tangy tzatzike sauce; hummus, a Middle Eastern dip made from garbanzo beans, sesame seeds, tahini and garlic; tabbouleh, a salad with parsley, bulgur wheat, green onions, tomatoes and cucumbers in a lemon-and-oil dressing; and falafel, consisting of deep-fried balls of spiced, ground chickpeas with tabbouleh and eggplant. Kabobs and gyro platters frequent a list of main courses that also includes moussaka, a ground lamb casserole; dolmades, grape leaves stuffed with beef, lamb and rice; and spanikopita, spinach pie in pastry. The Cazba is open Monday through Saturday for lunch and dinner.

The Cottage Tea Room
$ • 1031 E. 1st St., Meridian
• (208) 888-6829

Breakfast, lunch and afternoon tea are offered at this Old English restaurant inside the Cottage Expressions Gift Shop on the main run through Meridian. Finely upholstered chairs and Royal Doulton china set the tone for this proper and delightful place. Gourmet sandwiches, soups and salads are served with scones and gourmet coffee and tea. Two soups, such as cheddar cauliflower and tomato ravioli, are featured each day. The Tea Room is open for breakfast, lunch and afternoon tea Monday through Saturday.

The Den
$ • 1615 E. 1st St., Meridian
• (208) 888-1502

Okay, this joint is not elegant — broken, crowded, dusty, a former box burger drive-in. But is it not a perverse pleasure to enjoy a meal in such a place of meager promise and grand potential? Sohail Ishraq, a Pakistani who bought the dive a few years ago, still offers burgers to the forget-me-nots beside dishes from India, Pakistan and Afghanistan, Greek gyros and Mexican burritos. What's achar murgh? Pieces of whole chicken cooked in a blend of spices, garlic, tomatoes, onions and ginger. Kichree? Split chickpea cooked with basmati rice, spices and herbs. Mungi unday? Mung bean, garlic, ginger and spices simmered in green herbs. Get the idea, Adventure Tongue? The Den is open daily for lunch and dinner.

Doughty's Bistro
$$ • 199 N. 8th St. • (208) 336-7897

Located in the fine old sandstone Boise National Bank Building, this is the professional home of Chef Joyce Doughty, known for her local TV and radio cooking presence. It's a grand setting of marble floors and columns, awnings and cloth sails, modern art and leafy trees through the windows. Chef Doughty's eclectic menu includes specials such as noodle saute with bay, shrimp, carrots, snow peas, green onions and peanut sauce, and open-backed chicken parmigana with roasted vegetables ragu, goat cheese and sage. Doughty's is open for lunch and dinner Tuesday through Saturday.

The Gamekeeper
$$$$ • Owyhee Plaza Hotel, 1109 Main St. • (208) 343-4611

Caesar salads, flambeed meats and flaming desserts, such as cherries jubilee, are prepared tableside at a location known for its simple elegance and distinguished cuisine. Some of the best-known meals are duck a l'orange, Madagascar New York pepper steak and seafood fettuccine. Unusual appetizers such as scallops amaretto, which are bay scallops sauteed with wild chanterelle and porcini mushrooms in a sweet sauce of cream and amaretto liqueur, and warm, fresh-baked sourdough bread will get you off to a great start. Ikebana arrangements, brass chandeliers and wildlife watercolor paintings establish a comfortable but polished atmosphere. The Gamekeeper is open for lunch and dinner Monday through Friday and for dinner on Saturday.

Ibrahim Egyptian Cuisine
$$ • 500 W. Main St. • (208) 368-9844

The well-prepared Middle Eastern cuisine served here includes Cornish game hen, a chicken curry known as kebab hala, meat loaf in puffed pastry and roasted vegetable dishes. An appetizer of Tripoli mezza, served with freshly baked, raised Egyptian flat bread, includes hummus, which is mashed chickpeas, and baba ghanouj, which is mashed eggplant, blended with sesame tahini, lemon juice and garlic. Falafel, which is tangy deep-fried balls of mashed garbanzos and fava beans, and tabbouleh, a Lebanese parsley salad with tomatoes, onions, garlic and bulgur wheat in a lemony olive-oil dressing, are also offered. The restaurant has a vegetarian selection and a buffet. Desserts such as bird's nest, a pistachio-filled, honey-rich pastry, and k'nafe, a honey-glazed, layered sweet cheese topped with pine nuts, round out the menu. Belly dancers on the weekends add a bit of spice to the everyday decor of Egyptian art, tablecloths and chandeliers. Restaurant owner Ibrahim Ebed was a chef at the United Nations headquarters building in New York City. He is a native of Cairo and worked in restaurants in Lebanon, Saudi Arabia and Germany before coming to this country. The restaurant is open for lunch and dinner Monday through Saturday.

Koffee Klatsch
$ • 409 S. 8th St. • (208) 345-0452

Koffee Klatsch specializes in natural cuisine, offering organic, vegetarian and vegan meals. Organic means grown without herbicides, pesticides, inorganic fertilizers and preservatives; vegetarian refers to a non-meat-eater; and vegan means eating no animal products, including meat, dairy or even honey. That said, a lot can be done with what's left to offer, as this restaurant shows with its Thai curry specials, Mediterranean skillet, Punjabi wraps, avocado croissant sandwiches (stuffed with alfalfa sprouts, Swiss cheese, tomato, zucchini and red onion), homemade soups, and its "very veggie" and "Essene" juice bar. The coffee is excellent, and the elaborate ice cream dishes are the height of decadence. Music, plays, poetry and art shows that sometimes accompany the meals reflect the multicultural nature of the restaurant. Koffee Klatsch is open for breakfast, lunch and dinner Tuesday through Saturday and for breakfast and lunch on Sunday and Monday.

The Odyssey
$ • 904 W. Main St. • (208) 342-3230

Next door to The Book Shop in downtown Boise, wall murals depict ancient Greece at a restaurant that describes itself as "a Mediterranean dining experience." The lunch choices are Italian or Greek and include Mediterranean chicken salad, a Sophia Loren sandwich that features smoked turkey breast with melted brie cheese, and The Medicis panini, which is a gourmet ham-and-cheese sandwich. Nightly dinner specials may be Moroccan, Spanish or southern French recipes. Eggplant Parmesan and Israeli orange chicken have been two of the choices. The owners strive to present a menu that emphasizes health and nutrition. The Odyssey is open Monday through Friday for lunch and dinner and on Saturday for lunch.

Onati
$$ • 3544 Chinden Blvd., Garden City • (208) 343-6464

Boise is home to one of the largest Basque populations outside of Europe, and the old family recipes of these hardy, vigorous, independent people are available at this restaurant bedecked with paintings, photographs and costumes from the rugged Spanish-and-French enclave along the Atlantic Ocean. Family-style dishes often seasoned with garlic and olive oil are served at booths and long tables. The sauced lamb, solomo or pork with pimentos and garlic, and codfish are particularly good. The entrees come with homemade soups, salad and side dishes such as croquetas, a deep-fried blend of cream cheese, milk and flour. Fresh vegetables are cooked in olive oil, and pasta comes with tomato sauce, carrots and chorizo. The desserts include rice pudding and flan, which is custard

with caramel sauce. Onati is open for lunch and dinner Monday through Friday and for dinner only on Saturday.

Peter Schott's
$$$ • Hotel Idanha, 10th and Main Sts. • (208) 336-9100

Austrian chef and restaurant owner Peter Schott is well-known in Boise, since he has his own TV show and operates this highly rated European-style restaurant in the historic Idanha hotel. This place is for a special occasion or a big night out, the kind of place where visitors from more cosmopolitan areas will be impressed with the imaginative entrees, soups and salads. A visitor can start with a Thai poppy chicken appetizer dipped in peanut sauce, move on to Schott's signature Brie soup that is made with leeks, mushrooms, chicken stock and dry sherry with a golden cheese topping, and continue with beautifully prepared halibut, salmon, rahmschnitzel (escalope of veal with wild and domestic mushrooms in a rich cream sauce) or a number of other entrees such as pastas, buffalo rib eye with corn salsa, rack of lamb and pork. Peter Schott's is open for dinner Monday through Saturday.

Poulet Rouge
$ • 106 N. 6th St. and Main St. • (208) 343-8180

This breakfast and lunch location has constantly changing, imaginative menus that are chronicled on a chalkboard and an open, breezy, European-style ambiance. The food is healthy and tasty, and a range of vegetarian dishes is always available. The dish you order and pay for at a counter could be Southwest chicken-and-tortilla stew, eggplant parmigiana, mushroom stroganoff or asparagus-and-leek quiche. The likes of Creole jambalaya or African rice and peanut stew will send your taste buds into orbit. Saturday brunch offers cheddar-and-broccoli omelets, fruit salad, Denver quiche, gourmet coffee, espresso and past-

INSIDERS' TIP

During warm months, outdoor dining is popular at a number of restaurants on 8th Street downtown and beside the water at Lake Harbor.

ries prepared in-house. The Poulet Rouge is open for breakfast and lunch Monday through Saturday.

Richard's Bakery and Café
$$ • 1513 N. 13th St. • (208) 368-9629

Country French dinners are the specialty at this casual, eight-table restaurant run by Richard Langston, who learned his trade at the California Culinary Academy. Langston updates traditional French country ideas, using less cream and butter than the original recipes, more olive oils and lots of vegetables. His duck, leek and red bell pepper pancakes are topped with a sweet compote of pears in honey and ginger. His chicken is roasted with "40 cloves of garlic," his poached salmon is flavored by a frothy egg-white sauce, and his smoked trout lasagna has a lemon cream sauce and is sprinkled with fresh dill. Sunday brunch offers omelets of the day and French toast made from freshly baked challah, a Jewish yeast bread. Richard's is open for breakfast every day, for lunch Monday through Friday, for dinner Tuesday through Saturday and for breakfast and brunch on Sunday.

Italian

Boise

Amore
$$$ • 921 W. Jefferson St.
• (208) 343-6435

Excellent pasta dishes such as linguine congamberoni, with prawns in a cream sauce of vermouth and sun-dried tomatoes, and carciofi al panna, fettucine with chicken, artichoke hearts and ham, are the hallmark of this downtown restaurant that has an outdoor patio for use in warm weather as well as spacious indoor seating. The spinach lasagna has four layers with chicken, sausage, mushrooms, four cheeses, marinara sauce and salsa. Amore is also known for its extensive wine list and fabulous desserts, such as tiramisu, or brandy cake, and caramel ice cream sundae. It's a relaxing, well-run and friendly restaurant that has a considerable

local following. Amore is open for lunch and dinner Monday through Friday and for dinner on Saturday and Sunday.

Asiago's
$$ • Cole Village, 3423 N. Cole Rd.
• (208) 323-1469

You step into a vineyard-like atmosphere at Asiago's, where grapevines, wooden tables and twiggy menus await the visitor through stained-glass doors. The dress is casual, and the wait staff is professional but friendly. The freshly made pasta comes with a choice of 15 types of sauce such as tomato-pesto, spicy white wine and Gorgonzola. Daily specials include poached salmon with fettuccine, chicken pizza wraps and tri-tip sirloin with white bean ragout. A salad here can be a meal in itself. The Mediterranean includes artichoke hearts, roasted sweet peppers, tomatoes, crumbled feta and kalamata olives mixed in a sun-dried vinaigrette. The restaurant is named after a resort town in Italy where asiago cheese originated. It has an impressive wine list and microbrews. Asiago's is open daily for lunch and dinner.

Emilio's
$$$ • The Grove Hotel, 245 S. Capitol Blvd. • (208) 333-8000

This restaurant is in the main entrance of Boise's big new Grove Hotel and sports arena and across from the convention center so that it gets many out-of-town visitors who are impressed with its good hotel food. Chef Jonathan Mortimer presents Northern Italian grilled meats, seafood and pasta in light sauces, rainbow trout, and braised lamb, veal and chicken that are served with broths and vegetables. Lunch features salads, soups, sandwiches and thin-crust pizzas. Desserts are a knockout with the likes of hot berry cobbler à la mode, flan, chocolate cake and handmade wafflecones filled with ice cream.

Gino's
$$ • Capitol Terrace, 150 N. 8th St.
• (208) 331-3771

Restaurant tradition is strong here, where chef and owner Gino Vuolo is a fourth-generation Neapolitan chef. President Clinton ate at the restaurant of Vuolo's grandmother, Il Trono, in Naples, and Vuolo's parents ran a Manhattan, New York, restaurant for two decades. Vuolo's southern Italian cooking relies on fresh pastas, olive oil and piquant tomato sauces and less garlic and butter than is usual in the north. A half-dozen homemade pastas, such as pasta asparagus, gnocchi alla Sorrentinna, which is a potato pasta, and pasta with marinara sauce are offered. Vuolo serves fresh trout with vinegar, white wine and lemon. The ivied restaurant is situated in a small courtyard on the second floor that is decorated by a large neighborhood painting of Naples.

Louie's Pizza and Italian Restaurant
$ • 620 W. Idaho St. • (208) 344-5200

This comfortable restaurant has wholesome food and a friendly atmosphere. Wood floors, brick walls and ceiling fans create an easygoing ambiance. Traditional Italian fare includes spaghetti carbonara, chicken cacciatora, veal parmesan and pasta primavera. There's a broad range of pizza, salads, garlic bread and family-style combination dinners. The restaurant has nightly specials, takeout orders and makes deliveries. Louie Mallane founded the original Louie's in Ketchum in 1965, ran a Boise Louie's from 1983 to 1988, and returned to Boise to his present location in 1990, so that "the only Italian you have to know" has a long and varied Idaho restaurant history. The restaurant is open Monday through Saturday for lunch and every night of the week for dinner.

Mountain Thyme Pasta
$ • 7310 W. State St. at Glenwood St. • (208) 853-8513

Eat in or take out at this fast-food pasta restaurant owned by Boise orthopedic surgeon John Bishop, who thinks of it as a pilot store that could become a chain, offering an alternative to the usual fast-food fare. Customers select freshly made pasta, sauce and accompanying dishes at the counter. Some take pasta home and cook it for themselves. Favorites are Italian herb, lemon-pepper, carrot-dill and rosemary-garlic pasta. Bottled wine, beers, fresh breads, cheeses and dressings are offered as are a variety of des-

serts. Mountain Thyme is open daily for lunch and dinner.

Noodles
$$ • The Mode Building, 8th and Idaho Sts. • (208) 342-9300

Within the white walls of the classically sleek former The Mode department store is one of the most unusual restaurant layouts in Boise. Noodles wraps its tables in balcony fashion above climbing and descending escalators that must have served dress and beachwear shoppers at one time. But it also has four banquet rooms and a hardwood-floored bar where, evidently, nylons and sweaters once flourished. It's a canny, imaginative place, known for its creative and tasty Italian food, its music, its art and its meetings of authors and speakers on topical issues. The restaurant offers 11 traditional pasta dishes, including Jogger (fresh linguine with marinara sauce), Sprinter (mushrooms, artichoke hearts and sun-dried tomatoes with garlic, olive oil and Italian spices over fresh linguine) and Robie Creek, named after a killer local hill race (fresh fettuccine, chicken, mushrooms and garden vegetables in a light cream sauce). Entrees include eggplant parmesan, chicken saltimbocca and tortellini primavera. Two seafood and three veal dishes as well as nine gourmet and 16 select pizzas are also on the menu. Noodles is open daily for lunch and dinner.

Piatto Italiano
$ • Albertsons shopping center, 2448 S. Apple St. • (208) 344-3427

Red-and-white checkered tablecloths, travel posters, porcelain, chiles and garlic decorate this neat and simple 10-table restaurant. The food is prepared from fresh ingredients and served in generous portions. Seafood cannelloni and veal marsala are two of the popular dinner entrees, all of which come with soup and salad. Seven different pasta dishes are offered at lunch. The restaurant is open for lunch and dinner Monday through Friday and for dinner on Saturday.

Renaissance Ristorante Italiano
$$$$ • 110 S. 5th St. • (208) 344-6776

Candlelight, classical music, the historic Belgravia building and special little touches, such as lemon slices in the water glasses and chilled salad forks, point to a special dining experience in one of Boise's most romantic restaurants. Many people celebrate birthdays, anniversaries and other big occasions here. One of the restaurant's best-known dishes is Pollo Alla Fiorentina, which is chicken in bechamel sauce, herbs and white wine in a casserole with fresh spinach, mushrooms, tomatoes and linguine. The fire-roasted rack of lamb is flavored with garlic and rosemary, broiler-seared, then baked. The Gamberroni Della Casa consists of prawns sauteed in olive oil and garlic, spiced with saffron and served over linguine that has a light tomato bechamel sauce. Another seafood treat is the Idaho red meat trout al pescatore, a boneless filet trout topped with prawns, sea scallops, clams and mussels in a light saffron, lemon cream and caper sauce. Impeccable service and intelligent and imaginative preparation of each dish characterize the Renaissance, which concentrates on serving only dinner Monday through Saturday.

Smoky Mountain Pizza and Pasta
$ • 34 E. State St., Eagle
• (208) 939-0212

This is a casual but smart Italian hangout that is part of an Idaho restaurant group with similar eateries in Ketchum, McCall and Mountain Home that is run by a general manager of the group from Dublin, John Ryan. Red-and-white checkered tablecloths, forest colors and wood textures, and a tin roof hung above a 10-seat side bar accent the place. Among the inventive overtures of the restaurant are split pizzas — half "Smoky" style with pepperoni, bell peppers, red onions, jalapeno peppers, fresh tomatoes and garlic and half "California Designer" with basil pesto sauce topped with chicken, mushrooms and tomatoes. Other choices include lasagna, seafood and noodles; dessert features the likes of caramel apple crunch. Smoky Mountain is open for lunch Monday through Saturday and for dinner every night of the week.

Villano's Specialty Market & Deli
$$ • 712 W. Idaho St. • (208) 331-3066

This Old World-style deli is an espresso bar, gourmet retail market and catering center with various salads and dinner entrees for carry-out. It has a huge blackboard list of offerings, four tables, hardwood floors and additional seating in the Union Building lobby. Smoked turkey, pasta salad, Japanese noodle salad, minestrone soup, roasted lamb chops with orzo, vegetarian lasagna with goat cheese, and scallops with rosemary beurre sauce over pasta is just a sample of the tremendous menu. Owner Lisa Villano grew up in her grandfather's meat market in Denver, worked in restaurants to put herself through college, spent a decade working for others in restaurants after graduating from college, then studied the deli business in Seattle, San Francisco, Salt Lake City and Denver before opening her own place in Boise. One of her catering gigs is the jazz-and-wine brunches at Ste. Chapelle Winery (see our Annual Events and Festivals chapter). Villano's is open for breakfast, lunch and dinner Monday through Saturday.

Mexican

Boise

Chapala
$ • 3447 Chinden Blvd., Garden City
• (208) 342-5648
$ • 105 W. 6th St. • (208) 331-7866

These Mexican restaurants owned and operated by Margarito and Fabiola Marin, who are from Guadalajara, provide fast, tasty, inexpensive meals. The colorful decor at the Garden City restaurant takes you to Lago de Chapala, Mexico's largest lake; the historic upstairs, downtown Boise location is broad and spacious and brings back the past. Staffs at the restaurants are efficient, easygoing and knowledgeable. Meals begin with homemade tortilla chips, bean dip and salsas. Combination plates are big sellers. Chapala offers a beef taco, bean tostada and cheese enchilada; two burritos; a tamale and chile relleno; and a number of other choices. Menu entrees include carne asada burrito (skirt steak marinated with lime juice), pork carnitas, fajita salad, chicken mole, sopitos, chile verde and chile colorado. The Marins know their Mexican ingredients as well as the American palate and combine agreeable atmosphere with a brisk pace. Both restaurants are open daily for lunch and dinner.

Caldwell

Casa Elena's
$ • 2622 E. Cleveland Blvd.
• (208) 454-8609

The Martinez family has slipped an invented enchilada verde dish that is not typical of Mexico and homemade cinnamon rolls onto the menu. But that's okay. They're enjoyed as much as the Mexican dishes Jesus and Maria Martinez have been cooking for Canyon County restaurants since the 1970s. Now their daughter Maria Elena Martinez owns the restaurant where Jesus and Maria prepare Chihuahua enchiladas, made with three types of dried chiles blended with garlic, poultry broth, cumin seeds and other spices, and enchiladas nacional, which have three types of sauces that depict the colors of the Mexican flag in a dish that includes chicken, ground beef and cheese in a white cream sauce. This is a popular, colorful restaurant, where salsa onions, tomatoes and chiles are painted on the wall. Dessert includes a banana flauta split, which is a banana wrapped in flour tortilla, fried served on a plate with walnuts, coconut and honey, then topped with hot fudge and whipped cream. The restaurant is open Tuesday through Saturday for lunch and dinner.

Steak and Seafood

Boise

Angell's Bar and Grill
$$$ • One Capital Center, 9th and Main Sts. • (208) 342-4900

Restaurant co-owner and real estate developer Bob Angell trains his staff well, cuts them in on profits and is constantly changing his menu and the physical aspects of his downtown restaurant. Co-owner Kurt Knipe knows his grape and maintains a traditional and newly revealing wine list. This makes for a winning combination at this indoor and outdoor court-

yard patio location that features carpetbagger steak with fresh oysters and mushrooms, Cantonese chicken salad that is ordered by one in every five lunch guests, and a variety of fresh seafood. Daily specials include grilled chicken and ravioli stuffed with pesto and cheese that is topped by an alfredo cream sauce and served with olives, zucchini and carrots. Dinner is served nightly; lunch, Monday through Friday.

Chart House
$$$$ • 2228 N. Garden St.
• (208) 336-9370

The picture windows can be a bit distracting here. Anybody who visits is in jeopardy of buttering an arm or sloshing wine while gawking at the beavers and birds, the foliage and Boise River currents, so near and vivid on the other side of the glass. Inside, a resort theme presents waiters in Hawaiian shirts, waitresses in floral dresses, models of yachts hung from a high ceiling and navigational charts at the tables. The Chart House is a highly visual experience that includes an excellent salad bar, prime rib, New York pepper steak, chili chicken, grilled scallops and many other menu items. Dinner is served daily at the Chart House.

Duck's Grillhouse
$$$ • 415 E. Parkcenter Blvd.
• (208) 345-6700

Steaks and seafood are grilled over mesquite or apple wood and receive attractive presentation at this indoor and outdoor location. In warm months tree canopies and multicolored flowers engage diners on an outdoor patio; inside, green plants and duck-lined walls provide ambiance. Sourdough bread comes hot from the oven to be enjoyed with whisky crab soup or a soup du jour, such as steak-and-rice soup with oregano seasoning. Entrees include chicken cashew salad, plank-grilled salmon, pepper steak and prime rib. Stop by for lunch Tuesday through Friday or dinner Monday through Saturday.

Jaker's Steak, Ribs & Fish House
$$$ • 276 Bobwhite Court
• (208) 343-3430

Honey-glazed king salmon, "Filet à la Jaker's" served with asparagus, crabmeat and béarnaise sauce, 8-ounce prime rib sandwiches and blackened chicken pasta are some of the dishes offered at this pondside restaurant. Lighter dinners and "healthy choice" items are also available. Owner Jake Jones has been in the Boise restaurant business since 1975 and has other Jaker's restaurants in Twin Falls and Idaho Falls, Idaho, as well as Missoula and Great Falls, Montana. This restaurant is open for lunch Monday through Friday and for dinner every night of the week.

Lindy's Steak House
$$ • 12249 W. Chinden Blvd. at Cloverdale Rd. • (208) 375-1310

This down-to-earth eatery takes pride in its rib-eye steaks, finger steaks and pork chop sandwiches. It's an attractive restaurant decorated with hanging plants, wood trim and a shade of forest green. The mashed potatoes have lumps so that people know they are real; the steaks are choice, unseasoned Nebraska beef. Menu items include shrimp and steak, pork ribs and a broasted chicken sandwich. Lindy's is open for breakfast, lunch and dinner Monday through Friday and for lunch and dinner on Saturday.

Lone Star Steakhouse
$$$ • 8799 W. Franklin Rd. • (208) 377-5565

What you see is what you get in a meat case where you choose your own cut of beef and then eye decorative longhorns, saddle and rope, steer skulls and cacti. Looking for something to whet your whistle? Down a Rawhide Rita (Margarita) or two while your dinner cooks. Everything is big here — the house salad, the sweet potatoes, the 18-ounce rib eye marinated in Cajun spices for 60 hours, the whole shooting match, pardner. With the exception of the T-bones, all the steaks are cut fresh in-house. The service is casual, friendly and efficient. Country-and-western music accompanies the beef parade at Lone Star, which is open daily for lunch and dinner.

Milford's Fish House and Oyster Bar
$$$ • Eighth Street Marketplace, 8th and Broad Sts. • (208) 342-8382

Restaurant owner Wally Tamura won't settle for California scales, fins and filets because of less-than-perfect water temperatures off the West Coast. The halibut, king salmon, crab, oysters, prawns and other fish served at Milford's have probably been caught in Canada or Alaska because of their superior quality. The seafood chowder, Hood Canal oysters and prawns scampi go down well here. Milford's serves Cajun and Creole cooking such as Louisiana crawfish etoufee with the crustaceans baked with tomatoes, yellow and green onions, celery, green peppers and red potatoes surrounded by paprika rice. The house and Caesar salads as well as the soups and desserts are also well-received. New Orleans music and photos, maps and charts enliven the environment. Dinner is served nightly.

Murphy's Seafood and Chop House
$$$ • 1555 Broadway Ave. • (208) 344-3691

This is a handsome restaurant with a broad menu of well-prepared, strongly flavored, bold meals. The house salad is called "endless," because you can eat as much as you want. The jumbo prawns are immense. The seafood chowder doesn't skimp on the clams, crab, salmon and halibut, nor the potatoes, corn, celery and dill seasoning. The Louisiana prime rib is seasoned and blackened for three days as required by the recipe of Cajun chef Paul Prudhomme. Alaskan halibut and Jamaican jerk chicken are other popular items at this restaurant with clean, strong lines that's feathered with greenery. Murphy's is open daily for lunch and dinner.

Outback Steakhouse
$$ • 7189 Overland Rd. • (208) 323-4230

Drink a few Wallaby Darneds or Gold Coast Ritas, and the koala on a pole may wave to you on your way to the "tucker" or food in this rustic spread. A large photo of Paul Hogan beams down on your Drover's Platter, a rack of pork ribs piled with a chicken breast marinated in barbecue sauce and accompanied by Aussie chips (a.k.a. French fries) and cinnamon apples. The Prime Minister's prime rib comes with "shrimp on the barbie." The shrimp are grilled with cayenne pepper and sprinkled with parsley. Walkabout Soup, Great Barrier salmon salad and a 14-ounce heavily marbled

Rockhampton rib-eye steak are other menu eye openers. For dessert, the Cheesecake Olivia (Newton-John) is served with caramel sauce. The Outback is open for dinner every day.

The Sandpiper
$$$ • 1100 W. Jefferson St.
• (208) 344-8911

These people are so comfortable, confident and helpful, they seem to have been here forever. As it stands, The Sandpiper has been here since 1972 across from the tall, forest-like Boise Cascade headquarters and down the street from high, wide and modern Idaho Power. In a sealed-off enclosure decorated with beach and waterfront watercolors, beef takes center stage here, namely prime rib and steaks. The prime rib is corn-fed Colorado beef that is scored, basted with vodka, seasoned with bay leaf and other spices, crisped in a hot oven and then cooked for hours before au jus and horseradish sauce compliment its serving. Seafood dishes, chicken and pasta are also on the menu. The Sandpiper is open for lunch and dinner Monday through Friday and for dinner on Saturday.

Brewpubs and Sports Bars

Boise

Bolo's Pub & Eatery
$ • 602 S.E. 1st St., Meridian
• (208) 884-3737

A rarity in that it doesn't permit smoking, this pub offers an extensive selection of microbrews, TVs in every corner and a pool room at the rear. Philly cheesesteak and fresh-roasted turkey sandwiches, chicken wings with hot, spicy sauce, Big Sky chili and tacos are among the menu items. Bolo's serves lunch and dinner daily.

Buster's Grill and Bar
$ • 1326 Broadway Ave. • (208) 345-5688
$ • 6777 Overland Ave. • (208) 376-6350

Good-looking college women in T-shirts and miniskirts serve a largely male following at these two restaurants where televised sports events entertain. Owner Lou Pejovich's dad called him Buster "when he was angry at me," Pejovich explains, which led to the name of his first restaurant on Broadway in 1983 and the second on Overland in 1992. Pejovich's collection of sports memorabilia — photos, banners and trophies — covers the walls. The most popular menu items are the rotisserie chicken dinner, a bacon cheeseburger lunch and finger steaks. Six different cheese toppings are available for the burgers. Buster's is open daily for lunch and dinner.

Café Sport
$ • AJ's ParkCenter Health Club, 555 W. Parkcenter Blvd. • (208) 343-2288

Sometimes in strange places you find wonderful things. Between rocketing racquetballs contained by Plexiglas walls at the rear of AJ's Health Club is a café with delectable homemade soups, salads and sandwiches that is open to the public. The soup comes with fresh corn, onions, celery, green peppers and tomatoes as well as summer squash in a navy-bean broth. The house salad is made with red and green leaf lettuces, romaine lettuce, arugula, radicchio, baby spinach and red cabbage, greens that are tossed with carrots, tomatoes and grated romano. Almond chicken salad, homemade chicken enchiladas and vegetarian omelets are among other menu items offered by chef-manager Claudine Dorion, who was formerly a restaurant manager in Spokane, Washington. Café Sport is open for breakfast, lunch and dinner Monday through Friday and breakfast on Saturday.

Crescent Bar & Grill
$ • 413 N. Orchard St. • (208) 322-9856

The bar and grill's sign says "No Lawyers." That's because owners Butch and Jody Morrison were forced by a neighbor lawyer in their subdivision to spend $10,000 in legal fees to put in a swimming pool in an area that already had a dozen others before their neighbor tucked tail and withdrew his suit. Everyone in Boise who drives past remembers the sign. Its advertising appeal has become so hot that they sell shirts, hats and other items with the slogan "No Lawyers." They also offer excellent homemade soup and sandwiches such as smoked turkey with Swiss cheese, lettuce, tomato and mayonnaise on a croissant and peppered cream of potato soup with carrots, celery and onion. Crescent has 13 TVs wired to 27 sports channels, a horseshoe-shaped bar surrounded by dining tables, booths and pool tables, and walls decorated with National Football League memorabilia. The bar and grill is open from Monday through Saturday for lunch and dinner.

Dutch Goose
$ • 3515 W. State St. • (208) 342-8887

Steamer clams and finger steaks are a favorite in this gray and red concrete building where TVs broadcast sporting events; pool, Foosball, darts and video games offer more participatory pursuits; and an outdoor patio sports picnic tables, a lawn and horseshoes. The clams, flown in twice weekly from Boston, are steamed in white wine and onions and served with lemon wedges. The tender finger steaks are battered, deep-fried and served on a bed of curly fries. The Goose is open daily for lunch and dinner.

Ed's Abbey
$ • 650 Vista Ave. • (208) 331-1415

No, not the writer Edward Abbey, who wrote *The Monkey Wrench Gang*, silly! This eatery was named by owner Ed Carfora for the Belgian ales made by monks in abbeys. Carfora carries about 30 of these ales and lambics (spontaneously fermented wheat beers) in a nicely furnished, big-screen retreat with a well-appointed jukebox. A marinated chicken sandwich on a sesame bun, fish-and-chips, egg rolls, deep-fried pork and a huge Swiss ranch burger are on the menu. Ed's is open for lunch and dinner daily.

Harrison Hollow Brewhouse
$ • 2455 Harrison Hollow Rd.
• (208) 343-6820

Yes, they make their own brew here, such as Ginger Wheat, Western Ale, Raspberry Wheat and Hulaberry, and it's good, invigorating, tasty suds. But The Hollow attracts much of its following through its imaginative, spicy, eat-till-you-drop kitchen. Grilled polenta, seafood linguine, Mexican chicken salad, hot wings, German sausage with red beans, and Southwestern chicken breast are among the menu items that are served in generous portions and inevitably enjoyed with pints of beer, glasses of wine and other beverages. The sandwiches, salads and soups are hearty, stick-to-the ribs grub. A rough-hewn atmosphere is centered by a fireplace, and everything but the kitchen sink seems to hang from rafters and walls. Located at the base of Bogus Basin Road beneath the Bogus Basin Ski Area, this is a natural stop for snow people and mountain bikers, but its zesty food and spirits and laid-back nature draw customers from throughout the Treasure Valley. Harrison Hollow is open daily for lunch and dinner.

Harry's Bar & Grill
$ • 704 E. 1st St., Meridian
• (208) 888-9868

Finger food, burgers and other sandwiches are served in generous portions at this corner pub that offers sports TV, pool tables and electronic darts. A Wall of Fame touts the famous Harrys who gave the place its name — President Harry Truman, singer Harry Connick Jr., Clint "Dirty Harry" Eastwood and a Les Bois Race Track horse named "Hooten Harry." The owner's name happens to be Steve. Harry's is open for lunch and dinner daily.

Ram Family Restaurant and Sports Club
$ • 709 E. Park Blvd. • (208) 345-2929

Everything about this place is showtime — the high ceilings, big-screen TV and the large windows facing the Boise River; the paintings of athletes and celebrities; the names of the classic cocktails, Old Blue Eyes, The 007, Heart & Soul; and even the Margaritas, Horni Margarita, Cadillac Margarita, Green Iguana Margarita. It's like an indoor stadium for drinks and food beneath ceiling fans and high cabinets filled with bottles. A brass-trimmed bar, high tables and booths seat hundreds of customers during busy times. Appetizers, salads, soups, sandwiches, beef and chicken, seafood, pizza, burgers and Ram favorites, such as pan-fried oysters, jambalya, fish and chips and chicken and chips, will satisfy most any appetite. Games are played on the big-screen TV and five others as an ocean of noise from

Austrian Chef and Flying Pie
Show Boise How It's Done

One is a traditionally trained European cooking master, the other a cheeky and imaginative dough twirler.

Both speak of success on the ever more competitive Boise restaurant landscape where the chickens become fricassee and the bumblers turn into leftovers in a soup of red ink.

Growing up in the Austrian ski town of Kitzbuhel, Peter Schott, the longtime proprietor of a gourmet restaurant in the historic Idanha Hotel, knew when he was 6 years old that he wanted to be a chef.

At that tender age, if he was looking ahead at all, Joe Levitch, the vital force behind three Flying Pie Pizzarias, might have been eyeing medical adventure on a rescue helicopter rather than a future in the restaurant business.

By the time he was 14, Schott was an apprentice to a master chef in Kitzbuhel, where he worked long hours for low pay with no time off in kitchens with one small fan and huge stoves with four hot ovens. For his enthusiasm and energy, he got kicked around like a soccer ball by old, perfectionist chefs.

Levitch and his former Flying Pie general manager, Howard Olivier, to whom he sold the business in 1996, met at a Berkeley, California, nursery school, became immediate pals and have been playing games ever since. Knowing nothing about food or restaurants, Levitch was told a hard-luck story by his father, a general contractor, who heard it from an attorney in a Berkeley office building. In 1980 he came to Boise and paid $1 for two floundering Flying Pie stores.

Like so many other immigrants, Schott arrived in America looking for indepen-

— continued on next page

Joe Levitch paid $1 for two Flying Pie stores in 1980.

dence, wearing a white chef's hat and Chain des Retisseurs, a medallion of the world's oldest gourmet society. At Sun Valley, a ski town with similarities to his Kitzbuhel home, he was executive chef for Sun Valley Resort operations before opening his own Boise restaurant in 1979, just before Levitch got to town.

Now, Stromboli pizza is not Kaiser Schmarren, Eggs Husard has nothing in common with Pesto Primavera, and Calzone with sourdough crust won't be mistaken for Pfifferling Rahmschnitzel.

But these two men could shake hands on their flair for food, imagination and drive at a time when on one hand, Treasure Valley residents thought stuffing trout with asparagus and mushrooms was an obscene act, and on the other, almost all pizza was ordered from heavily advertised, national chains.

Schott all along had a vision with simple and honest criteria, which seems common to success in any field. Don't compromise on fresh ingredients such as fresh, unsalted creamery butter, make sure the wine is affordable but tops and, by all means, make the food look as good as it tastes. Dining is a total experience to the extent that Schott's restaurant interior was created by a Parisian interior decorator. And use the media to your advantage: Schott began a Boise TV cooking show back in 1979 that continues today.

The scrambling Levitch inherited $95,000 of debt with his $1 purchase of two floundering Flying Pie stores. To get by, he worked as a Life Flight paramedic for St. Alphonsus Regional Medical Center. In his spare Flying Pie hours he combined creative food with creative marketing to earn close to a cult following, open a third store and climb out of red ink.

The marketing tactics of Levitch and Olivier include building a computerized delivery system; selling Flying Pie pizza mix in stores in the Northwest, Midwest and Hawaii; having customers "capture" franchise coupons that are traded for rewards; setting up a customer message board in his restaurants; publishing a humorous and engaging restaurant menu; pioneering beer and wine delivery with pizza; teaching school and community classes how to make restaurant-quality pizza; and sending a pizza in 15 hours and 4 minutes to a man on an Alaskan island who usually waited three days to receive pizza from Anchorage — a scheme that cost nothing and received wide publicity.

Although traditional, Schott is bending with the times. While he continues his restaurant at the Idanha Hotel, he is opening the 7,500-square-foot Sports Pub and Grill next to Edward's 21 Cinemas that will feature a full bar, 10 microbrews, two 122-inch TVs and something Levitch can appreciate — a wood-fired pizza oven.

echoing talk off the stone and glass walls accompanies the socializing. Big Horn Brewing drinks include Idaho Blonde and Hefeweizen. A restaurant and bar are on the other side of a glass partition. Out front is a movie-type marquee that has dozens of yellow light bulbs beneath the white facade proclaiming the day's food special, and, appropriately enough, visible beyond the roof are the light standards from the Boise State University football stadium. The Ram is open daily for lunch and dinner.

Tablerock Brewpub Grill
$ • 705 Fulton St. • (208) 342-0944

Not so long ago this was the first brewpub in Boise. John Lemp, a German immigrant, brewer and early Boise mayor, inspired the founding of Tablerock, named for the mesa above Boise's eastern foothills. Camas Prairie barleys and Southern Idaho hops go into Depot Gold, White Bird Wheat, Razzberry Ale and other Tablerock beers made by brewmaster Terry Daniels in accordance with Reinheitsgebot, or the German purity law, which requires that only fresh ingredients and no additives or preservatives be used. A long bar with tables and a two-level restaurant offers an extensive menu of appetizers, sandwiches, chilis and soups, salads, burgers, sausages, side orders and pub specials. The latter include Rattlesnake Ribs, which are baby-back pork ribs baked in beer and jalapeno barbecue sauce and served with saloon slaw and spice rum applesauce; lasagna primavera, which has layers of fresh pasta, broccoli, zucchini, carrots, onions, mushrooms and peppers blended with alfredo, marinara and pesto sauces; fresh salmon; grilled halibut; smoked chicken and ravioli; and shepherd's pie, which is beef stew topped with oven-browned mashed potatoes and Parmesan cheese, served with French bread. This location has a clean, pleasant, wide-open atmosphere. Old Western portraits hang on the walls. Blond wood booths, tables and the bar provide views of the brewhouse, fermentation room and cold serving room through large windows. Tablerock is open daily for lunch and dinner.

Coffeehouses

Though many of the following coffeehouses do serve some kind of food in addition to their caffeine creations, it would be difficult to stretch these baked goods and other menu items into a meal to be represented by a price code.

Boise

Coffee-News Coffee-News
801 W. Main St. on the pedestrian mall • (208) 344-7661

All kinds of magazines and newspapers are offered with espresso and house blend coffee at a simple and friendly location near the convention center, the new Grove Hotel and sports arena. If it's screen instead of paper information that you are looking for, a computer kiosk offers Internet access. Baked breads, soups and bagels are also available. Coffee-News is open daily from early morning into the evenings and stays open late on Friday and Saturday nights.

Espresso Italia Hyde Park
1530 N. 13th St. • (208) 336-5122

This location has an excellent patio for people and dogs, who explore a treat jar while their owners sip two kinds of espresso and nibble muffins and cinnamon rolls. Its location near Camelback Park and the foothills draws bikers, hikers and other outdoor people as well as plenty of families with kids. Espresso is open from early morning into the evening every day. There are also six other locations around Boise.

Flying M Espresso & Fine Crafts
500 W. Idaho St. • (208) 345-4320

You'll feel like you've wandered into someone's living room, complete with couches, tables, reading materials and local art on the walls, at the Flying M in downtown Boise. Don't trip over the dogs and sun worshippers at sidewalk tables outside. Espresso, latte and mocha drinks are available along with muffins, rolls and sandwiches at a spot with a particularly healthy breakfast and lunch following. It opens early and closes late daily.

Giuseppe's Coffee House
219 N. 8th St. • (208) 336-5633

Giuseppe's serves 21 kinds of coffee from all over the world at a relaxing indoor location with outdoor tables. Coffee is roasted, ground and brewed daily on the premises. Sumatra, mochas and lattes are popular choices and can be enjoyed with fresh sandwiches, soups and frappes. Giuseppe's is open Monday through Friday from early morning into evening, on Saturday from early morning into late afternoon and from morning to mid-afternoon on Sunday.

Moxie Java
570 W. Main St. • (208) 343-9033
1750 W. State St. • (208) 389-9820

The downtown Moxie Java, a small place with outdoor tables that is popular with fast-moving students, workers and office people, was one of the city's first popular coffeehouses. The larger location on W. State Street in Albertson's Shopping Center draws a relaxed and conversational crowd indoors and out. Locally roasted White Cloud Mountain coffee with a variety of flavors along with muffins, croissants, cakes and cheesecakes are on the menu. Moxie is open early to late daily. There are a dozen locations throughout the Treasure Valley.

Soho Espresso Bar
6932 W. State St. • (208) 853-4641

This modern, nicely decorated coffee spot next to the Northgate movie theater features coffee from Italy, such as Palermo, Sardenia and Milano, as well as espresso made with a sweet chocolate mix. Visitors indulge in muffins, pastries and baklava with their coffee at tables and booths beneath imaginative paper chandeliers and clocks with Boise, New York and Milan time. Soho is open early to late every day.

Starbucks Coffee
1797 W. State St. • (208) 367-0781

Seattle's premier coffee maker arrived in Boise in 1998 at a comfortable, cafe-like location. It offers proven beans and friendly service. Bagels, scones, muffins and pastries are available with the Sumatra, House Blend and other coffee varieties. Starbucks is open early to late daily.

Wild West Bakery and Espresso
83 E. State Rd., Eagle • (208) 939-5677

A corner shop whose decor reflects its name, Wild West offers a wide range of coffee and espresso drinks along with sandwiches, soups, salads and pastries. Couches and tables provide conversational respite. Wild West is open early into evening every day except for Sunday when it is open early to mid-afternoon.

The greatest concentration of bars and nightclubs is in a 10-square-block section of downtown Boise, from 5th and Main streets in Old Boise to 10th and Idaho streets.

Nightlife

No one would mistake Boise for the nightlife capital of America. On the other hand, there are plenty of places to satisfy all but the most jaded night owl.

This is the town that spawned Paul Revere and the Raiders, one of the most popular bands in America in the late 1960s and early 1970s. It is the longtime roost of singer-guitarist Rosalie Sorrels, internationally acclaimed for her poetic folk stylings. It is the chosen domicile of pianist Gene Harris, whose mellow keyboard has earned him a position in the upper echelon of jazz circles. It is the hometown of Doug Martsch, whose alternative band, Built to Spill, has earned national critical acclaim since emerging in the mid-1990s.

And although there's no "Boise Sound" per se, the city has become known as one of the best blues towns in the country, with several annual festivals and its own Boise Blues Society, (208) 344-2583, supporting the work of numerous regional artists.

The greatest concentration of bars and nightclubs is in a 10-square-block section of downtown Boise, from 5th and Main streets in Old Boise to 10th and Idaho streets. Within this quadrant, or very near to it, you'll find at least 20 of the establishments listed in the following pages. But other nightspots are spread throughout the greater Boise area.

The drinking age is 21, and most bars only allow people 21 or older. You may be required to prove your age with a photo ID. Officially, bars close at 2 AM Monday through Saturday nights and at midnight Sundays. But on slow nights — which, at most locations, includes all but Fridays and Saturdays — many establishments will offer last call much earlier. Unless otherwise noted, all places listed in this chapter have a full bar.

Be exceedingly cautious about drinking and driving in Boise. The legal blood-alcohol limit in Idaho is .10 percent; any more and you can lose a lot more than your license. But even half that amount is enough to significantly impair your driving.

You'll normally be faced with a cover charge only at clubs that present live music and then often only on Friday and Saturday nights unless the band has been booked from another city. A typical cover charge is $3, although top-name entertainment may command as much as $10 in nonconcert venues.

There are several major divisions in the following listings.

The first category is concert venues. Nightspots with regular entertainment are classified according to the type of music they offer: rock, blues and jazz, country-and-western, and Latin, folk or world music. Following those listings are popular bars: brewpubs, wine bars, sports bars and other bars of special interest for one reason or another. You'll find more information on brewpubs, wine bars and sports bars in the Restaurants chapter, as many of these establishments have pretty tasty menus as well as libations and late-night entertainment. Also turn to the Restaurants chapter for listings of the Treasure Valley's coffeehouses. Many of them are open late and offer a quieter alternative to the bar scene. Toward the end of the chapter, we've included comedy clubs that will tickle your funny bone.

Finally, there's a short section on popular movie theaters in Boise. We have included only the largest and most popular theaters and those with a unique milieu.

For concise and timely entertainment listings, consult the "Scene" section, contained in every Friday morning's edition of *The Idaho Statesman*, or the *Boise Weekly*, a free publication distributed throughout the city each Thursday morning.

You can purchase tickets for events at Select-A-Seat outlets in Albertsons supermarkets, or order them by phone at (208) 385-1766. You might also inquire at leading independent compact-disk retailers such as the CD

Merchant, 601 W. Main Street, (208) 331-1200, or the Record Exchange, 1105 W. Idaho Street, (208) 344-8010.

Concert Venues

These locations are not exclusive, but they are the most likely spots to hear top touring musicians during the year. In summer you may find shows at various open-air sites such as Hawks Stadium (see our Spectator Sports chapter), where a recent lineup included Ziggy Marley, Carlos Santana and Big Head Todd.

Boise

Bank of America Centre
8th and Grove Sts. • (208) 331-8497

Downtown Boise's home of professional ice hockey and tennis is quickly converted to a concert hall accommodating 5,000. There's not a bad seat in the house, and that includes the private suites extending from The Grove Hotel. Musical offerings cover all bases, from classic rock (Allman Brothers Band, Kenny Loggins) to '90s alternative (Green Day, 311, Pantera) and from Latin crooner Julio Iglesias to Michael Flatley's highly acclaimed *Lord of the Dance*. Parking is available at the hotel, in nearby lots and on nearby downtown streets.

Boise State University Pavilion
1910 University Dr. • (208) 385-1766

Many top bands, primarily with student followings, perform in this three-tiered basketball arena. In 1997, the list of performers included country singer Alan Jackson and hard rockers Mötley Crüe and Rush as well as the vaunted Boston Pops Orchestra. Oldies-but-goodies such as the Eagles and the Beach Boys saw fit to include The Pavilion on their

1996 tours. Campus parking can be difficult. You may have to shell out a few bucks for a lot or walk a little ways if you park on the street.

DoubleTree Riverside Ballroom
Doubletree Riverside Hotel, 2900 Chinden Blvd. • (208) 343-1871

Seating in this hotel's convention space is limited to a few hundred guests, but that's just right for performers like Emmylou Harris, John Hiatt and Toad the Wet Sprocket who prefer playing in front of more intimate audiences.

Morrison Center for the Performing Arts
Boise State University, 2201 Campus Ln. • (208) 385-1609

Considered one of the finest civic theaters in the United States because of its marvelous acoustics, the Morrison Center seats 2,000 music lovers on its main floor and mezzanine deck for a variety of theatrical presentations and concerts. Recent performers have included violinist Itzhak Perlman, pianist George Winston, magician David Copperfield, folk artists John Prine and Peter, Paul & Mary, and popular singers Shawn Colvin and Lyle Lovett. You can order tickets directly from the Center's box office at (208) 385-1110. (See The Arts chapter for more information about the center's offerings.)

Union Block Concert Club
714 W. Idaho St. • (208) 381-0483

Since opening in mid-1997, this second-story ballroom in one of downtown Boise's most impressive restored historic buildings has featured a continuous lineup of emerging and established artists, many of them with a blues orientation to their music. The roster has included Mose Allison, the Freddy Jones Band and Reverend Horton Heat.

INSIDERS' TIP

For a small city, Boise has excellent concert halls. Morrison Center for the Performing Arts ranks among the best halls nationally for design as well as acoustics.

Photo: John Gottberg

Downtown Boise offers outdoor dining as well as entertainment.

Westpark Events Center
7071 W. Emerald St. • (208) 323-2107
   Performances at this west Boise concert hall are geared largely, though not exclusively, to a hard-rocking younger crowd: Bands like Helmet, Prong and Sister Machine Gun performed here recently.

Nampa

The Idaho Center
5000 Garrity Blvd. • (208) 468-1000
   Although it opened with a splash when the Moody Blues and ZZ Top came to town in mid-1997, this spacious 13,000-seat arena

is also used for rodeos, basketball games and monster truck rallies (see our Spectator Sports chapter). More bands are being booked: Peter Jackson, Eric Clapton's road manager, is The Idaho Center's events manager.

Music Clubs

Rock

Boise

Angell's Bar and Grill
999 W. Main St. • (208) 342-4900

Acoustic musicians provide pre- and post-dinner music in the lounge of this upscale downtown steak-and-seafood house. (See our Restaurants chapter for menu details.)

Bogie's
1124 Front St. • (208) 342-9663

One of the few clubs that admits those younger than 21, Bogie's is a spacious ballroom that frequently books acts that once made a national impact: For instance, Blue Oyster Cult and Randy Bachman recently took the stage. But the evening's entertainment is more likely to be provided by bands you've never heard of such as String Cheese Incident and Let's Go Bowling. There's dancing every Friday and Saturday night to music provided by a DJ, when the cover charge is $5. Cover charges for band performances range from $5 to $20.

Eastside Tavern
610 E. Boise Ave. • (208) 888-8700

Perhaps the only place east of Broadway Avenue with live dance music, this Eastgate Plaza tavern features bands on Friday and Saturday nights. There's a small cover. Other nights, patrons come to play pool and darts. The tavern serves beer and wine only.

Emerald Club
415 S. 9th St. • (208) 342-5446

"Yes, we are straight friendly" reads the marquee at this exceedingly popular club near the Eighth Street Marketplace. Thursdays are ballyhooed as "straight nights," but you'll find a mix of gays and straights waiting in line almost any night. The club boasts a large dance floor and a DJ who spins a continuous stream of contemporary hits.

Hannah's
621 W. Main St. • (208) 345-7557

The Rocci Johnson Band, which has held down the stage at this Old Boise nightclub for many years, has a loyal local following that comes to dance to its '70s and '80s rock offerings Tuesday through Saturday nights. An upstairs balcony overlooks the dance floor and band, and a big adjacent game room offers pool, darts and more. The clientele covers a wide range, from BSU students to those middle-age and sometimes beyond. There's no cover charge on Tuesdays and Thursdays. Men pay $2 on Wednesday, when it's ladies night. You'll pay $3 to get in on Fridays and Saturdays. Johnson, who is very active in the local women's arts scene, sometimes hosts special events at Hannah's.

The Interlude
213 N. 8th St. • (208) 342-9593

Though a long, narrow bar, The Interlude somehow finds space for rock bands on frequent weekend nights. At other times it offers sports on a series of small TVs and a pretty good bar menu (see the Restaurants chapter for more information). The Interlude tends to attract an older crowd.

Joe's Down Under
100 S. 6th St. • (208) 344-4146

DJs keep the volume turned high on techno-rock and disco, which dominate this dance club in the basement of Joe's All-American Grill (see our Restaurants chapter). It's very popular with the college and post-college crowds. On Friday and Saturday nights, the cover is $5; on Sundays and weeknights, $3.

Jones St. on Emerald
4802 Emerald St. • (208) 331-7800

If there's one place in Boise you'll be assured of hearing DJs spin good rhythm-and-blues music and perhaps a little rap, it's this club owned by a former BSU basketball star.

It's especially popular with student athletes and Boise's black population. Wednesday is ladies night. A cover is charged on Friday (when 18- to 21-year-olds are admitted) and Saturday.

J.T. Toad's
107 S. 6th St. • (208) 345-2505

Formerly Grainey's Basement, this casual club shares a low ceiling/floor and weekend cover with Tom Grainey's (see Blues, Jazz and Swing later in this chapter). A wide range of live music is presented here; often, but not always, it's alternative rock from out-of-towners. Twenty- and thirty-somethings gather around its central bar and in quieter alcoves.

Lock, Stock & Barrel
4705 Emerald St. • (208) 336-4266

Local favorites Tauge and Faulkner, a guitar and keyboard duo, are frequent stars in this steakhouse lounge. Conversation and light contemporary music that doesn't overwhelm pre- and post-dinner drinks are the main attractions. (Also see our Restaurants chapter.)

Murphy's
1555 Broadway Ave. • (208) 344-3691

The TVs may stay tuned to sports in the lounge of this upscale seafood house, but the volume is muted as soon as guitarist Wilson Roberts or another acoustic performer takes the stage. Roberts spins sets of light classic rock Thursday through Saturday evenings. (Read more about Murphy's in our Restaurants chapter.)

Neurolux
111 N. 11th St. • (208) 343-0886

Boise's leading alternative nightclub is the city's No. 1 hangout for the gothic set. On any given night as many as three different bands will perform sets one after another. Other nights might see DJ dancing, comedy performances or even fashion shows. Occasionally, national acts like the Wild Colonials will play here, and if you want to catch a rare appearance by Boise act Built to Spill, this is the place. There's no cover charge if there's no band playing. The cover is $3 for most bands; $5 is the maximum charge here.

Partners
2210 W. Main St. • (208) 331-3551

Boise's longest established gay club offers dancing with a DJ Wednesday through Saturday nights. Occasionally there's a live performance to draw an expanded crowd.

The Radio Room
Hoff Building, 802 W. Bannock St., 12th floor • (208) 345-1551

A revolving disco ball sends a rainbow of colors flickering through picture windows and across downtown Boise from the 12th floor of the art-deco Hoff Building. A DJ begins spinning '70s tunes around 9:30 PM nightly, when the dinner hour has come to an end. This atmospheric room is a little dressier than most Boise clubs, which can be casual to the extreme. (See the Restaurants chapter for more information.)

Rascals
Fairview Square, 5200 Fairview Ave. • (208) 378-7574

Patrons of this classic-rock club are treated to live music Wednesday to Saturday nights, with a cover charged on weekends. The big dance floor caters largely to a 30s-and-older set, who appreciate its off-the-beaten-track location in the Fairview Square strip mall near Orchard Street.

Sunshine Saloon at the Rodeway Inn
1115 N. Curtis Rd. • (208) 376-2700

Live contemporary and Top-40 rock for dancing is the formula that works on Friday and Saturday nights for a 30-and-older crowd. There's a $2 cover charge. Other nights, this cozy room is a quiet bar without a cover.

Caldwell

Victor's
211 21st St. • (208) 454-1497

This Caldwell restaurant has acoustic performers Wednesday nights and rock bands for dancing Fridays and Saturdays. It draws a wide-ranging clientele. There's no cover charge.

Blues, Jazz and Swing

Boise

The Blues Bouquet
1010 W. Main St. • (208) 345-6605

Perhaps Boise's most popular nightclub for dancing, this dark New Orleans-style establishment has a beautiful, long bar down one wall, pool tables by the front window and plenty of space for sitting and standing. There's even a small nonsmoking area at the rear of the club near the bandstand. House band The Hoochie Coochie Men or local favorite House of Hoi Polloi perform when top national touring blues artists like Charlie Musselwhite, Junior Wells or Maria Muldaur are not booked. Monday through Thursday and Sunday, there is no cover charge. Friday and Saturday performances usually cost $3. To see more well-known performers, the cover can be $8, $10 or $12.

Brando's Piano Bar
202 N. Capitol Blvd. • (208) 387-2395

A second-story corner turret above a Thai restaurant, just a couple of blocks from the State Capitol, is the home of this modern speakeasy, whose decor and mood are like something out of the Prohibition era. Jazz singer Kathy Miller and her trio are a mainstay on weekends, but a variety of other keyboardists and performers rotate through on a regular basis. There's never a cover charge. Ask about the regular cigar-and-cognac nights.

Gamekeeper Lounge
Owhee Plaza Hotel, 11th and Main Sts.
• (208) 343-4611

You'll hear everything from '40s swing to contemporary show tunes every night but Sunday at this elegant, dimly lit piano bar. This is not a place to visit in jeans and tennis shoes, as the clientele is older and tends to dress for an evening out.

Hyde Park Depot
1501 N. 13th St. • (208) 331-7007

A blues pianist or occasional light-jazz groups perform during the dinner hour at this casual North End restaurant with a vaguely

New Orleans-themed decor. (See our Restaurants chapter for more information.)

Noodles
800 W. Idaho St. • (208) 342-9300

Every Wednesday beginning at 5:30 PM and on other occasions, the Sandon Mayhew/Chuck Smith Quartet hosts a jazz jam at this second-story pasta eatery in downtown Boise's Mode Building. (See our Restaurants chapter for more information about Noodles.)

O'Michael's
2433 Bogus Basin Rd. • (208) 342-8948

Sing-along piano beside a roaring fireplace draws a clientele of North End regulars to this Irish-style bar adjoining a casual restaurant.

Tom Grainey's
109 S. 6th St. • (208) 345-2505

Look for Fat John and the Three Slims or The Rebecca Scott Decision at this Old Boise bar, one of the city's most popular. The clientele ranges from college students to middle-aged blues lovers. Seating is haphazard, but there's a good-size dance floor. J.T. Toad's is in the basement (see Rock in this chapter). A dual cover for both clubs is charged on weekends.

Country-and-Western

Boise

127 Club
127 E. Idaho Ave., Meridian
• (208) 884-0122

This very popular nightclub in downtown Meridian presents a country-and-western dance band Thursday through Saturday nights for the 30-and-older crowd. No cover is charged on Thursdays; a $2 cover is in effect on Fridays and Saturdays. There's a good-sized dance floor, plenty of seating and attentive bartenders. Several pool tables and dartboards are at the rear of the club.

Bill's Frontier Club
116 E. Broadway Ave., Meridian
• (208) 888-9034

Country-and-western bands play Friday and Saturday nights, but these sessions come in as a close second to Thursday's karaoke session, when would-be country crooners take their turn at the microphone. The otherwise nondescript bar is big with the darts-and-pool set.

Ranch Club
3544 Chinden Blvd., Garden City
• (208) 342-9546
Adjoining the Oñati Basque Restaurant, this cozy nightspot — distinguished by the rearing white palomino on its sign — has live country music for dancing Wednesday through Saturday. There is no cover charge. The club is also open without a band on Mondays and Tuesdays. (For details about the Oñati Basque Restaurant, turn to our Restaurants chapter.)

Shorty's Country & Western Saloon
5467 Glenwood St., Garden City
• (208) 323-0555
Easily the Boise area's largest and most popular country-and-western nightclub, Shorty's is *the* place to go if you wear Tony Lamas and drive a pickup truck. Situated opposite the Western Idaho Fairgrounds, it has two large bars, a huge dance floor and live music by the house band, Redstone, Wednesday through Saturday nights, when the cover charge is $2. Dance lessons are offered several nights a week. And if you time your visit right, you might stumble upon a tight-jeans or wet-T-shirt competition.

The Turf Club
4902 Chinden Blvd., Garden City
• (208) 373-0089
A friendly, slightly older clientele prefers dancing at this neighborhood bar to the frenzy of Shorty's (see the previous listing). This is a low-key nightclub with live country-and-western bands several nights a week.

Nampa

Hondo's
453 Caldwell Blvd. • (208) 465-4910
A spacious saloon and sports bar, Hondo's is undoubtedly the western Treasure Valley's best venue for swing and line dancing. There's a DJ Wednesdays and Thursdays, a live band Fridays and Saturdays, and country dance lessons are available early Friday evenings. A

cover is charged on weekends. Pool tables are always busy, and a series of TVs show rodeo whenever possible.

Latin, Folk and World Music

Boise

Acapulco Cantina
5181 Glenwood St., Garden City
• (208) 375-4896
The Margarita bar at this Mexican restaurant comes alive on Friday and Saturday nights when a DJ plays salsa, tejano and other Latin dance music.

Koffee Klatsch
409 S. 8th St. • (208) 345-0452
There's a different performer most evenings and Sunday midday at this natural-foods restaurant adjacent to the Eighth Street Marketplace. You never know what awaits your ears here: folk guitarists, chamber music, Indian ragas or French bossanova stylings. (See the Restaurants chapter for more information.)

Bars and Pubs

Brewpubs

Boise

Bittercreek Alehouse
246 N. 8th St. • (208) 345-1813
Not really the definition of a brewpub since it doesn't make its own beer, the Bittercreek nevertheless has the city's best selection of custom brews from pubs throughout the Northwest as well as a wide-ranging and delicious menu (see our Restaurants chapter for details). The clientele is primarily young professionals who prefer conversation to loud music.

Harrison Hollow Brewhouse
2455 Harrison Hollow • (208) 343-6820
A central fireplace sets the tone for this rustic establishment, whose location at the foot

of Bogus Basin Road makes it an especially popular stopover for skiers en route home after a day on the slopes. The brewpub, which has a new sister brewery on Maui, makes an excellent Hefeweizen, and its food offerings are creative and delicious (see the Restaurants chapter for more information).

Star Garnet Brewing
804 N. Orchard St. • (208) 388-8561

Ensconced in a former filling station, this brewpub is not yet in the forefront of the local brewing scene, but it's making rapid progress. A small cafe and beer garden share the premises, and a handful of area restaurants list Star Garnet beers on their menus.

Tablerock Brewpub Grill
705 Fulton St. • (208) 342-0944

This was Boise's first brewpub, and some argue it's still the best. Try the Nut Brown or Razzberry ales. Walking distance from downtown between the Eighth Street Marketplace and the public library, it supplements its beer selection with gourmet comfort food (see our Restaurants chapter for more information).

Nampa

Slick Rock Brewpub
111 13th Ave. S. • (208) 442-2565

New in mid-1997, the Treasure Valley's first brewpub outside of Boise has a spacious room in downtown Nampa, where it has been a hit with young professionals. The menu features prime rib, seafood, sausage and sandwiches. Beers include Red Hook, Anchor, Guiness, Table Rock Wheat and Sierra Nevada.

Wine Bars

Boise

Grape Escape Wine Bar
800 W. Idaho St. • (208) 368-0200

With its big glass windows at the northwest corner of 8th and Idaho streets and its outdoor patio open spring through fall, this is one of Boise professionals' favorite spots for people-watching. In addition to a handful of hors d'oeuvres from the deli, the menu fea-

tures a wide selection of epicurean wines by the glass. Or you can save a few dollars by buying any bottle from the racks and paying a corkage fee. (See our Restaurants chapter for more about the menu.)

Villano's Specialty Market & Deli
712 W. Idaho St. • (208) 331-3066

Imported vintages, especially Italian, are the specialty of this modern wine counter adjoining a specialty market and deli. (See the Restaurants chapter for more information.)

Sports Bars

Boise

Bolo's Pub & Eatery
601 E. 1st St., Meridian • (208) 884-3737

Nine TV sets carry sports events, rock music fills the air, a number of Northwest microbrews are available, and pool tables and video games take up the rear. Bolo's is smoke-free. (See the Restaurants chapter for details about the menu.)

Buster's Grill and Bar
1326 Broadway Ave. • (208) 345-5688
6777 Overland Rd. • (208) 376-6350

Buster's claims no alliance with the national Hooter's chain, but you wouldn't know it from the outfits donned by its college-coed service corps. The lounge is rife with televisions in every corner, one of them is a big-screen, and there are more TVs in the main dining room, which is decorated with BSU sporting memorabilia. (See the Restaurants chapter for more information.)

Crescent Bar & Grill
413 N. Orchard St. • (208) 322-9856

"No lawyers" is the credo of this neighborhood bar that nevertheless seems to attract a broad cross-section of the community. Thirteen big-screen televisions can pick up 27 separate sports channels by satellite transmission, so anyone who wants to watch a game is almost certain to find it televised here. A half-dozen pool tables are available for play free of charge to midday visitors. (See our Restaurants chapter for the grill side of this bar.)

The End Zone
1010 Broadway Ave. • (208) 384-0613

Students arrive late and stay later at this sports-oriented tavern opposite Bronco Stadium and the BSU campus.

Harry's Bar & Grill
704 E. 1st St., Meridian • (208) 888-9868

You may occasionally catch a blues performance in the evening at Harry's, but this Meridian main-street bar generally packs in patrons to watch TV sports or play pool and darts. A limited menu is offered. (See the Restaurants chapter for details.)

Old Chicago
730 W. Idaho St. • (208) 363-0037
Boise Towne Square, 350 N. Milwaukee St. • (208) 321-0033

Da Bears, Da Bulls, Da Cubs: These are the teams of choice for patrons of this Colorado-based chain. Chi-town sports memorabilia abounds, from autographed jerseys to game programs and Hall of Fame photos. There are plenty of TVs for any sporting event, and more than 100 bottled and draft beers from all over the world. An Italian-influenced menu focuses on pizzas.

Players Pub and Grill
5504 W. Alworth St., Garden City • (208) 376-6563

Adjoining a bowling alley near the fairgrounds, Players has the requisite big-screen TV and numerous smaller sets as well as a burger menu. Sports items on display here include several tied to horse racing and auto racing.

The Pocket
1487 N. Curtis Rd. • (208) 375-2474

Probably the biggest billiards hall in Boise, The Pocket features 22 pool tables as well as dartboards, numerous video games and a very large big-screen television. It costs $6 an hour to play pool and 50¢ a game for darts.

Ram Family Restaurant and Sports Club
709 E. Park Blvd. • (208) 345-2929

Boise's most popular sports bar is really four places in one. The main bar has a giant four-plex screen and at least eight other televisions as well as a huge bar with friendly and efficient bartenders. The Ram even makes its own beers, such as Buttface Ale and Total Disorder Porter. There's karaoke on selected nights, a DJ for late-night dancing and a National Trivia Network link at all hours. Adjoining is a family restaurant that extends to a wide outside deck where live music and parties often are held summer afternoons and evenings. The adjacent Stonehouse has a six-table pool hall and is used primarily for private parties. (See our Restaurants chapter for more information.)

Other Bars and Taverns

Boise

10th Street Station
104 N. 10th St. • (208) 344-2677

The basement of the Idanha Hotel is the home of this dark but well-frequented bar. Its decor focuses heavily on sports regalia, although the clientele is decidedly artistic and/or alternative.

Bill-N-Lynn's Place
35 E. Fairview Ave., Meridian • (208) 888-4075

Don't be fooled by this bar's location in a strip mall; it's a friendly and spacious room with all kinds of games. The owner describes it as a workman's bar that attracts a lot of construction workers. Shuffleboard, pool, darts and a jukebox keep patrons busy.

The Brews Brothers
Northgate Shopping Center, 6928 W. State St. • (208) 853-0526

This tavern in the Northgate Shopping Center is a favorite stop for shoppers or patrons of the adjacent cinema. It's a dark, comfortable location with a wide variety of suds, tables and a bar where it's quiet enough for conversation.

Cactus Bar
517 W. Main St. • (208) 342-9732

An Old Boise institution, this "dive" always seems busy — especially on Monday nights, when the rock group New Electric Peaches perform.

The Docksider
3000 N. Lakeharbor Ln. • (208) 853-2583

The sounds of Jimmy Buffett and Bob Marley prevail at this casual bar and grill beside Lakeharbor Pond. The Caribbean flavor is enhanced by a bar that's half indoors, half outdoors.

The Dutch Goose
3515 W. State St. • (208) 342-8887

The rear beer garden (with horseshoe pits) that's larger than the spacious bar itself is the best reason to visit the Goose. There are plenty of coin-operated pool tables and TVs and a stage for the live bands that perform occasionally. (See our Restaurants chapter for more information.)

Ed's Abbey
650 S. Vista Ave. • (208) 331-1415

There aren't too many places in the country where you'll find Belgian lambic ales on draft, but Ed's is one of them. These fruit-flavored "dessert beers" are made by monks in, you guessed it, abbeys. The activity focus here is darts; Ed's is a leader in city recreational leagues. (See the Restaurants chapter for details about Ed's menu.)

The Overland Bar
3907 Overland Rd. • (208) 336-4707

The karaoke crowd fights for the mike at this south-side bar. It's got a big stage and sing-along screen as well as tables where you can sit and watch or prepare for your premiere.

Pengilly's Saloon
513 W. Main St. • (208) 345-6344

Old Boise's favorite old-time tavern is a colorful and casual spot for friends to swap stories, either at the bar or in high-backed wooden booths.

The 'Piper Pub
Capital Terrace, 150 N. 8th St., 2nd Floor • (208) 343-2444

The city's most sophisticated see-and-be-seen bar for the suit set is on the second floor of the Capital Terrace complex. It's especially popular during the warmer months when conversations extend to an expansive deck overlooking Main Street.

Rider's Bar
1413 W. Idaho St. • (208) 342-0393

There always seems to be a Harley or three parked outside this near downtown bar, a well-maintained and not-overly-rowdy hangout for the chopper set.

Suds Tavern
1024 Broadway Ave. • (208) 345-9656

Next door to The End Zone (see our previous listing), Suds caters to a largely student clientele. It has a reputation as the last stop of the night before a return to campus housing.

The Symposion
2801 Fletcher St. • (208) 342-9420

There's an English pub flavor to this unusual establishment off Fairview Avenue just west of downtown. On one side of the entrance is the bar, which boasts a steady clientele; on the other side is a pool room where pet dogs have been known to hang out with customers.

The Trolley
Rose Hill St. at Jackson St. • no phone

A Boise Bench institution, this red railcar has housed a tavern since 1934. The quarters are tight, to say the least, but no one really seems to mind.

Comedy and Entertainment Clubs

Boise

Bacchus Cabaret
1519 W. Main St. • (208) 333-8505

Idaho's first professional female impersonation troupe, Lips Inc.!, does shows like "Glamazons" at this small club near downtown Boise. New shows are presented the first Friday and Saturday of each month; some people say they're a real "drag." Cover runs $10.

The Funny Bone
404 S. 8th St. • (208) 331-2663

Climb to the third level at the Eighth Street Marketplace, and you'll discover a spacious room that has done a booming business since opening its doors in 1996. George Carlin, Tommy Chong, Victoria Jackson and Bobcat Goldthwait are among the nationally known comics who have appeared here. The cover charge is $6 on Wednesdays and Thursdays, $7 on Fridays and Saturdays and $5 on Sundays. The club is closed on Mondays and Tuesdays.

Cinema

Boiseans' tastes in movies are generally quite mainstream and geared to the offerings of major studios. Even Academy Award winners like *The English Patient* have been forced to make their debuts at the city's lone arts theater. But groups like the Idaho Film Foundation, (208) 343-7120, sponsor touring film festivals over the course of the year, bringing some variety to the local cinematic scene.

Boise

Edwards 21 Cinemas
7701 Overland Rd. • (208) 377-1700

Boise's theatrical showcase opened in late 1997 with a splash. Each of the five main 450-seat theaters is themed to resemble a different classic Hollywood theater. Sixteen smaller theaters have about 140 seats each. The complex boasts 10 box offices, 7 miles of neon lighting and 24,000 square feet of imported granite and marble. Can moviegoing ever be the same again?

Admission is $6.75 for adults, $4.25 for ages 11 and younger as well as 55 and older.

Egyptian Theatre
700 W. Main St. • (208) 342-1441

This classic 1926 theater — the only cinema remaining in the heart of Boise — has seen the evolution of film from silent movies to contemporary film. Its original organ, which once accompanied the antics of Charlie Chaplin and Harold Lloyd, still gets a workout from time to time. But the Tutankhamen-inspired stage now shows mainly blockbuster movies. (See our Attractions chapter for more information about this theater.)

The Flicks
646 Fulton St. • (208) 342-4222

Traditionally the only Boise theater to show independent, foreign and arts films, The Flicks doubled its size in 1997 to four screens and now presents a wider choice of movies. A cafe and a wine-and-espresso bar are on-site, and yes, you are allowed to bring your drink into the theater. Look for film festivals and other special events that The Flicks hosts.

Tickets cost $6.50 for shows that start after 6 PM, $4 for those before. Seniors 65 and older, students with ID and children 12 and younger pay $4 after 6 PM.

Towne Square Cinemas
130 N. Milwaukee St. • (208) 323-0430

This six-screen Cineplex Odeon complex owes much of its success to its location across the parking lot from the Boise Towne Square shopping mall. Casual restaurants flank it on either side.

Tickets cost $6.25 for adults, $4 for ages 3 to 12 as well as 55 and older. Special rates include $4 for everyone for shows before 6 PM and $3.25 for all shows on Tuesdays.

Reflecting the territory, Boise is flush with sporting goods stores, and its intellect has been uncovered by a recent infusion of bookstores.

Shopping

Boise may surprise the newcomer who expects an isolated "Potato City" with its large, internationally known companies, its handsome Capitol, its good restaurants, nightlife, arts, parks, spectator sports and recreational opportunities. But shopping, well, let's just say we were a little behind the curve. The city didn't have a mall until a decade ago, and there was no substitute, no great concentration of wonderful, inspirational, independent city stores that appealed to hearts and pocketbooks.

That's changed radically with the construction of a first-rate mall, Boise Towne Square, and its satellite shopping plazas in west Boise, and with a renaissance of specialty shops, coffeehouses, galleries and restaurants that make downtown Boise a fun place to browse, eat, drink and pick up a few items. Big-bucks fashion connoisseurs still jet off to the likes of Nordstrom's, Macy's, Saks and Neiman Marcus in other locations. But Boise ain't bad for the average shopper. Reflecting the territory, it's flush with sporting goods stores, and its intellect has been uncovered by a recent infusion of bookstores.

The Downtown Boise Association has brought imagination and energy to the shopping scene with its First Thursday productions held every month that include free trolley rides and garage parking, a gallery stroll, music, food and drink, entertainment and demonstrations. Neighborhoods like Boise's Hyde Park and the historic section of Nampa and a self-guided tour through the produce markets and wineries in the area provide unusual shopping experiences.

Here we provide an overview of the shopping options in the Treasure Valley, beginning with the most concentrated and popular location, Boise Towne Square and its area, then moving onto downtown Boise, Boise's Eighth Street Marketplace, Hyde Park and Boise Factory Outlets. From there, we proceed to the city of Nampa and a self-guided farm-to-market agricultural tour. We finish off the chapter with a look at the area's specialty shops by category.

You'll find shops for children in the Kidstuff chapter and galleries in The Arts chapter.

Malls and Districts
Boise

Boise Towne Square
350 N. Milwaukee St., Franklin Rd. exit from I-84 • (208) 378-4400

The mall was opened in 1988 with The Bon Marche, Mervyn's California Department Stores, JCPenney and Sears as anchors and 180 other permanent stores. Although it is Boise's only mall, it's a good one, on par with the better malls in a large city. Parking is sufficient, stretching completely around the attached buildings so that it is often possible to park close to stores that a shopper is visiting. This is a smart, enclosed, well-organized, spacious but not cavernous, double-decker mall, with attractive benches for the tired or observant shopper scattered throughout, fountains and plants and a variety of restaurants, saloons, ice cream and cookie shops. It is well-lit, clean and well-maintained; there are no dark or unused shop fronts or building wings that need repair. Wheelchairs and baby carriages are available for rent. Occasional entertainment is provided by school musical groups and other organizations.

Popular stores include Eddie Bauer, The Limited, KB Toys, Bath and Body Works, B Dalton Bookseller, Victoria's Secret and Waldenbooks. Other shops sell Western apparel, furs, cards, gifts, home and kitchen wares, jewelry and sporting goods. Stalls and carts sell specialty merchandise.

The first expansion of the mall since it was built is underway. It includes another anchor —

a three-story Dillard's — and a 90,000-square-foot corridor that will house 20 more stores. Sears and The Bon are also expanding.

Surrounding the mall are stores Pier One Imports and Men's Warehouse and restaurants Café Olé and the Olive Garden. There's also the Towne Square movie complex. Retail stores located across Milwaukee Street include Toys 'R' Us, Gap and Future Shop. A short distance north of that is a 120,000-square-foot strip mall that features Ultimate Electronics, Borders Books and Music, Cost Plus, Zurchers Party and Wedding Outlet and other stores. Farther north on Milwaukee Street are Gart Sports and Barnes & Noble Booksellers.

Just west of Boise Towne Square, on Franklin Avenue, are large discount houses, such as Home Depot, Office Max, Petsmart and Costco.

Downtown Boise
Between State St. to the north, Myrtle St. on the south, 13th St. to the west and 5th St. on the east

An old comfortable pair of resoled and polished leather shoes that walk at a moderate pace beneath a modern and sometimes perplexing suit of new clothes — that is the architecture and rhythm of downtown Boise, which in one glimpse presents the venerable Capitol dome and classic old Egyptian Theater and, in another, the spiraling white rise of a newly constructed condo tower and heavy diagonal stone block of the West Coast Boise Hotel.

Most of all, downtown Boise is a friendly, pleasant, walking-and-talking place of shade trees, old brick, modern space and heights, outdoor tables, imaginative storefronts and gleaming business facades that is compact but large enough, in its surprising variety, for an afternoon of exploration or several days of browsing.

It is what downtowns used to be and are trying to be again: a true, lasting, personable focal point; a sense of identity unlike anywhere else, where you spend money for special occasions, knock about on weekends and proudly show off to visitors.

If shopping is an experience and atmosphere as well as a buy, then you'll want to visit the downtown blocks east and west of Capitol Boulevard, about a 59-square-block area of businesses, shops, restaurants, galleries and cafes that lie south of the Capitol building. A free map and directory of downtown Boise is available from the Downtown Boise Association, 300 N. 6th Street, (208) 336-2631.

The appeal of this area is a recent phenomenon. In 1990, 45 restaurants stood in the downtown core, and now there are 89 restaurants and more than 200 specialty shops that have poured in. Unlike the mall, you won't find every size, color, material and style here. But you might find something original, different and even unique and enjoy the spirit and passion of the independent entrepreneurs.

Two of the best-known shops are **The Bon Marche Downtown** at the corner of 10th and Idaho streets, a department store; and **The Book Shop**, 906 Main Street, (see our later listing under Bookstores in this chapter).

First Thursday
On the First Thursday of every month downtown shops stay open until 9 PM. Free trolley rides, free parking in public garages, special promotions, entertainment, food and drink and demonstrations are also offered. On a recent First Thursday, activities and treats, which were spread throughout the area, included a gallery stroll, book signings, prairie berry and saddlebag snacks, belly dancing, a one-act play, champagne and hors d'oeuvres, jazz, art presentations, Celtic band music, potato ice cream, a musical benefit for salmon and steelhead recovery, wines and a fashion show. For a current First Thursday pamphlet with a schedule of events and other information, contact the Downtown Boise Association, 300 N. 6th Street, (208) 336-2631.

Eighth Street Marketplace
Between Front St. on the north, Myrtle St. to the south, 9th St. on the west and Capitol Blvd. on the east

South of the Boise Centre on the Grove, the city's convention center, at 8th and Front

Albertsons®

FOOD & DRUG

- **909 East ParkCenter Blvd. — Boise**
- **1650 West State Street — Boise**
- **1219 Broadway Ave. — Boise**
- **10500 Overland Road — Boise**
- **10700 Ustick Road — Boise**
- **1520 North Cole Road — Boise**
- **7100 West State Street — Boise**
- **2625 Overland Road — Boise**
- **5100 Overland Road — Boise**

- **20 East Fairview — Meridian**
- **3301 West Cherry Lane — Meridian**

- **250 South Eagle Road — Eagle**

- **715 12th Ave. South — Nampa**
- **2400 12th Ave. Road — Nampa**

- **415 Cleveland Blvd. — Caldwell**
- **2500 Blaine Street — Caldwell**

streets and only a short distance from Main Street, is the renovated, turn-of-the-century warehouse district that is similar to The Cannery in San Francisco. It houses two dozen retail shops, restaurants and a movie theater. The Marketplace is a curious and relaxing place to visit, shop and dine — a solid, tasteful, architectural trip back into another era, with some quirky surprises such as The Funnybone Club, Boise's premier comedy club; nationally known leather-jacket entrepreneur Robert Comstock; and the one-of-a-kind World Sports Humanitarian Hall of Fame.

Frederick Shute has created sterling silver statuary at Mythological Images since 1982 (see listing later in this chapter). Milford's Fish House and Cafe Olé are among the restaurant options (see our Restaurants chapter). The Cineplex Odeon movie theater is on the main floor of the large brick building.

Hyde Park
Thirteenth St. north of Fort St. and south of Camelback Park

Hyde Park is a little oasis of times gone by. It's a mix of stores and houses going back a half-century on 13th Street, just north of downtown in Boise's North End. A half-dozen restaurants, five antique shops (including **American Nostalgia Antiques**, 1517 N. 13th Street; **Blue Moon Antiques**, 1611 N. 13th Street; **Collection Connection**, 1612 N. 13th Street; and **Forget Me Not Antiques**, 1603 N. 13th Street; all profiled later in this chapter) and six specialty shops stand beneath oak, maple and locust trees and near spacious Camelback Park. It's a place for patio dining and exploring shops behind flower gardens and in old storefronts. Street lamps cast an orange glow over the area.

Boise Factory Outlets
Southeast Boise at Gowen Rd., Exit 57 off I-84 • (208) 331-5000

This factory outlet mall has 39 stores, but not all the stores are "discount houses." Fashions, accessories, fragrances, dinnerware, housewares, luggage, shoes, books, party supplies and gifts are available. The names include Geoffrey Beene, Levi's, Van Heusen, Bass, Corning Revere and the Rocky Mountain Chocolate Factory.

Nampa

The Karcher Mall Shopping Center
Caldwell and Midland Blvds.
• (208) 467-7580

Until a decade ago this was *the* place to shop in the Treasure Valley. Although now overshadowed by the larger, more glittering Towne Square Mall in west Boise, it is the major Nampa, Caldwell and Canyon County shopping destination. More than 50 stores offer food, restaurants, jewelry and clothing. Anchor stores are The Bon Marche, the Emporium and the Hub. Other shops include Radio Shack, Nampa Furniture, Call Jewelers and Nampa Reel Cinema.

Downtown Nampa Historic District
11th and 14th Aves., 4th and Front Sts.

Hardwood trees, inlaid brick walkways and old architecture provide ambiance for restaurants, cafes, saloons, antique shops and enduring establishments such as Nafiziger's Men's Store, which opened its doors in 1946, at 1309 lst Street S. Two of the best used bookstores in the Treasure Valley, **The Yesteryear Shoppe** and **Twice Sold Tales**, are located here (see Bookstores later in this chap-

---

INSIDERS' TIP

Parking in downtown Boise is not difficult unless you insist on parking directly in front of the place you are visiting. The city has 18,000 public and private parking spaces. Seven garages and lots offer free parking with validated stamps available from participating downtown merchants; six offer conference parking for events at Boise Centre on the Grove, the city's convention hall. Metered parking is free on evenings and weekends. Old Boise has its own free parking lot, just south of Main Street on 6th Street.

ter). **Gifts International**, 1211-A lst Street, offers gifts from around the world, such as handcarved soapstone boxes, Guatemalan jackets and Peruvian pottery. **The Old Towne Antique Mall and Coffee House** is located in the First Street Marketplace, 1224 lst Street S., in three remodeled buildings that were busy 1920s grocery, bakery and Western Union enterprises.

Farm to Market Agricultural Tour

The Nampa Chamber of Commerce publishes an attractive free brochure for people who want to take a self-guided summer tour of Canyon County crops, fruit and produce stands and wineries. For information, call (208) 466-4641.

Although one of Idaho's smallest counties, Canyon County ranks among the top in producing sweet corn seed, sugar beets, hops, mint, onions, cattle and calves. Canyon County provides nearly 10 percent of the state's gross receipts for agricultural products, which in 1996 amounted to $278 million.

The climate, fertile soils and ample irrigation water all contribute to this excellent productivity. These factors as well as relative isolation facilitate the production of seed crops that cannot be produced elsewhere without problems such as disease.

A dry, high-desert climate, volcanic ash, cool nights and ungrafted vines contribute to the production of grapes with concentrated fruit flavors and high acidity. There are five wineries in the area. The two best-known wineries, which do not require appointments for visits, are presented here.

The tour includes the following locations, with a brochure map showing how to get there; other maps, of course, will take a person to one or more of these places.

The Berry Ranch
7998 Idaho Hwy. 20/26 at Franklin Rd.
• (208) 466-3860

A wide range of fruits and vegetables are grown and sold here. Visitors can pick strawberries, raspberries and pumpkins on a pickers hayride, or ranch personnel will pick them upon request. Also available are asparagus, sweet corn, tomatoes, melons, potatoes and winter squash. Picnic tables welcome you to

enjoy your purchase on the spot. Check out the antique machinery and the petting shed. U-Pick is available by appointment.

Karcher Ranch Market
2302 W. Karcher Rd. • (208) 467-2302

This market offers a wide variety of products including fruit, produce, dried fruit, nuts, health food, spices, gifts and fruit juice.

Pintler Cellar
13750 Surrey Ln. • (208) 467-1200

A 13-acre vineyard surrounds a handsomely-landscaped winery, making this an ideal place to savor Pintler's premium Idaho wines. Pintler Cellar hosts annual festivals, such as Mother's Day Wine and Food Festival, which draws thousands of wine enthusiasts for two days of music, wine and gourmet foods. The vineyard is open year-round to the public on Saturdays and Sundays from noon to 5 PM. Other tour times can be arranged by appointment. The free tours last about a half-hour. The vineyard produces Cabernet, Riesling, Chardonnay and Pinot Noir wines, among others.

Caldwell

Saxton Fruit Stand
16475 Lakeshore Dr. • (208) 459-7237

This roadside store offers cherries, apricots, peaches, plums, nectarines, prunes, pears and apples.

Ste. Chapelle Winery
19348 Lowell Rd. • (208) 459-7222

Ste. Chapelle overlooks the Snake River as it winds its way north through orchards and vineyards of the Sunny Slope area. From a small but successful beginning in 1978, Ste. Chapelle has grown to produce 100,000 cases of varietal wines each year. The winery is open 10 AM to 5 PM Monday through Saturday and noon to 5 PM Sunday, year-round. Free tours that begin on the hour and last 15 minutes as well as free winetastings are offered. The winery's best-known wine is a sweet Riesling. It also produces Chenin Blanc, Chardonnay, Cabernet, Merlot, Pinot Noir and other wines. "Jazz at the Winery," which features top performers such as pianist Gene Harris, is held

Downtown Boise has ample parking for shoppers and diners.

Photo: Idaho Power

Sundays in June and July, with a gate fee of $5 per person charged.

Symms Fruit Ranch
Idaho Hwy. 55 at Lowell Rd.
• (208) 459-2832

Symms Fruit Ranch specializes in asparagus, cherries, raspberries, apricots, peaches, nectarines, prunes, plums and apples.

Specialty Shops
Apparel
Boise

Central Park
601 Main St. • (208) 384-1167

Central Park offers women's contemporary clothing in natural fibers plus an outstanding collection of shoes, jewelry and accessories.

Daze Between
475 Main St. • (208) 331-3333

Tie-dyes, dresses, hats and T-shirts are featured here. You'll also find rock memorabilia that ranges from posters to tapestries and includes Grateful Dead merchandise. Knickknacks, jewelry and Phish Dry Goods are also available.

The Dragonfly
411 Main St. • (208) 338-9234

The Dragonfly has jewelry, gifts and a wide range of women's casual and more formal clothing.

Riebe's Hyde Park Shoe Shop
1413 N. 13th St. • (208) 342-2451

Riebe's not only repairs shoes, but also fits and makes custom work boots for loggers, packers and firefighters.

Swim and Run Shop

514 N. 16th St. • (208) 385-0105
8620 W. Fairview Ave. • (208) 321-0105

For active people, these two locations offer swimsuits, athletic wear, running apparel and shoes.

Treasure Valley Pendleton

Boise Towne Square, 350 N. Milwaukee St. • (208) 378-1244

offers quality woolen products manufactured by a company located just beyond the Blue Mountains in Pendleton, Oregon, about four hours away from Boise. Idaho's largest selection of Indian blankets is available here, as well as a full assortment of men's and women's apparel.

Antiques

Boise

American Nostalgia Antiques

1517 N. 13th St. • (208) 345-8027

American Nostalgia Antiques specializes in Depression-era glass. The shop is in an old storefront in Hyde Park.

Blue Moon Antiques

1611 N. 13th St. • (208) 336-5954

This shop, in a cottage behind a beautiful flower garden, offers Victoriana, jewelry, linen and kitchen items. Blue Moon buys as well as sells.

Boise Antique & Unique

Boise Towne Square, 350 N. Milwaukee St. • (208) 377-3921

Antiques from the eastern United States roll into this store by the truckload. It has authentic Indian jewelry, estate jewelry, rugs, antique glass, China, brass, copper and gift items.

Collection Connection

1612 N. 13th St. • (208) 343-6221

Pens, inkwells, glass, China, radios, lighters, toys and art deco comprise the stock at Collection Connection.

Forget Me Not Antiques

1603 N. 13th St. • (208) 344-0678

The unforgettable collection here includes country antiques, primitives, furniture, China and decor items.

Hobby Horse Antiques

231 Warm Springs Ave. • (208) 343-6005

This shop offers a variety of antiques and collectibles as well as furniture, glassware, clothing, silver, china and jewelry.

J. Elliott's

1006 Main St. • (208) 344-9775

J. Elliott's has 20th-century artifacts, antiques with a retro look that goes back to the 1930s through the 1960s. You'll find furniture, lamps, dishes and statues here.

Nifty 90s Antique Shop

2422 W. Main St. • (208) 344-3931

This shop buys and sells estates. It specializes in furniture, architectural and decorator items, jewelry, light fixtures and glassware.

Shabahang Persian Carpets

801 W. Bannock St. • (208) 336-0550

This store has a large selection of antique, contemporary, traditional, city and tribal carpets and kilims. Shabahang has for centuries taken pride in its knowledge of Persian carpets and Oriental rugs. Rugs are bought, sold and cleaned here.

INSIDERS' TIP

Combine a museum visit with books going back in time by visiting Nampa's historical district. Two of the Treasure Valley's best used bookstores, Twice Sold Tales and The Yesteryear Shoppe, are near each other on 1st Street. Just around the corner is the Oregon Short Line Depot, built in 1902, which is full of pictures, objects, exhibits, furniture, machinery and other items that go back to the settlement of the Treasure Valley.

Nampa

Old Towne Antique Mall
1212 1st St. S. • (208) 463-4555

Old Towne buys and sells furniture, glassware, sports equipment, clothes, jewelry and dolls.

The Village Square Antique Mall
1309 2nd St. S. • (208) 467-2842

The Village Square works with more than 50 dealers and has two floors filled with furniture, glassware, jewelry, collectibles and primitives.

Bookstores

Not so long ago, when you wanted a book in Boise, you headed downtown to the comfort and knowledge of The Book Shop, which ruled the shelf trade for an entire century. With the construction of Boise Towne Square in 1988 and the prosperity and growth of the '90s, the national chains began flooding the area: B Dalton Bookseller and Waldenbooks took root at the mall, Hastings Books Music & Video sprouted three locations, and most recently, brawny giants Barnes & Noble Booksellers and Borders Books and Music set up shop next-door to one another, tweaking each other's nose on Milwaukee Street just north of the mall. Discount heavyweights such as Costco skim the cream off the top with cut-rate bestsellers, while Dan Wilson, owner of The Book Shop, where it all started, proclaims with the anxiety of a man staring down a fleet of missile-laden warships, "We make bestsellers!" Yes, it's a lively scene as well as testimony to the written word that everything between hard and soft covers is up-to-date in River City.

Boise

Barnes & Noble Booksellers
1301 N. Milwaukee St. • (208) 375-4454

Barnes & Noble offers 150,000 titles in 35,000-square-feet of space and has about 50 employees. Its 7-foot-high book shelves create the intimate effect of a small, cozy place. There's a large selection of music and software, a separate children's area and a cafe.

The shop's monthly events and activities, which include lectures, discussions, author signings and storytelling for children, are listed in a store pamphlet.

The Blue Unicorn
1809 W. State St. • (208) 345-9390

The Blue Unicorn is a "holistic resource center" that offers books, gifts and music for the body, mind and spirit. It has an indoor water garden and, in addition to written materials, sells drums, jewelry, crystals, journals, incense and tarot.

Boise Books & Search
4210 Emerald St. • (208) 345-8670

This shop carries 35,000 to 40,000 used, rare and out-of-print books. It specializes in Western Americana and Northwest history and exploration. Chuck and Beryl Mary, who opened the shop in 1986, have extensive fly-fishing, photography and military selections. They search for titles in all areas of interest.

The Book Rack
10440 Fairview Ave. • (208) 322-9059

The Book Rack has thousands of low-priced, used paperback books, some new paperbacks and trades books.

The Book Shop
906 Main St. • (208) 342-2659

Portland has Powell's, Seattle has Elliott Bay Books and San Francisco has City Lights. Boise comes closest to those with The Book Shop, established more than a century ago by James Pinney. Jean Wilson started working at the store 30 years ago when her husband died, leaving her with five children. In 1979 she bought the store and, as a top independent knowledgeable about the industry and writing craft, became an advisor and influence for local writers, editors and publishers who wanted to get ahead. Recently Jean Wilson stepped aside and her son, Dan Wilson, who grew up in the shop, took over.

The Book Shop's employees have 150 years of combined bookselling experience, and they read like crazy. They get to know their customers' tastes on an individual basis and are always on the lookout for something their regulars might enjoy. The shop is particularly strong on Western Americana, books on Idaho, maps and travel guides, and it has a good selection of children's books. Through a side door is a deli and cafe that encourages lingering at the expense of less important matters.

Books Aloud
222 N. 9th St. • (208) 331-2229
Cole and Ustick Sts. • (208) 378-9691
Boise resident Linda Bianchi started Books Aloud five years ago and now has these two locations. The company has 3,000 book titles on tape for sale and rent that cover a broad spectrum of subject matter — contemporary bestsellers, classics, self-help, sci-fi and many others. Most of the tapes are on disk, although the stores do have some CDs. Travelers and people who like to listen to books while exercising, painting or gardening are loyal customers.

Borders Books & Music
1123 N. Milwaukee St. • (208) 322-6668
Borders has 110,000 book titles as well as a wide selection of music and software in 30,000 square feet of space that is staffed by 30 to 40 employees. The store's low bookshelves permit customers to see across the room, creating an open, casual atmosphere. Relax in the cafe, or turn your kids on to the joy of reading in the children's center. The shop's monthly events, which are listed on a flyer, include storytelling for children and a character that comes in to entertain, a quintet and other musical groups and four different reading groups.

Cornerstone Bookstore
1217 Broadway Ave., #101 (at Albertsons supermarket's Broadway Center) • (208) 336-1803
Cornerstone Bookstore offers Christian books, bibles and music. It's closed on Sunday.

Hastings Books Music & Video
7500 Fairview Ave. • (208) 375-3151
680 E. Boise Ave. • (208) 345-9750
10539 Overland Rd. • (208) 322-0314
Hastings bills itself as an "entertainment center" that has candy and refreshments and does a big rental-movie business. It also has hardcover, soft-cover and discount books on a wide variety of subjects.

The Paper Back Place
7011 Fairview Ave. • (208) 376-8100
This store buys, sells and trades used paperback books and new and used comics.

Parnassus Books
218 N. 9th St. • (208) 344-7560
Fifteen years ago Judith and Lorin Gaarder opened Parnassus Books, which now performs thousands of searches for out-of-print books each year. Parnassus Books has general stock and scarce and rare books on-site. It uses two electronic databases and advertisements in trade publications to track books for customers.

Reilly's
1021 Main St. • (208) 342-6100
Reilly's has many bible translations, children's books and religious gifts, retail and wholesale. It's closed on Sunday.

The Wild Hare Bookshop
Cole Village Shopping Center, 3397 N. Cole Rd. • (208) 377-5070
The Wild Hare Bookshop is about 2,000 square feet in size and has a selection of used books that is particularly strong in the arts, photography, metaphysics, fine literature and crafts.

Nampa

Nampa Christian Book and Supply
517 12th Avenue Rd. • (208) 467-9400
This locally owned store has been selling Christian gifts, bibles and books since 1977. It's closed on Sunday.

Twice Sold Tales
1215 1st St. • (208) 467-3329
This shop has a large inventory of used books that includes an entire room of children's books. It also has old games, magazines and mysteries.

The Yesteryear Shoppe
1211 1st St. S. • (208) 467-3581
This shop specializes in rare and out-of-print Western Americana, sci-fi and Idaho books. It carries 150,000 titles on 8-foot-high shelves, 25,000 old music albums that include

jazz, blues and rock 'n' roll, 10,000 comic books, autographs and rare postcards. Most of the books are in exceptional condition with their original dust jackets. Leather-bound classics start at $20. Numerous books are in limited editions, and many are autographed by their authors. Dave Gonzalez, the owner, and his son, Stephen Gonzalez, run the store and are members of the Antiquarian Booksellers Association.

Gifts and Novelty Items

Boise

The Guardian Angel
231 Warm Springs Ave. • (208) 343-6005
A specialty, year-round Christmas shop, The Guardian Angel features many one-of-a-kind ornaments and knickknacks.

Made in Idaho
Boise Towne Square, 350 N. Milwaukee St. • (208) 378-1188
This store carries products that are made, grown, manufactured or handcrafted in Idaho as well as U.S. products that enhance its Idaho product line. You'll find furniture, clothing, food and wine here.

Stewart's Gem Shop
2618 W. Idaho St. • (208) 342-1151
Stewart's opened in 1945. The star garnet, Idaho's official gemstone, is the shop specialty. It offers local gems, opals, jewelry, bookends, clocks and gifts. Also, it has polished rock, a rock yard and information and equipment for rock hounds.

Swiss Village Cheese Factory
4912 E. Garrity Blvd. (Exit 38 off I-84), Nampa • (208) 463-6620
For four generations Swiss Village Cheese Factory has produced cheeses of Old World quality from company-owned dairy cattle that graze in the Snake River Valley to the south.

Visitors watch cheesemakers cut and pack by hand Cheddar, Monterey Jack, Colby and other cheeses. Samples are available. The factory also has a country-style cafe, ice cream bar and gift shop that offers wine, Idaho and dairy souvenirs and gift packs. At its factory outlet store, a variety of products from company parent J.R. Simplot are offered at low, factory-outlet prices: locally grown produce, fresh and frozen potato and vegetable products, meats, snack foods, wine, ice cream and a Swiss Village specialty — Squeaky Cheese Curds.

Taters
249 S. 8th St. • (208) 338-1062
On The Grove plaza in the convention center building, Taters has Idaho and Boise souvenirs, including potato products, gift packs and T-shirts.

Zeppole Baking Co.
888 W. Fort St. • (208) 338-1381
Zeppole's makes excellent bread that is available at this address and at numerous other grocery and market locations in the Treasure Valley. Eleven kinds of bread are baked daily, including Ciabretta, a white chewy bread with rosemary, olive oil and sea salt on top, as well as sourdough, whole wheat and pumpernickel rye.

Jewelry

Boise

Frederick Shute Fine Diamonds & Jewelry
404 S. 8th St., Ste. 240 • (208) 385-0652
This store offers the custom-designed jewelry of Frederick Shute by appointment. Shute has 17 years of experience in precious stones and is Boise's Antwerp connection for fine diamonds that are sold at or below New York wholesale prices. He also specializes in rubies, emeralds and sapphires.

INSIDERS' TIP

Got a restless kid or a youngster who is glued to the TV set? You might try a book on tape to set the little devil's mind on fire.

Hal Davis Jewelers
130 N. 8th St. • (208) 343-6151

Hal Davis Jewelers offers Mikomoto Pearls; precious, colored gemstones; diamonds; Rolex, Tudor, Baume & Mercier and Raymond Weil watches; Lladro figurines; Waterford Crystal; and Mont Blanc pens.

Hi-Ho Silver
Boise Towne Square, 350 N. Milwaukee St. • (208) 378-1822

This store has sterling silver, 14-karat gold and gold fill, gem stones, authentic Navy American jewelry boxes and cleaners/polishes.

Perpetual Metals
807 W. Idaho St. • (208) 343-4055

Perpetual Metals features a custom jewelry/mineral gallery. It carries jewelry made by local and international designers and has mineral specimens from around the world.

R. Grey Company, Jewelry Gallery
818 W. Idaho St. • (208) 385-9337

R. Grey offers limited-edition designs, handcrafted jewelry, full-service jewelry repair and bead stringings and has a fine selection of gemstones and diamonds. The store is known for its creations taken from the imaginations of its customers.

Sporting Goods Stores

General

Great recreational opportunities in the city, valley and state, a rising population and more visitors are responsible for an infusion of sporting goods stores in the area. Boise now has more than 50 sporting goods retail shops, quite a few with several outlets, which means you find one every direction you look and stumble over others if you're not careful. Big, successful companies that boomed elsewhere, such as Gart Sports from Denver and Recreational Equipment Incorporated (REI) from Seattle, have come in with a flourish. They are making the entrenched locally owned businesses with longtime clientele expand into new territory as they become sharper and stronger in a ferocious

battle for survival. Here are a few of the better-known shops.

Boise

Benchmark
625 Vista Ave. • (208) 338-1700

Benchmark is a 15,000-square-foot shop with 12 full-time people that has a broad product mix in five areas: backpacking, hiking, rock climbing, fly-fishing and adventure sports. Emil Hutton has owned the shop for more than a decade, after 14 years in the business in Tucson and Prescott, Arizona. His staff is constantly going to schools for training to keep up with the latest information in their fields of expertise. Benchmark offers presentations by distinguished and sometimes internationally known sports people about sports travel experiences.

Bob Greenwood Ski Haus
2400 Bogus Basin Rd. • (208) 342-6808
1764 W. State St. • (208) 343-0282

The Ski Haus was started in 1957 by Bob Greenwood at the base of the 16-mile climb to Bogus Basin Ski Area. Greenwood, now in his 70s, skis 50 or 60 days each winter, leaving the shop in the hands of his son, John, Bill Tregoning and Carrie Gochnour. It's a shop created solely in the spirit of Alpine skiing and the only one that devotes itself entirely to skiing in the Treasure Valley. You'll find well-made and stylish outdoor winter clothes here, and its ski rental shop does big business. The State Street location sells apparel only.

Gart Sports
1301 N. Milwaukee St. • (208) 378-9590
670 Boise Ave. • (208) 344-2037
1031 Caldwell Blvd., Nampa • (208) 467-5711

These full-service sports stores have a wide range of products for individual and team sports, including tennis, golf, basketball, football and skiing.

Koppels Browzeville
3020 Fairview Ave. • (208) 344-3539

Koppels is a plain, simple, friendly store with endless shelves of every kind of sports and camping equipment at relatively low prices. Among the stock, you may find a surplus shipment of usable items you haven't seen for years or a bargain tent from China.

Idaho Mountain Touring
1310 W. Main St. • (208) 336-3854
5901 Fairview Ave. • (208) 377-0603

Idaho Mountain Touring has been in Boise since 1984. It specializes in summer outdoor equipment, especially in the areas of bicycling, climbing, backpacking and cross-country skiing. It carries high-quality products such as Trek bicycles and Dana-designed backpacks as well as cycling parts and accessories. It supports and helps maintain trails and other nonprofit activities that benefit all cyclists. Bicycle rentals cost $15 for 3½ hours and $25 for eight hours.

Idaho River Sports
1521 N. 13th St. • (208) 336-4844

All floating needs are fulfilled at Idaho River Sports, which sells and rents kayaks, canoes and rafts. A kayak package, which includes the kayak, paddles, life vest, helmet and spray skirt costs $30 a day. A canoe package, which includes helmet, life vest and paddle, costs $30 a day. An oar raft package, which includes equipment to lower the raft onto a river, costs $55 to $70 a day. Boise State University whitewater classes typically boats from here.

Intermountain Outdoor Sports
1375 E. Fairview Ave., Meridian
• (208) 888-4911
Vista Village, 900 Vista Ave.
• (208) 345-3474

Intermountain Outdoor Sports, the largest outdoor adventure store in Idaho, opened its original site in Meridian in 1993. That store is housed in a 60,000-square-foot retail, office and warehouse building on 6 acres of land. Both stores have bicycles, clothing and footwear as well as fishing, hunting, camping and outdoor gear. Owner Gary Sweet's mother and father arrived from Pennsylvania in 1976 and opened a hunting and shooting store that Sweet expanded with recreational products and accessories. There's a fly-fishing shop inside the large Meridian location.

McU Sports
2314 Bogus Basin Rd. • (208) 336-2300
822 W. Jefferson St. • (208) 342-7734

McU Sports has been in Boise since 1972. Its Jefferson Street location downtown sells a lot of casual clothing, in-line skates and athletic shoes and has a diversified line of camping, skiing and backpacking equipment. Its Bogus Basin Road location, next to Bob Greenwood's at the base of the 16-mile climb to the ski area, specializes in ski equipment and clothing and has mountain bike and ski rentals.

Newt & Harold's
1033 Broadway Ave. • (208) 385-9300

This store specializes in in-line skates and snowboard rentals. In-line skate rentals cost $5 an hour, $12 for three hours and $15 for the day. Snowboards rent for $20 a day. Newt & Harold's also has footwear, clothing and skateboards.

Play It Again Sports
1467 N. Milwaukee St. • (208) 378-0053

Play It Again Sports has "sports equipment that's used, but not used up." It buys, sells, trades and consigns used and new equipment. Areas include golf, exercise, hockey, football, watersports, in-line skating, baseball, softball, weights, skiing and yard games.

Recreational Equipment Inc. (REI)
8300 W. Emerald St. • (208) 322-1141

REI is the largest consumer co-op in the country. Its members own a share of the company and get 10 percent back on the price of a purchase. Nonmembers are also welcome to shop in this 25,000-square-foot store that is particularly strong in the areas of camping, climbing, skiing, cycling and paddling. Customers range from novices to experts.

Wheels R Fun
Boise River Greenbelt, 13th St. and
Shoreline Dr. • (208) 343-8228

This Greenbelt sports rental kiosk is open from Memorial Day through Labor Day and on weekends in April, May, September and October. A four-person raft rents for $24 for four hours. An eight-person raft rents for $36 for four hours. In-line skates rent for $5 for one hour, $12 for four hours and $18 for eight

Photo: William H. Mullins

Examples of turn-of-the-century style and late 20th-century architecture stand side by side in downtown Boise.

hours. Roller skates rent for $3 for one hour, $6 for four hours and $8 for eight hours. Bicycles are $5 for one hour, $12 for four hours and $18 for eight hours.

Cycling Shops

Bikes in Boise, with the Boise Front rising to the north, are most likely to be mountain bikes, even if pedaled by timid flatlanders who imag- ine themselves on the steeps. But the area does attract many high, hard pedalers, racers and dust eaters, and a common sight is a baby drawn behind a physically fit mom and/or dad, who would no sooner miss a vigorous workout than wolf lard and grease. The following stores cater specifically to cyclists, but biking enthusiasts can also find apparel, parts and equipment and rentals at some of the general sporting good stores we listed previously.

Boise

Bob's Bicycles
6112 Fairview Ave. • (208) 322-8042

Bob's has been here two decades and has more than 500 bicycles in stock. It specializes in suspensions and has a huge selection of bicycle accessories. It has mountain bikes, family bikes and racing/touring bikes. Bob's is also a BMX speed shop. Brands include GT Bicycles, Born in the USA and Powerlite, among others. The shop also services and repairs bikes.

George's Cycles and Fitness
1109 Broadway Ave. • (208) 343-3782
5809 Fairview Ave. • (208) 376-4526
1738 W. State St. • (208) 343-5617
5515 W. State St. • (208) 853-1964

George's sells road, mountain, BMX and kids bicycles. It has a large selection of parts, accessories, car rack systems and trailers. It also sells treadmills, home gyms and free weights. The shop offers one-day repair service for most small bike repairs.

Idaho Mountain Touring
1310 Main St. • (208) 336-3854
5901 Fairview Ave. • (208) 377-0603

This shop offers mountain, racing, touring and children's bikes. It has a large selection of accessories that include Nike shoes and clothing, Oakley sunglasses, Patagonia clothing and Burley and Blue Ski child trailers. The store has a special women's cycling section. It offers service and repair on all brands.

Idaho Tandem Cyclery
5809 Fairview Ave. • (208) 375-1107

Idaho Tandem Cyclery specializes in tandem, touring and recumbent bikes. It also offers custom frames.

Ken's Bicycle Warehouse
10470 W. Overland Rd. • (208) 376-9240

This shop has existed since 1980. It offers mountain, recreational and BMX bicycles manufactured by GT, Specialized and Raleigh USA. It also offers many accessories, including tubes, tires, sealants, pumps, helmets, bags, shorts, shoes, trailers and car racks.

Moo Cycles
1517½ N. 13th St. • (208) 336-5229

If you want a custom bike designed, Moo Cycles will connect you with custom builders throughout the United States, order frames and parts, and put it together for you. Prices have ranged from $1,200 to $4,000. Brands include Rocky Mountain, Serotta, Jamis, Breezer, Dean and Ibis.

Schwinn Cycling and Fitness
1015 Vista Ave. • (208) 336-2453

This is a family-oriented Schwinn store with more than 300 bikes in stock. It has new and used bicycles, takes trade-ins and repairs most models. It offers mountain bikes, exercise bikes, unicycles, BMX racing bikes and tandem bikes. The shop also sells baseball equipment, such as gloves, balls and bats.

Spoke N Wheel
6815 Fairview Ave. • (208) 377-2091

This shop opened in Boise in 1979. It offers mountain, BMX and freestyle bikes. It repairs bikes and takes trade-ins. The accessories it offers include helmets, car racks, tires and tubes.

World Cycle
180 N. 8th St. • (208) 343-9130

World Cycle has a wide selection of mountain, hybrid, tandem, recumbent and three-wheel bikes. Its accessories include Sidi and Shimano Shoes, Sugoi clothing, Terry Women's Clothing, Pearl Izumi, Bell helmets and Thule bike racks. It offers complete bicycle service from mechanics with eight or more years of experience.

Fly-Fishing Shops

If you read the Norman Maclean book or saw the Brad Pitt movie *A River Runs Through It*, you know the poetry of fly-fishing. If you've never looped an artificial lure by whippy rod above a murmuring stream, ask most anyone in Idaho, and they'll show you how. Okay, an exaggeration, but Boise does have four fly-fishing shops — not fishing, but *totally fly-fishing*, forget-everything-else shops — which tells you something about the local mentality and the countryside. They can all outfit you, but each has its special hook.

Boise

Bear Creek Outfitters
5521 W. State St. • (208) 853-8704

Bear Creek Outfitters, which specializes in Loomis equipment, is the only fly-fishing shop on the west side of town. Owner Rich Wallis and manager Tim Manfell spend plenty of time in the boondocks, so they can provide their customers with the latest fly-fishing intelligence. They provide fly-tying, fly-fishing and rod-building instruction at their 1,500-square-foot store that they have operated for seven years.

The Idaho Angler
1033 Bannock St. • (208) 389-9957

At 3,500 square feet, The Idaho Angler is the largest fly-fishing shop in the state, with the largest store inventory. It specializes in travel fly-fishing. It will book a trip for a customer anywhere in the world and provide every possible need in the way of equipment and clothes. Like the other stores, it offers fly-fishing classes, and it also has a loosely-knit group of about 30 women who like to fly-fish together that is open to newcomers.

The Rocky Mountain Angler
832 S. Vista Ave. • (208) 336-3336

This is a full-service fly shop that takes pride in its broad variety of fly-fishing equipment and service. Owner Warren Busse has been in Boise for more than five years and in fly-fishing for more than 15. He specializes in repairs, and while he's working on your equipment, he'll give you a loaner to keep you on-stream.

The Stonefly Angler
622 S. Vista Ave. (inside the Benchmark) • (208) 459-1102

If you're lucky when you stop by The Stonefly Angler, you'll get to speak with Clayne Baker, a lifetime Idaho fly-fisherman who has lived on the streams and may know more about the sport in Idaho than anyone else. "He's our biggest asset," says Tim Burke, who runs this shop that has a 75-foot casting pool in back where customers can try out products. Baker is president of the largest fly-fishing club for kids in the country, The Woolly Buggers, some 150 or 160 strong, who meet at the store, learn fly-tying, go on fishing outings and clean up streams.

Golf Shops

Boise

Bartlett's Golf Service
1771 N. Wildwood Rd. • (208) 322-5827

Bartlett's makes custom clubs, repairs clubs and has a computerized swing analyzer. It offers a full line of retail clubs and bags, club fitting and re-gripping, and demo clubs. It is a member of the Pro Golf Club Association.

Divotz
11350 Franklin St. • (208) 323-1135

Divotz is a golf shop and driving range. It offers lessons and has a snack bar. The shop sells name brand and custom clubs, shoes, bags and clothing, such as Ram, Spalding, Titleist, Bag Boy, Taylor Made, Wilson, Hogan, Nicklaus and Nike, among many others.

Las Vegas Discount Golf & Tennis
5226 Overland Rd. • (208) 343-4140

This shop has major brands and custom clubs. It also has a wide selection of clothing and shoes. Its on-site repair center offers one-day re-gripping, re-shafting, fitting and repairs.

Nevada Bob's
8011 Fairview Ave. • (208) 377-4996

Nevada Bob's is part of a chain of 300 stores worldwide. It has top-brand clubs, clothing and shoes, takes trade-ins and provides free club fitting. It repairs clubs and golf carts.

Pro Golf Discount of Idaho
6912 W. State St. • (208) 853-1450

This shop has a broad selection of men's and women's name-brand golf clubs, equipment and apparel. Its brands include Ping, Hogan, Mae Gregor, Palm Springs, Wilson, Nike and Bag Boy, among many others. It offers custom fitting, re-grip service and a complete club repair service.

Attractions

For a region whose lure to visitors and new residents is predominantly natural, Boise has a surprisingly diverse number of other attractions. Some say, in fact, the city has more museums per capita than any other city in the United States. There are museums of art and culture, museums of science and industry, even museums of sports. And there are many more in adjacent towns. An abundance of additional historic and architectural attractions are easily accessible on walking or driving tours.

We have been as accurate as possible in citing hours of operation and admission prices. However, many out-of-town attractions are open only during the summer months and may change their hours from year to year. We suggest calling for current hours before making a long drive.

Boise is a great city for walking or biking around, as you'll see plenty of folks doing at almost any time of year. So, we begin this chapter with a series of walking tours to help familiarize you with the lay of the city and point out some of Boise's architectural and historical highlights.

Boise

Walking or Driving Tours

Tour of Downtown Boise

The most recognizable hub from which to begin a circuit of the central city is the Idaho State Capitol.

Idaho State Capitol
700 W. Jefferson St. • (208) 334-2470

Certainly the most handsome edifice in Boise is the neoclassical state Capitol building, which dominates the downtown area from the head of Capitol Boulevard. Patterned after

the U.S. Capitol, construction of the 185,000-square-foot building began in 1905 but was not completed until 1920. Atop the 208-foot rotunda dome, its wings outstretched, stands a 4-foot-tall eagle, made of solid copper and plated with bronze. Total construction cost of the Capitol building was $2.3 million; it is estimated that replacing it today would require more than $100 million.

Most of the superstructure is native sandstone in 10-ton blocks, transported to the site by convicts then incarcerated at the foot of the Table Rock quarry. The interior incorporates four different types of marble: red from Georgia, green from Vermont, grey from Alaska and black from Italy. Sixty-foot Corinthian-style pillars of scagliola veneer dominate the main floor.

Join a free tour of the Capitol building, and you'll view four floors of historical and fine-art exhibits, as well as the state legislative chambers. On the first floor, you'll see the rare official state gem, the star garnet (the only place it's found outside of Idaho is south Asia), among a display of minerals; and a welded statue of a miner that pays homage to those who died in a 1972 mining disaster in the state's northern Panhandle.

The governor's office is on the second floor, as you might have guessed upon seeing a wall of portraits of every state leader since territorial times. The governor's 26 official place settings of china and silver also are on display. But the second-floor highlight, undoubtedly, is a statue of George Washington on horseback, handcarved from yellow pine by an Austrian immigrant and presented to the Territory of Idaho in 1869.

The third floor belongs to the Senate and House, lodged in the west and east wings, respectively. Entrance to the public galleries is from the fourth floor when the legislature is in session, from early January into April. Also on the upper floor are a series of murals that use dreamlike symbols to pay tribute to Idaho's heritage.

Several statues on the statehouse grounds are of note. A Pioneer Monument has stood near 7th and Jefferson streets since 1906 to remember the original Oregon Trail emigrants. A Union Army Monument honors Civil War conscripts on the west side of the state-house. At the foot of the Capitol staircase is a replica of the Liberty Bell (sans crack) presented by the U.S. Treasury in 1950. Facing the Capitol steps from a small park triangle across Jefferson Street is a statue of Frank Steunenberg, a turn-of-the-century governor whose 1905 assassination in the wake of labor strife turned national attention to Boise (see our History chapter).

The Capitol is open to visitors from 8 AM to 5 PM Monday through Friday.

A governmental complex of about eight square blocks extends to the east and north of the Capitol building. Most of these are mundane office buildings, but if you wander east along State Street, which runs along the north side of the Capitol, you'll see several structures of note.

The Ada County Courthouse
514 W. Jefferson St. • (208) 364-2000

The Fourth District Court sits here in a 1930s-era art-deco building raised by Franklin Roosevelt's Works Progress Administration. Indiana limestone encases the courthouse. The interior features WPA murals of local history. A jail that once held prisoners is now empty and no longer used.

The Idaho Supreme Court
451 W. State St. • (208) 334-2246

The court was built of travertine from eastern Idaho. It has granite floors, an extensive law library on the first floor and basement and a courtroom and justices' offices on the second floor. The public may use the library and attend court sessions, which are held here and at other state locations on a varying schedule.

Alexander House
304 W. State St. • (208) 334-2119

Nearby is the blue, Queen Anne-style, Alexander House, which was built in 1897 for the first Jewish governor in the United States, Moses Alexander. It is now home to the Idaho Commission on the Arts.

From the front steps of the Capitol you can look straight down Capitol Boulevard, which runs in a southerly direction for 1.25 miles across the Boise River to the former Union Pacific depot. Follow the boulevard three blocks to Main Street. On your left is the modern Boise City Hall.

Boise City Hall
150 N. Capitol Blvd. • (208) 384-3710

The hall has a streetside plaza that boasts the flags of all 50 states and the District of Columbia. The mayor's office and city council are located here in a modern and pleasant building. Council meetings are open to the public.

Egyptian Theatre
700 W. Main St. • (208) 342-1441

The 1926 Egyptian Theatre was built at the height of the Egyptian-revival fad that followed the discovery of King Tutankhamen's tomb. The images of Osiris, Anubis and Horus and accompanying hieroglyphs continue inside, where the theater's original pipe organ — which once provided music and sound effects for silent films — still occasionally is used on special occasions. Today the theatre shows first-run movies daily.

The southeast corner of Capitol Boulevard and Main Street is home to the Perrault-Fritchman Building (profiled later in our Old Boise Walking Tour). The building is quite a contrast to West One Plaza, which it faces on the southwest corner.

West One Plaza
101 S. Capitol Blvd. • (208) 383-7000

At 19 stories, West One Plaza has been Idaho's tallest building since 1978. It houses financial, law and other offices within a sleek, modern facade that is typical for big cities but unusual for Boise. West One Plaza stands at the edge of The Grove.

The Grove
8th and Grove Sts.

Much of downtown Boise south of Main Street was leveled in the 1970s in a fit of urban revitalization. Although the regional shopping center once envisioned here was placed elsewhere, the renewal made room for this traffic-free refuge. There's an open-air fountain at its heart and a bronze statue of children playing marbles that draws smiles from young and old. If you're here on any Wednesday night from mid-May to mid-September, you can join thousands of Boiseans who gather at The Grove to listen to live music and nosh on food from area restaurants during Alive After Five.

Boise Centre on the Grove
850 Front St. • (208) 336-8900

Boise's main convention hall is located on the southwest corner of The Grove. The facility has a multipurpose hall that accommodates up to 2,000 guests for conferences and banquets, plus another 10,000 square feet of flexible meeting space. A Visitor Information Center, (208) 344-5338, within the hall (and with a separate entrance directly off The Grove at 8th and Grove streets) has maps and other information on the city and region.

The Grove Hotel
245 S. Capitol Blvd. • 887-3438

This is downtown's newest and most impressive edifice. It opened for business just before New Year's Day 1998. The $32 million, 17-story hotel has 250 luxurious guest rooms crowned by private penthouses (see our Accommodations chapter).

Its Bank of America Centre seats 5,000 people for professional tennis, ice skating, ice hockey, boxing and other events (see our Spectator Sports chapter). Emilio's restaurant inside its main entrance is a popular Boise eatery (see our Restaurants chapter.)

A broad crosswalk takes you from The Grove across Myrtle Street to the Eighth Street Marketplace.

Eighth Street Marketplace
405 S. 8th St. • (208) 344-0641

A set of refurbished circa-1900 warehouses has been fully transformed with decorative masonry, arched entrances, skylights and much more. Within these structures you'll find shops, restaurants, a cinema, a comedy club, a variety of offices and the temporary home of the World Sports Humanitarian Hall of Fame (see Museums in this chapter).

For more information about the Marketplace, see our Shopping chapter.

Backtrack through The Grove to Main Street and turn left (west) to put yourself in the heart of downtown Boise's shopping and financial district. No building attracts more attention in this part of the city than the six-story Hotel Idanha.

Hotel Idanha
928 W. Main St. • (208) 342-3611

Built in 1900 in a loosely translated French chateau style with corner turrets and a crenelated rooftop, the hotel opened on New Year's Day 1901 with Idaho's first elevator (it was, after all, the state's tallest building). During its early years the Idanha hosted the likes of Theodore Roosevelt, Will Rogers and Clarence Darrow. Saved from the wrecker's ball, it lacks the financial base for a badly needed refurbishment but still welcomes guests (see our Accommodations chapter). A leading restaurant, Peter Schott's (see Restaurants), and a transcendental meditation center are among its tenants.

One Capital Center
999 W. Main St. • (208) 336-2110

This is the international headquarters of the J.R. Simplot Co., the world's largest privately owned agribusiness. Jack Simplot developed the frozen french fry to supply American troops during World War II, then tapped the McDonald's market and later branched into phosphate mining and other pursuits. Perhaps more than any other individual, he's responsible for putting the "famous" in the "Famous Potatoes" slogan you'll see on Idaho vehicle license plates. He's also the wealthiest man in Idaho, and his company employs 19,000 workers worldwide.

Tour of the North End

A short stroll through the blocks immediately north of downtown Boise yields a sense of the city's social life in the late 19th and early 20th centuries. Many of the churches and other buildings dating from that era still entertain their original uses.

St. Michael's Episcopal Church
518 N. 8th St. · (208) 342-5601

The congregation was organized in the mid-1860s and was blessed with the Treasure Valley's first bell a few years later. This church was dedicated in 1902. Built of local sandstone cut from Table Rock, a mesa above the foothills in east Boise, in English Gothic style, it has many exquisite stained-glass windows, the most notable a cluster of three signed Tiffany lancet glass windows denoting the Nativity that's located in the East Transept. Music has been important to worship in St. Michael's from the beginning of the church. The first organ was purchased for $500 and brought with an altar around Cape Horn at the tip of South America and up the Pacific Coast and overland to Boise.

Carnegie Library Building
815 W. Washington St. · no phone

This was once the site of Boise's first public school, built in 1868, and first public library. A new building constructed with an Andrew Carnegie grant went up in 1905. Much of the woodwork and marble of that building remain in the contemporary structure that now houses offices.

The First United Presbyterian Church
Tenth and State Sts. · (208) 345-3441

The church contains original furnishings brought to Boise by covered wagon and used in its original 1878 church on the site of the Idanha Hotel. This church went up in 1954. Its middle education building dates back to 1929, and Lindsay Hall, also part of the complex,

Photo: Idaho Botanical Garden

In an odd twist, Idaho Botanical Garden is snuggled up against the Old Territorial Penitentiary.

was built in 1967. The church is known for its modern stained-glass windows.

Congregation Beth Israel Synagogue
1102 State St. • (208) 342-7247

This synagogue has the distinction of being the oldest Jewish temple west of the Mississippi River that is still used by its original congregation.

Boise High School
1010 W. Washington St. • (208) 338-3575

Boise High School, whose campus takes up three city blocks between Washington and Franklin, 10th and 13th streets, had a first graduating class of two students after it opened in 1884. Rebuilt in 1912, it was the city's only high school until 1958.

East and west of the school, residences along Washington and Franklin streets display variations on Queen Anne-style architecture, many of them turreted. Two more houses of worship here are worthy of note.

The First United Methodist Church
Eleventh and Franklin Sts.
• (208) 343-7511

Also known as the "Cathedral of the Rockies," this is a grand structure of modern Gothic style surrounded by stained-glass mosaics that were designed and created by the Willet Studios in Philadelphia. The choicest handblown pot-metal glasses and Norman slabs of great thickness went into the windows, creating a vibrant, jewel-like effect as light passes through them. One window depicts episodes of local history.

The cathedral is built of Arizona flagstone with Indiana sandstone trim. Its 153-foot spire rises above an avenue of hardwood trees. At night, floodlights illuminate the intricate tracery of its stone and metal pattern that climbs to an 8-foot cross on top. The cathedral has a lovely courtyard, 75 public rooms and a sanctuary that seats 1,000 people.

St. John's Cathedral
804 N. 8th St. • (208) 342-3511

Built of sandstone in 1905, St. John's is the central cathedral for Boise's Roman Catholics; its elaborate interior features vaulted ceilings decorated with oil paintings, marble floors and a profusion of statues and altars.

Tour of Old Boise

The two-block-long core of Boise's original downtown, extending along Main Street from Capitol Boulevard to 5th Street, is known today as Old Boise. A good place to begin a short jaunt through this historic district is outside the Perrault-Fritchman Building, at the southeast corner of Main Street and Capitol Boulevard.

Perrault-Fritchman Building
104 S. Capitol Blvd. • (208) 342-6320

Built of local sandstone in 1879, it is the oldest commercial building in downtown Boise and today houses a boutique on its ground floor and attorneys' offices upstairs.

As you stroll east along the south side of Main Street, you'll pass a series of restaurants, galleries and quaint shops behind century-old facades of brick and stone. From Capitol Boulevard to 6th Street, the north side of Main Street is taken up by City Hall, but in the next block, both sides of Main Street fairly

INSIDERS' TIP

The Basque people — or Euskaldunak, as they refer to themselves — came to the northern Great Basin region from the Basque Country in the late 19th century and initially found work raising sheep and other livestock. Now fully assimilated into the general population, southwestern Idaho's 20,000 Basques still maintain strong ties with their traditional homeland along the mountainous Atlantic coast of Spain and France. Even there, they are an anomaly: Their unique language, for instance, has no known linguistic relatives.

hum with the spirit of yesteryear. With its plethora of bars and night clubs (at least nine of them), Old Boise attracts throngs of university students and other young people. Streetside hotdog vendors have learned to take up mobile residence to capture their late-night business, while Boise police also gather to keep a wary eye.

Across 5th Street on the right is a medieval-looking sandstone building called The Belgravia.

The Belgravia
5th and Main Sts. • no phone

The Belgravia was Boise's first apartment house when it was built early in the 20th century. It's a medieval building with stone walls as thick as 2 feet and bay windows and balconies. Today it is an office building with a fine Northern Italian restaurant, Renaissance Ristorante Italiano, in its basement (see our Restaurants chapter for more information).

C.W. Moore Park
Fifth and Grove Sts.

This park is a quiet square where you can see artifacts of structures long ago demolished — 19th-century cornerstones, for instance, and a waterwheel that turned on one of Boise's earliest canals.

Two blocks east, across 3rd Street on the north side of Main Street, is the old U.S. Assay Office.

U.S. Assay Office
210 W. Main St. • (208) 334-3861

Some $75 million in gold and silver ore passed through the two-foot-thick sandstone walls of this imposing, cube-like structure between 1872, when it was built, and 1933. A designated National Historic Landmark, it is now the home of the Idaho Historical Society, and served as exhibition space for the Society's collection of gemstones.

Tour of the Warm Springs District

Boise's original upper-class residential district extends easterly along Warm Springs Avenue for more than a half-mile beyond Broad-

way Avenue. As you walk or drive past these stately Victorian mansions, keep in mind that this was America's first geothermally heated neighborhood. (These are private homes, so tours are not offered.)

Moore-Cunningham House
1109 Warm Springs Ave. • no phone

The Moore-Cunningham House was the first geothermally heated house, built in French chateau style in 1891. It served as the residence of the family of C.W. Moore, president of the hot water company who helped establish Idaho First National Bank. Scions of the family still live in the home. This splendid house has three floors appointed with oak, cherry and redwood.

G.W. Russell House
1035 Warm Springs Ave. • no phone

The Russell House is the district's oldest residence, built in 1868 in Greek revival style. Its builder, George W. Russell, founded the city's first electric streetcar company.

C.C. Anderson House
929 Warm Springs Ave. • no phone

This 1925 English country-style manor that is the designated home of the president of Boise State University. It was built by C.C. Anderson, whose Golden Rule retail store became the present Bon Marche department store, now with downtown and Boise Towne Square mall locations.

Just off Warm Springs Avenue, about a mile from Broadway Avenue, detour to the north into Quarry View Park.

Quarry View Park
Bacon Dr., west of Hot Springs Dr. • (208) 384-4240

The park has a restored pump house. Since 1890, 700,000 gallons of 172-degree water have been pumped each day from a well drilled into a rhyolite aquifer beneath this site. The 400 homes and eight government buildings that receive this steam heat are not likely to change this process anytime soon: The cost to them is about half that of natural-gas heating.

Museums

Basque Museum & Cultural Center
607-611 Grove St. • (208) 343-2671

Boise boasts the largest population of people of Basque heritage of any city in the world, outside of this nationality's European homeland. It comes as no surprise, then, that the only museum in the United States devoted entirely to the colorful Basque culture should be here, a scant five blocks from the State Capitol building.

This museum is lodged within Boise's oldest brick building — the Cyrus Jacobs-Uberuaga House, a former boarding house for Basque immigrants built in 1864 — and an adjacent exhibit hall.

The brick home is in the process of conversion to a living-history showcase. The exhibit hall features displays on the Basque experience in Europe and through more than 100 years in Idaho. Of particular interest is a sheep wagon, still stocked as it would have been when a herder lived in it around the turn of the 20th century. You'll also find a library and gift shop, here.

The museum is the centerpiece of the so-called Basque Block that encompasses the south side of Grove Street between Capitol Boulevard and 6th Street. Also on the block are the Basque Center, a gathering place that sponsors the internationally acclaimed Oinkari Dancers; Bar Gernika, a newly expanded Basque restaurant and tavern; and a fronton for playing pelota, a traditional form of handball similar to jai alai.

Museum and gift shop hours are 10 AM to 4 PM Tuesday through Friday and 11 AM to 3 PM Saturday. Admission is $1 for adults, 50¢ for seniors and students.

Discovery Center of Idaho
131 Myrtle St. • (208) 343-9895

Idaho's premier interactive science-and-technology museum, with hands-on exhibits and educational programs for the entire family, the Discovery Center is located just off the north edge of Julia Davis Park. Some 170 permanent exhibits encourage experimentation in electricity, magnetism, motion and other physical sciences. It also has a fascinating shop with science-related toys and games (see our Kidstuff chapter for more information).

Museum hours are 10 AM to 5 PM Tuesday through Saturday and noon to 5 PM on Sunday; it opens an hour earlier on weekdays during the school year. Admission is $4 for adults, $3 for seniors and $2.50 for children 3 to 18.

Idaho Museum of Military History
4040 W. Guard St., Bldg. 303
• (208) 422-6006

Boise's newest museum tells the story of Idahoans who have served in America's wars, especially the two world wars, Korea and Vietnam. Highlights include the General Patch College of World War I memorabilia, an exhibit of military firearms and an apparently anomalous display on Idaho naval history: The U.S. Navy had a submarine testing facility in Boise during World War II, and today continues to experiment with sonar in deep Lake Pend Oreille in northern Idaho. Located in the industrial zone south of Gowen Field, the museum also offers exhibits on the evolution of the airfield and of the Idaho Army and Air National Guard.

The Museum of Military History is open 9 AM to 5 PM, Wednesday through Sunday, between Memorial Day weekend and Labor Day, and 1 to 5 PM Friday through Sunday in winter. There is no formal admission, but donations are appreciated.

Idaho Museum of Mining & Geology
2455 Old Penitentiary Rd.
• (208) 368-9876

This small museum's exhibits focus on the state's mineral resources, past and present. Archival photographs and artifacts portray 19th-century gold- and silver-mining settlements, particularly in the Boise Basin area. Other displays pinpoint existing pockets of wealth throughout Idaho's varied landscape.

Situated at, but independent of, the Old Pen, the mining museum occupies the prison's New Trusty Quarters, built outside its walls in 1928 as a dormitory for trusted inmates with supervisory responsibilities.

This museum opens Saturdays and Sundays from noon to 5 PM only. Admission is $2 for adults, $1 for seniors and students.

Idaho State Historical Museum
610 N. Julia Davis Dr. • (208) 334-2120

Idaho history is vividly presented at this modern museum, whose well-considered exhibits bring to life native prehistory and the early days of white settlement. Displays focus on the fossil past, traditional Shoshone Indian culture, the fur-trade and gold-rush eras, up to the early beginnings of urban Boise. Special emphasis is placed on the lives of ethnic minorities, including Chinese miners and Basque sheepherders.

Re-creations of a blacksmith's forge, a settler's kitchen, an Old West saloon and a Chinese apothecary shop evoke a sense of "being there," especially on designated living-history days when volunteers re-create pioneer lifestyles. Their demonstrations extend to the adjacent Pioneer Village, to which several adobe, log and wood-frame dwellings — dating from the 1860s through the early 20th century — have been relocated.

The Historical Museum, located at the edge of Julia Davis Park near the Boise Art Museum, is open 9 AM to 5 PM Monday through Saturday and 1 to 5 PM Sunday. There is no admission, but donations are appreciated.

Old Idaho Territorial Penitentiary
2445 Old Penitentiary Rd.
• (208) 334-2844

Boise's foreboding Old Pen is one of only three territorial prisons still standing in the United States. And it was only in 1973, after more than a century of continuous use, that this gothic structure closed its imposing stone walls.

Located 2 miles from downtown at the east end of the Warm Springs district, the Old Pen got its start in 1870 as a single cellhouse, constructed by the convicts themselves of hand-cut sandstone quarried from adjacent Table Rock.

During its 103 years of operation, more than 13,000 prisoners did time in the Old Pen. Over the years, their labor built the high turreted walls and sandstone buildings that make the Old Pen such an intriguing museum today. It was finally replaced by a new prison (on Pleasant Valley Road, due south of the Boise Air Terminal) after a series of riots in protest of poor living conditions. When you

tour this archaic landmark, admitted to the National Register of Historic Places in 1974, you'll have some idea of why the prisoners complained.

A tour of the Old Pen grounds — which you can make either by yourself or with a guide — begins with an 18-minute slide show recounting various episodes of prison history. Then you'll be off to explore numerous cell blocks, including the claustrophobic women's ward; the solitary confinement chambers known to inmates as "Siberia" and "The Corner Pocket;" and the gallows used for Idaho's only hanging (in 1957).

Don't miss the museums within the museum. An exhibit of prison tattoo art, with photos and replicas of inmates' skin designs (frequently either demonic or erotic), is said to be the only one of its kind. A display of weapons confiscated within prison walls is shocking. The History of Electricity in Idaho Museum, lodged in the former commissary, begins with Ben Franklin's kite-flying experiments and carries through Thomas Edison's invention of the light bulb to the modern hydropower industry. The Idaho Transportation Museum, in the prison's former shirt factory, presents an array of vehicles ranging from a pre-Lewis-and-Clark Shoshone Indian travois (a two-pole sled dragged by a dog) to horse-drawn carriages, classic cars and early farm machinery.

Owned by the Idaho State Historical Society, the Old Pen is open 10 AM to 5 PM daily in the summer (Memorial Day to Labor Day) and noon to 5 PM the rest of the year. Admission is $4 for adults, $3 for children 6 to 12 and seniors 60 and older.

World Sports Humanitarian Hall of Fame
404 S. 8th St. • (208) 343-7224

Sports stars most often are known for their achievements on the field or the court, rarely for what they've contributed to society as a whole. It's the goal of this museum to change that perception. Established in 1994, the Hall has inducted three members a year for a total of 12 by 1997.

Charter members include Arthur Ashe (tennis), Roberto Clemente (baseball), Julius Erving (basketball), Rafer Johnson (decathlon), Dale Murphy (baseball) and Chi Chi

Rodriguez (golf). Each has been recognized for his endeavors to better the human condition by applying his fame and resources to charitable causes.

Ground was broken in the fall of 1997 on a permanent museum site adjacent to the Boise Outlet Mall, not far from Interstate 84's Gowen Road exit at the southeast edge of Boise. In the meantime, the Hall of Fame maintains an interim museum in the Eighth Street Marketplace. Memorabilia of each member athlete is showcased. It's open 9 AM to 4 PM Monday through Friday, and donations are welcomed.

The Humanitarian Bowl — Boise's late-December college football game between the champion of the Big West Conference and an at-large team — gets major support from the World Sports Humanitarian Hall of Fame ... and vice versa.

Construction of the Capitol began in 1905 but wasn't completed until 1920.

Natural Attractions

You'll also find information about natural wonders around Boise in our Parks and Preserves and Recreation chapters.

Boise River Greenbelt
Headquarters at 1104 Royal Blvd.
• **(208) 342-4240**

Extending for 19 miles from southeast to northwest through the heart of the city, this network of walking and biking paths is an integral part of city life. Discovery State Park, Barber Park, Municipal Park, Julia Davis Park, Boise State University, Ann Morrison Park, Kathryn Albertson Park and Veterans Memorial State Park are all linked by this riverside byway. See our Parks and Preserves chapter for more information.

Idaho Botanical Garden
2355 Old Penitentiary Rd.
• **(208) 343-8649**

Situated outside the southeast wall of the Old Idaho Territorial Penitentiary, this lovingly maintained garden remains in bloom from late April through mid-October, when the season's first freezes hit the Treasure Valley.

Each of the 11 separate theme and display gardens has a character of its own. For viewers with particular floral interests, there are heirloom rose, historical iris and peony

gardens. There's a herb garden, a water garden, a cactus garden and a garden devoted to plants indigenous to Idaho. One garden has been planted especially to appeal to children, another to lure butterflies and hummingbirds. A Chinese garden encourages meditation, while the Basque garden and contemporary English garden inspire reflections on Europe.

The gardens are open from 9 AM to 5 PM Tuesday through Friday and noon to 8 PM Saturday and Sunday, from mid-April to mid-October. Adults pay $3, seniors and students $2, while children younger than 6 are admitted free.

Morrison-Knudsen Nature Center
600 S. Walnut St. • (208) 368-6060

Imagine a gently flowing mountain stream pouring from a wetland pond, with underwater windows for nature lovers to study the behavior of its denizens, and you'll have some idea of the unique scope of the M-K Nature Center. Located behind the headquarters of the state Department of Fish & Game adjacent to Municipal Park, it allows visitors to observe, in compact scale, the life cycle of trout and other fish from developing eggs to full-size adults. Muskrat, mink, beaver and other riparian species also inhabit the wetland environment, best viewed by following a winding trail on a self-guided tour past a series of interpretive signs.

A small visitor center at the site has a museum of natural history that educates visitors on the fundamentals of stream hydraulics and riparian ecology. The visitor center is open from 11 AM to 5 PM Tuesday through Sunday. Admission is 50¢. It's free to stroll along the outdoor walkway, which is open daily from sunrise to sunset.

World Center for Birds of Prey
566 W. Flying Hawk Ln. • (208) 362-8687

Few attractions warrant the label "unique." But the World Center truly is one of a kind. Established in 1984, this is the world's largest and most sophisticated private facility for breeding threatened and endangered raptor species, as well as for conducting scientific research to their benefit and educating the public about birds of prey.

Operated by the conservationist Peregrine Fund, the World Center already has succeeded in hatching and nurturing more than 4,000 hawks, eagles, owls and falcons of 22 different species. These birds have then been reintroduced to native habitats as far apart as the Philippines, Madagascar ... and Idaho. In 1997 a rare harpy eagle was born here. Visitors who join guided tours in the interpretive center can observe the incubation process, then spend time with active adults in the Tropical Raptor Building and view a demonstration with live birds on an outdoor stage.

The World Center for Birds of Prey is located 6 miles south of Boise off Interstate 84 via S. Cole Road. It's open 9 AM to 5 PM daily in summer, 10 AM to 4 PM in winter. Admission is $4 for adults, $3 for seniors and $2 for those ages 4 to 16.

Zoo Boise
355 N. Julia Davis Dr. • (208) 384-4260

Boise's city zoo isn't one of the world's great wildlife repositories, but it's a pleasant place to while away a couple of hours on a sunny afternoon. More than 200 animals of 90 species, the vast majority native to the Rocky Mountain and Pacific Northwest states, are displayed here. See our Kidstuff chapter for more information.

The zoo is open 10 AM to 5 PM daily except on holidays. Admission is $3 for adults, $1.50 for seniors and students, with Thursday admission at half-price.

Other Attractions

Boise State University
1910 University Dr. • (208) 385-1011

Idaho's largest institution of higher learning occupies a 110-acre campus on the south bank of the Boise River, between Capitol Boulevard and Broadway Avenue. Its 15,000 students stroll back and forth across a footbridge that connects the campus to Julia Davis Park.

A highlight of campus tours — offered on a regular schedule (call for times) — is the Morrison Center for the Performing Arts (see The Arts chapter), renowned for its marvelous acoustics: The center had the same designer as the Lincoln Center in New York City.

The white-clapboard Christ Chapel, the oldest Protestant church in Idaho, was built in 1866 and moved to its present location (on Broadway Avenue at the Boise River bridge) in 1964. It has been restored by the Sons and Daughters of Idaho Pioneers. No regular services are held here, but it is frequently reserved for wedding ceremonies. Call (208) 385-1442.

Additional points of interest on campus include:

Hemingway Center, (208) 385-1999, a small building next to the BSU library on Campus Lane, boasts a collection of memorabilia from late author Ernest Hemingway, a resident of the Sun Valley area, and archives of all films made in Idaho since 1920.

The Idaho Wild Bird Exhibit, on the second floor of the Science Education Building, (208) 385-3262, also on Campus Lane, displays 300 mounted avians native to the state. The collection was begun in 1936 by employees of the U.S. Biological Survey.

The Edward F. Rhodenbaugh collection of rocks, crystals and minerals can be found on the first floor of the Old Science Building on University Drive, (208) 385-3262.

Gallery I, on the first floor of the Liberal Arts Building on University Drive, (208) 385-1562, features displays of student and faculty art.

The 12,000-seat BSU Pavilion is used for basketball and concerts alike, while 30,000-seat Bronco Stadium is home to the university's football team (see our Spectator Sports chapter).

Fort Boise Reserve
5th and Fort Sts. • (208) 384-4486

In 1863 a U.S. Army post was built on this 67-acre site to defend travelers between the fledgling supply center on the Boise River and the rich new mining settlements in the nearby Rocky Mountain foothills. Even before the fort was raised, however, soldier John O'Farrell constructed a simple log cabin for his 17-year-old bride. The O'Farrell Cabin, regarded as Boise's first, stands in its original location at 4th and Fort streets. It later was used as Boise's first school and for its first Roman Catholic Mass.

You can visit old Fort Boise today on your own. You'll enter the quiet grounds past the original sandstone guardhouse. You can still see a medical complex, quartermaster's building and officers' dwellings around the perimeter of the loop road. Admissions is free.

The fort closed in 1912. In 1938, it became the site of the Idaho Veterans Home, 320 Collins Road, (208) 334-5000, and Veterans Administration Hospital, 500 W. Fort Street, (208) 422-1000.

Eighty-six percent of the fort's land (449 acres) was donated in 1954 to the City of Boise, which turned much of that space into softball fields and other recreation grounds. They are administered from the Fort Boise Community Center, 700 Robbins Road, (208) 384-4486.

National Interagency Fire Center
3833 S. Development Ave.
• (208) 387-5512

So you think the life of a firefighter is all blaze and glory? Think again. Thousands of dedicated men and women put their lives on the line each summer and fall when forest fires, grassland infernos and other wild fires ravage state and federal lands throughout the West. Here in Boise, off Airport Way on the east side of the Boise Air Terminal, is their logistics support center.

Tours of the facility, offered by appointment at no charge, preview some of the high-tech equipment used in sustaining teams that work from New Mexico to Alaska. Of special interest are an automatic lightning-detection system, an infrared mapping system and state-of-the-art radio-communication systems.

Nampa

Canyon County Historical Museum
1200 Front St. • (208) 467-7611

Railroad memorabilia are the highlight of this four-room museum in the town's 1902 Oregon Short Line Depot, which sits beside the tracks in the downtown historic district. Said by some to be Idaho's finest example of Baroque revival architecture, the depot displays a fascinating assortment of whistlestop artifacts as well as other items from more than 100 years of Nampa-area history. It was built with separate waiting rooms for men and women, so that "the fairer sex" could maintain decorum and not be offended by men swearing and spitting tobacco on the waiting-room floor.

The museum is open 1 to 5 PM Tuesday through Saturday. Admission is by donation.

Deer Flat National Wildlife Refuge
13751 Upper Embankment Rd.
• (208) 462-9278

More than 200 species of resident and migratory birds, including waterfowl, raptors and songbirds, live along the banks and in the woodlands of this refuge. One of America's first, it was created by the executive order of President Theodore Roosevelt and completely surrounds pretty Lake Lowell. The lake originated in 1909 with the diversion (for irrigation) of the New York Canal from the Boise River. Today a handsome visitors center on the southern shore has exhibits that describe many of the refuge's most common avian species, as well as frequently seen mammals and other denizens. Up to 100,000 ducks and 10,000 geese congregate in late autumn on the lake, which is open seasonally for hunting and fishing. (See our Parks and Preserves chapter for more information about the refuge.)

Caldwell

Albertson College of Idaho
2112 Cleveland Blvd. • (208) 459-5011

The name of Joe Albertson, the late supermarket magnate, was conferred upon the former College of Idaho when he bequeathed millions of dollars of his fortune to his alma mater upon its centennial in 1991. One of the West's most highly esteemed private, four-year, liberal-arts colleges, Albertson was founded by a Presbyterian minister, William Judson Boone, but is today a nonsectarian institution. Annual enrollment is just more than 700.

The Boone Hall science building, 2102 Fillmore Street, 459-5507, on the handsome campus quadrangle is of special interest to visitors for its museum-quality exhibits. The Orma J. Smith Museum of Natural History boasts a research collection from throughout the western United States and Baja California. The Glen and Ruth Evans Gem and Mineral Collection has more than 5,000 mineral specimens from around the United States and 100 foreign countries. Whittenberger Planetarium and H.M. Tucker Herbarium are popular field-trip destinations for local schoolchildren.

Our Memories Museum
1122 Main St. • (208) 459-1413

For the antique lover, Our Memories recreates a 19-room turn-of-the-century home furnished with late 19th and early 20th century bric-a-brac: "stuff," as the owners call it. There's a kitchen, a pantry, a parlor, two bedrooms and many other living areas. The museum is open from 10 AM to 4:30 PM Fridays and 1 to 4:30 PM Sundays. Admission is by donation.

Van Slyke Agricultural Museum Memorial Park
S. Kimball and Irving Sts.
• (208) 459-7493

Two 1864 log cabins with period furnishings, a variety of antique farm machinery and tools and a pair of circa-1950 railroad cars (a caboose and a freight car) are featured in this open-air museum. The site is open by appointment only, but it's always on display for those willing to peer through the chain-link fence.

Warhawk Air Museum
Caldwell Industrial Airport, 4917 Aviation Way • (208) 454-2854

Antique aircraft enthusiasts from all over the United States drop into Caldwell (some of them quite literally — as skydivers) to see the collection at the town's general-aviation airport. Several World War II aircraft and an exhibit of wartime uniforms, photographs and rare souvenirs and artifacts are on display daily from 10 AM to 4 PM..

Some of the planes — including a Fokker tri-plane replica and two Curtiss P-40s — come out of their hangars in June during Caldwell's annual air show, a function of the museum. Admission is $2.

Elsewhere in the Region

What follows are just a few of the attractions outside the Boise-Nampa-Caldwell area. For other destinations, see our Daytrips chapter.

Gem County Historical Museum
501 E. 1st St. at Hawthorne St., Emmett • (208) 365-9530

This complex of five pioneer buildings in the Payette River orchard town on Payette River, incorporates exhibits on early Shoshone Indian culture with the heritage of early settlers and the evolution of local industries, including fruit-growing and wood products.

The museum is open from 1 to 4 PM on Saturday and Sunday in the summer and other times by appointment. Donations are welcomed. Emmett is 31 miles northwest of Boise at the junction of Idaho highways 16 and 52.

Old Fort Boise
E. Main Ave., Parma • (208) 722-7808

The original Fort Boise was a Hudson Bay Company's trading post at the confluence of the Boise and Snake rivers. Built in 1834, it grew to become a key provisioning place for westward emigrants after the Oregon Trail was established four years later. A flood destroyed the adobe fort in 1853, and although a ferry service operated from the same location between 1864 and 1902, the only evidence remaining today is a solitary marker.

Five miles east, however, at the east end of the small town of Parma, a replica of the original fort recaptures some of its spirit. The concrete walls are guaranteed to withstand a rush of water like adobe could not. Within the fort are a pioneer cabin, furnished in mid-19th-century fashion and a historical museum whose nine rooms include a recreated school-room, chapel and pioneer kitchen.

The museum is open from 1 to 3 PM Friday, Saturday and Sunday from June through August and by appointment. A $1 donation is requested. Parma is 39 miles west of Boise on U.S. highways 20, 26 and 95.

Payette County Historical Museum
90 S. 9th St., Payette • (208) 642-2362

The name of French-Canadian trader François Payette, who ran old Fort Boise in the 1830s and '40s, was bestowed upon the Payette River and the town built near its mouth in 1867. Historic downtown Payette has preserved 85 buildings from as early as 1885, most notable of which is a Gothic revival-style Methodist Episcopal Church that was built in 1904. That church now houses this museum, whose volunteers gladly provide visitors with information for a walking tour of other historic structures.

Apart from displays of vintage clothing and antique furniture, the Payette museum is of special interest to baseball fans for its exhibit on native son Harmon Killebrew. Born in Payette in 1936, Killebrew became one of baseball's greatest sluggers in a 22-year major-league career spent mainly with the Washington Senators and Minnesota Twins. His 573 career home runs — a total surpassed only by Hank Aaron, Babe Ruth, Willie Mays and Frank Robinson — earned him permanent membership in the Baseball Hall of Fame after he retired in 1975.

The museum is open from 1 to 4 PM Sundays in the summer or by appointment. Payette is 55 miles northwest of Boise on U.S. Highway 95.

Parents anxious to find places for their kids to play, to learn or to interact with nature and technology will find a wealth of opportunities in Boise.

Kidstuff

When it comes to children, the Boise area is no different from most other cities. Parents are anxious to find places for their kids to play, to learn, to interact with nature and technology. They want shops to buy clothes, toys and books. Sometimes, they even want places to leave the little imps to give them some time alone.

In this chapter, we offer a range of choices for kids in almost every area except education and healthcare, which have their own chapters.

A terrific source of information on any child-related question is *Boise Family Magazine*, published 10 times a year and distributed free throughout the area. If you can't find a copy or want a subscription mailed to your home, write P.O. Box 3178, Boise, ID 83703, or call (208) 853-2516. The magazine also publishes an annual *Kids' Pages* resource directory.

Out and About Town

Boise

Discovery Center of Idaho
131 Myrtle St. • (208) 343-9895

Did you ever wonder why magnets attract metal, or how an electrical current is passed? You can learn answers to these and hundreds of other questions by performing simple experiments at this hands-on museum dedicated to science and technology.

Exhibits and educational programs, including weekend science classes and summer day camps, are set up for the whole family to share. Visitors are encouraged to initiate action in some 170 different displays that demonstrate principles of physical science. A series of theme-related exhibits — motion in 1997-98, weather in 1998-99 — rotate with the school year.

The Discovery Center, established in 1988, occupies a former inland Naval barracks and submarine training facility at the northern edge of Julia Davis Park. Hours are 10 AM to 5 PM Tuesday through Saturday and noon to 5 PM on Sunday. It opens an hour earlier on weekdays during the school year. Admission for children 3 to 18 is $2.50, while Mom and Dad pay $4 and Grandma and Grandpa pay $3.

Idaho Botanical Garden
2355 Old Penitentiary Rd.
• (208) 343-8649

The Children's Garden is under expansion and reconstruction at this writing. In the meantime, the Butterfly and Hummingbird Garden is sure to please youngsters. The gardens are populated by plants who nectar and color attract butterflies and hummingbirds.

The gardens, situated outside the southeast wall of the Old Idaho Territorial Penitentiary, are open 9 AM to 5 PM Tuesday through Friday and noon to 8 PM Saturday and Sunday, from mid-April to mid-October. Children younger than 6 enter free; students pay $2, as do seniors; and adults pay $3. (See our Attractions chapter for more details.)

Idaho State Historical Museum
610 N. Julia Davis Dr. • (208) 334-2120

While younger children may find the everyday exhibits at this fine museum a bit on the dry side, no one should miss visiting when there's a living history day. You can watch sparks fly as the blacksmith forges horseshoes and, perhaps, a good hunting knife; marvel at the intricate weaving produced by the woman seated at the old hand loom; or plug your ears when mountain men compete in a black-powder shoot. Many other folks go about settlers' lives in Pioneer Village, a collection of late 19th- and early 20th-century homes next to the museum on the edge of Julia Davis Park.

The Historical Museum is open 9 AM to 5

PM Monday through Saturday and 1 to 5 PM Sunday. There is no admission, but donations are appreciated. Call for information on living-history days. (See our Attractions chapter.)

Old Idaho Territorial Penitentiary
2445 Old Penitentiary Rd.
• **(208) 334-2844**

"If you're not a good boy or girl, you could wind up in a place like this!" Well, not any longer, but Idahoans of the past may have used this cautionary phrase with their children. A tour of the imposing Old Pen, which closed in 1973 after more than a century of continuous use, might still send a shiver up their spines.

Built in 1870 by the very prisoners held here, the Old Pen is remarkable for its thick sandstone walls topped by turrets where its guards kept watch. Visitors tour cell blocks, solitary-confinement chambers and the gallows where Idaho's only hanging took place. Among other exhibits, older children might be intrigued by those on contraband weapons and prison tattoo art (but be warned: it deserves an "R" rating). The prison also contains small museums on the development of electricity in Idaho, and on the evolution of transportation through the centuries. (See Attractions for more information.)

The Old Pen is open 10 AM to 5 PM daily in summer (Memorial Day to Labor Day), noon to 5 PM the rest of the year. Admission is $4 for adults and $3 for children 6 to 12 and seniors 60 and older.

Nampa

The Berry Ranch
7998 Idaho Hwy. 20/26 • (208) 466-3860

City kids can head out to the farm where, depending upon the season, they can pick their own strawberries and blackberries or take a hayride to the pumpkin patch and select their own jack o' lantern-to-be. Several farm animals are sequestered in a petting shed, and fresh produce is available for sale in the barn.

The ranch, on Chinden Boulevard 10 miles west of Eagle Road, is open 4 to 7 PM Fridays, 10 AM to 7 PM Saturdays and Sundays. Admission is $2 for preschoolers, $2.50 for those in kindergarten through 2nd grade, $3.25 for 3rd through 6th graders and $4.25 for junior high students through adults.

Caldwell

Warhawk Air Museum
Caldwell Industrial Airport, 4917 Aviation Way • (208) 454-2854

Those weird airplanes you've seen in old movies and cartoons — such as the Fokker triplane the Red Baron might have flown against Snoopy — are on display at this museum, along with an interesting exhibit of World War II uniforms and souvenirs. Kids won't want to miss the June air show when some of the planes, including a Fokker triplane replica and two Curtiss P-40s come out of the hangar. The museum is open 10 AM to 4 PM daily; admission is $2. For more details, see the Attractions chapter.

Cool Critters

Boise

Morrison-Knudsen Nature Center
600 S. Walnut St. • (208) 368-6060

This is the place to go if you want to learn about fish, and other animals who love the water, without leaving the city. The state Department of Fish & Game has re-created a mountain pond and stream, stocked it with trout in various stages of life, and installed underwater windows where you can watch the development of fish from eggs to full-size adults. A trail winds past the pond where beaver, mink and muskrat live, and a small visitors center includes a museum of natural history. (See our Attractions chapter for more information.)

Photo: Andrew Rafkind

A young fire chief tries on his hat at the Boise River Festival.

The outdoor walk, open daily from sunrise to sunset, is free. The visitors center is open from 11 AM to 5 PM Tuesday through Sunday; admission is 50¢.

World Center for Birds of Prey
566 W. Flying Hawk Ln. • (208) 362-8687

If you think hawks and owls are just big mean birds who prey on defenseless small rodents, you'll have a totally different view after your visit to the World Center. At this, the largest private raptor research and breeding facility on earth, you will have a chance to learn more about these great birds and their place in the ecosystem. You'll also see how the Center helps rare eagles and hawks, whose natural homes may be thousands of miles away in the tropics, reestablish their declining populations; and you'll watch a live bird show with golden eagles and peregrine falcons.

The Center is 6 miles south of Boise off Interstate 84 via S. Cole Road. It's open 9 AM to 5 PM daily in summer, 10 AM to 4 PM in winter. Admission is $3 for students and seniors, $4 for adults. (See our Attractions chapter for more information.)

Zoo Boise
355 N. Julia Davis Dr. • (208) 384-4260

Boise's city zoo isn't one of the world's great zoological gardens, but it is a pleasant place to pass an afternoon. More than 200 animals of 90 species, most of them native to Idaho and the greater Rocky Mountain-Pacific Northwest region, are residents of the zoo, which sits in the heart of Julia Davis Park.

You'll see bears, deer, elk, moose, bighorn sheep and many smaller animals, including an extensive display of native birds. Among the exotic animals in Zoo Boise are camels, zebras, monkeys, ring-tailed lemurs, cheetahs and a Bengal tiger.

Younger children appreciate the petting zoo and the new Jack and Esther Simplot Education Center, which exhibits bugs and other interesting wildlife. The zoo also has an excellent gift shop, known as the Zootique, and a snack bar named the Coati Cafe.

Zoo Boise is open 10 AM to 5 PM daily but is closed on holidays. Admission is free for children 3 and younger, $1.75 for kids 4 to 12,

$4 for teenagers and adults and $2 for seniors (62 and older). Thursdays are half-price.

Room to Run

Boise

Boise City Parks
Boise Parks & Recreation Department, 1104 Royal Blvd. • (208) 342-4240

Fifty-five individual parks are part and parcel of the city parks system, all of them great places to take the kids. Twenty-three parks have both playgrounds and restrooms, both generally regarded as essential facilities for younger kids. (For more information on the area's parks, turn to our Parks and Preserves and Recreation chapters.)

In downtown Boise and the adjacent North End, these include Camelback Park, 1200 Heron Street; Elm Grove Park, 2200 Irene Street; Fairview Park, 2300 W. Idaho Street; Fort Boise Park, 600 W. Garrison Street; Julia Davis Park, 700 S. Capitol Boulevard; and Memorial Park, 900 N. 6th Street.

In northwest Boise, visit Sunset Park, 2625 N. 32nd Street, and Willow Lane Park, 4623 Willow Lane, off W. State Street.

In northeast Boise, there's Municipal Park, 500 Walnut Street, and Quarry View Park, 2150 Old Penitentiary Road.

In southeast Boise, try Ivywild Park, 416 Ivywild Street; Manitou Park, 1951 Manitou Street; and Williams Park, 300 Williams Street.

On the south Boise bench, take the family to Borah Park, 801 Aurora Drive; Bowden Park, 3249 Edson Street; Cassia Park, 4600 Camas Street; Owyhee Park, 3400 Elder Street; Phillippi Park, 2299 S. Phillippi Street; and Shoshone Park, 2800 Canal Street.

In west Boise, go to DeMeyer Park, 5100 Tumbleweed Place; Fairmont Park, 7925 Northview Street; Mountain View Park, 7006 Ustick Road; or Winstead Park, 6150 Northview Street.

There are parks-administered swimming pools at Borah and Fairmont parks, as well as at the historic Natatorium & Hydrotube, 1811 Warm Springs Avenue; Lowell Elementary School, 1601 N. 28th Street; South Junior High

School, 921 Shoshone Street; and the Westside Sportsplex, 14400 W. McMillan Street.

Many Boise parks also have tennis courts, baseball or softball fields, basketball and volleyball courts. In addition, areas at two urban parks have been set aside for skateboarders and in-line skaters: Hobble Creek Park, 5835 N. Discovery Street, in west Boise, and Rhodes Park, 1555 W. Front Street, under the freeway connector in downtown Boise.

Parks are open from sunrise to sunset, except where lighted facilities exist.

Nampa

Nampa City Parks
Nampa Recreation Center, 131 Constitution Way • (208) 465-2215

Nampa has seven city parks, every one of them with playground equipment and basketball courts. The largest is Lakeview Park, Garrity Boulevard and 16th Avenue N., north of downtown, whose facilities include a playground and swimming pool, basketball and tennis courts, softball fields, an archery range, even a duck pond and a 1,000-seat amphitheater. Older kids also enjoy looking at the military jet and M-60 tank displayed in the park near the BMX track.

Lions Park, Davis Avenue and Winther Boulevard in northwest Nampa, also has a playground and extensive recreational facilities, including a swimming pool. Other kid-oriented parks are City Acres Park, 4th Road N. and 4th Street N. Extension; Hunter Park, 9th Avenue N. and Phyllis Canal; Housing Project Park, 2nd Street N. and 17th Avenue N.; Liberty Park, Constitution Way and Juniper Street; and West Park, Lone Star Road and Midland Boulevard. See Parks and Preserves for more information.

Caldwell

Caldwell City Parks
618 Irving St. • (208) 455-3060

The Oregon Trail Centennial Greenway offers Caldwell residents and visitors a greenbelt alongside the Boise River that is similar to Boise's own greenbelt but with historic markers along the way.

The city also has seven other parks. Memorial Park, S. Kimball Avenue at Irving Street, has a playground, a swimming pool and a variety of sports facilities. See Parks and Preserves for more information.

Activity Centers

Boise

Discovery Zone Fun Center
8567 W. Franklin Rd. • (208) 375-3000

For birthday parties or any other special occasion, Discovery Zone — lodged in a strip mall beside PetsMart near Boise Towne Square — delights children as well as their parents. It has an inflatable play park and a variety of other games, as well as a video arcade and, perhaps best of all, private rooms when it's time for the cake and ice cream.

The Zone is open 11 AM to 8 PM Monday through Thursday, 10 AM to 9 PM Friday and Saturday and 11 AM to 7 PM Sunday. Admission is $3.99 for children up to the age of 4 and $5.99 for older kids.

Downtown Boise Family YMCA
1050 W. State St. • (208) 344-5501

Boise's original Y has recently been refurbished and expanded, but it still offers the same

---

INSIDERS' TIP

Every child finds something special at the Boise River Festival in late June. Two giant parades, one of them at night, a fireworks extravaganza and a hot-air balloon rally (with giant inflatables of popular cartoon characters) are just the most visible events. Other activities include children's concerts and plays, a carnival, sports and games, comedy and storytelling, face painting, a maze and a sand sculpture contest.

variety of activities for children and parents. Kids of all ages can take lessons and participate in swimming and diving, basketball, soccer, running programs, martial arts, dance classes and more. A fitness gym with weight training, aerobics classes and a climbing wall is appropriate for older youngsters. For the toddlers, there are child development programs. There are day camps for all.

Annual memberships start at $22 for individual youths (age 7 to 18), with no joining fee; Y officials pledge that "no youth will be turned away for inability to pay." Parents and families, of course, pay more. Hours are 5 AM to 10 PM Monday through Friday, 7 AM to 6 PM Saturday and noon to 6 PM Sunday.

West Family YMCA and Boise City Aquatic Center
5959 N. Discovery Pl. • (208) 377-9622

Like its downtown forebear, the new West Y offers programs in a great range of physical activities, including basketball, soccer, running, dancing and strength and aerobic training. Its aquatic center sets it apart: Nowhere else in the state, certainly, have a YMCA and a city parks department formed a partnership of this nature. Because of its extensive pool space, space for recreational swimming is available at all times, even on Mondays and Wednesdays when an almost constant series of lessons is offered.

Daily fees that include lockers and showers are $3 for children 18 and younger, $6 for adults and $15 for families. Residential monthly fees are $12 for children, $30 for adults and $60 for families. Nonresidents pay $18 per child, $45 per adult and $90 per family. The West Y is open 5 AM to 11 PM Monday through Friday, 7 AM to 8 PM Saturday and noon to 6 PM Sunday.

Wings Center
1875 Century Way • (208) 376-3641

The Planet Kid inflatable play park is but one element of this amusement center for children 2 to 10, but in itself is worth the price of admission: Kids can safely take part in boxing, jousting, climbing a Velcro wall or spring back from a bungee run. You'll also find miniature golf and more advanced rock climbing, and classes are available in swimming, gymnastics and dancing. It's another popular place for birthdays and other parties.

Wings Center is located just south of the Cole/Overland exit from I-84. Planet Kid is open 10 AM to 8 PM Monday through Thursday, 10 AM to 9 PM Friday and Saturday and noon to 6 PM Sunday. Admission is $4.95 per child up to the age of 10. There are additional charges for minigolf and rock climbing.

Nampa

Nampa Recreation Center
131 Constitution Way • (208) 465-2288

There may be no other place in the Treasure Valley that maintains the nonstop energy rush of the Nampa Rec Center. The beautiful facility at Liberty Park is one of the largest and finest civic recreation centers in the United States. Where else could children find six pools and three full-size basketball courts?

The pools include an Olympic-size lap pool, a deep pool for diving and scuba lessons, a water aerobics pool, a hydrotherapy pool, a wading pool and a children's playground pool. There are also exercise and weight rooms, racquetball and handball courts, a .2-mile indoor running track and an impressive climbing wall where local search-and-rescue teams train. In addition, the Rec Center has a children's play center and an adjoining senior citizens' center.

The $8.8 million Rec Center is unique as a civic facility in that it was built totally with private donations, with no tax dollars involved. Thirteen thousand Idahoans became charter

---

INSIDERS' TIP

Children love the Boise River Greenbelt, which extends 19 miles from the southeast to the northwest through the heart of the city. Riverside facilities include Wheels R Fun, at the end of S. 13th Street, (208) 343-8228, which rents bicycles and in-line skates for excursions up and down the network of paved paths.

members for annual passes before its doors even opened. Five thousand more have since joined.

Daily (youth $4, adults $6), summer and annual passes are available. The Center is open 6 AM to 10 PM Monday through Saturday and 1 to 6 PM Sunday.

Amusing Diversions

Boise

Fun Center
5290 Franklin Rd. • (208) 345-1898

An 18-hole miniature golf course, pool tables, table tennis and air-hockey tables, a video arcade and a snack bar are the highlights of this indoor amusement center in the Franklin Shopping Center (at the corner of Orchard Street).

It's open 10 AM to midnight Sunday through Thursday and 10 AM to 1 AM Friday and Saturday. There's no admission fee, but each activity has a charge.

Game World
7709 W. Overland Rd. • (208) 376-3833

This brand-new, 9,000-square-foot video arcade, featuring numerous virtual-reality and simulation games as well as more commonplace amusements, opened in December 1997 next door to a new cinema complex. Hours are 11 AM to midnight Monday through Thursday; 11 AM to 1 AM Friday and Saturday; and 11 AM to 11 PM Sunday.

Golf Mountain
1801 N. Wildwood St. • (208) 327-0780

The Treasure Valley's only outdoor miniature golf complex has three separate 18-hole courses with all of the obstacles minigolf players come to anticipate. It also has horseshoe pits and basketball and sand-volleyball courts, which make it a popular place for family outings.

Located north of Fairview Avenue near Five Mile Road, it's open from March through November, 3 to 7 PM Tuesday through Friday, noon to 7 PM Saturday and noon to 5 PM Sunday. Greens fees are $5 for 18 holes, $7 for 36 holes and $10 for 54 holes per player.

Po-Jo's Food-n-Fun
7736 Fairview Ave. • (208) 376-6981

Idaho's only indoor carousel — visible from Fairview Avenue through giant glass windows — highlights Boise's longest established amusement center. Ticket-redemption games, a huge video and pinball arcade (including one section in which all games cost just a nickel to play), four virtual-reality pods and a bumper-car arena add to the fun. Po-Jo's Carousel Cafe serves a wide selection of burgers, pizza and ice-cream desserts.

The arcade is open 10 AM to 1 AM Monday to Saturday, 11 AM to 1 AM Sunday.

Q-Zar of Boise
2110 Broadway Ave. • (208) 342-6265

Techno-rock music and a light-enhancing mist are special features of Q-Zar's 4,000-square-foot arena, which welcomes players of all ages (although usually not younger than 5) to play laser tag. Teams of anywhere from one to 20 players join in 15-minute games, trying to accumulate the top score of the month and win free games. Q-Zar also has a video arcade, ticket-redemption games and a full pizza parlor.

The amusement center is open 11 AM to midnight Monday through Thursday, 11 AM to 1 AM Friday and Saturday and noon to 10 PM Sunday. Standard rates are $5 per person per game, or $15 for an all-day pass. Group rates and discounts are also available.

Ray Sorensen Family Fun Center
3883 S. Orchard St. • (208) 344-2008

Golf, baseball and go-carts: This facility holds its greatest appeal to teenage youth. There's a nine-hole pitch-and-putt course, a driving range, batting cages, a go-cart track and — especially for younger children — bumper cars. The Family Fun Center also has a snack bar.

It's closed from November to mid-February, but otherwise opens from 9 AM to 6 PM in spring and fall, 8 AM to 10 PM in summer. Call for specific hours and activity fees.

Tilt
Boise Towne Square, 350 N. Milwaukee St. • (208) 375-5054

Video games, pinball and driving and flying simulators keep young hands busy at this arcade, where Mom or Dad might be tempted to leave Junior for an hour or two while they shop. Hours are 10 AM to 9 PM Monday to Saturday, noon to 6 PM Sunday.

Actual Reality Laser Tag
9115 Chinden Blvd., Garden City
• (208) 377-9966

A 3,000-square-foot maze arena, complete with fog and black lights, provides the setting for teams of 10 players who seek and destroy opponents with infrared laser guns. Relax, parents: It's the newest slant on what we used to call "cowboys and Indians." The amusement center, which is fully handicapped-accessible, also has a video arcade, snack bar and viewing room to watch the laser-tag activities.

Hours are noon to 10 PM Monday through Thursday, 11 AM to midnight Friday and Saturday and 1 to 6 PM Sunday. Standard rates are $5.50 for one game, $10 for two, but a wide range of group rates and discounts — including a birthday party special — are available.

Paintball Sports
37 E. Broadway Ave., Meridian
• (208) 887-7707

Talk about taking out frustrations: This is the place to do it! Players wander through a strobe-lit labyrinth within this 50,000-square-foot building, crossing catwalks, finding their way through castles and pyramids, as they track opponents and shoot them with paintballs.

A day pass, priced at $25, gives players a gun, a mask and 100 rounds of ammunition. Each additional 100 rounds cost $6. The facility is open 11 AM to 11 PM daily.

Nampa

Po-Jo's Cookies-n-Cream
Karcher Mall, Caldwell and Midland Blvds. • (208) 466-7660

Video games, pinball and arcade games — Skee-Ball, water-gun marksmanship and the like, in which tickets earned can be redeemed for prizes — keeps kids occupied while parents shop. It's open 10 AM to 10 PM Monday through Friday, 10 AM to 9 PM Saturday and 11 AM to 6 PM Sunday.

Reading Hour

Boise

Barnes & Noble
1315 N. Milwaukee St. • (208) 375-4454

Don't be surprised if you see Winnie the Pooh or the Cat in the Hat wandering through the aisles of this huge bookstore. They're some of the celebrities who occasionally make appearances to promote the store's 14,000-plus children's titles, as well as kid-oriented books on cassette, computer software and compact discs. There are story times every week at 7:30 PM Thursdays and 1 PM Saturdays, and special holiday events might include Easter egg painting and Halloween mask making. Pick up a copy of B & N's free monthly events calendar for details.

Boise Public Library!
715 S. Capitol Blvd. • (208) 384-4200

If you thought a library was just books … guess again! Boise's central library, across the street from Julia Davis Park, has all kinds of events for kids. Preschoolers are especially well catered to, with regular story hours during the day, and a variety of programs that include singing, puppet shows and sometimes short films. Plus, youngsters can check out "Kid Packs" on particular subjects (dinosaurs, for instance, or frogs) that include books, a movie, a puppet, a puzzle and an activity board.

Throughout the year, weekend programs and parties themed to holidays are designed to appeal to elementary-school children. Library volunteers often visit schools to discuss books, and classes through high school are welcomed en masse to the library, where they can check out films and cassette tapes as well as books.

The Library! — its exclamation mark was donated by a local pizza-parlor chain — is open 10 AM to 6 PM Mondays and Fridays, 10 AM to 9 PM Tuesdays, Wednesdays and Thursdays and noon to 5 PM Saturdays and Sundays. It's closed on Sundays during the summer.

Library cards are free to Boise residents, who benefit from an open-access agreement with the libraries of Ada County, 10664 W. Victory Road, (208) 362-0181; Caldwell, 1010 Dearborn Street, (208) 459-3242; Eagle, 67 E. State Street, (208) 939-6814; Garden City, 201 E. 50th Street, (208) 377-2180; Meridian, 1326 W. Cherry Lane, (208) 888-4451; and Nampa, 101 11th Avenue S., (208) 465-2263.

Borders Books & Music
1123 N. Milwaukee St. • (208) 322-6668

With more than 20,000 children's titles in stock and a wide choice of music to boot, Borders is a great destination in its own right. Literary activity gets a boost from weekly and monthly events planned just for young 'uns. Story times for 3- to 8-year-olds, at noon Saturday and 7 PM Wednesday, are visited monthly by costumed characters like Arthur the Aardvark and Corduroy the Bear. Young adults attend occasional theme-related parties, like one in late 1997 for author Brian Jacques' "Redwall" series. Once a month a children's musician performs. Advance sign-up is requested only for seasonal craft events such as the making of Christmas ornaments. See Borders' free monthly events calendar for details.

Kid Stuff Books 'n' Gifts
803 W. Bannock St. • (208) 336-1122

Boise's best child-oriented bookstore also sells audio and video tapes, CD-ROM discs for computers, puzzles, puppets, games and much more. Special orders are welcomed. The downtown store is closed Sunday and Monday.

The Joys of Toys

Boise

The Children's Store
137 Benjamin Ln. • (208) 322-4366

Educational and European-import toys that you're unlikely to get at large franchise outlets are the stock here. There are French dolls and accessories, German craft kits, model trains from Switzerland. The inventory also features scientific toys, books and puzzles geared to a more affluent and well-

educated clientele than less-expensive toy stores. Brand names include Playmobil, K'Nex and Rainbow Play Systems.

Hobby Town USA
501 N. Milwaukee St. • (208) 376-1942

A full-line hobby store, Hobby Town specializes in model trains, plastic model kits, radio-controlled cars and airplanes, launch rockets, pine-car supplies and the like. There are also collectible sports cards, games and coin-collecting supplies. While the clientele is largely adult, children from the age of 8 or 9 usually find something of interest.

Kay-Bee Toys
Boise Towne Square, 350 N. Milwaukee St. • (208) 377-1720
Boise Factory Outlet Mall, 6904 S. Eisenman Rd. • (208) 331-1964

One of the country's largest toy franchises, Kay-Bee has a wide range of toys from U.S. and Asian manufacturers, many of them at discounted prices.

Learning Express
The Marketplace, 1746 W. State St. • (208) 389-9911

Preschoolers through junior high-age children will find lots of great things in this new store: arts-and-crafts starters, science and nature kits, European-made construction sets and much more. There's a small but prominent selection of educational books and music, puzzles and games, and for toddlers, a full wall of developmental toys.

Ralph's Toys & Hobbies
Overland and S. Five Mile Rds. • (208) 376-0027

A child-oriented hobby shop, Ralph's stocks things like paint-by-number kits, graph sketch boards, Barbie dolls and accessories, model cars and planes, chemistry sets, telescopes, pottery wheels, rock tumblers, hacky sacks and a wall full of board games.

Scientific Wizardry
9925 Fairview Ave. • (208) 377-8575

High-quality educational toys — including such construction toys as Legos and Robotix, a range of art supplies, science kits with microscopes and telescopes — keep this store at a higher standard than most. Books, games and puzzles are also sold. The store is closed Sundays.

Toycrafters World
276 N. 8th St. • (208) 345-2971

Collector teddy bears, Russian nesting dolls, German cuckoo clocks and novelty dolls are among the specialty items you'll find at this intriguing store in downtown Boise. There's also a range of high-quality educational toys and games, including Playmobil and Lego sets at competitive prices.

Toys 'R' Us
131 N. Milwaukee St. • (208) 322-1915

The superstore for toy shoppers, Toys 'R' Us has made its name on size. The Treasure Valley store, for instance, across the street from Towne Square Mall, covers 45,000 square feet. All top manufacturer brands are carried here, but because buying is done exclusively at the corporation's New Jersey headquarters, there is no local control over purchasing.

Clothes Encounters

Boise

Carter Childrens Wear
Boise Factory Outlet Mall, 6998 S. Eisenman Rd. • (208) 336-4224

Carter and Baby Dior clothing to size 6 is carried by this factory outlet store. Don't expect to find anything for children older than kindergarten age.

Esse Baby
800 W. Idaho St. • (208) 331-2255

Designer clothing, shoes and accessories for the newborn to kindergarten set are the focus of this shop in downtown Boise's Mode Building. There is talk of expanding the inventory to include older children in 1998.

The Gap Kids
347 N. Milwaukee St. • (208) 378-8173

Children from newborn to age 16 can be garbed at the Boise store of this worldwide

clothing company. The inventory, which turns over every six weeks, tends toward casual but includes less formal dress clothing: corduroys, button-down shirts and ties, for instance. The store is located across the street from Boise Towne Square.

Once Upon a Child
Westpark Plaza, 435 N. Milwaukee St. • (208) 376-1077

Children's clothing, equipment and accessories are bought and sold at this exchange store, which advertises "kids' stuff with previous experience." You'll get real bargains here on brand-name apparel, shoes and bedding, as well as cribs and strollers, swings and bouncers, changing tables and car seats, lamps and dressers, toys and play equipment. The shop is closed Sundays.

Other Mothers
10470 Fairview Ave. • (208) 376-4855

Children's garments (size 0 through 14) and maternity attire are sold at this west Boise clothing exchange, as well as baby furniture and pre-owned toys. It's closed on Sunday.

Touch the Moon
821 W. Idaho St. • (208) 367-1644

Local designers, such as Muktuk and Lulu's, have contributed heavily to the inventory of this upscale children's store in downtown Boise. The clothes for newborns through preteens (size 14) tend toward casual for school and play, but dressier holiday garb is also available. You'll find shoes, socks and hats here, a few toys and children's music on CD and tape.

The Gang's All Here

Boise

Boy Scouts of America
Ore-Ida Council, 8901 W. Franklin Rd. • (208) 376-4411

The regional Boy Scout headquarters is the clearinghouse for information on Cub Scout, Boy Scout and Explorer programs

Photo: William H. Mullins

These wranglers are ready to ride!

for youth 8 to 18 years old. The council has several summer camps in addition to providing supervision for dozens of Scout troops.

4-H Club, Ada County Extension
Western Idaho Fairgrounds, 5880 Glenwood St. • (208) 377-2107

Young farmers, horticulturists and homemakers ages 5 to 19 are actively involved with this club and its rural orientation. The raising of livestock, vegetables and fruit, and home-oriented projects like cooking, crafts and clothing production, are popular activities, with the year's successes showcased at the state fair in August. The club costs $7 a year.

Silver Sage Girl Scout Council
1410 Etheridge Ln. • (208) 377-2011

Brownies (age 8 to 11) and Girl Scouts (11 to 17) are under the jurisdiction of this regional council. Summer camps are popular, and most troops have weekly and monthly activities.

Boys & Girls Club of Ada County
610 E. 42nd St., Garden City • (208) 321-9157

This small after-school club beside the Boise River in Garden City is open to all youth 6 to 18 years old, with an annual membership

fee of just $10. Kids enter into a large game room with pool and Foosball tables; there's a computer room, an arts-and-crafts room, dance and movie clubs and more. Like similar clubs in other parts of the United States, it is located in a less-affluent part of the metropolitan area and emphasizes wholesome activities quite apart from any gang-related involvement. It's open 3 to 8 PM Monday through Friday during the school year, 11 AM to 6 PM in summer, and extended weekend hours are anticipated.

Learning Opportunities

Boise

Ballet Idaho Academy of Dance
501 S. 8th St., Ste. A • (208) 336-3241

Children age 3½ and older are welcome to enroll in ballet, tap, jazz and modern dancing classes under the tutelage of professional dancers. The best are invited to dance with the Ballet Idaho Youth Company. In addition to this academy, there are (at current count) nine other dance schools in the Boise area. (For more information about Ballet Idaho, see The Arts chapter.)

Boise Parks & Recreation
1104 Royal Blvd. • (208) 384-4240

A year-round series of evening and weekend classes — geared mainly to youngsters and teenagers, but on a smaller level also to adults — is offered by the parks department. Classes include arts and crafts, dance, basketball, golf, karate and swimming. In addition, the parks department sponsors city league play in basketball and volleyball and supports soccer and softball leagues. Most classes are held at the Fort Boise Community Center, 700 Robbins Road, (208) 384-4486.

Ceramica
598 W. Main St. • (208) 342-3822

This corner shop in Old Boise invites drop-ins to make their own pottery, from wheel and kiln to glazing and painting. Children of all ages are welcome to join their parents in the process. It's open 10 AM to 5 PM Tuesday through Saturday and noon to 5 PM Sunday.

Gem State Gymnastics Academy
5420 W. State St. • (208) 853-3220

Continuing gymnastics classes for kindergarten through 8th graders are the mainstay of this school after school. But classes in dancing, swimming and self-defense also are offered here. It's the best known of five gymnastics school in Boise.

Idaho Theater for Youth
Eighth Street Marketplace, 404 S. 8th St. • (208) 345-0060

Is there a child actor in your midst? The Drama School offers a series of youth acting classes that lead to work with the theater's performing company, known as ITY Mainstage. Classes are given for 2nd graders up to age 18. (See The Arts chapter for more information.)

PCS Edventures
2675 W. Main St. • (208) 345-8606

Children take a rapid step into the 21st century with PCS, which offers training in computers, the Internet, robotics, lasers, engineering and other high-tech "stuff." The young learners' program welcomes preschoolers (3 to 6), while older children come for PCS' after-school enrichment programs.

Off to Camp

Boise

Adventures Unlimited
10317 Barnsdale Dr. • (208) 376-9773

Youngsters and their parents join this summer outdoor adventure camp to take part in horseback riding, whitewater rafting, wind surfing, water skiing, mountain biking and backpacking.

Downtown Boise Family YMCA
1050 W. State St. • (208) 344-5501

Spring and winter day camps and summer residence camps are part of the annual program both at this Y and the West Family YMCA, 5959 N. Discovery Place, (208) 377-9622. Day-camp centers set up during school holidays are in Boise, Eagle, Meridian and Garden City. Weeklong summer camps in Idaho's national forests include such activities as swimming, canoeing, archery and evening campfires. See Activity Centers in this chapter for more information about the Ys' daily programs.

Gem State Gymnastics Academy
5420 W. State St. • (208) 853-3220

Summer camps for children ages 5 to 12 incorporate not just gymnastics activities, but also swimming lessons, crafts making, science instruction and field trips. A teen camp incorporates swimming and gymnastics with hiking and biking trips. See Learning Opportunities in this chapter for more information on the academy.

INSIDERS' TIP

It should go without saying, but never leave a child (or pet) alone in a vehicle, even for a few minutes, during the heat of summer when temperatures inside a car can rise to 150 degrees in a matter of minutes.

Idaho Botanical Garden
2355 Old Penitentiary Rd.
• (208) 343-8649

A half-day nature camp for children 5 to 9 is offered for two weeks each August from 9 AM to noon. See Out and About Town in this chapter to learn more about the garden.

Log Cabin Literary Center
801 S. Capitol Blvd. • (208) 331-8000

Boise's center for the literary arts offers half-day summer camps in July that encourage children in three different age groups, from elementary to high school, to express themselves through the written word. Some scholarships are available. The center also has programs for adults. See The Arts chapter for details.

Wings Center
1875 Century Way • (208) 376-3641

Day camps are offered in winter, spring and especially summer for school-age children. They include swimming and gymnastics, and for older children, miniature golf and rock climbing. See Activity Centers in this chapter for more details on Wings Center.

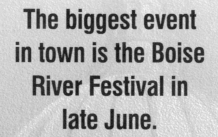

The biggest event in town is the Boise River Festival in late June.

Annual Events and Festivals

Boiseans love their music. They love their food. They love their arts and their cultural heritage. They *really* love their outdoor sports: running, bicycling, rafting, skiing.

It comes as no surprise that these are the passions that inspire Boise-area citizens in a series of festivals and events that extend throughout the year.

The biggest event of all is the Boise River Festival in late June. Established in 1991, it has grown in a few short years to be ranked as one of the top-10 summer festivals in the United States. (See the Close-up in this chapter for more information.)

But myriad other events also capture Idahoans' hearts, depending upon what time of year it may be. Some festivals are traditional country-town harvest festivals, such as Payette's Apple Blossom Festival and Emmett's Cherry Festival. Some acknowledge the region's cultural heritage, such as Cinco de Mayo and the Basque Festival of San Inazio. Others pay tribute to cowboy history (the Snake River Stampede) or Oregon Trail Days (the Three Island Crossing re-enactment).

Bicycle races, a whitewater carnival, ski competitions and the nation's largest women-only run/walk — the Idaho Women's Fitness Celebration — underscore the city's devotion to recreational sports.

Some occasions focus on culture: the Idaho Shakespeare Festival, Art in the Park. Some highlight music: Jazz at the Winery, the National Old-Time Fiddlers Contest.

But the most popular events seem to be merely fun: the Western Idaho Fair, the McCall Winter Carnival and "Alive After Five," a Boise civic celebration held every Wednesday from May to September.

In this chapter, we describe many of the annual celebrations that bring spark to life in Idaho's Treasure Valley. We give approximate dates to most, but you should call event organizers to confirm dates before making plans to attend, as dates and locations sometimes change.

Outdoor events are generally free; we'll let you know if there is an admission charge. A typical festival has many free attractions and a few that charge admission, such as a concert or a street dance; we've designated these, "Free admission to most events." But even at free events, you should make sure you have cash on hand for food booths and souvenir vendors.

For up-to-the-minute information on events, be sure to look at the Friday "Scene" section of *The Idaho Statesman* in Boise, the Thursday "More" section of Nampa's *Idaho Press-Tribune*, or the alternative *Boise Weekly*, which hits newsstands on Thursday mornings.

January

Meridian Chili Cook-off
Meridian Speedway, 335 E. 1st St., Meridian • (208) 888-2817

Judges insist that the hottest Texas-style stews in Idaho are produced during this winter warm-up that draws about 1,500 tasters to Boise's commuter suburb. The cook-off is held on Super Bowl Saturday, the last Saturday in January. There is a limit of 20 teams that participate; registration begins in October. Entry fees are $25 to $75, with businesses, individuals and community organizations charged different amounts. Tasters pay a $3 admission fee.

McCall Winter Carnival
McCall • (208) 634-7631

A world-class ice sculpture competition near the shores of Payette Lake highlights this community-wide fest that annually attracts some 20,000 people to the little resort town of McCall. For 10 days beginning the last Friday in January or the first Friday in February, there are parades and fireworks, sled-dog and snowmobile races, ski competitions and a climactic Snowflake Ball, where people dress up in their fanciest clothes for dancing and celebration. Residents also enjoy the beard and hairy-leg contests and a tongue-in-cheek variety show. Most of the activities are free.

McCall is 100 miles north of Boise on Idaho Highway 55, which runs through the center of town, where activities and events are held.

February

First Security
Winter Games of Idaho
Various locations • (208) 393-2255

Weekend athletes from 6 to 106 participate in three weeks of alpine and nordic ski racing, snowboard, snowmobile and other competitions. The principal venues are the Bogus Basin and Brundage Mountain ski areas, but one of the big events — the Boulder Mountain Tour — runs from Galena Lodge to the Sawtooth National Recreation Area north of Ketchum. This 30-kilometer cross-country race, which is part of the Great American Ski Chase, attracts Olympic-caliber contestants from around the country. The games are free to spectators; entry fees range from $10 to $40.

Valentines for AIDS
Flying M Espresso, 500 W. Idaho St., Boise • (208) 345-4320

Well-known area artists and celebrities sub-

mit valentines they've made for a silent auction in an event that began in 1993 and has grown to more than 100 entries. In 1998 about $10,000 was raised for the Idaho AIDS Foundation. The event spans four days in February beginning on the first Thursday of the month.

Idaho Boat Show
Western Idaho Fairgrounds, 5610 Glenwood St., Boise • (208) 323-1500

About 10,000 visitors turn out for the largest boat show in Boise, which is held Wednesday through the second weekend in February. Admission is $3. Powerboats, sailboats, pontoon boats and many others are on display. The Coast Guard Auxiliary is there with information, and people can sign up for boating safety classes.

Winter Gem Show
Western Idaho Fairgrounds, 5610 Glenwood St., Boise • (208) 323-1680

Traditional and creative jewelry shares the exposition hall with gem dealers and rockhounds. The retail show features the gems of 15 dealers. Displays are judged by the Idaho Gem Club. Demonstrations include working silver, polishing rocks and glass blowing. This is the perfect place to see the star garnet, Idaho's state gemstone.

The show is held on a weekend in late February. Admission is $3.

March

NAIA Men's National
Basketball Tournament
The Idaho Center, 16200 Can-Ada Rd., Nampa • (208) 467-8011

Northwest Nazarene College is the annual host of this well-attended championship tourney in mid-March. Thirty-two teams from 22 states, members of the National Association of Intercollegiate Athletics, competed for the national championships in 1998. Tickets for a four-game session cost $7. For general admission to all the games, the cost is $50; for reserved seating, $80. About 27,000 people attended in 1998.

Boise Home and Garden Show
Western Idaho Fairgrounds, 5610 Glenwood St., Boise • (208) 939-6426

One of the most popular annual events at the fairgrounds, this exhibition, as its name implies, displays all manner of products for gardeners and interior decorators. There is special pricing for the show, so it's a good place for bargains. Seminars on topics, such as fixing your own plumbing and closet arrangement, are also part of the event. Hundreds of exhibits draw a crowd of about 30,000 each year.

The show is held over a four-day period that includes a weekend in mid-March. Admission is $4.

April

Earth Day
Julia Davis Park, Capital Blvd. and River St., Boise • (208) 345-8077

Earth Day is always held the Saturday before the national recognition of Earth Day on April 22. It is sponsored by the Northern Rockies Preservation Project, which has about 400 volunteer members. The event features five or six rock, jazz and blues bands. Tables with information about the environment and political issues are set up around the park. Vegetarian and other healthy foods are for sale. Don't leave the kids at home! They get a tree to plant and can participate in painting a mural.

Mercy Community Sale
Nampa Recreation Center, 131 Constitution Way, Nampa • (208) 467-1171

An estimated 20,000 people attend this giant rummage sale in mid-April that is organized by the Mercy Medical Center to benefit the Healthy Nampa, Healthy Youth program. Anyone can donate items for this sale: The donation of furniture, household items and toys is especially encouraged. A silent auction, live auction, raffle and jewelry sale are included in the one-day event. About $76,000 was raised in 1998.

Photo: Idaho Shakespeare Festival

The words of the Bard come to life in Boise at the summer Idaho Shakespeare Festival.

BSU/Gene Harris Jazz Festival
Several venues in Boise • (208) 385-1596

Headlined by world-renowned pianist Gene Harris and sponsored by Boise State University, this festival, inaugurated in 1998, includes a series of workshops for high-schoolers. About 6,000 people attended the performances in the first year. Plans are that the event will continue to be held over four days the second week of April.

Several downtown Boise establishments present music on Wednesday night; concerts are held Thursday at the Bank of America Centre and Friday at the BSU Pavilion. Table seats at the Bank of America Centre and BSU Pavilion cost $40 to $50; seats in the stands run $14 to $25. Restaurant cover charges are $5.

May

Cinco de Mayo Festival
Caldwell Memorial Park, Kimball and Grant Sts., Caldwell • (208) 454-1652

This Mexican national holiday celebrates the

Battle of Puebla, when an outnumbered Mexican-Indian force defeated the French in 1841. The festival is always held on May 5, but the location has switched back and forth between Nampa and Caldwell in recent years. In 1998 it was held in Caldwell, and it is anticipated that Caldwell will be the site in 1999. A live band, folkloric dancing, children's activities, softball, golf and speeches made by political leaders and candidates make this a full day of events.

Apple Blossom Festival
Payette • (208) 642-2362

Rural Payette, surrounded by fruit orchards, celebrates the apple bloom with a wide range of activities, including the Great Payette Balloon Classic of hot-air vessels. Events feature the expected — a parade, a carnival, a rodeo, an arts-and-crafts exhibit — and the unexpected — an apple-bobbing race, a pie-eating contest, a pretty baby contest and the Apple Core Open Golf Tournament. The festival is held over two weeks in the middle of the month, and most activities are free.

Flower of the Desert
Spring Festival
City Park, between 1st St. N. and 2nd St. N. off Main St., Marsing • (208) 896-4122

The sage-speckled farming community of Marsing, on the Snake River at the edge of the Owyhee Desert, celebrates spring in rural fashion, with a parade, entertainment and arts and crafts displays on a Friday and Saturday in mid-May. A barbecue on Friday night is a treat for the taste buds; admission is $6 for adults, $3 for ages 5 to 12 and $1.50 for children 5 and younger. The parade is on Saturday.

Alive After Five
The Grove plaza, 8th and Grove Sts., Boise • (208) 336-2631

From mid-May through mid-September, downtown Boise's central plaza jumps with live bands, food and beer booths and plenty of mingling after work on Wednesdays. Crowds ranging from 3,000 to 7,000 attend. Rock, blues and jazz are featured during the 18 Wednesdays of the schedule. Artists perform from 5 to 7:30 PM. Different restaurants offer food, desserts and beverages on the plaza each week.

June

Greek Food Festival
St. Constantine & Helen Greek Orthodox Church, 2618 W. Bannock St., Boise
• (208) 345-6147

Balkan entertainers perform from 11 AM to 9 PM on the first Saturday and Sunday of the month as celebrants munch on dolmades, spanikopita and baklava. Attendance approaches 5,000. The festival began in 1981 and is held inside the church and on the surrounding grounds. Admission is $1 for adults; children 12 and younger get in free.

Old Fort Boise Days
Fort Boise Replica, Parma
• (208) 342-0777

This is the site of the original Fort Boise, built of adobe in 1834. The fort eventually became a Hudson Bay Company trading port and later a haven for many Oregon Trail travelers. It was wiped out by flood waters in 1853 and rebuilt as a smaller fort in 1854. After another flood whisked it downstream, it served as a ferry location for nearly 40 years.

Old Fort Boise Days are held near the site of the original Oregon Trail fort on the first weekend in June. Events include a tractor pull, mud volleyball, chili cook-off and a variety of other rural activities as well as a parade, carnival and tour of the fort itself.

Owyhee Outpost Days
Murphy • (208) 495-2319

Demonstrations of lost pioneer skills and crafts highlight this local celebration the first Sunday in June, which benefits the Owyhee County Historical Museum. There are food booths and a horned toad race. The event is held behind the courthouse of this small town on Idaho Highway 78.

An auction of donated items — paintings, photos, antiques, quilts — is the main attraction. Local kids catch horn-toad lizards, name them and enter them in the race. The toads are put in a bucket and let loose. The first one out of the bull's-eye circle wins his proud owner a toad trophy. Food includes baked potatoes, barbecue ribs, hamburgers and ice cream. As many as 3,000 people have attended.

Eagle Fun Days
State St., Eagle • (208) 939-5588

Eagle Fun Days are held on a Friday and Saturday in early June. A golf tournament is held Friday, and Saturday begins with a pancake breakfast, parade and car show. A carnival runs through the day. Tickets bought ahead of time are $10 for an all-day pass; at the carnival, they're $17. What carnival organizers claim is the world's largest Rocky Mountain Oyster Feed — also called "The Nut Feed" — begins Saturday afternoon.

The location is about 10 miles from downtown Boise. Follow State Street through the middle of Eagle, where the events are held.

Cherry Festival
Johns and Main Sts., Emmett
• (208) 365-3485

The Payette River community of Emmett celebrates its annual cherry harvest with pie-eating and cherry pit-spitting contests, yacht and hot-air balloon races. There's also a carnival, a Civil War encampment, a quilt show and a horseshoe-pitching competition. In the evening, square dancers do-si-do to a live band. Most activities are free.

The Cherry Festival is always held the second full week in June, with most activities scheduled for Wednesday through Saturday.

Dairy Days
Meridian • (208) 888-2817

The west Boise suburb of Meridian recalls its dairy-farming heritage with events that include a pancake feed, a community auction, a fun run, a parade and a carnival. Area farmers are joined by members of the 4-H Clubs and Future Farmers of America in exhibiting their finest dairy cattle. Most activities are free during these four days in mid-June.

National Old-Time Fiddlers' Contest and Festival
Weiser High School, Weiser
• (208) 549-0452, (800) 437-1280

America's most prestigious country fiddlers' contest attracts 330 to 350 of the top nonprofessional fiddlers in the country. It is held Monday through Saturday of the third full week in June. To reach Weiser from Boise, take Interstate 84 N. to U.S. Highway 95 N.

onto State Street in Weiser. Turn left on Indian Head Road, which leads to Weiser High School. Weiser is 72 miles from Boise.

The contest has eight categories of competition — small fry, junior juniors, junior, young students, adults, seniors, senior seniors and grand champions. Six judges from across the United States choose the most fabulous fiddlers.

Tickets for the preliminary competition cost $2. Tickets for the evening final rounds and accompanying entertainment cost $6 to $12. Though the competitions are very entertaining, perhaps the best shows of fiddling expertise are the jam sessions in the parking lot and parks around town that start in the early morning and go on until 2 or 3 AM. The jam sessions are free. A Saturday parade through Weiser and arts and crafts booths set up in Weiser are also part of the festivities.

Jazz at the Winery
Ste. Chapelle Winery, 19348 Lowell Rd., Caldwell • (208) 459-7222,
(800) 743-9549

Jazz pianist Gene Harris, swing band leader Gib Hochstrasser and blues favorites Fat John and the Three Slims are among the top-flight performers at the winery's outdoor amphitheater on Sunday afternoons from mid-June to mid-August. Folks come from miles around to spread their blankets on the grass and enjoy picnic lunches with bottles of Ste. Chapelle's own fine vintages. Admission is $5, except when Gene Harris and his full band are playing. When Gene is playing alone, admission is $10.

Idaho Shakespeare Festival
5657 Warm Springs Ave., Boise
• (208) 323-9700, (208) 336-9221 box office

The play's the thing at Boise's version of Shakespeare under the stars. For more than 20 years this band of thespians has brought the Bard's words to life from mid-June to Labor Day. A new (in 1998), outdoor amphitheater in northeast Boise offers 600 seats to festivalgoers.

Each year, the festival committee presents three of Shakespeare's works plus a more recent work. Recently the festival featured *Romeo* and Juliet, Cymbeline and A Midsummer Night's Dream. For reserved seating, call the box office at the previously listed number.

Tickets for individual plays cost $18 to $26. A season's ticket costs $64 for adults, $60 for seniors 60 and older and $44 for full-time students.

Hewlett-Packard International Women's Challenge
Boise and surrounding highways • (208) 345-7223

This bicycle race attracts close to 150 female competitors from around the world. Past winners include Australian Anna Wilson and Lithuanian Rasa Polikevicinte. The race is done in stages from Boise to Stanley, in the Sawtooth Mountains north of Sun Valley, over a distance of hundreds of miles. Spectators are estimated at 50,000 total. The event is held over a full week in late June, and there's no charge to cheer your favorite cyclist on to victory.

Boise River Festival
Morrison and Davis parks and downtown Boise • (208) 338-8887

Boise's signature celebration extends for four days around the last weekend in June. More than 300 family-oriented events include the largest inflatable parade west of the Mississippi, a major hot-air balloon rally and music and entertainment on seven separate stages. Best of all, every event, including major concerts, is free. See this chapter's close-up for more details.

Bite of Boise
Outdoors on The Grove, 8th and Grove Sts., Boise • (208) 336-2631

Presented simultaneously with the River Festival, Bite of Boise brings together 16 or more Boise restaurants, each of whom offer menu samples, and eight leading local rock, blues, and jazz bands, who perform for two to three hours each on Thursday and Friday from 4 to 10:30 PM and Saturday from 10:30 AM to 10:30 PM over the last weekend of the month.

Alive After Five
The Grove plaza, 8th and Grove Sts., Boise • (208) 336-2631

Looking for something to rejuvenate you in the middle of the work week? Well, come on down to the Grove for bands, booze and buddies on Wednesdays from mid-May to mid-September. (See our entry under May for more information.)

July

Independence Day Celebrations
Various locations • (208) 344-7777

Pyrotechnic displays shower Ann Morrison Park, the Western Idaho Fairgrounds and other locations throughout the Treasure Valley, as Idahoans pay tribute to their nation's independence. Many people watch the fairgrounds fireworks from the Bench, or bluffs, west of Chinden Boulevard. Mountain View Drive is also a popular spot.

BSU SummerFest
Centennial Amphitheater, Boise State University, 2201 Campus Ln., Boise • (208) 385-1596

The Boise Chamber Orchestra, the Boise Big Band and other artists perform pops and classical music during this outdoor event organized by the Boise State University Music Department. The festival is held during the three weekends in the middle of the month in a beautiful outdoor amphitheater beside the Boise River. Spectators are apt to bring picnic dinners and beverages. Tickets cost $8.50 for

---

INSIDERS' TIP

First Thursday, so named because it's held the first Thursday of each month, is an after-work gallery walk sponsored by downtown Boise merchants. Free wine, hors d'oeuvres and light musical entertainment are offered by the owners and employees of many establishments, who welcome the opportunity to meet shoppers in a relaxed atmosphere.

each night's performance or $22 for three performances on successive weekends.

Payette Whitewater Rodeo
Payette River, at Banks and Horseshoe Bend • (800) 292-RAFT

Cascade Raft and Kayak, 26 miles north of Boise between Horseshoe Bend and Banks on Idaho Highway 55, is the headquarters and sponsor of this event that takes place the first weekend after July 4. Possibly the only "junior" rodeo in the country for kayak racers younger than 18 takes place Friday morning at The Gutter, across from the cemetery in Horseshoe Bend on the Payette River. Friday evening in Banks features a river rescue presentation. Adult racers compete at Otter's Slide," 2 miles north of Banks, Saturday and Sunday. Top amateur and a broad range of recreational racers compete in expert, intermediate and beginner classes. Entry fees are $25 for two events, and entrants receive a T-shirt. There is also a raft challenge. A beginner's kayak race that has attracted celebrities such as Boise Mayor Brent Coles is held on Saturday afternoon. Saturday night features a casual dinner/dance at Cascade Raft and Kayak, where well-known Boise band Fat John and the Three Slims perform. The cost is $7.50 per person. Hundreds of spectators line the river to watch the events. There's no charge to watch the race.

Western Idaho Powwow Association Powwow
Horseshoe Bend High School, Idaho Hwy. 55, Horseshoe Bend • (208) 343-1528

About 200 Native American dancers from Idaho, the West Coast, North and South Dakota and other locations compete in dancing competitions over a three-day weekend the second week of July. The grand entrance on Friday and exit on Sunday are particularly popular spectator events. Admission is $5 for adults; $3 for students and for seniors 55 and older.

Snake River Stampede
The Idaho Center, 16200 Can-Ada Rd., Nampa • (208) 466-8497, (208) 468-1000

Ranked as one of the top 25 rodeos in the United States (it rated 21st in prize money in 1996), the Stampede moved indoors for the first time in 1997 and was better than ever. In addition to arena events — which include bareback and saddle bronc riding, bull riding, calf roping, steer wrestling and barrel racing — the Stampede includes a parade through downtown Nampa, a Good Old Days street fair, a buckaroo breakfast, with flapjacks, eggs, potatoes and sausages, and evening concerts by some of America's foremost country-and-western stars. The fun lasts for five days over the third weekend in July.

Canyon County Fair
Canyon County Fairgrounds, 1122 S. 22nd Ave., Caldwell • (208) 459-9266

This five-day fair spilling into a weekend in late July goes back to 1887.

A livestock competition features the animals of students in 4-H and FFA organizations. Agricultural exhibits and a three-day horse show reinforce the county-fair feel. Performances are staged by local rock and Christian bands as well as by Hispanic and Basque dancers. Admission is $1 per person.

McCall Folk Music Festival
University of Idaho Field Campus, Ponderosa State Park, McCall • (208) 634-7631

Established in 1979, this festival offers three nights of music beside Payette Lake during the last weekend in July. Thursday is Locals' Night, featuring homegrown talent. Folk and bluegrass performers from other parts of the Northwest perform on Friday night. On Saturday night, world music holds forth: In 1997, a Brazilian dance-and-percussion troupe wowed the audience. Tickets cost $8 for a night's performances or $21 for the full weekend.

First Security Twilight Criterium
Downtown Boise • (208) 393-2255

This circular road race between 9th and 6th and Main and Idaho streets was first held in 1986. The streets are closed off, and the race begins at twilight. About 150 competitors, who are registered with the U.S. Cycling Association, come from around the country and abroad. The main event has a $10,000 purse and $3,000 for first place; winners in lower categories win watches and gift certificates. An estimated 10,000 spectators line the streets for this event, held on the last Saturday of July or first Saturday of August.

Jazz at the Winery
Ste. Chapelle Winery, 19348 Lowell Rd., Caldwell • (208) 459-7222, (800) 743-9549

Spend the afternoon wining and dining the one you love. Sundays from mid-June through mid-August at Ste. Chapelle feature performances by jazz, swing band and blues musicians accompanied by vintages produced at the winery. (See our entry under June for more information.)

San Inazio Basque Festival
601 Grove St. and other locations, Boise • (208) 343-2671

San Inazio (St. Ignatius) is the patron saint of Europe's Basque Country, and the observation of his July 31 birthday (held over the closest weekend to July 31) gives local Basques a good reason to close off Grove Street in front of the Basque Cultural Center for Saturday afternoon demonstrations of music and dance, sports and games. In the evening, San Inazio's Mass is celebrated at St. John's Cathedral. Families gather for a Sunday picnic at Municipal Park, and there are dances on Grove Street Saturday and Sunday nights. Most activities are free.

Alive After Five
The Grove plaza, 8th and Grove Sts., Boise • (208) 336-2631

In cities across the nation, everyone is working for the weekend. But in Boise, everyone's working for Wednesday — Alive After Five Wednesdays that is. From mid-May through mid-September, downtown Boise's central plaza offers weary workers munchies, music and mingling. (See our May entry for more information.)

Idaho Shakespeare Festival
5657 Warm Springs Ave., Boise • (208) 323-9700, (208) 336-9221 box office

Fools and fairies, heroes and hellions entertain and enlighten during performances held from mid-June to Labor Day. Each summer the

players present three of Shakespeare's works as well as a more contemporary piece. (See our entry under June for more information.)

August

Three Island Crossing Re-enactment
Three Island State Park, Glenns Ferry • (208) 366-2394

During the second weekend in August, horses and riders recreate an 1840s fording of the Snake River by a pioneer wagon train on the Oregon Trail. Although there were perils involved with such a crossing, the desert transit along the south side of the Snake, west of here, was even more dangerous … and these three sandbars were the safest place to cross the river. The celebration also features a mountain-man rendezvous with black-powder shooting demonstrations, an ice-cream social, a Western barbecue, arts-and-crafts exhibits and a parade through downtown Glenns Ferry. Admission is free.

Glenns Ferry is 78 miles east of Boise on Interstate 84; signs at the freeway exit lead to the park.

Caldwell Night Rodeo
Rodeo Grounds, 2301 Blaine St., Caldwell • (208) 459-2060

Five consecutive nights of bull and bronco riding, roping, wild-horse racing and clowning around in mid-August has grown so big that even ESPN airs its finals. First held in 1924, it is now the 20th-ranked rodeo in the United States with annual prize money exceeding $200,000. The Miss Rodeo Idaho contest is held in conjunction with these events.

Adult tickets cost $10.50 Tuesday through Friday, $12.50 on Saturday. Tuesday and Wednesday offer a special rate of $8.50 to seniors 65 and older. Children younger than 12 get in for $4.50 Tuesday and Wednesday, $7.50 Thursday through Saturday.

Idaho Shakespeare Festival
5657 Warm Springs Ave., Boise • (208) 323-9700, (208) 336-9221 box office

The Idaho Shakespeare Festival presents a full summer of the Bard from mid-June to Labor

The River Giants parade is one of many events held during the four-day Boise River Festival.

Day. Recent past performances have included *Macbeth*, *The Taming of Shrew*, *Romeo and Juliet* and *A Midsummer Night's Dream*. (See our entry under June for more information.)

Jazz at the Winery
Ste. Chapelle Winery, 19348 Lowell Rd., Caldwell • (208) 459-7222, (800) 743-9549

Ste. Chapelle's amphitheater comes alive with wine and music lovers Sunday afternoons

from mid-June through mid-August. Enjoy the mellow melodies of blues, jazz and swing bands while you sample one of Ste. Chapelle's own vintages. (See our entry under June for more information.)

Western Idaho Fair
Western Idaho Fairgrounds, 5610 Glenwood St., Boise • (208) 376-3247

Idaho's oldest (founded in 1897) and largest (250,000 attendance) fair still follows a tried-and-true formula. The nine-day event, which begins on the third Friday in August, features trade and agricultural exhibits, a large carnival and food court and almost-nightly concerts by rock and country stars. The animals are the big draws: horses, cattle, swine, sheep, poultry, rabbits, llamas and enough other creatures to keep you at the fair until the cows come home. Admission is $5 for adults, $2 for children 6 to 11 and seniors.

Alive After Five
The Grove plaza, 8th and Grove Sts., Boise • (208) 336-2631

Celebrate the middle of the work week at Alive After Five. Held on Wednesdays from mid-May through mid-September, these minifestivals soothe jangled nerves with refreshments and entertainment. (See our entry under May for more information.)

September

Boise City Arts Celebration
Downtown Boise • (208) 336-4936

Starting in front of City Hall on First Thursday, when downtown merchants sponsor their monthly gallery walk, the City Arts Celebration features free performances by many of Boise's "highbrow" performing arts groups: the Boise Philharmonic, the Idaho Shakespeare Festival, the Idaho Dance Theatre, Opera Idaho, Ballet Idaho, Idaho Theater for Youth and the Master Chorale. The Mayor's Awards for Excellence in the Arts are delivered the following Wednesday during a luncheon at the Boise Centre on the Grove. Events continue throughout the month.

Idaho Shakespeare Festival
5657 Warm Springs Ave., Boise
• (208) 323-9700, (208) 336-9221 box office

This is your last chance of the year to catch Shakespeare under the stars. Thespians of the Idaho Shakespeare Festival present the tragedies, histories and comedies of the Bard from mid-June through Labor Day at an amphitheater in northeast Boise. (See our entry under June for more information.)

Air Force Appreciation Day
Carl Miller Park, Mountain Home
• (208) 587-4334

Residents of Mountain Home, a city southeast of Boise, pay tribute to the adjacent Mountain Home Air Force Base with a parade, street fair and barbecue. Held the first Saturday after Labor Day, the highlight is a "fly-by" of jet aircraft from the base.

Art in the Park
Julia Davis Park, 700 S. Capitol Blvd., Boise • (208) 345-8330

Up to 150,000 people attend this three-day, end-of-summer arts-and-crafts festival held the weekend after Labor Day. Selected visual artists from Idaho and the intermountain West come to display — and, hopefully, to sell — their work at this outdoor festivity. You'll also find musical performances, children's activities and food booths

Gene Harris' 8th Street Block Party
Eighth and Idaho Sts., Boise
• (208) 342-9300

Idaho's premier jazz pianist and his band, the L.A. Connection, take center stage — literally — as a four-block zone of downtown Boise is closed to traffic for Harris' free two-hour concert. Nearby outdoor cafes and a tent dispensing Idaho wines and beers do a booming business. The party is held the second Thursday of the month.

Hyde Park Street Fair
Camelback Park, 13th and Heron Sts., Boise • (208) 388-8615

The North End's quintessential neighborhood pulls out all the stops for this two-day event during the second weekend in September. You'll find more than three dozen musical entertainers of all genres on two stages. Also look for more than 100 arts-and-crafts vendors, a food court, a beer garden and a small children's carnival.

Alive After Five
The Grove plaza, 8th and Grove Sts., Boise • (208) 336-2631

September marks your last opportunity of the year to enjoy these outdoor festivals that celebrate Wednesday — not a particular Wednesday, just Wednesday. From mid-May through mid-September, downtown Boise's central plaza comes alive with Boiseans of every occupation mingling, eating and imbibing their way over the hump of the work week. (See our entry under May for more information.)

Idaho Women's Fitness Celebration
Ann Morrison Park, Americana Blvd. just south of the Boise River, Boise
• (208) 331-2221

The largest one-day, women-only fitness event in the United States, this festivity, held the third Saturday of the month, is built around a 5-kilometer (3.1-mile) run/walk. Thousands of women of all ages and abilities — from 3 to 93, some of them in wheelchairs — take part in the footrace, which concludes with a celebration in the park. More than 17,000 women have participated in recent years, and numbers continue to climb. Entry fees cost $18 for an individual and $15 per member for a team of 10 women. The event recently raised $50,000 for 10 charities. ESPN televises the festivities to 100 countries. Close to 98 percent of participants are local to the area.

Floats, Fireworks and Fun Are Hallmarks of Boise River Festival

How does a city stage a $1.2 million festival with more than 300 separate events, draw hundreds of thousands of people to take part and not charge a penny for anything?

Ask Steve Schmader, president of the Boise River Festival. He's the one who pulled the four-day celebration together in late June 1991, and he's the one who holds the reins today.

"We have three things going for us here," says Schmader.

"One, we have an unusually strong corporate sponsorship base in Boise. We have some 750 corporate sponsors, many of whom make in-kind donations. There is not a company of any size in Boise that's not involved in some way.

"Two, our parks and other resources, such as museums and art centers, are concentrated along the Boise River. There can be few other cities that have an asset to compare to our Greenbelt.

"And three, there is a strong volunteer attitude in this city. We estimate that our 3,700 volunteers put in more than 40,000 hours to make this festival happen."

The Boise River Festival has been acclaimed "one of the top three new events, worldwide, created in the last 10 years" by the International Festivals and Events Association. Media have cited it as "one of the top 10 summer festivals in the United States" and "America's finest family festival."

Two parades are the festival's central events. The Idaho Statesman River Giants Parade, which runs from 10 AM to noon on Saturday, is the largest helium-inflatables

— continued on next page

Photo: William H. Mullins

Hot-air balloons take to the skies over Boise.

parade west of the Mississippi River. Boasting balloons as tall as 62 feet, it winds through downtown Boise, beginning and ending at Bronco Stadium.

At 10:30 PM on Friday and Saturday, the Albertsons Nite-Lite Parade — designed by the same Southern California company that puts together Pasadena's annual Rose Parade — dazzles downtown Boise with a dozen brightly lit floats and a half-dozen mobile show stages.

In its earliest years, the River Festival had a floating night parade down the Boise River. But the impossibility of predicting the river level led to its replacement by the Nite-Lite Parade. "We could have drought or flood," said Schmader. "It was unique but not practical. On top of that, there were a great many safety and ecology questions. Now, we have more control over the quality of the parade."

More than 100 separate entertainment acts perform on seven stages over the course of the festival's four days, including several big-name performers — although, warns Schmader, "Anybody your kids can name, we can't afford." The list in recent years has included John Tesh, Lou Rawls, the Commodores, and country singer David Lee Murphy.

Hot-air balloons always catch public imagination. The River Festival boasts the largest pre-dawn launch in the United States, featuring more than five dozen inflatable craft. In fact, rallies are held every morning throughout the festival, and late Saturday, pilots light up their balloons for an eerie "Niteglow" at Ann Morrison Park.

The River Festival includes a wide range of children's activities, including a carnival, sports and games, comedy and storytelling, face painting and a maze.

For sports lovers, there are competitions in golf, basketball, softball, bicycling, running, in-line skating, table tennis, bowling and some lesser-known pursuits like water volleyball and frisbee golf. Skydivers, sand sculptors, quilters, gardeners and classic car enthusiasts all have their opportunities to shine.

A different nation is featured each year in the festival's "World Showcase" of entertainment and exhibits; in 1997, it was New Zealand. On the short list for upcoming festivals, according to Schmader, are Italy, Malaysia, Mexico and Turkey.

— continued on next page

The festival concludes with a Sunday night Fireworks Extravaganza, a pyrotechnic display that exceeds those held throughout the Treasure Valley a week later for Independence Day.

With aggregate attendance at festival events exceeding 1 million in 1997, representing perhaps a quarter-million different individuals, infrastructure is an essential concern. More than 100 food-and-drink vendors provide sustenance in three large food courts and several other festival locations. Medical and security staffs provide assistance in case of any emergency. Park-and-ride shuttles minimize parking crunches near festival venues. Special parking areas, as well as wheelchair rentals, are available for handicapped individuals.

What is the future of the River Festival?

"We're never ones to sit still," says Steve Schmader. "There are always new floats and entertainment. We're expanding the kids' activities. We're planning something special for the millennium. And we *will* remain free."

Beach Party
Downtown Nampa, 2nd St. between 12th and 13th Aves. • (208) 466-0992

You won't believe all there is to see and do at this get-together — a car cruise, sand sculptures, dog Frisbee — and that's just the tip of the iceberg — or sand dune as the case may be. A band playing tunes from the late '50s through the '60s keep crowds twisting, and beach movies transport them to the land of killer waves and summer romances between Gidget and Moondoggie. Surf's up the last Friday and Saturday of the month.

Museum Comes to Life
Idaho State Historical Museum, 610 Julia Davis Dr., Boise • (208) 334-2120

Volunteers garbed in 19th-century clothing make Boise's past come alive with special exhibits in the museum and the adjacent Pioneer Village. Reprising early settlers, they demonstrate the lost arts of spinning and weaving, blacksmithing, quilting, broom-making, flint-knapping and more. They'll also teach children some old-fashioned games and perform a round or two of country dancing. The event is held the last Saturday in September.

Renaissance Faire
Western Idaho Fairgrounds, 5610 Glenwood St., Boise • (208) 342-5754

The Junior League of Boise holds this biennial weekend event in late September or early October. In 1998 the dates are the last Saturday and Sunday in September.

A 16th-century village, Castle Creek Glen, has a stage for magicians, jugglers, a comedy group and other performers. There are soothsayers, astrologists, street dancers and a 24-foot catapult that hauls objects 600 feet. The league makes 200 costumes for crafters, merchants and volunteers. Children's crafts, games and equestrian events — all harkening back to the 16th-century — are also part of the fun. Turkey legs, pig in a poke and "popcorn," now know as corn of the cob, are for sale. Admission is $5; children 5 and younger are admitted free.

October

Boo at the Zoo
Zoo Boise, Julia Davis Park, 700 S. Capitol Blvd., Boise • (208) 384-4216

Children's activities are the focus of this Halloween celebration, where the joy of visiting with animals and birds replaces the some-times-dangerous tradition of door-to-door trick-or-treating. A story corner, spook alley, costume contest, pumpkin contest, jumping castle, bat game and face painting are all part of the fun. Ribbons are given for all costume and pumpkin participants, and prizes are awarded to the winners.

The event takes place the last Saturday of the month. Children 4 to 11 pay $1.75; adults, $4. Children 3 and younger and seniors 62 and older are admitted free.

November

Beaux Arts for Christmas Fair
Boise Art Museum, 670 Julia Davis Dr., Boise • (208) 345-8330

The Christmas Fair started in 1967 and continues to be held every year from early to mid-November. Close to 350 artisans from different parts of the country display their works for sale during this benefit for the Boise Art Museum. Artisans donate 30 percent of their sales to the museum, which recently totaled $350,000, with a profit of $90,000.

More than 15,000 art-lovers attend the nine-day holiday event to find unique handcrafted gift items. Nine rooms are filled with specific types of items — pottery, kitchen goods, jewelry, fibers, collectors items, etc. A $1 donation is charged at the door. There are also special nights — preview, corporate, jazz — where wine and appetizers are sold for $1 to $3.

Festival of Trees
Boise Centre on the Grove, 8th and Grove Sts., Boise • (208) 367-2797

The City of Trees' Festival of Trees is a holiday fund-raising event for St. Alphonsus Regional Medical Center that's always held during Thanksgiving week. One hundred lav-ishly decorated evergreens are sponsored, and six are auctioned off. Admission is $5 for adults, $4 for seniors 60 and older and $1.50 for children 12 and younger. A black-tie dinner with cocktails costs $150, and the close to 1,000 people who attend purchase their tickets within two weeks of them going on sale in mid-October. A fashion lunch, children's programs and senior programs are part of the five-day schedule. In 1997 St. Alphonsus raised more than $416,000 from this event.

At the same time, Nampa celebrates the Canyon County Festival of Trees at the Nampa Civic Center, 311 3rd Street S., (208) 465-2252.

December

BSU Christmas Concert
Morrison Center for the Performing Arts, Boise State University, 2201 Campus Ln., Boise • (208) 385-1596

BSU's combined student choirs, percussion ensemble and the University Community Orchestra get together to offer this 90-minute family concert in the acoustically superior Morrison Center. Beginning at 6:30 PM on the first Sunday of the month, the festive presentation includes holiday medleys, sing-alongs and modern arrangements of traditional hymns, with a distinct children's orientation. Admission is $5.50 for adults, $3.50 for students. Children younger than 5 get in free.

Holiday Lights Tour
Boise • (208) 345-4357

Choose an open-air Boise Tour Train or an enclosed trolley car for this tour in mid-December of creatively decorated homes in the Warm Springs and North End neighborhoods near downtown Boise. Reservations are required.

INSIDERS' TIP

Every five years — the next time will be in 2000 — the San Inazio Basque Festival is superceded by Jaialdi, an international fest that brings dancers, musicians and athletes to Boise from throughout the American West and from the Basque homeland in Spain and France.

Humanitarian Bowl

Bronco Stadium, Boise State University, 2201 Campus Ln., Boise

• **(208) 338-8887**

Boise's own college football bowl game, featuring the champion of the Big West Conference (in which BSU plays), was inaugurated in 1997. Attendance at the first bowl was more than 16,000 when the University of Cincinnati defeated Utah State University 35 -19. The event is held close to January 1 annually. The name reflects the presence in Boise of the World Sports Humanitarian Hall of Fame. Tickets are $30.

Boise is blessed
with creative energy,
wealthy patrons and
facilities that make the
arts communities of
larger metropolises turn
green with envy.

The Arts

Boise takes a backseat to few other cities of similar size when it comes to cultural activities. Blessed with creative energy, wealthy patrons and facilities that make the arts communities of larger metropolises turn green with envy, the Idaho capital can present a year-round program of outstanding music, dance and theater as well as fine presentations of visual and literary arts.

You can get up-to-date information on all major arts events in the greater Boise area by reading the Friday "Scene" section of *The Idaho Statesman*.

Tickets for most events can be obtained from Select-A-Seat, (208) 385-1766, which has outlets in all Albertsons grocery stores. Select-A-Seat also operates an entertainment information line at (208) 385-3535.

Performing Arts

Support Organizations

Despite Boise's interest in the arts, it often seems that state and city agencies have their work cut out for them when it comes to funding for arts programs. The leaders in this effort, who combine national endowments and other sources for national support follow.

Boise City Arts Commission
Boise City Hall, 150 N. Capitol Blvd., Boise • (208) 336-4936

This is a city department with a staff of three and a commission of 15 volunteers appointed by the Boise Mayor that meets monthly and advises the city council on public art as well as organizes events and activities and works on arts projects. Boise public art overseen by the commission includes plaza and sidewalk sculpture and paintings in the Boise Centre on the Grove, which is the convention center. An example of an event organized by the Commission is the pedestrian-oriented First Night Boise held downtown on New Year's Eve, where the cost of a $6 to $8 button provides entry into a number of downtown arts-related locations such as the Boise Art Museum, The Log Cabin, Boise Centre on the Grove and arts shops at the Eighth Street Marketplace was well as participation in children's activities and a procession. A current project is attempting to turn Downtown Boise into a cultural district.

Idaho Commission on the Arts
304 W. State St., Boise • (208) 334-2119

This commission distributes National Endowment for the Arts and State of Idaho grants in three different areas: for public education arts programs, for individual artists and for arts organizations throughout the state. The Idaho Theater for Youth, for instance, has received grants that allow it to perform for communities around the state. A funded Artist in Residence program, which has shown good results, establishes a four-to-six-week residency at a school for an artist who attempts to channel in a creative way the energies of students at risk. Every two years a state writer in residence is chosen. The writer receives a cash award and conducts readings throughout the state. Dramatic artists, block printers and musicians are among those who have won individual grants. Arts organizations around the state may receive grants for reviving or establishing arts centers or for operating expenses. The commission has 10 full-time and two part-time employees at work in a beautiful blue Victorian house just blocks from the Capitol.

Very Special Arts Idaho
802 W. Bannock St., Boise • (208) 333-0122

This agency provides people of all ages who have disabilities opportunities to participate in the arts. It receives $20,000 each year in federal funding and raises additional money through state and other grants. It has been involved in dance programs, has made murals for Julia Davis Park, has had a playwriting program, has provided art classes for families, has worked with arts educators in schools around the state and has been involved in many other activities and projects. A current project is gathering cultural data to let people with disabilities know what is available to them around the state. People with disabilities join others without disabilities in many of the activities, so that thousands of people are involved in programs each year.

Caldwell Fine Arts Series
(208) 454-1376

This organization provides local arts programming in the western Treasure Valley. In particular, it offers classes, art workshops and theater performances in schools throughout the area.

Venues

Boise

Esther Simplot Performing Arts Academy
516 S. 9th St. • (208) 345-9116

The Boise Philharmonic, Ballet Idaho and Opera Idaho are based at the Esther Simplot Performing Arts Academy. Their offices and rehearsal space are located in this building, where they promote and prepare performances that are given at the Morrison Center and at other community locations. Recitals are staged here occasionally.

Morrison Center for the Performing Arts
Boise State University, 2201 Campus Ln. • (208) 385-1609, (208) 385-1110 box office

Renowned for its outstanding acoustics, the Morrison Center for the Performing Arts is considered one of the finest civic concert theaters in the United States. Occupying a site beside the Boise River on the campus of Boise State University, the 2,014-seat arts center hosts numerous performances every month by symphonies, dance and theatrical troupes and others, including touring national musical stage companies.

The center sees as many as 140 performances a year. *Cats*, *Les Miserables*, *The King and I* and *Fiddler on the Roof* have been performed here. The Boise Philharmonic performs nine or 10 times a year. Opera Idaho stages its big performance here, and Ballet Idaho's *Nutcracker* is a delight during the holiday season.

Nampa

Nampa Civic Center
311 3rd St. S. • (208) 465-2252

The Boise Philharmonic, Ballet Idaho and various touring dance troupes and theater companies perform at this fine new complex in downtown Nampa.

Caldwell

Langroise Center at Albertson College
2112 E. Cleveland Blvd. • (208) 459-5836

A new $6 million facility for the performing and fine arts, the Langroise Center boasts a 192-seat musical recital hall and a 120-seat theater. Nearby Jewett Auditorium has another 850 seats for major concerts.

Music and Dance

Ballet Idaho
516 S. 9th St., Boise • (208) 343-0556

Ballet Idaho began in 1972. Classical and contemporary ballets are the fare of the 20-member company that has a professional partnership with the Eugene (Oregon) Ballet Company. It is the only professionally touring company in the state, and it gives performances at schools throughout Idaho. The 35-week season extends from September into May. Toni

Pimble, artistic director and choreographer, combines the styles of ballet, modern and ethnic dance to create innovative yet thematically linked works. A title classical piece and two shorter contemporary pieces make up most programs. Most shows sell out — especially the Christmas-season *Nutcracker* — so it's wise to get tickets early. The company's Academy of Dance offers classes to children 5 and older.

Boise Master Chorale
100 W. State St., Boise • (208) 344-7901

The multifaceted harmonies of these songsters are frequently backed by the Boise Philharmonic or are part of Opera Idaho productions. But the Chorale also presents its own series of concerts throughout the year. The symphonic choir consists of 110 men and women who perform with other groups up to four times a year. The chorale sings "The Messiah" with the Boise Philharmonic during Christmas at the Morrison Center for Performing Arts. Auditions are held in August for this semiprofessional group, although interested parties can request an audition at any time.

Boise Philharmonic
516 S. 9th St., Boise • (208) 344-7849

Leading guest artists accentuate a concert season that extends from September to May. (A recent season featured violin virtuoso Itzhak Perlman.) Conductor James Ogle mixes staples of symphony repertoires with a selection of lesser known works.

BSU Music Department
Boise State University, 2201 Campus Ln., Boise • (208) 385-3980

Faculty, students and guest musicians often perform recitals at the Morrison Center, most frequently on smaller stages within the complex. These are usually held during the college year. Student recitals are free; faculty and guest performances cost $3 to $5. The department stages a summer festival at the BSU outdoor campus amphitheater three weekends in July. A symphony orchestra plays two weekends, and a concert band performs the third weekend. (See the BSU Summerfest in the Annual Events and Festivals chapter for more information.)

Idaho Dance Theatre
928 W. Main St., Boise • (208) 331-9592

You're as likely to find this company, which focuses on modern dance and music, in schools statewide as on any other stage. Interactive dance and movement performances are its bread and butter; during a recent season, the troupe worked on "defiance of gravity."

Oinkari Basque Dancers
2418 Pendleton St., Boise
• (208) 336-8219

Idaho's most renowned troupe of folk danc-

Photo: William H. Mullins

The Boise Basque Museum hosts many special events that feature dancing and authentic Basque cuisine.

1998
Sept. 18/19
Oct. 16/17
Nov. 06/07 — *Just for the h--- of it*
1999
Jan. 22/23 — *Musical Morphings*
Feb. 19/20 — *Amazing Amadeus*
Mar. 19/20 — *American Graffiti*
April 16/17 — *Season Finale*

**Boise
Philharmonic**

For Tickets and Information Call 344-7849

ers has been featured at national dance festivals, often accompanied by Gaupasa, a six-member band whose instruments include guitar, accordion, tambourine, tambor (drum), txistu (Basque flute) and ttun ttun (a long, box-like stringed instrument). The colorful dancers perform in Boise at annual Basque festivals and other special events; inquire at the Basque Museum and Cultural Center, (208) 343-2671, for more details.

Opera Idaho
516 S. 9th St., Boise • (208) 345-3531

This burgeoning company, which began in 1961, presents three operas a year at the Morrison Center. Traditional works by Mozart, Puccini and other classical composers are presented, but the company also experiments with forms that combine conventional opera with contemporary theater. Professional singers from the East and West coasts as well as local vocalists come together during presentations that are usually 40 to 60 performers strong. Auditions are held in the spring and fall. The

opera has a choir for children, beginning at the age of 7. Its artistic director, Timothy Lindberg, directs the University of Southern California training program and has worked with the New York Metropolitan Opera.

Theater

With the exception of the summerlong Idaho Shakespeare Festival (see our Annual Events and Festivals chapter), the Treasure Valley's various community theater companies perform a wide range of productions during the September-to-May season.

Boise Actors Guild
308 E. 36th St., Garden City
• (208) 323-8431

This community troupe, which presents dramas as well as comedies, often works with the nearby Boys & Girls Club of Ada County in its productions. Plays are performed at the Garden City Playhouse, 308 36th Street, and are free.

INSIDERS' TIP

The largest university in Idaho, Boise State University, is an arts magnet. Its music and arts departments, Morrison Center for the Performing Arts and Visual Arts Center are constant sources of shows, concerts and events that are often free or reasonably priced.

Boise Little Theater
100 E. Fort St., Boise • (208) 342-5104

This is one of the oldest continuously performing community theater groups in the country, dating back to 1948. It performs seven shows from the beginning of September to mid-June. The shows are comedies, mysteries, musicals and, every couple of years, a children's favorite. *Nunsense, Cabaret* and *Arsenic and Old Lace* are some of the plays that have been performed at the domed theater, which seats more than 360 people. Tickets cost $7.50 to $10.

BSU Theatre Arts Department
Boise State University, 2201 Campus Ln., Boise • (208) 385-3980

Experimental works and rarely seen older plays are forums for drama students to hone their acting skills. Performances typically are presented on smaller stages at the Morrison Center.

Idaho Performing Arts
910 W. Main St., Boise • (208) 343-6567

Musical theater, including Broadway productions, comes to Boise primarily courtesy of this agency. The likes of *Ain't Misbehavin'*, *Cats, Damn Yankees, Evita, West Side Story* and *The Will Rogers Follies* have been presented in recent years at the Morrison Center to thunderous applause.

Idaho Theater for Youth
404 S. 8th St., Boise • (208) 345-0060

Schools throughout Idaho are blessed with live productions by this touring company, whose repertoire often deals with serious issues affecting the young people of today, such as substance abuse, teenage pregnancy and depression. The company performs a one-hour play that is followed by an open discussion. Professional actors from Idaho and sometimes guest actors from elsewhere are in the touring cast that never exceeds four people since a small van is used to reach remote rural areas. This company also presents two plays for adults each year, usually at the Morrison Center, at Christmas and in May. Tickets cost $8. *The Last Paving Stone*, a world premiere, *Charlotte's Web* and *Little Lulu* are a few of the past shows presented. The group has appeared at the Russian Theater Festival and at the Kennedy Center in Washington, D.C.

Knock 'em Dead Dinner Theater
807 W. Idaho St., Boise • (208) 385-0021

Boise's lone dinner theater has found its greatest success with classic musicals such as *Man of La Mancha. Love Letters* and *You Can't Take it With You* have been performed more recently. Plays run for nearly two months and are presented on Thursdays, Fridays and Saturdays. Thursday ticket prices are $10. Friday and Saturday tickets, with dinner included, are $25 to $30.

Stage Coach Theatre
2000 Kootenai St., Boise • (208) 342-2000

This nonprofit community theater group is run entirely by volunteers. It focuses on contemporary comedies and musicals such as *And You Want to Give Up Show Biz?* The company presents eight-show runs at its stage in the Hillcrest Shopping Center at Overland Road and Orchard Street. Tickets are $7 to $9.50.

Visual Arts

Art Museums and Centers

Boise Art Museum
670 S. Julia Davis Dr., Boise • (208) 345-8330

Neon streamers welcome visitors to Idaho's only public art museum, situated at the west end of Julia Davis Park. The museum is home to the Glenn C. Janss Collection of American Realism, one of the nation's most highly regarded collections of that genre.

The museum also presents an annual calendar of more than 15 touring exhibitions, featuring the work of regional and national artists in a broad range of themes, from abstract oils to photography, Classical to Impressionist. A recent exhibit featured 50 painted ceramics by the late Pablo Picasso. Upcoming exhibits include watercolors and pastels from the National Museum of American Art in Washington, D.C., paintings by American artists of the 1980s and '90s from the Milwaukee Art Mu

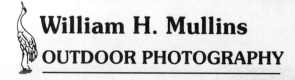

seum and a sculpture court featuring Northwest metal craft.

Sixteen galleries, a sculpture garden and a new education wing are among the benefits of a $1.8 million museum expansion completed in late 1997. A small but excellent gift shop sells prints of noted masterpieces, art books, jewelry and various other arts and crafts.

The museum takes an active part in the Boise community, sponsoring several well-attended events each year, including the outdoor Art in the Park each September; a Museum After Hours wine-and-cheese affair with live music on Wednesday evenings in autumn; and, in conjunction with its Beaux Arts Societé, an Arts for Christmas Sale and Wine Festival.

The Boise Art Museum is open 10 AM to 5 PM Tuesday through Friday and noon to 5 PM Saturday and Sunday year round; in the summer, it's also open 10 AM to 5 PM Monday. Admission is $3 for adults, $2 for seniors and students, $1 for kids in grades 1 through 12 and free for younger children.

Boise State University Visual Arts Center
Gallery 1, Liberal Arts Building, 1874 University Dr., Boise • (208) 385-1230
Gallery 2, Public Affairs West Building, 2100 University Dr., Boise
• (208) 385-3994

Students and faculty exhibit their finest work in these two campus galleries. Their presentations are sometimes augmented by regional or national shows of contemporary and traditional art. Both galleries are open Monday through Friday from 9 AM to 5 PM; admission is free.

Galleries

If there's a "best time" to take yourself on a Boise gallery walk, it's the first Thursday of any month. That's when downtown merchants get together for a First Thursday event that keeps most galleries and other shops open until 9 PM. Many stage special openings or winetastings to coincide with the date. Call (208) 336-2631 for information.

The following listings are by no means exclusive, but they do demonstrate the breadth of galleries in the Boise area.

Boise

Art Source Gallery
609 W. Main St. • (208) 331-3374

This Old Boise gallery, which stocks original work by local artists, is one of the city's largest and most diversified. Not only will you find paintings (watercolors, oils, acrylics and pastels), but also fiber and wearable art, jewelry, photography, woodcarvings and quilts. Art Source Gallery has a large collection of three-dimensional work including handthrown pottery, carved gourds, hand-inlaid wooden boxes and clocks.

Basement Gallery
928 W. Main St. • (208) 333-0309

Local and regional artists, with styles ranging from contemporary to traditional, are on display here. Mark Bangarter — a Boise resident half the year, when he's not in Russia or France, and a painter of modern figurative realism all year — opened this gallery in the basement of the historic Idanha Hotel in late 1997. Shows change monthly.

Brown's Gallery
1022 W. Main St. • (208) 342-6661

This is Idaho's largest and longest established gallery. Brown's Gallery started out as The Art Mart in 1962. George and Gloria Brown have been operating it as Brown's since 1971. It features international and local painters, sculptors, potters and textile artists as well as consultation, framing, restoration and appraisal services.

Cole/Marr Gallery
404 S. 8th St., Ste. 152 • (208) 336-7630

Creative photography is the thrust of this gallery in the Eighth Street Marketplace. Photography classes, rental darkrooms and exhibits round out the offerings.

Cynthia Wearden Gallery
404 S. 8th St., Ste. 154 • (208) 336-3380

A wide-ranging collection of painting, pottery, jewelry, furniture and more, all by artist/designer Wearden, shares floor space with works by modern American Indian and Idaho artisans.

DecorCreations Art and Furniture Gallery
1020 W. Main St. • (208) 336-6775

Raku and glazed ceramics and various glass arts are featured at this downtown gallery. Individual artists may be present to discuss their work.

Fritchman Galleries
112 N. 6th St. • (208) 385-0279

Archie B. Teater, who makes his home in a Frank Lloyd Wright-designed house above the Snake River in Idaho's Hagerman Valley, is perhaps the best-known artist to have his work displayed here. Look for his Idaho landscapes and his New York cityscapes. Delbert Jifh, a member of the American Watercolor Society, is the other painter whose work is displayed here. The gallery itself, established in 1935, occupies an 1885 law office that is the oldest building in historic Old Boise.

Gallery 601
850 W. Main St. • (208) 336-5899

The nationally acclaimed work of Jane Wooster Scott, a modern American folk artist who makes her home in Sun Valley, is the big attraction of this gallery. But many other painters, including those of national acclaim, are presented here as well.

Galos Fine Arts
601 W. Main St. • (208) 385-7995

Original work by contemporary regional painters, sculptors and ceramicists are the highlight of this Old Boise gallery, which also presents limited-edition prints by nationally acclaimed painters.

INSIDERS' TIP

Believe it or not, Boise has had some pretty big names and performances roll through. Broadway productions of *Cats* and *Les Miserables* as well as concerts by Shania Twain, Eric Clapton and James Taylor have graced the stages of the capital city.

Homespun Crafters' Mall
5110 W. Franklin Rd. • (208) 336-2090

More than 200 crafters and antique collectors display their wares here in 3,000 square feet of exhibit space at the corner of Orchard Street. Crafters here work with wood, make furniture, do copper punching, make angels and craft and mold jewelry.

J. Crist Gallery
461 W. Main St. • (208) 336-2671

A variety of contemporary art, including furniture by celebrated Los Angeles architect Frank Gehry and ornate book pages by San Francisco artist Charles Hobson, are presented at this gallery in Old Boise's historic, granite Belgravia Building. Numerous regional artists are represented as well.

Jefferson House Gallery
1515 N. 13th St. • (208) 345-7001

Work by G. Harvey, Thomas Kincaid, Sandra Kuck, Lena Lieu and other prolific American artists are the mainstay of this Hyde Park gallery. Jefferson House Gallery also offers framing and interior design consultation.

Lindley Glass Studio
603 W. Main St. • (208) 342-8024

Nearly three decades of experience in original etched crystal and glasswork, custom-leaded panels, windows and lamps are on display at this Old Boise studio. Limited editions are signed and numbered.

Mountain Buffalo Gallery
1105 W. Main St. • (208) 385-0774

Western and American Indian art, especially that of Southwestern tribes, keeps this downtown gallery busy. You'll find pottery, basketry and jewelry as well as cowboy-style sculptures, paintings and paper-art creations.

Orient East
819 W. Idaho St. • (208) 344-6232

Prices at this gallery of contemporary and antique art from the countries of East and South Asia may start low but run upwards of $20,000. Artifacts and jewelry made of jade, ivory and pearls are among the priciest. You'll also find furniture and numerous precious knickknacks.

The Potter's Center
110 Ellen St., Garden City
• (208) 378-1112

The handthrown work of more than 20 Idaho potters — from functional to one-of-a-kind sculptures — are displayed in this gallery that also sells pottery supplies and equipment.

SandStone Gallery at Sinclair Studio
615 W. Main St. • (208) 338-1454

Landscapes, portraits and occasional abstract work in color and black-and-white photography are showcased at this gallery. Photographic methods of every kind, including the latest in digital technologies, can be seen on display; the work of Boise-area cameramen most often takes center stage.

Caldwell

Rosenthal Gallery at Albertson College
2112 E. Cleveland Blvd. • (208) 459-5321

The work of Albertson College of Idaho faculty and students is presented here at a gallery that has been converted from a theater stage. The bulk of a permanent collection is prints — etchings, lithographs and photos. Five to six free exhibits are presented during the college year between mid-September and the end of May. One-person exhibits given by artists in the community and region show photographs, paintings and ceramics.

The gallery is open from 1 to 4 PM Tuesday through Saturday when exhibits are being presented.

Literary Arts

Log Cabin Literary Center
801 S. Capitol Blvd., Boise
• (208) 331-8000

A focal point for writers of nonfiction, fiction and poetry, the Log Cabin offers a series of readings and classes as well as a weeklong summer writing camp for youth. Established in 1995, it is developing an outreach to schools and communities throughout Idaho.

Boise's most popular parks are named after women of prominent Boise families.

Parks and Preserves

The most popular Boise parks are joined together like a bracelet on the Greenbelt and named after women of prominent Boise families — Kathryn Albertson, wife of Joe Albertson, the supermarket king; Ann Morrison, wife of Henry Morrison, the Morrison-Knudsen founder who built dams and other construction projects around the world; and Julia Davis, who with husband Tom Davis, owned thousands of acres of farmland and property along the Boise River.

These three and the other most notable of 69 city parks, Camelback Park and Quarry View Park Shelter, are explored in this section, as are three state parks in the Boise area — Eagle Island, Lucky Peak and Veterans Memorial. We round out the chapter with a look at two national parks, Boise National Forest and Deer Flat National Wildlife Refuge. For more information check with The Idaho State Parks office, 5657 Warm Springs Avenue, (208) 334-4199. The office publishes a free, 64-page guide with information about state parks, maps, diagrams and photos, and also has other brochures and pamphlets that relate to parks and recreation.

Some of the attributes of these natural areas are covered in more detail in other chapters. Centers and museums located within the parks and the World Center for Birds of Prey are detailed in the Attractions chapter. Zoo Boise is highlighted in Kidstuff. You'll also find the recreational opportunities of each park discussed more fully in the Recreation chapter.

Unless otherwise noted, the parks and preserves in this chapter are open daily from sunrise to dark.

Boise City Parks

Camelback Park
13th St. and Heron St. • (208) 383-4240
A high brown hump that is delightedly "con-

quered" by hiker types, scrambling kids and exhausted dogs led to the name of this park. Below it is a broad green swath fitted with tennis courts and a playground with madly twisting slides. It's a good spot for Frisbee, kites and football. Because of its contours, size and variety, this park is well-used.

Quarry View Park Shelter
2150 Penitentiary Rd. • (208) 384-4240
This park offers an informal starting point for hiking on Castle Rock and is close to the Idaho Botanical Garden and the Old Idaho State Penitentiary museum (see our Attractions chapter). The shelter has eight picnic tables and two cooking grills. Tennis courts, basketball courts, playgrounds and a multipurpose field surround it.

Boise River Greenbelt

Think of a string of eight parks and a golf course linked together beside a sweetly flowing river, populated by songbirds, ducks, blue heron, geese, quail, owls, hawks and bald eagles. Muskrat, beaver, fox and deer are observed on pathways that stretch more than 20 miles through 163 acres of greenery. Inhabitants of the two-legged variety include walkers, bikers, joggers, skaters and runners.

The most vigorous participants follow the tar ribbon more than 11 miles east from Capitol Boulevard to Discovery State Park, near Lucky Peak Dam.

In the middle of Boise, anglers pull out rainbow trout and occasionally large brood steelhead planted by Idaho Fish & Game. Large brown trout and whitehead are also caught in this part of the river.

About 300,000 people float a 4-mile stretch of the Boise River each year, using inflated tire tubes and rafts between Barber Park and downtown Boise. Thousands more ride the river in a canoe. The river's 63 miles of water stretching from Discovery State Park to the confluence of the Snake River west of Parma offer fun for beginners as well as experts. There are many canoeing accesses, and almost all of them can be reached by major roads, which makes for simple shuttles. Wildlife is abundant along the river, and the hundreds of people traveling the river through Boise by inner tube are left behind.

(For more information on the recreational opportunities of the Boise River Greenbelt, see the Biking, Fishing, Hiking and Tubing sections of the Recreation chapter.)

See this and many other **Insiders' Guide®** destinations online — in their entirety.

ducks and nesting birds, and sodded lawn is favored by hungry Canadian geese, wigeons and rabbits.

Waterfowl, game fowl, owls and herons have found their niches here. Raccoons, beavers, rabbits, voles and other animals reside at this park in the middle of the city. Red foxes merely visit.

The Eyrie Gazebo, The Rookery Gazebo, the artistic use of huge boulders and rocks, a Russian Olive Grove and other magnificent trees make this a lovely, quiet refuge for people as well as wildlife.

Kathryn Albertson Park
1000 block of Americana Blvd.
• (208) 384-4240

Kathryn McCurry, a Boise native, met her future husband, Joe Albertson, founder of Albertsons, Inc., supermarkets, at what was then known as the College of Idaho in Caldwell. Kathryn spilled an acid solution on her leg in chemistry class, and Joe came to her rescue. They were married on New Year's Day in 1930. With success that has made Albertsons the fourth largest and most profitable supermarket chain in the country, the family has become one of the community's largest benefactors. Huge contributions to the college where Joe and Kathryn met have led to a name change — Albertson College of Idaho — and Kathryn Albertson Park would warm the heart of the meanest-spirited curmudgeon.

Dedicated in 1989 the park is home to resident and migratory wildlife and welcomes people seeking a luxuriant outdoor escape. Vegetation offers food from ground level to treetops as well as nesting cover and protection for wild animals. Shallow ponds stimulate the growth of aquatic insects and plants that in turn become food for many kinds of wildlife. Islands offer loafing and roosting spots for

Ann Morrison Park
Americana Blvd., just south of the Boise River • (208) 384-4240

Across Americana Boulevard from Kathryn Albertson Park is 153-acre Ann Morrison Park, a wide-open space for roaming that is known for its swarms of ducks, geese and swan that command ponds just inside its entrance and its long stretch of riverside ambiance on the opposite, northern side.

The park features a reflecting pool with water cascading from an illuminated spray fountain, gardens, Candy Cane Playground, tennis courts, lighted softball diamonds, soccer and football fields and a picnic pavilion. It is Boise's largest park, and the riverside location allows for easy access to float trips, fishing and views of wildlife.

The woman the park is named for grew up as Anna Daly in the Idaho mountains and came to Boise when she was 16. She married Harry W. Morrison, founder of Morrison-Knudsen Company, who was pictured on the cover of *Life* magazine as the person who had done more than anyone else to change the face of the world.

As the first lady of construction, Ann Morrison traveled with her husband to projects

INSIDERS' TIP

Frugal outdoor enthusiasts know that biking the 10 miles along the Greenbelt and a paved bike path to Sandy Point State Park saves them $2 since they are not required to pay the park's motorized vehicle fee.

Sandy Point, at the foot of Lucky Peak Dam, is popular with kids of all ages.

throughout the world. The guest of presidents, kings and diplomats, she did not let the brilliance and pageantry of her life change her. She was known locally for her great civic interest and friendliness. She died in 1957.

Julia Davis Park
700 S. Capitol Blvd. • (208) 384-4240

This 87-acre emerald expanse is in the heart of the city, with Boise State University on one side, Boise Library on another, and the giant Morrison-Knudsen building complex on a third.

The long, slender park houses animals at Zoo Boise, science at the Discovery Center, the past at the Idaho State Historical Museum and creative impressions at the Boise Art Museum. It also has a rose garden, a band shell for concerts and other musical celebrations, tennis courts and the only horseshoe pits in the city system. The Boise River courses down its entire southern side, separating it from BSU.

The woman the park is named for was born Julia McCrumb. She came to the Boise Valley from Ontario, Canada, to visit relatives in the summer of 1869. Two years later she and Tom Davis were married. They ran a sizable farm operation and also owned land on the river.

Julia was known for her kindness and gracious hospitality and welcomed and assisted travelers as they stopped their wagons on the river for relief from their high-desert travel. It was after helping one of these travelers that she fell ill and died in 1907. Her husband deeded approximately 40 acres of riverside land in memory of his wife, a piece that has more than doubled as parkland on the Greenbelt.

Municipal Park
500 Walnut St. • (208) 384-4240

The Boise River and Greenbelt run next to the park, and the Morrison-Knudsen Nature Center is nearby. The park has a year-round restroom, parking for about 300 vehicles, six drinking fountains and a softball field. It also has 10 open picnic areas and one shelter available for rent that can accommodate 50 people.

Picnic and Garden Reservations
(208) 384-4240

Park space may be reserved for family picnics, corporate barbecues, wedding ceremonies, anniversary parties and the like at a number of city park settings that include the Rose Garden at Julia Davis Park, a shelter at Ann Morrison Park or a private evening at Zoo Boise.

Picnic areas and shelters are rented in four-hour time blocks. Fees range from $30 to $75 for Boise residents and $45 to $112.50 for non-residents. Zoo Boise is available for large gatherings with prices starting at $500. Also, the band shell may be reserved for large events, and volleyball equipment may be rented for $10 a day.

State Parks

Eagle Island State Park
2691 Mace Rd., Eagle • (208) 939-0696 summer, (208) 939-0704 winter

This day-use park on the Boise River offers a popular swimming beach, concessions, grassy picnic areas with tables, a group shelter and a water slide. The beach is about a football field long and 30 to 40 feet wide; there is no lifeguard on duty. Admission to the park is $3.

Lucky Peak State Park
Idaho Hwy. 21, 10 miles southeast of Boise • (208) 344-0240 summer, (208) 336-9505 winter

This park is divided into three parts that are all located in or near Lucky Peak Reservoir, just outside Boise. Lucky Peak Reservoir begins 10 miles southeast of Boise. Traveling on Idaho Highway 21, you'll go over a bridge that crosses the body of water, with the reservoir exit just north. The reservoir has 12 miles of water and a perimeter shoreline of 42 miles. This is a scenic waterway, surrounded by hills, rock cliffs and faces and crowded with powerboaters, water-skiers and Jet Skiers on summer weekends. The lake perimeter offers walking, hiking, picnic and fishing opportunities. Idaho Fish & Game planted 840,000 fish in 1997, including three species of rainbow trout, steelhead, perch and chinook and coho salmon. Bird watchers have counted 176 species living here and flying through.

Sandy Point, at the foot of towering Lucky Peak Dam, has a pretty white-sand beach beside a calm swimming area and, above that, spacious grass slopes with picnic tables, grills and concessions. It's a gem of a retreat that is ideal for families. Admission is $2.

Discovery State Park, which also has an admission fee of $2, juts out into the Boise River beneath, which in spring and summer is

a creamy, powerful gush of water through huge dam pipes. The park offers shaded picnic tables and fishing in the Boise River.

Above the dam, Spring Shores Marina is a boating haven with docks, ramps, boat trailer parking, concessions, beaches and picnic tables. It has 300 boat slips and boat rentals.

(For more information about what Lucky Peak Reservoir and Lucky Peak State Park offers outdoors enthusiasts, turn to the Boating, Fishing and Swimming sections of the Recreation chapter.)

Veterans Memorial State Park
960 Veterans Pkwy., Boise • (208) 334-2812

Bordered by two busy city streets, this park is a broad and deep getaway to the Boise River and Greenbelt pathways. Cottonwood trees rise above walkers, cyclists and families playing on gentle contours. As the name implies the park honors our nation's veterans. It is a popular site for ceremonies, and a number of plaques and memorials commemorate veterans, including America's first POW memorial.

There's no admission fee to the park. It's about a 10-minute walk on asphalt trails to the Boise River. Wide-open grassy areas are good for Frisbees or a game of catch.

National Forests and Refuges

Boise National Forest
1249 S. Vinnell Way, Boise • (208) 373-4007

Forested waterways and sagebrush hills rise to evergreens on the northern incline of the Treasure Valley, about a mile up to heavily antennaed, 7,590-foot Shafer Butte. That's about 75,000 acres of land between Boise Ridge and Boise River. This magnificent natural playground is laced with primitive roads, four-wheel drive, motorcycle and ATV stretches and hiking, biking and horseback trails. Mountain bike trails spiced with creeks, wild flowers, shaded gullies, rock faces and panoramic views rank with the best in the country. There are three primitive roads, four multiuse four-

Photo: Idaho Department of Parks and Recreation

Headed to Eagle Island State Park? Don't forget your bathing suit!

wheel-drive trails, six multiuse motorized trails not open to four-wheel-drives, three pedestrian-only trails and 22 trails for mountain bikers, hikers and horseback riders.

One of the most popular and informative hiking trails is Hull's Gulch Interpretive Trail. Signs along the way identify flora and fauna and cite historical facts about the park.

There is no admission to this area.

(See the Recreation chapter for more detailed information about Biking, Hiking and Horseback Riding in Boise National Forest.)

Deer Flat National Wildlife Refuge
13751 Upper Embankment Rd., Nampa
• (208) 467-9278, (208) 888-5582

The 11,430-acre Deer Flat National Refuge is 4 miles southwest of Nampa. It is composed of Lake Lowell and Snake River islands north on the Snake River near Weiser and south of Brownlee Reservoir, which provide habitat for large numbers of wintering waterfowl, especially mallards and Canadian geese.

The Lake Lowell portion of the refuge was established by executive order of President Theodore Roosevelt in 1909.

Water diverted from the Boise River fills 9-mile-long Lake Lowell, which offers a wide variety of game fish. Most of the lake is encircled by trees and marshland in a rural, agricultural setting made picturesque by the Owyhee Mountains and Snake River canyons to the south. Large numbers of birds begin to move into the area in September and by the first of December, up to 10,000 geese and 100,000 ducks may be present.

The refuge visitors center/headquarters is open from 7:30 AM to 4 PM weekdays, except holidays. There are four boat launching spots, water-skiing docks and designated swimming areas. Lake winds make this one of the best sailboarding areas in the Treasure Valley.

(See the Bird-Watching, Boating, Fishing and Swimming sections in the Recreation chapter for more information on what the refuge has to offer.)

Broad foothills, valley woods, fields and the refreshing tongue of the Boise River — these natural blessings stoke recreational fires.

Recreation

A broad foothills wall rises brown, green or white, depending upon the season, north above the Capitol dome and jigsaw puzzle shapes of Boise's new, high buildings. Through valley woods and fields flows the refreshing tongue of the Boise River. These natural blessings stoke recreational fires.

Hiking, mountain biking, skiing. Fishing, skating, canoeing, tubing. It's all right in our own backyard, beneath the nose of commerce, government, abstract educational theories and military wings. Boise is a western recreational boom town, wearing a white collar and suit over its sportswear. It's a working city of vehicles outfitted with sports racks, golf clubs in the trunk, closets stuffed with fishing rods and bike shops everywhere you look.

Boise recreation is active as flower garden bees and barbecue wasps, and the city is the state gateway for the best array of whitewater adventures in the world and fishing, hunting, backpacking and hiking on a grand scale.

The ease of participation and harmonious spirit of this enjoyment bind the local culture like the spine of a book. Any recreation seems possible in the water-fed, grass-walled, high-desert Treasure Valley, whose name could be a nod to its wealth of participatory sports as much as anything else.

In the Park and Preserves chapter, we introduced you to Boise's major natural areas, such as the Boise River Greenbelt, Lucky Peak State Park, Boise National Forest and Deer Flat National Wildlife Refuge. These parks will come up over and over again throughout this chapter, so it may be worth your while to take a quick pass through the Parks and Preserves chapter to get a general overview of what these areas offer.

Here we've broken the chapter down by recreational activity. So, if you're interested in Hiking, for instance, you'll find all the information on hiking opportunities detailed in that one section. We hope that this organization allows for less time researching your recreational options and more hours enjoying Boise's great outdoors.

Happy Trails!

Resources

Several organizations provide information on the parks and activities in the area. From maps of hiking trails to activity guides chock-full of programs for kids as well as adults, these agencies have a wealth of resources to choose from.

Boise

**Boise Parks &
Recreation Department**
1104 Royal Blvd. • (208) 384-4240
Boise Parks & Rec publishes a free, 50-page activity guide three times a year that provides information on programs for youths, teens, and adults as well as events and accessibility. It also includes a facility map and list of amenities at each location. The department has many other brochures and pam-

INSIDERS' TIP

Ramps, viewpoints, picnicking, fishing and boating are made possible for the handicapped by specially designed facilities at a number of Treasure Valley and southern Idaho locations. For information and a pamphlet, contact Physically Challenged Access to the Woods, Treasure Valley Chapter, (208) 939-5587 or (208) 345-4802.

phlets that deal with parks, wildlife, activities, outings, etc.

Bureau of Land Management
3948 Development Ave. • (208) 384-3300

The BLM manages 43,000 acres between Idaho highways 55 and 21, up to 6,000 feet, where Boise National Forest begins. These are the Boise Foothills, where hiking, biking, horseback riding and dog walking are popular on trails and fire roads. Maps that show the trails, fire roads and contours of the landscape are available for $4 for an old version or $5 for a new version. You can pick one up at the previously mentioned address or at 1387 Vinnell Way.

www.insiders.com

See this and many other **Insiders' Guide®** destinations online — in their entirety.

Visit us today!

Convention & Visitors Bureau of Boise
168 N. 9th St. • (208) 344-7777
Boise Air Terminal, 2739 Airport Way
• (208) 385-0362
Boise Centre on the Grove, 850 W. Front St. • (208) 344-5338

These bureaus have recreation information, brochures and pamphlets for Boise and the state that cover a wide variety of subjects, including activities, events and lodging.

Idaho Fish & Game Department
600 S. Walnut Ave. • (208) 334-3700

This resource in the East End near Morrison-Knudsen has guides, brochures and pamphlets with information about fishing, hunting, camping and boating throughout the state.

Idaho Department of Parks and Recreation
5657 Warm Springs Ave.
• (208) 334-4199

The department has state guides on hunting, fishing and boating and brochures and

pamphlets on a number of recreational activities in Boise and throughout the state. It's between the city of Boise and Lucky Peak State Park.

Travel Council
700 W. State St. • (208) 334-2470

The Travel Council is on the second floor of the JR Williams Building, north across the street from the Capitol building. The department has an extensive array of brochures and pamphlets addressing Boise and state recreation.

Recreation Centers and Programs

Boise

Boise Parks & Recreation Department
1104 Royal Blvd. • (208) 384-4240

The department is just west of Boise State University. Twelve youth programs for kids ages 2 to 14 include art, karate and swimming. Basketball, late-night Fridays and dance classes are offered to teens ages 12 to 17, and adults enjoy programs in fitness, golf and volleyball, among others. But these focuses are only a sampling of what the department offers. Three times a year Boise Parks & Recreation publishes an extensive, free activity guide detailing all the programs being offered during that season. The department also has numerous brochures and pamphlets covering team and individual recreational activities for those that are interested. Drop by the office or give them a call to get a copy of this season's activity guide or more information about a particular program.

INSIDERS' TIP

A person of any age in reasonably good physical condition can tube the gentle 4-mile stretch of the Boise River from Barber Park upstream to Ann Morrison Park in the middle of the city.

Photo: William H. Mullins

Mountain bikers will enjoy the trails Boise and its environs have to offer.

Fort Boise Community Center
700 Robbins Rd. • **(208) 384-4468**

The renovated Fort Boise Community Center, which is run by Boise Parks & Recreation, offers physical fitness and workout equipment and instruction, dance classes, Saturday adventure outings, basketball, pool, Foosball and table tennis. A newly built, 4,500-square-foot arts area offers more than 80 art classes that include sculpting, drawing, stained glass, ceramics and photography. The center is be-

hind Elks Rehab and next to the Boise Senior Center. It's open 7:45 AM to 10 PM Monday through Thursday and late night (7 to 11 PM) for teens only on Fridays. Hours on Saturday are 9 AM to 3 PM; Sunday, 10 AM to 4 PM.

Daily drop-in costs are $2 for ages 12 to 17 and $3 for those 18 and older. A monthly open gym pass costs $22.05 for a resident and $33.08 for a nonresident. The pass includes use of the weight room, drop-in gym and locker room as well as strength training instruction.

Nampa

Nampa Recreation Center
131 Constitution Way • (208) 465-2288

The Nampa Recreation Center is a smash hit in Canyon County. A 140,000-square-foot sweat palace, the center houses the largest indoor rock-climbing wall in Idaho, three collegiate-size basketball courts, six racquetball courts, an indoor running track, three dance studios, a large gymnastics floor, five swimming pools, a spa, sauna, steam room and Senior Center. A daily pass for those 18 and older is $6; for those 12 to 17, $4; 6 to 11, $3; and younger than 6, $1. Annual pass rates are $265 for an individual and $477 for a family.

Hours are 6 AM to 10 PM Monday through Saturday and 1 to 6 PM Sunday.

Ballooning

Widespread Treasure Valley airspace and a high-desert climate that attracted long, federally-financed airport runways for World War II bombers and the National Interagency Fire Center are also excellent for feathery, scenic balloon rides.

A balloon rally at the Boise River Festival (see Annual Festivals and Events), held on the last weekend in June, is the big hot air balloon event of the year.

Boise

Footelights
Western Idaho Fairgrounds, 5610 Glenwood St. • (208) 362-5914

Rides are provided year-round on weekends, weather permitting. Up to four passengers may ride together on these tours that usually last an hour. The balloons are launched from Ladybird Park at the fairgrounds. Winds usually blow the balloon over the Boise River toward Eagle. Champagne or cider and a buffet celebrate the landing, wherever it may be. The cost is $125 per passenger.

Quackerjack Balloons
Western Idaho Fairgrounds, 5610 Glenwood St. • (208) 343-5969

This company offers weekend flights, weather permitting, between January and the end of October. Rides, which begin at Ladybird Park at the fairgrounds, last about an hour and generally follow the Boise River toward Eagle. A champagne ceremony during which participants are awarded with a certificate follows the flight. Up to four people may ride together. The cost is $125 per passenger.

Bicycling

Shops that rent bicycles as well as sell accessories and provide repair services are listed in the Shopping chapter under Sporting Goods Stores.

Resources

The Idaho Transportation Department
3311 W. State St., Boise • (208) 334-8272

Publishes a free, statewide *Idaho Bicycling Guide*, with a map, state information, advice and contacts. To request a guide, call the previously listed number.

In the Parks

Boise River Greenbelt

The Boise River Greenbelt has 22 miles of pathway stretching from Garden City on the west to Discovery State Park on the east. The pathway follows the course of the Boise River as it meanders through eight parks and passes a golf course. City sections are heavily wooded and provide bridges that make riding possible on both sides of the river. Stretches to the east are flat and wide-open. To the west, tree-lined corridors follow the river. Walkers, dog walkers and in-line skaters also use this pathway.

The pathway is accessible from Harbor Lane, Willow Lane, Veterans Memorial State Park, Garden Street, Riverside Park, Shoreline Park, Capitol Boulevard, Julia Davis Park, Boise State University, Municipal Park, Barber Park, and at many points on Warm Springs Avenue east of Barber Park.

For information about the Boise River Greenbelt pathways and a brochure with a map, contact the Boise Parks & Recreation Department, 1104 Royal Boulevard, Boise, (208) 384-4240.

Wheels R Fun
Shoreline Dr. and S. 13th St.
• (208) 343-8228

Wheels R Fun has bicycle as well as tube, raft, in-line skate and roller-skate rentals. It is open from Memorial Day through Labor Day and on weekends in April, May, September and October. The shop's location couldn't be more convenient as it's located right on the Greenbelt. Rental bikes, roller skates and in-line skates cost $5 an hour or $12 for four hours.

(See Tubing in this chapter for more information.)

In the Mountains

Sagebrush hills that rise to evergreens on the northern incline of the Treasure Valley make for excellent mountain-biking territory. Twenty-two trails situated as high as a mile above the valley are spiced with creeks, wild flowers, shaded gullies, rock faces and panoramic views. Intermediate to expert terrain may be reached by riding from the city up 8th Street to Hull's Gulch trails; by riding up Brumback Street to the Crestline Drive trail; by riding up Reserve Street to the Mountain Cove Road Trail; and by starting from trails that cut off from Bogus Basin Road, which climbs to the top of the Boise Foothills.

Information and maps of this terrain are available from Boise National Forest, 1249 S. Vinnell Way, Boise, (208) 373-4007. The Boise Parks & Recreation Department, 1104 Royal Boulevard, Boise, (208) 384-4240, publishes a free trail guide. For details on Boise Front mountain-biking trails as well as others in the region see *Mountain Biking in Southwest Idaho*, by Stephen Steubner and Stephen Phipps, a 97-page paperback published by High Mountain Adventures.

Throughout the State

Only 1.2 million people inhabit Idaho's dusty and green, plunging and climbing 83,557 square miles — the 13th largest in the nation. More than two-thirds of the land is federal and state-owned, with much of that included in forests, parks and the largest wilderness area in the Lower 48. Road and mountain biking are excellent in many areas.

Bird-Watching

The Southwest Idaho Travel Association produces a free *Casual Birdwatching Guide* for 15 areas of Boise and the region, which includes a map, photos and detailed information about habitat and birds. To obtain a guide contact the association at P.O. Box 2106, Boise, ID 83701, (800) 635-5240.

Lake Lowell
Deer Flat National Wildlife Refuge, 13751 Upper Embankment Rd., Nampa
• (208) 467-9278, (208) 888-5582

At Lake Lowell, part of the Deer Flat National Wildlife Refuge, large numbers of birds begin to appear in September. By the first of December, up to 10,000 geese and 100,000 ducks may be in residence. Mallards predominate, but small numbers of pintail, American widgeon, green-winged teal, wood duck, common merganser and northern shoveler are also present.

Winter concentrations of waterfowl at Lake Lowell attract bald eagles that move into the area to feed on weak and injured birds. Other raptors found during the fall and winter include the red-tailed hawk, northern harrier, American Kestrel, goshawk, Cooper's hawk, rough-legged hawk, prairie falcon, great horned owl and peregrine falcon.

INSIDERS' TIP

The **World Center for Birds of Prey** provides a perfect introduction for bird watchers headed south into the Snake River Birds of Prey National Conservation Area. This Bureau of Land Management-administered area is most easily approached from Boise at Swan Falls Dam, 35 miles southwest via Kuna. More than 800 pairs of raptors of 15 species nest within the 81-mile-long reserve, the largest concentration of nesting birds of prey anywhere on earth.

World Center for Birds of Prey
566 W. Flying Hawk Ln., Boise
• (208) 362-8687

For a closer look at big and unusual birds, visit the Peregrine Fund's World Center for Birds of Prey in south of Boise. Through one-way glass, you can see young peregrine falcons as well as tropical raptors, such as the giant harpy eagle with a wingspan of nearly 7 feet. The center offers exhibits, interactive displays, multimedia presentations and live bird interactions. (For more information see our Attractions chapter.)

Snake River Birds of Prey National Conservation Area

An 81-mile stretch of the Snake River Canyon is designated as the Snake River Birds of Prey National Conservation Area. Nearly constant updrafts allow raptors, such as hawks and eagles, to hunt the desert floor and proliferate like nowhere else on earth. To reach this area, take I-84 to Exit 44 at Meridian and proceed south on Idaho Highway 69 through Kuna to Dedication Point and Swan Falls Dam.

Boating

Lake Lowell
Deer Flat National Wildlife Refuge, 13751 Upper Embankment Rd., Nampa
• (208) 467-9278, (208) 888-5582

Lake Lowell has four boat launching spots, water-skiing docks and designated swimming areas. Lake winds make this the best sailboarding area in the Treasure Valley. The rural lake is ringed by woodland and grasslands. It's about 10 miles long and 3 miles across at its widest point. Motor and sailboats may use Lake Lowell during daylight hours from April 15 through September 30.

Lucky Peak State Park
Idaho Hwy. 21, 10 miles southeast of Boise • (208) 334-2679

Lucky Peak Reservoir has 12 miles of water and a perimeter shoreline of 42 miles. It is a scenic waterway surrounded by hills, rock cliffs and faces that is used mostly by powerboaters, water-skiers and Jet Skiers. Sailboarders show up early for the best winds.

Because of space confinement, sailboats avoid summer weekends but can sail freely during the week and in spring and autumn.

At Lucky Peak, Spring Shores Marina, (208) 336-9505, offers boat docks, ramps, boat-trailer parking, a marina and concessions services. It has 288 slips that are hart to get: There is a waiting list of 50. Yearly rentals for an 18-foot boat cost $309; for a 24-foot, $412; and for a 28-foot, $515.

Canoeing

Canoeing is good for beginners to intermediates on a stretch of 63 Boise River miles from Discovery State Park (below the dam of Lucky Peak Reservoir in Lucky Peak State Park) to the confluence of the Snake River west of Parma. There are many river accesses, and almost all of them are reached on major roads, which makes for simple shuttles. Popular access points include Notus and Parma on U.S. Highway 20/26 and at Old Fort Boise Road, west of U.S. Highway 95, just after the Boise River feeds into the Snake River. Wildlife is abundant, and the hundreds of people floating the river by tube through Boise in the hot summer months are left behind.

There are several canoeing options in Boise are not too far away. Parkcenter Pond, located at Parkcenter Boulevard between Bobwhite Court and Mallard Drive, is good for beginners. Quinn's Pond, located west of the end of Pleasanton Avenue, where you park and portage to the Boise River Greenbelt, is deeper and colder than Parkcenter Pond. Veterans Pond also offers good canoeing, beside the river at Veterans Memorial Parkway.

Other canoe-accessible areas include Arrowrock Reservoir, on a dirt road east of Lucky Peak State Park, which is 10 miles southeast of Boise on Idaho Highway 21. It's a big, beautiful lake with few motorboats. Discovery State Park, below the dam of Lucky Peak Reservoir, has enough current to get in and out of eddies and ferry across the Boise River current. The North Fork of the Boise River, accessible at the Idaho Highway 55 bridge on the south side of Cascade, 94 miles north of Boise, has class I canoeing with gentle currents, no whitewater and lots of wildlife. And to reach the Middle Fork of the Payette River, put in at the Tie Campground, just after the pavement ends about 12 miles north of Crouch, which is 52 miles north of Boise and east of Banks. It's a spring and early summer run of three to four hours to the Banks-Lowman highway bridge through a pretty valley. It's rated class I+/II.

Fishing

Fishing is a popular Boise activity. Below we've highlighted a few of the favorite fishing holes in and immediately around Boise and throughout the state.

A one-year fishing license for residents costs $16.50. The cost for a nonresident is $51.50 or $7.50 for one day and $3 for each additional consecutive day. Anyone 14 or older must have a fishing license. Nonresidents 13 or younger must fish with a license-holder, but residents in this age group are not required to do so. Fishing licenses may be obtained at sporting goods stores (see our Shopping chapter), Rite Aid and Wal-Mart stores as well as at the Idaho Fish & Game Department.

Catch-and-release is always encouraged to preserve the fish population.

For more information about wielding a rod and reel in the area, contact the Idaho Fish & Game Department, 600 S. Walnut Avenue, Boise, (208) 334-3700. The department publishes a free, 28-page *Official Guide to Fishing in Idaho*. When requesting it by mail, enclose a self-addressed stamped (55¢) 9 X 12 envelope to Fishing Guide, IDFG, Front Desk, P.O. Box 25, Boise, ID 83707.

In the Treasure Valley

Boise River

In the middle of the city, anglers fishing from the shore or in waders pull rainbow trout and occasionally large brood steelhead planted by the Idaho Fish & Game Department out of the Boise River. Large brown trout and whitehead are also found on the river. In 1992 a brown trout weighing 20 pounds was caught in Boise. Anglers often fish near the Broadway Avenue, Capitol Boulevard, Americana Boulevard and Glenwood Street bridges that cross the river in the city. They are also found at many spots along the 22-mile Greenbelt pathway that follows the course of the river.

Lake Lowell

Deer Flat National Wildlife Refuge, 13751 Upper Embankment Rd., Nampa
• (208) 467-9278, (208) 888-5582

Lake Lowell offers a wide variety of game fish such as largemouth bass, bullhead, crappie, trout, perch, bluegill, smallmouth bass and channel catfish. Fishing during waterfowl season (early October to mid-January) is permitted only within 200 yards of the Upper and Lower Dams.

Lucky Peak State Park

Idaho Hwy. 21, 10 miles southeast of Boise • (208) 334-2697

Lucky Peak Reservoir also has fishing, mainly from its 42 miles of shoreline. The lake is filled with motorboats, water-skiers and jet boats during the warmer months, so quiet, less busy areas must be sought out. The Idaho Fish & Game Department planted 840,000 fish in Lucky Peak Reservoir in 1997, including three species of rainbow trout, steelhead, perch and chinook and coho salmon. For information call Spring Shores Marina at the reservoir, (208) 336-9505.

Throughout the State

Idaho has more running water than any state in the continental United States. Devoted fly-fishers test their skill against wild, selective trout on such legendary waters as the Henrys Fork of the Snake River in eastern Idaho, Silver Creek, Kelly Creek, Teton River and the south forks of both the Snake and Boise rivers. (For more information on fishing some of these waters, see Recreation in the Sun Valley chapter.)

In cold water the experienced, or lucky, angler will snag brook trout, brown trout, bull trout, chinook salmon, cutthroat trout, kokanee salmon, lake trout, rainbow trout, steelhead, whitefish or sturgeon. Warmer waters are home to largemouth bass, smallmouth bass, bluegill, bullhead catfish, channel cat, crappie, perch, walleye and northern pike.

Golf

New courses are going in as Boise increases its appetite for golf. Generally dry, sunny weather and mountain views make the

A-Good-Walk-Ruined sport a natural for the Treasure Valley. There are 11 public course in the area, allowing easy visitor access and play for resident hackers who don't want to spend their lives or a great deal of money at the links but like to get out now and then.

As elsewhere, summer weekends are the busiest golf times, and reservations a week ahead of time are recommended. For play during the week, reservations at least several days ahead are prudent. However, it is possible to walk onto a public course during the week and tee off a short time after.

Boise

Boise Ranch Golf Course
6501 S. Cloverdale Rd. · (208) 362-6501

The course is architecturally designed to accommodate average to excellent playing skills. It has seven lakes and strategically placed roughs, moguls and mounds. Fees for 18 holes Friday through Sunday are $20; Monday through Thursday, it's $15. A cart rental for 18 holes is $18.

Foxtail Executive Golf Course
990 W. Chinden Blvd., Meridian
· (208) 887-4653

This is a short, easy 18-hole course with panoramic views. It's good for a warm-up round and coddles beginners. Foxtail has 12 par 3 holes and a 483-yard par 5 18th hole. Fees are $7 for nine holes or $11 for 18 holes seven days a week. Carts cost $6 for nine holes or $12 for 18 holes.

The Golf & Recreation Club
3883 S. Orchard St. · (208) 344-2008

This is a true par 3, nine-hole course, ideal for working on the short game or tuning up for that corporate tournament. The course is particularly good for beginners and kids. Course fees are $7.35 every day. A pull cart rents for $1.

Indian Lakes Golf Club
4700 Umatilla Ave. · (208) 362-5771

This nine-hole course is particularly good for beginners and seniors. It has two demanding par 3 holes and a true three-shot par 5. Hardwood and pine trees complement the

Photo: Idaho State Parks

Hot summer afternoons are made for a relaxing float — or soak — in area waters.

mountain backdrop. Course fees for 18 holes Monday through Thursday are $15; Friday through Sunday, $18. The cart rental for 18 holes is $18.

Quail Hollow Golf Club
4520 N. 36th St. • (208) 344-7807

Nestled in the foothills, Quail Hollow is an up-and-down course rated as one of the five best in Idaho by *Golf Digest*. Vistas and canyons give the course a back-country atmosphere. Most people opt for carts on this rugged terrain rather than shouldering their bags over some fairly steep inclines. The course has water on 10 holes and 60 bunkers. Course fees are $18 weekdays and $22 on weekends. Carts cost $9 for 18 holes.

Warm Springs Golf Course
2495 Warm Springs Ave.
• (208) 343-5661

This flat course with large greens is on the Boise River Greenbelt. Four holes are on the river and six have water hazards. The course is convenient, scenic and playable to anyone's level. Course fees are $15 weekdays and $17 on weekends. Carts rent for $5 for nine holes, $9 for 18 holes.

Nampa

Centennial Golf Course
Centennial Dr. • (208) 467-3011

With a mix of rolling terrain and flat surfaces, the course has scenic mountain views throughout. It also has wide fairways, water on 12 holes and large, fluctuating greens that are difficult to read. Course fees are $12 for nine or 18 holes every day. Carts rent for $9 for nine holes or $15 for 18 holes.

Ridgecrest Golf Course
3730 Ridgecrest Dr. • (208) 888-3730

Idaho's newest public golf course, Ridgecrest

blends the character and tradition of Scottish links courses into the gently rolling corn fields of Nampa. Its high ground offers a spectacular panorama of the Owyhee Mountains and Boise Foothills. Course fees are $16 weekdays and $19 weekends. A cart rents for $18.

Caldwell

Fairview Golf Course
816 Grant St. • (208) 455-3090

This nine-hole course is practically in downtown Caldwell. Golfers are personally liable for damage done to houses and shop fronts. The course is filled with mature Russian olive, maple and pine trees. The course is flat, the greens are small, and slopes are slight. No tee times are taken, so just come on over and tee up. Fees are $10 for nine holes, $12 for 18 holes; a cart rents for $7.75 per each nine holes.

Purple Sage Golf Course
15192 Purple Sage Rd. • (208) 459-2223

The course has flat, tree-lined fairways, water on nine holes, 27 bunkers and mountain and desert views. It is a layout that the average golfer can enjoy. Course fees are $12 weekdays and $14 on weekends. A cart rents for $16.

Health Clubs

Treasure Valley health clubs typically have physical fitness equipment and training, playing courts, pools, tanning and physical therapy.

Boise

AJ's Health Clubs
ParkCenter, 555 West Parkcenter Blvd.
• (208) 343-2288

This club has about 5,000 members and charges $45 to $55 per month. Facilities include seven racquetball courts, free weights,

---

INSIDERS' TIP

Bogus Basin Ski Area can have very different weather conditions than the Treasure Valley, about a mile below, so check out conditions before you start up the road. If you don't see a snowflake on city streets, that doesn't mean the skiing isn't spectacular above. Call (208) 332-1500 to check conditions.

cardiovascular equipment, a swimming pool and a steam room and sauna.

Gold's Gym
8650 Fairview Ave. • (208) 377-4653

Gold's Gym is strictly a physical fitness center. It tailors programs for individual members. Classes include spinning (a bicycle workout), aerobics and body pump, which uses 3 to 17 pound weights during the one-hour group workouts. Gold's has 1,700 members. Monthly charges vary from $17 to $75.

Caldwell

Idaho Athletic Club
3410 Blaine St. • (208) 459-0729

This club features five racquetball courts, a 60-foot pool, an aerobics room, a large variety of weights and 10 treadmills. It has 1,200 members who pay $399 for the year or $39 per month.

Hiking

Hull's Gulch Interpretive Trail
Boise National Forest, 1249 S. Vinnell Way, Boise • (208) 373-4007

An excellent, informative hike for people of all abilities is Hulls Gulch Interpretive Trail, which begins from the dirt road 3.5 miles beyond the end of the N. 8th Street pavement, has 3.5-mile and 2.5-mile self-guided, interpretive loops and has signs that address wildlife, history, soils, vegetation and ecology. Many plant species are identified along the trail. Rabbits, squirrels, lizards, snakes, mule deer, skunks, porcupines, badgers and coyotes inhabit Hull's Gulch. Trees and shrubs along the trail include Rocky Mountain maple, Hawthorn, Water, Birch, Chokeberry and Syringa, the Idaho state flower. The Hull's Gulch Interpretive Trail is limited to walkers.

Hull's Gulch is part of the Boise Front, which is an incline of 75,000 acres that rises about a mile above the Treasure Valley to 7,590-foot Shafer Butte. This magnificent natural playground is laced with primitive roads and trails that make for good hiking. Twenty-two of the marked trails are set aside for hikers, mountain bikers and horseback riders.

These are dirt trails that are part of a huge labyrinth that covers the foothills above Boise. You can go for a short, easy walk or a long, rugged hike. The hills are covered with sagebrush and creeks that can be forded or are dry. At higher levels, you'll see softwood and hardwood trees. City and valley views are excellent from these many trails.

Here are several of the best trail access points to follow. Drive up 8th Street to trails below and above Hull's Gulch Interpretive Trail; drive up Brumback Street to Crestline Drive trail; take Reserve Street to the Mountain Cove Road Trail. In each case you can park beside the road or in a lot. To get on top of the Boise Front for varied hiking and walking possibilities, drive 16 miles up Bogus Basin Road to Bogus Basin Ski Resort. This is a difficult, zigzag road that requires patience but has scenery and recreational opportunities that make it worth the ride.

For information about Boise Front trails contact the Bureau of Land Management, 3948 Development Avenue, Boise, (208) 384-3300, or Boise National Forest, 1249 S. Vinnell Way, Boise, at the previously listed number.

Boise River Greenbelt

The 22-mile riverside pathway of the Greenbelt offers a nearby hiking/walking opportunity. A short getaway in the middle of the city or a day's trek are possible. Greenbelt access points are at Harbor Lane, Willow Lane, Garden Street, Riverside Park, Veterans Memorial State Park, Shoreline Park, Capitol Boulevard, Julia Davis Park, Boise State University, Municipal Park, Barber Park and at many points on Warm Springs Avenue east of Barber Park.

For information about trails that connect to the Greenbelt as well as a Greenbelt brochure with a map, contact the Boise Parks & Recreation Department, 1104 Royal Boulevard, (208) 384-4240.

Horseback Riding

The hilly, wide-open, water-fed Treasure Valley offers easy access to trail riding and has good facilities for riding lessons and horse shows. You can stable your horse close-in to the city and find a good ride within a half-hour of downtown. Trail maps are available from the Boise National Forest, 1249 S. Vinnell Way, Boise, (208) 373-4007, and the Bureau of Land Management, 3948 Development Avenue, Boise, (208) 384-3300.

The challenge in accommodating riders is the limited parking for horse trailers on many trails near Boise. It's an important question to ask when seeking trail and other riding information.

A monthly, all-breed horse publication, *Just Horses*, (208) 336-6707, is available for free at area tack shops, horse-related businesses and by subscription. It carries feature stories, columns and a calendar of events.

Stables

Boise

D Bar P Roping Arena
65 W. Hazel St., Meridian
· (208) 888-2126

This 20-acre property is known for its real cowboy stuff — cutting and roping and team penning. Owner Dave Stucker is a professional outfitter who teaches a packing school for back-country riders and hunters in spring and fall and a team roping school in the spring.

In addition to boarding and arena rentals, the D Bar P teaches beginner riding lessons that stress confidence, learning and enjoyment of the horse. Group lessons for beginners cost $15 per student. There is barn space for about 30 horses that are boarded for a fee of $175 per month.

Dusty Acres
6343 E. Columbia Rd. · (208) 336-7469

This 20-acre retreat is on the high-plains desert behind Micron Technology, the computer-chip maker and largest Boise employer. It has a 105-foot-by-140-foot outdoor arena that is large enough to play cowboy polo. An indoor barn stables between 40 and 60 horses. The monthly stable fee is $170, and horse-back-riding lessons cost $20 an hour.

Dusty Acres is owned by Andrew and Susan Isaac who have been around horses all their lives. Trina McGowen acts as manager, trainer and salesperson. Billy Blackchex, a stal-

lion, is available for stud services. Novice and expert equestrians enjoy the wide-open territory, where they can ride along the Oregon Trail, through Lucky Peak Reservoir and to the Boise River.

The Idaho Equestrian Center
9400 N. Pierce Park Rd. · (208) 853-2065

Owner and senior instructor Gretchen LaPointe worked at the Headley Thoroughbred Farm near Seattle and studied with Melissa Beardsley in the 1980s. She began teaching at the Girdner Ranch in Meridian before establishing this equestrian center on a hilly back road covered with sagebrush and woodland only 10 minutes from the Capitol.

The 10-acre riding facility includes large and small outdoor arenas, a trail, clubhouse, barn, pastures and covered paddocks. Located in the Boise Foothills, the stables have access to hundreds of miles of federal land for trail and endurance riding.

Services include private and semiprivate lessons; training and conditioning; and horse rental, leasing, boarding and sales.

Pasture board is available for $135 per month; indoor barn stalls with paddocks are $195; a breezeway barn with partially covered paddocks runs $165. Board rates include twice daily feeding and use of large and small outdoor arenas and a round corral.

Two introductory lessons cost $50, a three-lesson package costs $85, and a five-lesson package costs $135. An individual 45-minute lesson costs $32, and an individual semiprivate lesson, with two or three students, costs $27.

Summer camps for kids, group outings and special events are also offered at The Idaho Equestrian Center.

Once Upon a Horse
2880 N. Eagle Rd., near Beacon Light Rd., Eagle · (208) 939-0785

Owners Ernst and Janet Herrmanns are known in Western dressage circles: Ernst as a judge, Janet as a competitor at the highest level and both as teachers. Dressage is a judged performance with a horse. The Herrmanns' 32-acre Eagle stable location has an indoor riding arena and outdoor arenas for dressage, jumping and cross-country jumping.

Fifty horses are stabled here at a cost of $300 per month. English riding, dressage and jumping lessons are offered at prices ranging from $20 to $35 a lesson, depending on length and whether the lessons are individual or group. A good school program is offered that has many beginners taking mostly dressage classes.

Riding Clubs

Local riding clubs go on outings, stage shows and competitions and sponsor many events that are open to the public. Their biggest event is an annual Horse-A-Thon held the last weekend of May. Participants trailer their horses to Eagle and take part in 8-mile and 12-mile rides. More than 300 riders showed up in 1997 and raised $30,000 that was donated to the Idaho Diabetes Association.

Here are the contact numbers for the local riding clubs: Black Canyon Riding Club, (208) 365-4062; Boise Foothills Trail Riders, (208) 387-2658; Boise Saddle and Jump Club, (208) 939-6483; Eagle Valley Riders, (208) 459-2608; Eh-Capa Bareback Riders, (208) 939-9158; Idaho Cowboy Association, (208) 549-1397; Idaho Mounted Orienteering, (208) 585-3948; Idaho State Horseshow Association, (208) 466-6940; Intermountain Region Pony Clubs, (208) 939-8848; Kuna Kave Riding Club, (208) 888-7645; Les Bois Dressage Club and Combined Training Association, (208) 362-0084; Payette Valley Riders, (208) 642-9416; Snake River Team Penning Association, (208) 362-9042; Southwest Idaho Trail and Distance Riders, (208) 336-9413; Ten Mile Riding Club, (208) 922-4741; Treasure Valley Back Country Horsemen of Idaho, (208) 495-2302; Treasure Valley Leather Slappers, (208) 454-8045; and Western Riding Club, (208) 286-0955.

Trail Rides

Boise

Bogus Creek Outfitters
1015 Robert St. • (208) 336-3130
This company of licensed outfitters and guides, started in 1989, provides summer horseback trail rides and chuck-wagon din-

ners, winter sleigh rides and dinners at Bogus Basin. It is the only company of its kind on the mountain.

Summer trail rides cost $18 per person for an hour and $30 for two hours, with a pre-ride lesson provided. A summer chuck-wagon dinner costs $59. A winter sleigh ride and dinner that includes cowboy poetry and live music costs $59.

Hunting

Hunting is popular in the Treasure Valley, as it is throughout the state of Idaho. Deer, elk, black bear, mountain lion, wild turkey, waterfowl and upland game birds may be hunted in hills, mountains and along rivers only a short distance — within an hour or two — of downtown.

State geography ranges from canyons and flat, sagebrush-covered deserts in the south to forested, high mountains in the center to smaller and lushly vegetated mountains in the north. It provides sustenance and cover for elk, mule deer, bighorn sheep, antelope, bear, moose, cougar, mountain goat, white-tailed deer, upland game birds and waterfowl. And an elk population growing across the state attracts as many as 100,000 hunters a year, making it the most hunted species.

Hunters must purchase a general hunting license and a tag for each hunted species. An annual resident license costs $7.50, a nonresident license $101.50. The cost of resident hunting tags for deer is $10.50; elk, $16.50; bear, $7.50; mountain lion, $26.50; wild turkey, $7.50; and antelope, $28. The cost of nonresident hunting tags for deer, bear, mountain lion and antelope is $226.50 for each tag; for elk, $326.50; and for wild turkey, $36.50. Idaho's hunting seasons are as long as 65 days in many areas and overall success rates are high.

For information contact the Idaho Fish & Game Department, 600 S. Walnut Avenue, Boise, (208) 334-3700. You can learn a lot about Idaho's wildlife by subscribing to *Wildlife*, the award-winning, Idaho Fish & Game Department magazine.

For information about outfitters and guides, contact the Idaho Outfitters and Guides Association, 711 N. 5th Street, Boise, (208) 342-1438 or (800) 847-4843.

Skiing

Downhill

Boise

Bogus Basin Ski Area
2405 Bogus Basin Rd. • (208) 332-5100

The Boise foothills are crowned by one of the finest nonprofit, community-run ski areas in the country. Bogus Basin's 2,600 ski acres offer a great variety of terrain, particularly long, intermediate runs, and night skiing that with its forest passageways, back-mountain, black-diamond drop and valley views could be the best in the country. With the addition of a quad chairlift to go with seven double chairs serving a 1,490 vertical and 58 trails, everything is up-to-date at Bogus Basin.

Prices are less than at other comparable areas. Adult ticket prices are around $30, and from 4 to 10 PM prices are around $20. As at other resorts snowboarding has caught on big and is seen all over the mountain. The sport has its own halfpipe, activities and events. A Nordic Trail that provides lessons and rentals and has splendid views is located less than a mile past the base area.

Food is available at the Bogus Creek Lodge and Pioneer Lodge. A sports shop offers rental, repair and retail of skis and snowboards. Ski-in, ski-out lodging is available at Pioneer Inn Condominiums, where hot tubs, saunas and a game room are on-site.

The only drawback of Bogus Basin is the 16-mile zigzag road climb to get there, which takes 30 to 45 minutes under good conditions and can be icy and treacherous. Take it slow — we guarantee you'll be hitting the slopes in no time.

Throughout the State

If Grand Targhee, just over the Wyoming border, is counted, Idaho has nine good and widely different downhill ski areas. Sun Valley (see our Sun Valley chapter), located 153 miles east of Boise, has been ranked the top down-hill resort in the country. Targhee is known for its tremendous snow accumulations and Old West, Teton Mountain grandeur. Far-flung

Schweitzer Mountain, in Sandpoint to the north, overlooks the state's largest lake, Pend Oreille, and Brundage Mountain, 106 miles north of Boise in McCall, overlooks Payette Lake. Bruce Willis and Demi Moore have bought and improved Soldier Mountain, a small resort at a gorgeous location with Old America ambiance. Soldier Mountain is in the Camas Valley, halfway between Boise and Sun Valley. Pomerelle, south of Burley, has snow when it's scarce elsewhere; Silver Mountain is in the old mining town of Kellogg; and Pebble Creek, east of Pocatello in the southeast, is the ultimate small-town community resort.

All of these areas have ski schools and rent ski and snowboard equipment.

Brundage Mountain
McCall • (208) 634-4151

McCall is calling all skiers to its 1,800-foot vertical drop at Brundage Mountain. Two double chairs, two triple chairs, one poma lift and one handle tow guide the way to the start of 44 runs. Adults pay $28; ages 13 to 18 and 65 and older, $23; and ages 7 to 12, $17. Kids 6 and younger ski free.

Grand Targhee
Alta, Wyo. • (307) 353-2300

This area lives up to the "grand" in its name with a vertical drop of 2,200 feet, two quad chairs, three double chairs, one surface lift and 62 runs. Tickets are $36 for adult; $22 for children 6 to 14 and seniors 62 to 69. Children 5 and younger and those 70 and older ski for free.

Pebble Creek
Inkom • (208) 775-4452

Twenty-four runs line the 2,000-foot drop at Pebble Creek, which has two double chairs and one triple chair. Adults pay $22; those ages 13 to 18 and seniors 65 and older, $18; and children 12 and younger, $14.

Schweitzer Mountain
Sandpoint • (208) 263-9555

One quad run and five double chair lifts get skiers to the start of Schweitzer Mountain's 55 runs. Momentum and gravity get them down the 2,400-foot vertical drop. Tickets are $34 for adults, $20 for children 7 to 12, and $27 for students 13 and older and seniors. Are you

Photo: World Center for Birds of Prey

At the World Center for Birds of Prey, you can view hawks, eagles, owls and falcons.

new to the world of downhill skiing? There's a beginner's lift ticket for $15.

Silver Mountain
Kellogg • (208) 783-1111
Access to 50 runs is provided by a gondola, quad chair, one of two triple chairs, one of two double chairs or a surface tow at this resort with a vertical drop of 2,200 feet. Tickets are $31 for adults, $24 for students and seniors and $18 for children. A perk for parents: kids 6 and younger ski free.

Soldier Mountain
Fairfield • (208) 764-2526
More than 40 runs grace the 1,400-foot vertical drop at Soldier Mountain, the snowy pride and joy of Bruce Willis and Demi Moore. Two double chair lifts, one handle pull and one rope tow get you to the top, or at least to the highest point you'd like to brave. Tickets are $18 for adults, $14 for children.

Cross-Country

Numerous state parks, U.S. forests, municipalities and private ski operators in Idaho provide cross-country skiing opportunities. The state offers a cross-country ski guide in conjunction with its Park N' Ski permit program. An annual permit costs $15 and a three-day temporary permit is $7.50. The Idaho City area, 21 miles northeast of Boise, has a number of first-rate trails, which are detailed in the Park N' Ski Idaho City Area guide that is available from the Idaho Department of Parks and Recreation, 5657 Warm Springs Avenue, Boise, (208) 334-4199, or Ada County Park N' Ski Committee, P.O. Box 3232, Boise ID 83702, (208) 345-4855.

Banner Ridge
Idaho Hwy. 21, 23.5 miles north of Idaho City
Banner Ridge has 14.5 miles of marked trails for intermediate to expert skiers. Off-trail skiing is also offered. There are restrooms and a plowed parking lot, and trails are groomed weekly.

Gold Fork
Idaho Hwy. 21, 20 miles north of Idaho City
Gold Fork has 14.9 miles of skiing. Begin-

ners should be able to handle this area, except for steep downhills that can challenge experts. Restrooms and a plowed parking area are on-site, and trails are groomed weekly.

Whoop-Um-Up
Idaho Hwy. 21, 18 miles north of Idaho City

Some sections of the 6.6-mile trail complex are challenging and require advanced skills. Trails are marked but not groomed.

Snowmobiling

Of Idaho's 44 counties, 24 have designated snowmobile areas, and there is a score of very active state clubs that work to improve the snowmobile experience. The most popular area is Island Park, just over the hill from West Yellowstone in northeast Idaho, about 300 miles east of Boise. The second-most popular area is Valley County, where the towns of McCall, Cascade and Smith's Ferry are located, about 100 miles north of Boise. For information, contact Idaho Department of Parks and Recreation, 5657 Warm Springs Avenue, Boise, (208) 334-4199.

Skydiving

Skydive Idaho
Caldwell Industrial Airport, Exit 29, I-84, Caldwell • (208) 455-0000

This company is open year-round, seven days a week. It has 10 instructors. Skydivers make jumps from Cessna 182 and Beechcraft King airplanes from 10,000 to 13,000 above the airport. The cost for tandem jumps with an instructor is $150. Included in the price are instruction, a videotape and your jumpsuit. The company supervises about 500 tandem jumps a year, and about 4,000 jumps are made from its planes each year.

Snake River Skydiving
4005 N. Can-Ada Rd., Star
• (208) 286-7912, (800) 860-JUMP

Snake River Skydiving offers training and jumping on the same day, tandem and static line instruction and free-fall videos and still photos. The company has five instructors and

uses a Cessna 182 for taking up jumpers. It sees more than 400 first-time jumpers and 3,000 skydives each year. The cost for a tandem jump with an instructor is $129 weekdays and $149 weekends.

Swimming

Lakes, Rivers and Reservoirs

Lucky Peak State Park
Idaho Hwy. 21, 10 miles southeast of Boise • (208) 334-2679

Sandy Point is one of three units that make up Lucky Peak State Park. Beneath the huge wall of Lucky Peak Dam, it has a beautiful white sand beach that curves against a pond-like swimming area, a grassy overlook with grills and picnic tables and concessions. It's an excellent family spot. A motorized vehicle entrance fee of $2 is charged regardless of how many people are in the vehicle. Visitors entering the park without a vehicle do not pay. The park and beach are generally open Memorial Day through Labor Day. There is no lifeguard on duty.

For information about Lucky Peak and other Idaho state parks, visit or contact Idaho Department of Parks and Recreation, between the city of Boise and Lucky Peak, at 5657 Warm Springs Avenue, (208) 334-4199.

Lake Lowell
Deer Flat National Wildlife Refuge, 13751 Upper Embankment Rd., Nampa
• (208) 467-9278, (208) 888-5582

Lake Lowell has designated swimming areas at its upper and lower dams. There are no lifeguards. Lake Lowell is a rural body of water surrounded by woodlands and grasslands that is about 10 miles long and 3 miles across at its widest point.

Eagle Island State Park
2691 Mace Rd., Eagle • (208) 939-0696

Eagle Island, in the middle of the Boise River, has a sand beach and a water slide, but there is no lifeguard on duty. Admission to the park is $3.

Pools

Boise

The Boise City Aquatic Center
West Family YMCA, 5959 N. Discovery Pl. • (208) 377-9622

The Boise City Aquatic Center offers year-round public swimming at an Olympic-size pool, a kiddie pool with slides and a big turtle mountain, and a rehabilitation and therapy pool. Daily fees that include lockers and showers are $3 for children ages 18 and younger, $6 for adults and $15 for families. Monthly fees are $12 for children, $30 for adults. Nonresident, monthly prices are $18 for children, $45 for adults. Resident families pay $60; nonresident families, $90.

Three-week session swimming lessons are offered in September, October, November and December. For ages 3 to 5, lessons cost $22 for residents and $33 for nonresidents; for ages 6 to 14, $30 for residents and $45 for nonresidents; and for adults ages 15 and older, $35 for residents and $52.50 for nonresidents.

Outdoor swimming pools at the following locations are open to the public during June, July and August. Pool hours are generally 1:30 to 5:30 PM and 7 to 9 PM daily except for Sunday night when they are closed. Prices per visit are $1.50 to $2 for ages 11 and younger; $2 to $2.50 for ages 12 to 18; and $3 to $3.50 for adults.

For information about Boise public swimming, contact Boise Parks & Recreation, 1104 Royal Boulevard, Boise, (208) 384-4240.

Borah High School, 6001 Cassia Street, (208) 322-3855

Fairmont Junior High School, 2121 N. Cole Road, (208) 322-3835

Lowell School, 1507 N. 28th Street, (208) 338-3478

Natatorium & Hydrotube, 1811 Warm Springs Avenue, (208) 345-9270

South Junior High School, 805 Shoshone Street, (208) 338-3565

Ivywild Pool, 416 Ivywild Street, (208) 384-4486

Nampa

Nampa Recreation Center
131 Constitution Way • (208) 465-2288

The Nampa Recreation Center is open year round and offers five swimming pools for exercise and recreational enjoyment. It has a diving well with a depth of 9 to 10 feet; a 10-lane, 25-meter lap swimming pool; a recreational pool equipped with spraying fountains; a pool for young children; and a hydrotherapy pool that is designed for therapy exercise classes and recreational swimming.

Fees include access to the entire 140,000-square-foot center, which has among its activities indoor rock climbing, basketball and racquetball courts, a running track, a gymnastics floor and a spa, sauna and steam room. Daily passes are $6 for those 18 and older, $4 for those 12 to 17, $3 for kids 6 to 11 and $1 for children 6 and younger. Annual pass rates are $265 for an individual and $477 for a family.

Tennis

Boise has 101 public courts at 17 parks, nine schools and Boise State University. All players must wear tennis shoes. Black soled shoes are prohibited. No reservations are taken. Play is limited to one hour when other players are waiting. School teams have weekday priority until 5:30 PM. Players 18 and older have priority after 5:30 PM daily and all day on weekends and holidays. Courts may be reserved for special events, but one court at each reservation location must be kept open for general public play.

INSIDERS' TIP

If you are visiting Idaho for an outback fishing, hunting or whitewater experience, take a few days to explore the arts, history, dining, nightlife and spectator sports in surprisingly sophisticated Boise. Likewise, if you are visiting Boise for business, it's an easy, spectacular step into the outback.

For reservation information call (208) 376-1052. The Boise Parks & Recreation Department, 1104 Royal Boulevard, Boise, (208) 384-4240, lists parks with tennis courts in its free activity guide.

You'll find public courts at the following locations.

Boise

Ann Morrison Park, 900 block of Ann Morrison Drive

Boise High School, 13th and Washington streets

Boise State University, University Drive off Broadway Avenue

Borah High School, 6001 Cassia Street

Camelback Park, 13th and Heron streets

Capitol High School, 6055 Goddard Road

Cassia Park, 4500 Camas Lane

Castle Hills Park, 6000 Eugene Street, off Castle Drive

Elm Grove Park, 23rd and Irene streets

Fairmont Junior High School, 7925 Northview Street, off Cole Road

Fairview Park, 23rd and Bannock streets

Fort Boise Park, Reserve and Fort streets

Hillside Park, 36th Street and Hill Road

Ivywild Park, 2300 Division Avenue, off Melrose Street

Julia Davis Park, 500 Capitol Boulevard, across from Myrtle Street

Les Bois Junior High School, Apple Street and Boise Avenue

Lincoln School, 3rd and Fort streets

Manitou Park, 600 S. Manitou Avenue

North Junior High School, 15th and Fort streets

Owyhee Park, 3131 S. Owyhee Street

Quarry View Park, off Penitentiary Drive and Warm Springs Avenue

Shoshone Park, 2800 Canal Street

South Junior High School, Cassia and Shoshone streets

Sunset Park, 32nd Street and Sunset Avenue

West Junior High School, Curtis and Emerald streets

Williams Park, 200 block of Williams Street

Winstead Park, 6150 Northview Street

Tubing

From Memorial Day to Labor Day each year about 300,000 people tube a 4-mile stretch of the Boise River between Barber Park and downtown Boise. They float through a string of parks that are inhabited by songbirds, ducks, blue heron, quail, geese, hawks, owls and bald eagles and past a people parade on Greenbelt pathways that includes walkers, joggers, bikers, skaters, runners and anglers.

Bus service is provided from 11 AM to 9 PM daily by Laidlaw Transportation between Barber Park, upstream at 4525 S. Eckert Road, and downstream at the take-out point, Wheels R Fun, located on the Greenbelt at Shoreline Drive and S. 13th Street, across from the main Boise post office. The bus arrives at Barber Park every hour on the half-hour and at Ann Morrison Park every hour on the hour.

If you go tubing, remember that even on hot summer days the river water can be cool, so bring cover-ups as well as sun protection.

Tubes may be rented for $5 from Wheels R Fun, (208) 343-8228, and from the rental office at Barber Park, (208) 343-6564.

Whitewater Adventures

There are people in Idaho who think the "Famous Potatoes" on the license plate should be replaced by "The White-Water State." The proponents may be sodden and wear lopsided grins from too much time spent in eddies, waves and water holes, but it is true that Idaho's 3,300 whitewater miles are about 1,000 more than California, the next highest state.

Idaho offers every kind of whitewater excursion, from white-knuckled roller coaster rides to serene drifts through cottonwoods. Commercial rafting began here a half-century ago. The

---

INSIDERS' TIP

Idaho has splendidly long fall and spring seasons — times when the recreational crowds of summer can be avoided in the state's marvelous outdoors.

first successful trip through the tumultuous Middle Fork of the Salmon was made in 1936 in plywood and Masonite boats. Rubber rafts, kayaks, canoes, drift boats, jet boats and do-it-yourself paddleboats are now used on trips ranging from a few hours to a few weeks.

One hundred world class rapids make the Middle Fork of the Salmon Idaho's most famous stretch of river. Its full 100-mile length is federally protected as a wild and scenic waterway. Also in the wild and scenic category are the main Salmon River, the Lochsa, the Selway, the St. Joe and Hells Canyon of the Snake River. Together, they comprise a wild river system of 236 miles in length.

Closer to Boise the Payette is known for rafting, kayaking and paddleboating. The South Fork of the Payette, east of Banks and continuing through Lowman on Idaho Highway 21, has some of the best kayaking in the country and is only 45 minutes from Boise.

Idaho Outfitters and Guides
711 N. 5th St., Boise • (208) 342-1438, (800) 847-4843

This nonprofit organization that has existed since the 1950s represents 70 percent, or 270 outfitters and guides in Idaho. It provides information on whitewater trips, fishing, hunting, mountain biking, guest ranches, jetboating and other outdoor activities that could range from a two-hour trail ride to a seven-to-eight-day rafting trip to two weeks at a guest ranch. The organization sends out two directories — one for water and one for land activities. Call (208) 342-1919 for a directory.

With the recent construction of two professional sports centers in Boise and Nampa, the Treasure Valley spectator sports menu has gone from good to outstanding.

Spectator Sports

With the recent construction of two professional sports centers in Boise and Nampa, the Treasure Valley spectator sports menu has gone from good to outstanding.

Football and basketball at Boise State University, Nampa and Caldwell rodeos, horse racing at Les Bois Racetrack and auto racing in Meridian and near Emmett are traditional big draws.

In 1989 Diamond Sports, Inc., built 4,000-seat Memorial Stadium for its Boise Hawks minor league baseball team, and park ambiance and championship teams resulted in record-setting attendance.

A women's professional bicycle race, the Nike Boise Open golf tournament, and World Team Tennis spice the summer agenda.

Now things have gotten truly exciting for the avid sports fan with the 1997 opening of the 5,000-seat Bank of America Centre in downtown Boise, which with a constant slate of events that includes minor league ice hockey, figure skating, tennis and boxing, is acting the part of a "Little Madison Square Garden," *and* the opening of the 7,773-seat Idaho Center in Nampa, where the Idaho Stampede hosts 28 Continental Basketball Association professional games.

Although world-class athletes like John McEnroe and Kristi Yamaguchi show up for special events, no one would mistake Boise for The Big Cheese of spectator sports. Boise State University is not in the Big Ten any more than the Idaho Steelheads are in the National Hockey League.

But as far as the enjoyment of spectator sports — reasonable cost, ease of attending, the comfort of the arenas and stadiums, the quality of the presentations, including extras such as bands, mascots and dancers, and the color and enthusiasm of participants and crowds — Boise rates very high.

Auto Racing

Firebird Raceway
5 miles north of Boise on Idaho Hwy. 44 to Idaho Hwy. 16 toward Emmett
• (208) 344-0411

Championship drag racing begins with the National Hot Rod Association of America Ignitor during the April-through-October racing schedule. The Nightfire Nationals in August, which attracts autos from all over the western United States, is the state's largest auto racing event, with a purse of $125,000. Dragsters hit speeds of 280 to 320 mph on the half-mile track. Spectator capacity is 7,500, and about 100,000 attend in a season. Specialty events, such as motorcycle racing, Chevy makes and models, and Ford Day, are held throughout the season.

Meridian Speedway
335 E. 1st St., Meridian • (208) 888-2813

This quarter-mile, paved oval with 4,000

---

seats has racing every Saturday night and on four other days between mid-April and the end of September. It averages 2,400 to 2,500 fans for its 27 races. Its biggest race, the two-day Diamond Cup held at the end of May, is the biggest super-modified event west of Oswego, New York.

In addition to the super-modifieds, which are open-wheel cars with wings that weigh 1,750 pounds and are pushed to 100 mph by 850 horsepower motors, the speedway's racing classes are IMCA, Street Stockcars, Future Stocks, Super Stocks, Bomber Stocks (for people off the road with cages and seat belts), Legend Cars (quarter-size, 1200cc mid-'30s Fords, Chevys and the like) and mini pickups.

Traditionally there is a Memorial Day race and July 4th fireworks.

Baseball

The Boise Hawks
Memorial Stadium, 5600 Glenwood St., Boise, on the edge of the Western Idaho Fairgrounds • (208) 322-5000

One of the most delightful ways to spend a summer evening in Boise is to take in a minor league baseball game at Memorial Stadium, which is clean, well-maintained and organized, with high banks of seats that are close to the field, concession stands and an open-air restaurant behind third base. The view beyond the outfield fences is of the Boise Front Range and its foothills, which hold sunshine late into the games.

The Hawks play a "short-season" schedule of 76 games, half at home, that begins in mid-June and runs to the beginning of September. They are in the A Northwest League beneath minor league AA and AAA classifications. League playoffs each year lead to a championship series that the Hawks won in 1991, 1993, 1994 and 1995.

Many league players just graduated from college or were signed from high school and are in their first pro year. The Hawks are owned by the major league Anaheim Angels and have

sent 22 players to the "bigs." The Hawks generally lead the league in attendance at 4,700-seat Memorial Stadium, where the 1997 total was 154,891. If you go to a game, try to get a ticket on the third base side of the stadium, as the descending sun can cast a fierce glare on the first base side.

Diamond Sports, which also owns the Bank of America Centre, the Idaho Steelhead hockey team and professional Idaho Sneakers tennis team, is known for integrating entertainment into its sports events. At Memorial Stadium there is an irreverent Hawk mascot, between-inning contests, activities and presentations, and a humorous scoreboard with sound effects.

Basketball

Idaho Stampede
Can-Ada Rd. at Exit 38, I-84, Nampa • (208) 468-1000

The Idaho Stampede of the Continental Basketball Association began play at the new 7,773-seat Idaho Center in November 1997, with 28 home games in a schedule that ran through the third week of March.

Idaho joined La Crosse, Quad City, Sioux Falls and Yakima in the National Conference; the American Conference consists of Connecticut, Fort Wayne, Grand Rapids and Rockford. Playoffs and a championship series are held at the end of the season.

The Continental Basketball Association is filled with players not quite good enough to play in the country's top pro basketball league, the National Basketball Association, but hoping to get there — or make their way back. In 1996-97, 47 CBA players were called up to the NBA.

The Stampede is coached by Bobby Dye, who had a 213-133 record in his 12 years of coaching Boise State University and had an overall 531-297 record at the four colleges and one high school where he coached.

Players include Rusty LaRue, a 6-foot 2-inch guard from Wake Forest who averaged 12 points a game with Connecticut in 1996-97 and was called up by the NBA Chicago Bulls

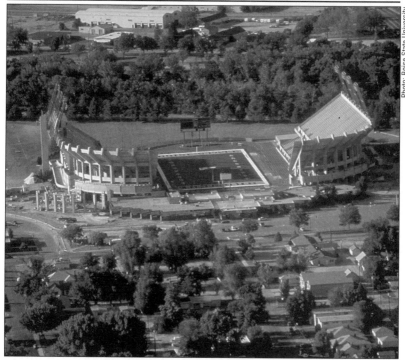

Photo: Boise State University

The 30,000-seat Bronco Stadium is home to BSU's football team.

at the start of the 1997-98 season; Jared Pickett, a 6-foot 9-inch rookie who was the second player in University of Kentucky history to play on three NCAA Final Four teams; Devin Davis, a 6-foot 7-inch forward and the Stampede's top draft pick who averaged 15 points per game at Miami, Ohio; Nate Huffman, who averaged 17 points and 11 rebounds a game at Central Michigan; Nate Erdmann, a 6-foot 2-inch guard who averaged 20 points a game in his senior year at the University of Oklahoma and was drafted in the second round by the NBA Utah Jazz; Ashrat Amaya, a 6-foot 8-inch forward who spent two years in the NBA; and Deryl Cunningham, a three-year CBA veteran and top-20 shot blocker.

BSU Pavilion
1910 University Dr., BSU campus, Boise · (208) 385-1285

Boise State University plays in the Big West Conference at 12,380-seat BSU Pavilion, one of the finest basketball arenas in the West. The $17.5 million structure went up in 1982, doesn't have a bad seat, has the latest scoreboard and computer message boards, an enthusiastic student and local following, acrobatic cheerleaders, a fired-up band and the attractive and imaginative Mane Line Dancers.

In its 15 years in the Pavilion, BSU has averaged 12 home wins a season and has picked up victories better than 75 percent of the time. The team's conference average attendance of 7,900 fans is second only to New Mexico State. BSU is in the conference's Eastern Division along with Idaho, Nevada, New Mexico State, North Texas and Utah State. Members of the Western Division are Cal Poly SLO, Cal-State Fullerton, Long Beach State, Pacific, UC Irvine and UC Santa Barbara.

BSU Coach Rod Jensen had a 46-39 three-year record at the end of the 1997-98 season. The school's best-known former player is National Basketball Association guard Chris Childs.

The Pavilion hosted an early NCAA tournament round in spring 1998, as it did in 1995, 1992, 1989 and 1983. From victories by top-ranked Virginia and Ralph Sampson, to UCLA and Tyus Edney's improbable 4.8 second coast-to-coast lay-up to beat Missouri in 1995 when the Bruins won the national championship, Boise has become one of the most popular and respected NCAA regional sites.

Tickets are available for most BSU games, and it is a top sports night out at a primo location.

Bicycling

Hewlett-Packard International Women's Challenge
(208) 345-7223

This is a premier event in women's professional cycling consisting of road races, time trials and criterion races during an 11-day period in mid-June, which attracts competitors from all over the world. Altogether, 12 stages are held in Idaho and Utah, with $100,000 in prize money. Events are staged at community locations that lend themselves to outings with families and friends and might be combined with picnics, hikes, sight-seeing and other such activities. Race sites include a circuit around the Capitol in downtown Boise, the steep, Bogus Basin Road zigzag that reaches to the ski area, and a Sun Valley climb over 8,701-foot Galena Summit.

Football

Boise State University
Bronco Stadium, 1910 University Dr.,
BSU campus, Boise • (208) 385-1285

Boise State University's football fortunes have gone up and down like a trampoline in recent years, with participation in a Division II championship game; the poignant death from cancer of popular coach Pokey Allen followed by a season of team gridiron collapse; a revival of enthusiasm, spirit and performance by new coach Houston Nutt; and just when things looked good again, the loss of Nutt after only a year to the University of Arkansas, his alma mater, where he was an outstanding player

and close to athletic director and former Razorback coach Frank Broyles.

New BSU coach Dirk Koetter, previously offensive coordinator at the University of Oregon, is coming to a city that greatly enjoys and has been a strong supporter of college football. When Bronco Stadium was built in 1970, it had 14,500 seats; with a second expansion in 1997, capacity is 30,000. Season ticket sales run 12,000 to 13,000, and about 5,000 students attend the games, so more than 20,000 generally turn out, except for the game with arch-rival University of Idaho, when it's standing room only.

Boise State, now in its third year of playing in the top 1-A NCAA Division, is a member of Big West Conference, which includes Cal State Northridge, Weber State, New Mexico State, North Texas, Utah State, Nevada and Idaho. In 1997 it played against two top-25 teams, nearly defeating the Big Ten's University of Wisconsin in Madison and getting flattened by the Pac 10's Rose Bowl representative, Washington State, in Pullman.

The most striking thing about Bronco Stadium games is the blue Astroturf football field, the only one in the country and possibly the world. From an airplane it looks like an immense swimming pool. On a sunny day, the blue gradually changes color as the sun crosses the sky, going from a deep royal blue to lighter shades of the South Pacific.

A Bronco game is spiced by a Bronco horse and rider waving a huge flag, trailed by a "Pokey helmet" that is a VW bug, which circle the field after a BSU touchdown; a wildly-enthusiastic, orange-bereted Bronco band; a little Bronco black dog that dashes out to retrieve the kicking tee; the halftime pizzazz of the Mane Line Dancers; formations of geese flying above autumn trees beside the adjacent Boise River and Greenbelt; and a cannon that when fired issues white puffs of smoke that float up into the sky.

Humanitarian Bowl
Bronco Stadium, 1910 University Dr.,
BSU campus, Boise • (208) 338-8887

With an expanded 30,000-seat Bronco Stadium and community zeal that has made the summer Boise River Festival a success, in 1997 Boise hosted its first bowl game, which was

From Harvest Sideshow to Big-Time Rodeo

President Franklin Roosevelt at his home in Hyde Park, New York, pressed a golden telegraph key that opened the 1937 Snake River Stampede for the first time under lights and as a separate event from the annual Nampa Harvest Festival. The telegraph key pressed by Franklin, which was studded with the first 22 nuggets of gold found in Alaska and had been used by Presidents for opening the Panama Canal and Boulder Dam, marked a new era of rodeo standing alone as a popular spectator attraction that continues today, often with extra attractions, in an urban society when most people are unfamiliar with horses and bulls.

 Close-up

The first local rodeo-type competition was staged with the Nampa Harvest Festival in 1911, which featured crop and stock exhibits, prizes for the best products of Nampa farms, orchards and gardens, sports and contests, special attractions and free amusements. This festival may be looked upon as a predecessor of the state fair, with the original bucking contests gaining in popularity and joined by calf roping and bulldogging over the years. Ed Moody herded bucking stock overland from his ranch north of Horseshoe Bend for what was called "the buck show" in 1923 and continued to furnish stock for the Rodeo and Buck Show until 1937.

In 1937, cued by Roosevelt's telegraph signal, the rodeo separated from the harvest festival and moved its dates from September to July. It became a member of the Professional Rodeo Cowboy Association and, following a contest, was called the Snake River Stampede. Lights were installed on the rodeo grounds so that it was changed from an afternoon to night show, and professional stock contractor Leo Cremer of Montana brought his stock to the rodeo by train.

In 1950 a new green, horseshoe-shaped arena that seated 10,000 people was constructed that would serve the rodeo well for 46 years. This was a period when cowboy singers were big, and Gene Autry, a TV gunslinger with a guitar, was the first star of the Snake River Stampede and filled the stands every night. Many people who couldn't get inside the arena stood outside and listened to Autry sing. Others who followed Autry included Roy Rogers and Dale Evans, Rex Allen, Doc and Festus of *Gunsmoke* and the Sons of the Pioneers.

With the 1970s and 1980s, country singers replaced the spurred variety as rodeo draws. Reba McEntire, popular today, made her debut as a headline entertainer at the Snake River Stampede. Glen Campbell and Barbara Mandrell were among other nationally known country crooners who hiked the gate. In the late 1980s musical twang subsided in favor of more rodeo events. The stars disappeared, and ladies

— continued on next page

Photo: William H. Mullins

Don't try this at home.

barrel racing and team roping, and Wrangler bullfighting featuring bullfighting clowns, were added.

In the 1990s an event for kids ages 5 to 7, mutton busting, joined the lineup. The Miss Rodeo Idaho contest and large Nampa horse parade also became part of the Stampede rodeo week. And in 1997 the Stampede went inside, to the new 10,000-seat, air-conditioned Idaho Center, also the home of the Idaho Stampede professional basketball team and site of rock and pop music concerts. With the hot summer sun blocked out, a matinee performance was added to the rodeo schedule for the first time since 1936, and summer rain outbursts that occasionally plagued the event were no longer a force to contend with.

carried live by ESPN2. The University of Cincinnati defeated Utah State 35-19.

Designed as an annual late December event that offers a pot of at least $750,000 to each participant, the bowl matches the champion of the Big West Conference, which was Utah State in the inaugural, against an at-large team, which was the University of Cincinnati the first year.

Big West Conference champions previously played in the Las Vegas Bowl against the champion of the Mid-America Conference. The Las Vegas Bowl was earlier known as the California Raisin and California Bowl. Big West Conference teams have played in 20 bowl games altogether.

It might be noted that most bowl games are held in warmer climates such as Florida, California and Arizona, so the Humanitarian Bowl, contested during the ski season at Bogus Basin above white hills that are visible from the stadium, and watched by people who might otherwise be occupied by snowmobiles, snowshoes, or ice fishing, may be considered an unusual venture.

Golf

Boise Open
Hillcrest Country Club, 4610 Hillcrest Dr., at the intersection of Overland Rd. and Orchard St., Boise • (208) 343-1769

The Boise Open is a four-day, Nike Tour event played in mid-September by touring minor league golfers who are trying to rise to the top Professional Golf Association (PGA) circuit. The top-15 Nike finishers each year move

into the company of Tiger Woods, Ernie Els, John Daly and other luminaries on the world's most prestigious tour. Els and Daly both played in the Boise tournament.

The $45,000 Boise Open winner's share and $100,000 purse are 25 percent more than the average in the 30 or so Nike events. Expected players for the next Boise open include tour leaders John Wilson, Casey Martin and Chris Riley.

Boise Open attendance rose from 31,000 in 1993 to 50,000 in 1997 at Hillcrest Country Club, which has three holes that are among the 25 most difficult on the Nike Tour. The course is flat, interspersed with trees and has 11 water holes and 57 bunkers. Its luxurious clubhouse sits on a "bench" that overlooks the city of Boise and foothills of the Boise Front.

Horse Racing

Les Bois Park
Western Idaho Fairgrounds, at the intersection of Glenwood St. and Chinden Blvd., Boise • (208) 376-7223

The largest mixed horse racing events in the Northwest occur at Les Bois Park from the end of April through mid-August when thoroughbreds take part in 70 percent and quarter horses 30 percent of the action. A slate of 10 to 12 races is presented three times a week at a three-quarter-mile oval where an average turnout of 2,600 people bet $110,000 to $120,000.

A grandstand, clubhouse and Turf Club are open to all visitors, and restaurant and concession food are available. Simulcast broadcasting of horse races throughout the country, with bets placed at Les Bois going into the total at the originating track, and winnings coming from the sum of money funneled into that same place from all over, are presented year-round, seven days a week, on 165 Les Bois screens.

Two of the best-known jockeys in the world, thoroughbred racer Gary Stephens and quarter horse racer Kip Didericksen, grew up in Boise and learned their trade at Les Bois Park. In 1991 each finished at the top of his standings in this country. Stephens has made a name for himself at the Kentucky Derby.

Ice Hockey

The Idaho Steelheads
Bank of America Centre, Capitol Blvd.
and Front St., Boise • (208) 331-8497

The Idaho Steelheads began West Coast Hockey League play in 1997-98 with a mid-October to end of March 64-game season, followed by playoffs and a championship series. Half the games were played at the team's brand-new, 5,000-seat arena in downtown Boise, where a great deal of enthusiasm greeted a brawling team with sellout crowds and cries for mayhem and goals.

The Steelheads face Anchorage, Reno and Tacoma in the North Division and Bakersfield, Fresno, San Diego, Phoenix and Tucson in the South Division of the professional minor league, and play exhibitions against the likes of the Red Army team from Russia.

Steelhead coach Dave Langevin is a straightforward, no-nonsense tough guy who wants the most intimidating team in the league. Langevin played on four Stanley Cup winners in his 11-year National Hockey League career, and wants "character players" willing to go into the corner and get the puck.

The Bank of America Centre has luxury boxes on the third level that hold up to 100 guests. Diamond Sports also offers a dinner-game package, with a meal served in the Grove Hotel's Grand Ballroom and a stroll downstairs into the arena, which is in the same building, afterwards.

Rodeos

Caldwell Night Rodeo
2301 Blaine St., Caldwell
• (208) 459-2060, (208) 459-7493

This outdoor, mid-August rodeo celebrates its 64th year in 1998 at the 8,500-seat Caldwell Events Center. It is one of the top 20 Professional Rodeo Cowboy Association events of the year and in recent years awarded $200,000 in prize money in the following competitions: bareback bronco riding, steer wrestling, saddle bronco riding, calf roping, bull riding, team roping and barrel riding. A Rodeo Queen Contest takes place during the week of the event, in which contestants are judged on appearance, poise, speaking ability and horsemanship, with the winner advancing to the Miss Rodeo America competition.

Restaurant-quality food is offered by local service clubs, with tacos and super-nachos particularly popular. Beer is available on the rowdy side of the stadium — children sit on the opposite side. This is known as a pure Western, cowboy rodeo, without specialty acts. The rodeo has been carried on delayed broadcasts by ESPN the last four years.

Snake River Stampede
Can-Ada Rd. at I-84 exit 38, Nampa
• (208) 442-3232

After 81 years in an outdoor arena, in 1997 the Snake River Stampede moved indoors with its "wildest, fastest show on earth" to the new air-conditioned, 10,000-seat oval at the Idaho Center. The week-long, mid-July event begins on a Saturday with one of the largest horse parades in the West through downtown Nampa. Buckaroo Breakfasts, which are traditional Western breakfasts accompanied by

INSIDERS' TIP

The Boise State University football bleachers are placed right against the end zones and offer a good close-field view for the most inexpensive ticket price.

Photo: Boise State University

All together now — Goooo Broncos!

entertainment, are served at Nampa's Lakeview Park during rodeo week.

The rodeo is one of the top 20 Professional Rodeo Cowboy Association events in the country and includes all eight PRCA approved events — bareback bronco riding, steer wrestling, saddle bronco riding, wrangler bull fighting, calf roping, bull riding, team roping and barrel racing. The rodeo features the Wrangler bullfighters tour, in which nationally known bullfighter clowns compete by fighting bulls "the cowboy way"; Mutton Busting, in which children 5 to 7 years old are timed and judged on eight-second sheep rides; the Miss Rodeo Idaho contest; and "The One Arm Bandit" John Payne, whose trained horses and dogs annually earn him Specialty Act of the Year on the PRCA circuit.

Tennis

The Idaho Sneakers
Bank of America Centre, Capitol Blvd. and Front St., Boise • (208) 331-8497

The Sneakers are in their fifth season of World Team Tennis play, which takes place in September to the beginning of October. They compete against the Delaware Smash, Kansas City Explorers, Milwaukee Racqueteers, New York OTBZZ, Sacramento Capitals, Springfield Lazers and St. Louis Aces in a league that does not have the top contemporary Wimbledon and U.S. Open players, but has presented some of the biggest all-time names, such as Jimmy Connors, Bjorn Borg and Martina Navratilova.

INSIDERS' TIP

Don't miss the Mane Line Dancers during halftime of both Boise State University football and basketball games. The good-looking, award-winning group presents energetic and sparkling revue-like numbers that may take more conditioning and rehearsal than the plays on the field or court.

Amy Frazier, the top Sneakers player who has been with the team since its inception, has been a top 20s singles and doubles player in world tour standings and has been as high as No. 5 singles player in the United States. She's a crowd favorite with a stellar, two-hand backhand, who is described by Sneaker coach Greg Patton as "beautiful, smart and tenacious."

Patton, who also coaches at Boise State University, where he has lifted the Bronco team to the top 10 in NCAA rankings, has in recent years been named coach of the year by World Team Tennis and the Intercollegiate Tennis Coaches Association. He is one of the most colorful, quotable, knowledgeable and effective coaches in the world. His goals with the Sneakers are getting them into the playoffs and getting the community to feel a strong sense of pride in the team. "They feed each other," he says. "The bottom line is: These Sneakers don't stink."

WTT events are different than typical tournament tennis play. Five events, or sets, are played in women's singles, women's doubles, mixed doubles, men's singles and men's doubles, with overtime played if the trailing team wins event 5, and a supertiebreaker played when the teams are even after event 5 or after overtime.

In any direction you
go, you'll be seduced
by natural wonder,
whether it's a high,
cascading waterfall,
rock-ledged canyons or
towering, sparkling
Alpine country.

Daytrips

Boise is a launch pad for excellent daytrips north, south, east and west. These different directions could give you the feeling of traveling in four separate states or territories — that's how much things change. The constants are Idaho's sparse population and scenic variety, which add up to very good driving loops from Boise with unusually striking, often memorable and sometimes stupendous stops along the way. The Oregon Trail makes a crescent through southern Idaho, emphasizing the state's vital link to Western history. Its old mining towns, Idaho City and Silver City, were once the prospector's rage, and a magnificent Oregon Trail Interpretive Center is located just across the state line in Oregon, west of the country's deepest gorge — take that, Grand Canyon, a punch in the nose! — known, aptly, as Hells Canyon.

In any direction you go, you'll be seduced by natural wonder, whether it is a high, cascading waterfall, rock-ledged canyons as remarkable as Arizona's, towering and sparkling Alpine country, or places that speak for themselves, such as Craters of the Moon National Park, City of Rocks and the Bruneau Dunes. If that all seems too pure and wholesome for you, never fear. Nevada is close by, with its casino gambling and stage shows in Jackpot, where they run on Idaho time because they're in the back pocket of Twin Falls.

In this chapter we take you in four different directions from Boise, beginning with two northern routes, one to Idaho City and two splendid driving loops beyond, and one to sparkling, snowcapped McCall and glittering lake country. The second direction is south, a wide-open, sagebrush and volcanic territory that features the highest sand dune in North America at Bruneau, where sharp ridge lines, shapes and textures conjure visions of elephants and dinosaurs; the spectacular sweep of Owyhee County, where remote but reachable Silver City lies creaking in the clouds;

and the fantastic canyon color of Leslie Gulch, which beckons from an Oregon flank. The third azimuth points east to the Three Island Crossing at Glenns Ferry, Malad Gorge, Hagerman Fossil Beds and the deep white veils of Shoshone Falls. In opposite directions from there are the City of Rocks and Craters of the Moon National Monument. Or you can drop straight down from there to Cactus Pete's in Jackpot, Nevada. To the west of Boise, our final direction, are the rugged, lion-colored shoulders of Hells Canyon that frame jet boats and rafts on a curling canyon floor, and farther west beneath high Oregon peaks, sitting on a prominent sagebrush hill where wagon ruts are still visible, the Oregon Trail Interpretive Center.

Have we forgotten something? Could it be that we've overlooked Sun Valley? Actually we've dedicated a whole chapter to Sun Valley, Ketchum and the Wood River Valley, which at 2½ to three hours away from Boise, could also be a daytrip.

North

Idaho City

It's a sweet drive past the mansions on Warm Springs Avenue east along the Boise River on two-lane blacktop that becomes Idaho Highway 21. Several miles out, near Diversion Dam, a new connecting road from Interstate 84 bridges the river and joins Idaho 21 for the climb over Lucky Peak Reservoir and the 45-minute, 39-mile trip to Idaho City.

Take it easy on this winding road, where reckless drivers push their luck and many deer are killed crossing to More's Creek, the delicious silver thread that runs beside the road.

Just 1.5 miles southwest of Idaho City, at Mile Post 37.5 on Idaho 21, is **Warm Springs Resort**, (208) 392-4437. In 1862, the same year that gold was discovered in the Boise Basin, George W. Thatcher discovered the natural artesian warm springs that became the resort. The resort began in an old house that provided laundry services, baths and swimming for Boise Basin Gold Rush miners and early pioneers. It also served as an overnight stage stop for early travelers. The resort has been a saloon and dance hall, a hospital and an inn. The current owner acquired Warm Springs in 1961, remodeled and enlarged the old bathhouse, put in a snack bar and dressing rooms, and converted rock piles left by early dredge mining into a picnic area and campground.

The resort is open year-round. The water in its outdoor pool rises from about 2 kilometers in the earth and is 109 degrees at ground level. Pool water is cooled to 94 degrees in the summer and maintained at 97 degrees for winter use. The water is naturally soft and carbon-dated to more than 10,000 years of age. Daily swimming fees are $4 for those 13 and older, $2 for children ages 3 to 12 and free for those 2 and younger. Cabins rent for $40 a night and $200 weekly; RV parking costs $18 a day and $90 weekly; camping costs $6 a unit.

Just up the road stands **Idaho City** that with the discovery of Boise Basin gold in 1862, became the largest town in the Idaho Territory. In its heyday in the 1860s, the town boasted more than 250 businesses, including opera and theater houses, music stores, tailors, breweries, bowling alleys, barber shops, bakeries, pool halls, drugstores and, of course, numerous saloons. It was a bawdy, lusty town, where whiskey was cheaper than water. Life was cheap, too. Men went armed at all times and were quick to defend themselves. Winners in disputes often spent time in the stout log jail. Losers were carted off to Pioneer Cemetery.

Within three years of its start, Idaho City's 6,200 population surpassed Portland, Oregon's, making it the most populous city in the Northwest. More than $250 million worth of gold was mined there. Within a few years of the first gold strike by three prospectors pan-

ning on Grimes Creek (7 miles north of Idaho City), the precious yellow metal became harder to find and more difficult to mine. The population rapidly decreased, and fires ravaged the community in 1865, 1867, 1868 and 1871. But because of the wealth extracted from gold, Idaho City was always rebuilt, and many early buildings remain today.

Excellent examples of early brickwork and woodwork exist in Idaho City. Planked boardwalks lead past restaurants and shops to the **Boise Basin Mercantile Co.**, a general store that opened in 1865 at its present location on Main Street and never closed. This general store still provides groceries, household items and a wide variety of merchandise to locals and visitors. The town's **Masonic Temple**, built in 1865, is the oldest Masonic Hall in the West, and the **Idaho World Building**, at Main and Commercial streets, was home from 1867 to 1918 to Idaho's longest running newspaper, *The Idaho World*, still published as a weekly. **The Boise Basin Historical Museum**, 402 Montgomery Street, which goes back to 1867, is a visit to photographs and memorabilia passed down by the descendants of gold miners, saloon owners and other townspeople. The museum is open from 11 AM to 5 PM on weekends in May and September and daily from Memorial Day to Labor Day. Admission is $2 for adults and $1 for students and seniors. Inquire here as well for information on walking tours of Idaho City, from its planked boardwalks to its Pioneer Cemetery. Don't miss **Pioneer Cemetery**, on Centerville Road, filled with ancient headboards that tell intriguing tales from the past.

Idaho City is surrounded by **Boise National Forest**, (208) 364-4100, a vast territory of timbered mountains, crystal-clear creeks and rivers, dams, reservoirs and bridges. Mule deer and Rocky Mountain elk find large areas of summer range here, native trout live in the lakes and streams, while oceangoing salmon and steelhead inhabit the many tributaries of the Salmon River. Excellent cross-country skiing, snowmobiling, mountain biking and hiking are possible on the many dirt roads, trails and pathways in and around Idaho City. At

3,900 feet Idaho City is more than 1,000 feet higher than Boise, which sits at 2,704 feet. Snow often blankets the ground when none is found in Boise and the Treasure Valley. (For more information on Boise National Forest, see our Parks and Preserves chapter.)

About 300 people live in Idaho City today. They work for the U.S. Forest Service, commute to jobs in Boise, and run the town's five restaurants, five lodging places, shops and museum.

Kayak Country

Idaho Highway 21 climbs from 3,900 feet of elevation at Idaho City to Mores Creek Summit at 6,118 feet, then takes a zigzag plunge into the Canyon of the South Fork of the Payette River, which was charred, blackened, devastated and ravaged by a 1992 forest fire but is now coming back nicely. Lowman sits at the crossroads, and a turning west from here, toward Garden Valley and Banks, takes you above the South Fork of the Payette River, which is popular with kayakers and rafters. Many places along the river are good for picnicking and watching the adventurous boaters in May, June, July and August. Those on the water are captivated by the beautiful scenery and the fabulous rapids. The road through the area is above and removed from the river, which allows kayakers and other water enthusiasts to enjoy the wilderness without the distractions of the modern world.

It's 23 miles from Lowman to Garden Valley and another 10 miles to Banks, where a left turn to the south on Idaho Highway 55, beside the North Fork of the Payette River, takes a visitor back through Horseshoe Bend to Boise. There is a wonderful little beach with picnic tables in the trees just south of Banks on the west side of Idaho 55 where you park beside the road. Bring your swimsuit and sandwiches for a refreshing summer stop.

Photo: Idaho Department of Parks and Recreation

Bruneau Dunes State Park has lake, marsh, desert, prairie and dune habitats.

This entire loop from Boise to Idaho City and around through Garden Valley and Banks back to Boise is about a three-hour drive. In winter the roads can be icy and treacherous, and avalanches and mudslides sometimes close Idaho 21 above Idaho City.

Idaho City's visitors center is at Idaho 21 and Main Street, (208) 392-4290.

Stanley and Sawtooth National Recreation Area

The coldest, most beautiful place in Idaho is Stanley. In warm months, it's just as striking but much more amenable to outdoor activities. Continuing on Idaho Highway 21 past Idaho City, heading east at Lowman and continuing on Idaho 21 along the South Fork of the Payette River over 7,056-foot Banner Summit, Stanley is 131 eye-dancing miles from Boise. Not too long after turning east at Lowman, you'll come upon Kirkham Hot Springs, where thermal vents in the river heat a series of rock pools. Pipes carry the water to four tubs that exist, virtually, at roadside. Picnic tables are also on-site at the Boise National Forest campground, (208) 364-4100.

Farther on, the marvelous, rising, snowclad spires of the Sawtooth Mountains, which do cut the sky, as well as creeks and wildflowers that color broad open meadows, and the deep, whispering woodlands tell you that you have arrived at one of those special places on earth that no photo, drawing or written description can honor. **Stanley** is a cluster of wood buildings, stores and shops set at an elevation of 6,260 feet above sea level beside the Salmon River. Seventy-one residents brave the subzero temperatures of January and February and snow depths that typically reach 80 feet to walk outside into a panorama of staggering beauty in warmer months.

Stanley has 22 lodging choices, ranging from motels to resorts to ranches and cabins. It offers many recreational activities, including camping, cross-country skiing, river trips, horseback riding, snowshoeing, snowmobiling, llama packing and water-skiing. For an information packet, call (800) 878-7950. For additional information about area services and lodging, call (208) 774-3411. For campground reservations in Stanley, call (800) 280-2267.

Many visitors from Boise turn this visit into a two-day getaway, spending the night in Stanley or nearby and continuing the second day south on Idaho Highway 75 over Galena Summit, through Ketchum/Sun Valley, west on U.S. Highway 20 through the Camas Valley to Mountain Home and back to Boise on Interstate 84. The round-trip total is 342 miles — 131 miles to Stanley, 61 miles to Sun Valley and 150 miles back to Boise — or six to seven hours of driving.

Stanley is enveloped by the Sawtooth Mountain Range, Boulder Mountains and the White Cloud Peaks, all of which are contained within the 1,180-square-mile **Sawtooth National Recreation Area**, (800) 260-5970, (208) 727-5013, (208) 727-5000. More than 300 Alpine lakes are tucked into this vast territory, where 42 chiseled mountain peaks rise above 10,000 feet in elevation to tower above the Middle and East forks and main Salmon rivers, the North and South forks of the Boise River, the South Fork of the Payette River and the Big Wood River. Hunters, anglers, horseback riders, backpackers and hikers frequent the mountains during much of the year. The deep indigo waters of Redfish Lake, framed by craggy peaks and surrounded by pine forests, is the single most popular destination in the Sawtooths.

Driving south from Stanley on Idaho 75, you'll quickly come to the **Sawtooth National Fish Hatchery**, (208) 774-3684, which at 6,600 feet of elevation is the highest hatchery in the United States. It breeds more than 3,000 chinook salmon each year and provides summer tours. Farther south you'll rise above Galena Summit (see our Sun Valley chapter) and come to the headquarters of the Sawtooth National Recreation Area, which is 8 miles north of Ketchum and has an exhibition room that features wildlife, geography, botany and history.

South of Ketchum, Sun Valley and Wood River Valley, which are highlighted in our Sun Valley chapter, a turn west on U.S. 20 provides the most scenic way back to Boise. The wide-open **Camas Valley** is the habitat for many species of waterfowl and other birds beneath 10,095-foot-high Smoky Dome to the south and 10,174-foot-high Baker Peak to the north. Fairfield, located 50 miles from Sun Valley and 100 miles from Boise, is home to Soldier Mountain Ski Area, (208) 764-2526, owned by Bruce Willis and Demi Moore. It's a fine little hill with a 1,400-foot vertical drop, 42 runs, a double pull, a handle pull and a rope tow. (See our Recreation chapter for more Soldier Mountain ski information.)

Thirty-six miles west of Fairfield and 21 miles from Interstate 84 driving east from Mountain Home (covered later in this chapter), is the turnoff for **Anderson Ranch Reservoir** (Mile Post 116). When completed in 1950, Anderson Ranch Dam, at the foot of the reservoir above the South Fork of the Boise River, was the world's largest earth-filled dam. The reservoir is 17 miles long with 50 miles of shoreline that lead back into the Trinity Mountains and 11 high alpine lakes. This is fishing and snowmobile country. Small mouth bass of more than 6 pounds and rainbow trout of more than 10 pounds have been caught in the reservoir, and some of the best fly-fishing in the state is found along the South Fork of the Boise River beneath the reservoir. A 250-mile groomed snowmobile trail system with a warming hut is high in the Trinity Mountains. For information about this area, contact the **Mountain Home Chamber of Commerce**, (208) 587-4334.

McCall

Idaho Highway 55 heads north from State Street on a climbing, 100-mile, riverside course to the town of McCall, a lakeside community of 2,600 residents with a gorgeous mountain backdrop that has long been a summer escape and winter high for Boise people. It's a pretty, sometimes very curvy, two-lane ride that can be heavy with jockeying traffic on weekends. The Long Valley opens wide, high and handsome south of **Cascade Reservoir**, a long body of water with 110 miles of shoreline that was created in 1948 by a Bureau of Reclamation dam on the Payette River's North Fork. Today the lake is popular with campers (600 sites), boaters (24 launches) and anglers (trout, salmon, whitefish and perch). Contact the Boise National Forest, (208) 364-4100, for information.

The town of **Cascade**, with a population of 1,050, is 30 miles south of McCall on Idaho 55. Established shortly after the turn of the century as a service center for mining, agriculture and the timber industry, it received its name from the cascading waters of the North Fork of the Payette River, which meanders in and around the town.

McCall curls along the banks of Lake Payette, a 6-mile-long deep-blue body of mountain-fed water that is popular with boaters, water-skiers and trout anglers. It's a breezy, friendly little town filled with restaurants, shops and only one route through, Idaho 55, which can move like a turtle. The dominating destinations here are Ponderosa State Park, Payette National Forest and Brundage Mountain, 8 miles north of town.

Ponderosa State Park, (208) 634-2164, covers most of a 1,000-acre peninsula that juts into Payette Lake just outside McCall. From Idaho 55, fork right (east) at the lake on Lake Street and turn left on Davis Avenue to reach the park. The character of the park is molded by its diverse topography. Within minutes one can go from arid sagebrush flats to a lakeside trail; from flat, even ground to steep cliffs; and from dense forest to spongy marsh. Nature trails and dirt roads have been developed for visitor enjoyment. The 630-acre North Beach Area has the largest sandy public beach on the lake. The park has 170 campsites that are open from spring to early fall for RVs and tents. Some of the sites can be reserved.

INSIDERS' TIP

Heading out of Boise into the great Idahoan unknown? Don't forget to bring your favorite pastime along. If you fish, bring your rod. If you bicycle, take your bike. If you hike, make sure you have your walking shoes. Wherever you're headed in the state, chances are you'll find places to enjoy these activities either at your final destination or along the way.

The park's namesake, the 150-foot-tall ponderosa pine, is the most noticeable species of tree. Douglas and grand fir, lodgepole pine and western larch also grow in the park. Birds often sighted include osprey, red-tailed hawks, bald eagles, Canada geese, wood ducks and mallards, along with a variety of songbirds, woodpeckers, hummingbirds and ravens. Deer, red fox, beavers, muskrats and bears also live in the park. An interpretive trail at Meadow Marsh is rich in wild flowers. Day entrance to the park is $3 per car. Campsites cost $12 without electricity or $16 with electricity.

The **Payette National Forest**, (208) 634-0400, surrounds McCall with 2.3 million acres of rugged, forested, remote land. It is bordered by two of the deepest canyons in North America — the Salmon River Canyon on the north and Hells Canyon of the Snake River on the west. On the eastern border is the Frank Church Wilderness area, which covers 2.4 million acres and is the largest wilderness area in the lower 48 states.

In the forest, a primitive loop road goes through McCall, Warren, Big Creek, Yellow Pine, over Lick Creek Summit and back to McCall, following old mining routes. The forest has wonderful campgrounds with parking spurs, tables, fire rings, cooking grills, drinking water and restrooms. Activities include day hikes, backpacking, fishing, rock-climbing, river running and swimming. Wildlife in the area include endangered species such as the gray wolf, chinook salmon, bald eagle and peregrine falcon. The forest is blanketed with snow from November to May, making it popular for skiing and snowmobiling.

Brundage Mountain, (208) 634-4151, located 8 miles north of McCall, has spectacular views of the Salmon River Mountains, Oregon's Eagle Cap Wilderness, the Seven Devils towering over Hells Canyon and Payette Lake with McCall nestled on the south shore. It's a good ski mountain with an 1,800-foot vertical drop and 44 runs that are served by a quad lift, two double chairs, a triple chair, a poma lift and handle tow. The resort has a comfortable day lodge and ski and rental shop. (See our Recreation chapter for more information.)

There are several hot springs in the McCall area. **Burgdorf Hot Springs**, 36 miles north of McCall and 14 miles past Upper Payette

Lake, is the best-known. Stop at the Payette National Forest Service, 106 W. Park Street, McCall, (208) 634-8151, for a map and directions to Burgdorf and other hot springs. The Burgdorf settlement was developed as a spa in 1865 by German immigrant Fred Burgdorf, who ran a 20-room resort there for 20 years. Today Burgdorf's hot spring pools remain open year-round. They are accessible by car in summer and snowmobile and cross-country skiing in winter. Primitive cabins and camping sites are available.

Other hot springs in the area include Zim's Hot Springs, Last Chance, White Licks Hot Springs, Molly's Hot Springs, Vulcan Hot Springs and Trail Creek Hot Springs. **Zim's** is 4 miles north of New Meadows on U.S. Highway 95. It's a family facility with a picnic and RV camping area, snack bar and showers.

Last Chance is 2 miles beyond the Brundage Mountain turnoff on Idaho Highway 55. The hot springs is off the campground road, about a half-mile walk along Goose Creek starting before you cross the bridge.

The other hot springs are located in the Donnelly, Council and Cascade village areas. Check at the Payette National Forest office for more information.

McCall's best-known annual event is its **Winter Carnival**, a 10-day, early February celebration that attracts as many as 100,000 visitors. It started in 1924 when an army of volunteers created snow sculptures all over town to reduce the boredom of the long McCall winters. The snow sculptures are still the main focus of current celebrations, with 60 entries in a judged contest that has some very sophisticated, artistic creations. (See our Annual Events and Festivals chapter for details about the Winter Carnival.)

For information about McCall, contact the **McCall Area Chamber of Commerce**, (208) 634-7631.

South

Mountain Home

Some of the driest, most forlorn and deceiving landscape in the state is observed during the 48-mile Interstate 84 drive southwest from Boise to **Mountain Home.** That barren land is a misleading preface to geographic highlights that will stir your soul. Mountain Home is the opposite of its name, a town of 7,500 residents situated on a flat sagebrush desert 13 miles north of the Snake River. A stagecoach driver pining for the cool climate of his own mountain home gave it the misleading name: It's actually the warmest place in the state. Mountain Home is known for its large **Mountain Home Air Force Base**, (208) 828-2111, located 11 miles southwest of town on Idaho Highway 67. The entrance is marked by a sign and a gate. The base was established in 1942 as a training school for World War II bomber crews and is now home to the U.S. Air Intervention Composite Wing, a division of the Tactical Air Command. Crews at the base, which are on immediate call for duty anywhere in the world, have recently served in the Persian Gulf, Somalia and Bosnia. A free tour of the base may be arranged by calling the previously listed number for an appointment.

The Elmore County Historical Museum, (208) 587-6847, in Mountain Home, has artifacts that go back to the 1882 founding of Mountain Home on Rattlesnake Creek by Oregon Short Line railroad construction crews. Within a couple of decades it became an important shipping point for 1 million pounds of wool a year.

Bruneau Sand Dunes

A visitor to the **Bruneau Dunes State Park**, (208) 366-7919, 20 miles south of Mountain Home and about a 1½-hour drive from Boise, may take Exit 90 from I-84 west of Mountain Home, bypassing the town, or take Exit 95 to go through the town. Either way, Idaho Highway 51 leads to the largest single structured sand dune in North America with a peak that rises 470 feet above a lake surface. Several rugged, wild and weathered dunes may be climbed, hiked, observed and photographed for various effects as the light changes. These are immense, intriguing piles of sand that in their rise, lines and texture resemble great elephants or prehistoric animals and make dots of human beings as they walk into the sky. They provide great family fun for tumblers, slid-

ers and runners who challenge their flanks and stout exercise for visitors who ascend their ridge lines for "crossings" of the dunes.

The dunes are unique in the Western Hemisphere in their formation and are in vivid contrast to the surrounding plateaus. Other dunes in the Americas form at the edge of a natural basin; these form near the center. The combination of a source of sand, relatively constant wind activity and a natural trap have caused sand to collect in this semicircular basin for about 15,000 years. Unlike many dunes, they do not drift far. The two prevailing winds blow from the southeast 28 percent of the time and from the northeast 32 percent of the time. The two prominent dunes cover about 600 acres.

Park habitat includes lakes, marsh, desert prairie and dunes. Fishing for largemouth bass and bluegill is allowed from nonmotorized boats and the shore. Wildlife includes blacktailed jackrabbit, Western whiptail lizard, ruddy duck, Great Basin gopher snake, magpie, desert horned lizard, muskrat, coyote, burrowing owl, marsh hawk and mallard.

An equestrian trail, 5-mile trail, nature trail and self-guided marked trail are available in the dunes. The park, which covers 4,800 acres, is open all year. A picnic area, restrooms, sun shelters and tent and trailer sites are available.

Silver City

Owyhee County, a vast open space with a population of fewer than one resident per square mile, fills the southwest corner of the state with a gorgeous calm. South of Boise, its mountain peaks spread across the horizon. The Bruneau Dunes, discussed previously, are on the edge of the county, just south of the Snake River. If you'd like a very full day of sightseeing, it is possible to take in both the dunes and Silver City on the same outing, but we wouldn't recommend it. The dunes are so much fun and a great place to relax, and Silver City is a rare hideaway that deserves a foot tour for soaking up its Old West atmosphere. Each deserves at least a day of exploration in its own right.

For those on the run, Idaho Highway 78 west of Bruneau connects with Grand View, 16 miles away. As Idaho 78 continues west toward Murphy, there is a marked turnoff for Silver City. Those coming from Boise to Silver City should take Idaho Highway 69 or Idaho Highway 45 south through Nampa, turn east on Idaho 78, south of the Snake River, and drive through Murphy to the turnoff.

Murphy, with a population of 75, is notable for two reasons. It has a single parking meter, in front of its court house, and if you don't pay up, they'll nab you. It is also the home of the **Owyhee County Historical Museum**, 190 Basey St., (208) 495-2319, which displays a reconstructed mining-stamp mill, an old-time schoolhouse and a homesteader's cabin with an untouched kitchen just like it was back then. The museum is open from 10 AM to 4 PM Wednesday through Friday and noon to 5 PM Saturday and Sunday, May through August. Admission is by donation.

From Murphy, it takes about an hour to ascend the rough, winding, 23-mile dirt road from Idaho 78 to Silver City, which passes through desert, foothills, spectacular canyon lands and forest-covered mountains. For stretches the road does not have space for cars passing both ways. A normal passenger car, driving slowly and carefully, can make the trip, but high-suspension and four-wheel-drive are preferable. About halfway up to the 6,179-foot elevation, a creek crosses beneath the road and makes for a good stopping point and picnic area. It is also possible to reach Silver City from the west by exiting U.S. Highway 95 east of Jordan Valley, Oregon. This is a 25-mile climb that is not nearly as scenic or interesting as the rise from Idaho 78, but for the most part, it's an easier drive, with very rough going just below Silver City.

Silver City, (208) 583-4104 or (208) 583-2402, is worth the tough climb. It is surrounded by the picturesque, 8,000-foot-high Owyhee Mountains and contains about 75 structures that date from the 1860s to the early 1900s. The Idaho Hotel, Post Office-Drugstore and School House-Museum are open to the public for a nominal fee during the summer months. It is not advisable to visit on the last weekend of July, when the Idaho Cattleman's Association fills the town. A good time to visit is the second weekend in September, when 10 buildings are open to the public. During the Open House weekend money is raised by people who reside in Silver City during the warm months to pay a winter watchman. The watchman is necessary because vandals have shot up the town in the past, causing great destruction to properties that have otherwise endured. The town's water is cut off each year from mid-October to mid-April.

Between 1863 and 1865, more than 250 mines operated in the area, and hundreds more were developed later. Through 70-odd years of mining, more than 60 ore-processing mills gleaned rich rewards in tons of gold and silver. Large stacks of gold and silver ingots were photographed for posterity. At least $60 million worth of precious metals was taken from the area. More than two dozen camps provided shelters, supplies and amusement for the thousands of people who came to the mountains seeking their fortunes. Almost a dozen cemeteries and many more remote burial sites attest to the hard and sometimes dangerous and violent lives led by many. Hundreds of mines pockmark the territory; one had upwards of 70 miles of tunnels laboriously hand-dug through it.

During its glory, Silver City had a dozen streets, 75 businesses, 300 homes and a population of 2,500. It was the Owyhee County seat from 1866 to 1934. Some of the largest stagecoach lines in the West operated in the area, and Silver City had the first telegraph and first daily newspaper in the Oregon Territory in 1874. Telephones were in use by 1880, and the town was "electrified" in the 1890s. There are four separate burial grounds near Silver City with large and elaborately carved stones.

It is possible to spend the night at the **Idaho Hotel**, (208) 583-4104, which has been likened to "camping out indoors with antique accessories." Room rates are $20 to $40. Over-

---

INSIDERS' TIP

Driving in Idaho is easy and fast. The roads are good, the population is sparse, and on some interstate sections 75 mph is the speed limit.

night guests should make reservations several days in advance and must provide their own bedding or sleeping bags and towels. Since there is no electricity in the area, the hotel has no laundry facilities. The bedrooms have vintage furniture and most are unheated. A shower, 12-volt lights, handwashing sinks and compost toilets are available. A fully furnished Silver City house, (208) 583-2510 or (208) 922-5918, is also available for rent.

The hotel was built in 1863 a mile below in Ruby City. When Ruby City lost its county seat to Silver City, the hotel and other buildings were transported above to capitalize on the business generated in the new government center. The hotel's barroom was ornamented with the costliest and handsomest mirror ever brought to Silver City in 1874. All of the interior woodwork was handgrained in 1882 and a billiards parlor-gambling room was added in 1889.

Today the hotel serves snacks, soft drinks, beer, wine and cocktails and offers family-style meals with reservations of a week in advance.

Owyhee Loop and Leslie Gulch

A wonderful day's outing for those who like the back-country, easy, leg-stretching hikes, creekside picnics and fanciful rock formations that you would more expect in Utah and Arizona has Grand View for a take-off point. **Grand View**, on Idaho Highway 67 south of Interstate 84 and the Mountain Home Air Force Base, lives up to its name, with sweeping prairie and mountain views. Continue on Idaho 67 south as it changes to a two-lane road called Owyhee Uplands Back Country Byway on a map, although you may not find a road sign. You can't get lost, because it's the only road there. It has magnificent rock formations, broad meadows and forest retreats. Waterfowl, bluebirds, deer and the glimpse of a cougar are not beyond the question of what you might spy. As the road curves north toward Jordan Valley, Oregon, it crosses the North Fork of the Owyhee River, one of several excellent stopping points along the way. It is roughly 100 miles of relaxed scenic driving between Grand View and Jordan Valley

that is spiced by the peaks of South Mountain and War Eagle Mountain to the north and east and the Jarbridge Mountains of Nevada to the south and west. You'll probably only see a couple of other vehicles along the way.

After you continue through Jordan Valley, Oregon, north on U.S. Highway 95, look for a sign for the Leslie Gulch Succor Creek Byway. This comes before the turn and sign for Marsing, Idaho, which has a Snake River crossing, and is the way back to Boise. **Leslie Gulch**, (503) 473-3144, has the high, irregular, orange-pink, multicolored, angular rock chunks, turrets, arches and spires that demand hushed contemplation and the clicking of cameras. It's a great place to climb and roam and wander and wonder. You probably won't see many other people, because it's not well-known.

A bowl the size of a football stadium in Leslie Gulch marks the explosion of a volcano some 15 million years ago. Usually when a volcano explodes, the force spreads debris through a wide area, but here, the explosion was so quick, everything got trapped in the bowl. This makes it a fascinating hiking area. It also provides shade and shelter for bighorn sheep, wild horses, raptors and lizards. Rocks that look like owls, Buddhas, camels, Popeyes and pumas peer down.

Flaming red Indian paintbrush, white prairie stars, wild roses, red bitterbrush, juniper and 300-year-old curl leaf mountain mahogany grow in Leslie Gulch, which was named for a cattleman who was killed there by lightning in 1882. Exploring Leslie Gulch is most popular in fall and spring — it heats up like an oven in summer. Boating is possible in a reservoir where anglers fish for crappie.

East

Glenns Ferry

A smooth ribbon of highway, Interstate 84, connects Boise with **Glenns Ferry**, 78 miles east. For the fur trappers, explorers, and pioneers coming the other way in the 19th century there was no such easy corridor. They followed the south bank of the Snake River on the Oregon Trail until they came to Three Island Crossing at Glenns Ferry. Here they were faced with a difficult decision. Should they risk the dangerous crossing of the Snake River or endure the dry, rocky route on the south side of the river? The rewards of a successful crossing were a shorter route, more potable water and better feed for their stock. About half the emigrants chose to attempt the crossing by using the gravel bars that extended across the river. Not all were successful; many casualties are recounted in pioneer diaries. The Three Island ford was used as early as 1811 by fur trappers and explorers, and up to 1869 by pioneers when Gus Glenn constructed a ferry about 2 miles upstream and had the town named after him.

Today 513-acre **Three Island State Park**, (208) 366-2394, which is reached by following signs from I-84 in Glenns Ferry, coddles visitors with a grassy, tree-shaded campground and picnic areas. It also offers historic interpretive programs at a fascinating, air-conditioned interpretive center. You can take the self-guided tour, see replica wagons and dangle your feet in the Snake River where emigrants made their historic crossings. Every August, the park hosts a re-enactment of the crossing that features horse-drawn covered wagons.

Malad Gorge

Farther east from Boise than Three Island State Park and also on Interstate 84 is **Malad Gorge State Park**, (208) 837-4505. Many people pass the park in the blink of an eye, never guessing the spectacular canyon views that await them just a mile off the highway. The distance is 96 miles, or about 90 minutes, from Boise, and a day's visit could be combined with a stop or stops at Three Island State Park, listed previously, and/or the Hagerman Fossil Beds, our next entry. To visit Malad Gorge, take the Tuttle exit, which is Exit 47, turn south and follow the signs. To get to the interpretive area and footbridge that spans the gorge, follow the loop road through the park.

A steel footbridge spans the 250-foot-deep canyon above a 60-foot waterfall called the Devil's Washbowl. The cascading water is an impressive sight, but the main act is the gorge itself. Its dizzying proportions defy comprehen-

sion. Cracks and folds of rock along the canyon cliffs record the movements of earth, lava and water. Indians piled rocks along the rim to capture bison and other game. The historic Kelton Trail runs through the park, providing Western history buffs with excellent wagon ruts and traces of the Kelton Stage Stop.

Birds that frequent the 652-acre park include eagles, great horned owls, barn owls, kestrels, harriers, prairie falcons, red-tailed hawks, orioles, pigeons and cliff swallows. On the ground or in the water, you're apt to see deer, coyotes, beaver, porcupines and marmots. For those who follow the trails to the bottom, the wild rainbow trout fishing can be surprisingly good.

In addition to hiking trails, the park has areas for mountain biking and horseback riding. An interpretive center near the footbridge provides information about the area's history and geology. The river was named by French trappers, who called it the "malad," or sickly river, after becoming ill from eating the tail of a beaver there. Faint traces of petroglyphs remain on some of the rocks where Indians herded animals over the edge to their deaths. There are no railings along the rim, so watch children closely here.

The park is open all year from sunrise to sunset. There are no campsites, but there are picnic tables, grills, a shelter, restrooms and a scenic, 2-mile loop road. Tours may be arranged with advance notice by calling (208) 837-4505.

Hagerman Fossil Beds

Only a few miles from Malad Gorge, on U.S. Highway 30 south of Interstate 84, is the town of Hagerman, where the park headquarters for **Hagerman Fossil Beds National Monument**, 221 N. State Street, (208) 837-4793, is located. A visitors center offers information and fossil displays. The 4,281 acre monument is composed of 600-foot-high bluffs west of Hagerman across the Snake River.

The monument is most famous for the horse that is Idaho's state fossil. It is most significant for its variety, quantity and quality of fossils, which are evidence of animals or plants present in the earth's crust. No other fossil beds preserve such a varied land and

Photo: William H. Mullins

Cross-country skiing in the Sawtooth Wilderness is
a peaceful way to spend a winter afternoon.

aquatic species from the time of the Pliocene Epoch, which dates back 1 to 12 million years, and was the era when modern plants and animals were developed and mountains formed in western America. More than 140 animal species of both vertebrates and invertebrates and 35 plant species have been found here first. The Hagerman Horse, *Equus simplicidens*, exemplifies the quality of the fossils. From these fossil beds have come both complete and partial skeletons of this zebra-like ancestor of today's horse.

Mastodons, sabre-tooth cats, beavers, muskrats, otters, camels, antelope, deer, ground sloths and hyena-like dogs as well as fish, frogs, snakes and waterfowl lived here during the Pliocene Epoch. The sediment levels where fossils are found from river level to bluff tops span some 550,000 years — from 3.7 million years old at river level to 3.15 million years old atop the bluff. These layers were deposited when rivers flowing into ancient Lake Idaho flooded the countryside.

For an easy view of the monument, drive south from Hagerman on U.S. 30. A quarter-mile past the road to Wendell take a right turn, marked "Sportsman's Access." Follow the signs to the Bell Rapids boat dock on the Snake River for fishing, watersports or viewing birds along the scenic shoreline. The monument, across the river, includes 7 miles of shoreline.

To reach a wheelchair-accessible boardwalk overlook, drive south from Hagerman on U.S. 30, cross the Snake River, turn right on Bell Rapids Road and drive 2.8 miles. The parking lot is on the right just after you enter the monument. The boardwalk, with wayside exhibits, provides a commanding view of the fossil beds and Snake River and is a good place to watch waterfowl. Farther along this road white stakes mark the Oregon Trail. Do not move or take any fossil, rock or plant from the monument. If you see a fossil, report its location to a ranger, so information can be gathered. Many fossils are fragile and must be protected by trained experts before they can be moved safely.

Twin Falls

U.S. Highway 30 from Bliss to Twin Falls is nicknamed Thousand Springs Scenic Route for the dozens of waterfalls that trickle and pour from sheer black cliffs along the northeast canyon wall. Irrigation diversion has significantly reduced their numbers from the several hundred springs seen by pioneers.

The top stop in Twin Falls, a city of 30,000 people located 128 miles, or about 2½ hours, east of Boise, is the **Buzz Langdon Visitors Center**, (800) 255-8946. It is on Blue Lakes Boulevard south of the Interstate 84 exit for Twin Falls and just south of Perrine Bridge, which crosses the Snake River Canyon. Observation decks present an awesome panorama of a canyon carved 15,000 years ago by the great Bonneville Flood. Palisades rise as high as 600 feet above two golf courses and a city park that occupy the canyon floor. The **Perrine Bridge**, 933 feet long and 486 feet above the canyon, was the world's highest bridge when it was built in 1927. In 1974, Evel Knievel tried to rocket across the Snake River Canyon on a motorcycle, a couple of miles upstream from Perrine Bridge. The Montana stuntman couldn't make it across and parachuted to the canyon floor.

A little farther upstream, on Shoshone Falls Road, is **Shoshone Falls**, known as The Niagara of the West. Bathing the area in a cool rainbow mist, its waters pour down 212 feet — 52 feet more than Niagara — over a horseshoe-shaped, 1,000-foot-wide basalt face. Spring is the best time to visit, when the Snake River is swollen from snowmelt.

The Northwest's largest Gigistar II planetarium opened in November 1996 at the **Herrett Center** on the College of Southern Idaho campus in Twin Falls, 315 Falls Avenue, (208) 733-9554 Ext. 2655. The planetarium, said to be the most modern in the world, has a Sutherland Digistar II computer-graphic projection system, Sony projector with a Conic pan-tilt video head, 49 Kodak EKTA-Pro 7000 slide projectors, laser disk players wrapped in a five-channel digital audio system, and a 50-foot aluminum dome that has more than 40 million perforations that allow air and sound movement through the theater. Audience members lay back and look upward at the dome and are totally surrounded by subject matter.

Shows in the 154-seat theater have included *Through the Eyes of the Hubble Telescope* and *Innerspace*, which explores the human body. The Herrett Center also has an extensive pre-Columbian collection, contemporary art and a natural history gallery with 14,000-year-old remnants of Pleistocene mammals from Idaho.

Jackpot, Nevada

Do you like to play blackjack? How about a roll of the dice — is that your fancy? Or would a dinner show with country-and-western, rock or pop music performers who climbed the charts in the '60s, '70s or '80s be more to your liking? The Great Casino Escape for Boise is **Jackpot, Nevada**, about 60 miles south of Twin Falls, or about 190 miles, and three to 3½ hours by car, from Boise. Take Interstate 84 east to the Twin Falls, U.S. Highway 93 exit, and drive south on U.S. 93 to Jackpot, just over the Nevada border.

The main action is at **Cactus Pete's**, (800) 821-1103, an award-winning resort that, at a quiet and remote location far from the rush and crowds of the big theme gambling houses in Las Vegas and Reno, is almost cozy. The 26,000-square-foot casino floor has more than 800 slot machines and video games, three gaming pits that offer blackjack and other card games, craps, roulette, a poker room, keno and a spacious sports-book area where bets from $5 to $5,000 are taken on sporting events.

Dinner and cocktail stage presentations are offered Tuesday through Sunday and feature people and groups that were big in the past, such as Chubby Checker, Lacy J. Dalton and The Coasters. The shows are presented in a 275-seat theater and are well-staged. At the dinner show, entrees run $12.95 to steak and lobster at $29.95; cocktail shows run $10, with two drinks or coffee and dessert offered — otherwise there is no cover charge.

■ INSIDERS' TIP

Okay, a day in Idaho may not be a day at the beach, but it is still possible to get sunburned and bitten by mosquitos. However, both are less likely than in most other places because of the dry climate, scarcity of sand beaches and northern latitude.

Cactus Pete's has two hotels under its one roof, with about 300 rooms that range from standard to luxury and living room suites that cost from $55 to $175 per night. A large outdoor swimming pool, hot tub and Jacuzzi and two outdoor tennis courts are available for use. A scenic, well-maintained, 18-hole golf course that is owned by the casino is just a short distance away.

Jackpot has about a half-dozen other smaller casinos and motels.

Craters of the Moon National Monument

Idaho has no national parks, but **Craters of the Moon National Monument** has been discussed as a possible addition to the national park category, because of its unusual attributes. "The strangest 75 square miles on the North American continent," was the description of one early traveler." Others deemed it "a weird lunar landscape," "an outdoor museum of volcanism" and "a desolate and awful waste." Virtually unknown until 1921, the area was made a national monument in 1924, and today embraces 83 square miles.

To get there from Boise, take Interstate 84 south to Mountain Home and U.S. Highway 20 east through the Camas Valley and past a number of tiny villages all the way to the monument, which is about 175 miles away — a three-to-3½-hour drive. It's a beautiful route that is embellished with high mountains, broad meadows, ponds and reservoirs.

In earlier times the Shoshone Indians hunted in the Craters of the Moon area. Pioneers in covered wagons skirted the lava flows, cattle ranchers stayed away, and miners staked claims beyond its reaches. Geologists predict the landscape will erupt again. Instead of one volcano, lava flowed out through fissure vents and volcanic cones about 15,000 years ago and continued to do so until about 2,000 years ago.

A 7-mile loop road leads to spatter and cinder cones, lava flows and lava tube "caves." You will be amazed at the life that inhabits this alien, moonlike landscape — 2,000 insect species, 148 birds, 47 mammals, eight reptiles and a lone amphibian, the western toad. Mule deer are sometimes seen, and bobcats and great horned owls hunt here. Plant life is also amazingly abundant. Wildflowers carpet the park from early May until late August. In all, 300 species of plants decorate this apparently desolate stretch. Sagebrush, antelope bitterbush and rubber bitterbrush are established on the older lava flows. On the younger flows, mockorange and tansybush fill deeper crevices where soil and organic matter have accumulated.

The park's loop road is open from April to mid-November, when it is closed by snow. A visitors center, which offers displays, a dramatic video about erupting volcanoes, and history, is open year-round, except for holidays in winter. A campground is open from May to October. In winter the loop road makes an excellent trail for cross-country skiers. For information about the park, call (208) 527-3257.

City of Rocks National Reserve

"We encamped in the city of the rocks, a noted place from the granite rocks rising abruptly out the ground," James Wilkins wrote in 1849. "They are in a romantic valley clustered together, which gives them the appearance of a city." Wilkins was among the first wagon travelers to fix the name City of Rocks to what looked like "a dismantled, rock-built city of the Stone Age." The area's historical and geological values, scenery and opportunities for recreation led to its designation as **City of Rocks National Reserve** in 1988.

City of Rocks offers scenic walks near the historic California Trail and opportunities for watching wildlife, taking pictures and participating in world-class technical rock climbing. Picnic areas and camping sites are also available. The reserve's range of elevation in a compact area creates varied patterns of vegetation and wildlife habitat. Pine and fir exist at high elevations; aspen, mountain mahogany and cottonwood occupy middle elevations; and sagebrush, pinyon pines and juniper dominate the lower elevations. Deer, mountain lion, coyotes, badgers and bobcats are among the wildlife. Over head, you may spot eagles, falcons, hawks and vultures.

City of Rocks is most known by rock climbers. It rivals Yosemite National Park in California as a western favorite for technical climbing. International climbers come to the reserve to climb Rabbit Rock, Morning Glory Spire and Bread Loaves. The degree of difficulty scale for rock climbing runs from 5.0 to 5.14. A great number and variety of climbs are 5.13 and better.

Park elevations range from 5,500 to 8,867 feet atop Graham Peak. Camping is permitted in designated primitive sites. Overnight lodging, meals, gasoline and groceries are available in nearby communities. Although reserve facilities are primitive, restrooms are located throughout.

To reach City of Rocks from Boise, take Interstate 84 to the Declo exit, drive south on Idaho Highway 77 through Albion, and leave Idaho 77 for the road to Almo, where the reserve is located. The distance is more than 200 miles, or about a four-hour drive from Boise. For information call (208) 824-5519.

West

Hells Canyon

Hugging the borders of northeastern Oregon and western Idaho, **Hells Canyon National Recreation Area**, (208) 628-3916, is a rugged, 652,488-acre cleft in the earth split by the Snake River beneath cliffs and mountains that rise nearly 8,000 feet above. This is a tawny, brawny, bruiser of a place that rises from sandbars and desert to Alpine lakes and snowcapped peaks. Tiny pika, cougars, bobcats, elk, deer, mountain goats and bighorn sheep live in Hells Canyon's lush forests and craggy ridges. Prehistoric Native American tribes, Chief Joseph's band of Nez Perce Indians, and 19th-century gold miners and homesteaders found refuge here. Indian pictographs and petroglyphs as well as the remains of settlers' homes are found today. World-class whitewater rapids and glass-smooth pools of water describe the course of the Snake River, which continues from here through Lewiston and on to the Columbia River and Pacific Ocean. The area presents many opportunities for hiking, fishing, boating, horseback riding, picnicking and observing from lookout points.

Perhaps the best way to visit from Boise is to begin at the **Hells Canyon Visitor Center**, about a three-hour drive away. Drive west on Interstate 84 and take the Fruitland exit and U.S. Highway 95 north. At Cambridge turn left or west on Idaho Highway 71. From there it is 28 miles to Brownlee Dam, 40 miles to Oxbow Reservoir and 62 miles to the road's end at Hells Canyon Creek, where the center is located.

The center features permanent and changing exhibits and videos on the fish, archaeology and other aspects of the canyon. A 20-minute trail leads from the parking lot along Hells Canyon Creek to waterfalls. A second trail follows the Snake River past a prehistoric rock shelter and a Native American pit house, a depression in the ground that was once part of a prehistoric village.

You can also jet boat, fish or spend the night at nearby campgrounds. Or, you can visit the Brownlee Power Plant.

Oregon Trail Interpretive Center

A gleaming, silvery structure perched on a basalt cap above the vast Baker Valley, which has a 360-degree view of the sagebrush flanks and dirt trails taken by the pioneers of the last century. This is the $10 million **Oregon Trail Interpretive Center**, (541) 523-1843, located outside Baker City, Oregon, 140 miles and two to 2½ hours from Boise. Take Interstate 84 north from Boise to the Oregon state line at Ontario, continue to just north of Baker City and go east, on Oregon Highway 86 for 5 miles to reach the center. Admission is $5 for adults and $3.50 for children age 17 and younger. The center is open every day but Christmas and New Year's days.

INSIDERS' TIP

Rivers and creeks run along many of Idaho's highways, providing excellent picnic opportunities and a sparkle to any daytrip.

One of the spectacular things about the center is its remote character: It's a sky capsule surrounded by rough, high, angular terrain where you imagine the creak of covered wagons, the whinny of mules and horses and the curve of women's bonnets. Here you can taste the wind and come upon actual ruts going back to the last century.

The 23,000-square-foot visitor complex has a 150-seat indoor theater, a multiple use room for conferences and traveling exhibits, two outdoor living history displays and a trail system. The themes presented are the trail experience, mining and the West, explorers and fur traders, natural history of northeastern Oregon and Native American history. They are not presented via TV or computer graphics but with a triumph of theater over slick gadgetry, of immaculate and imaginative design over special effects, of photos and the written word and sculpture and costumes over splashy revelation. The Oregon Trail figures seem more real than the people eyeing them.

This is a place to relax and spend the day, to enjoy history and the magnificent natural surroundings. Hells Canyon (listed previously) is just east. You can take Ore. 86 from the center east to Richland, Oregon, and then south on an improved, unpaved road that takes you high above the canyon, for excellent views, as you nose back to Interstate 84 and your return to Boise.

**Tree-lined
reservoirs and rivers
enhance the settlements
of Boise, Nampa
and Caldwell.**

Neighborhoods and Real Estate

Boise is compact, easy to see and get around. Its arms open to a smart, tucked-away isolation that will always surprise the first-time visitor after many miles of sagebrush flats, sparse ridge lines and mountains. The current metro population of 372,210 is expected to approach a half-million by 2010.

An air view of the Treasure Valley presents a sagebrush plain between the Owyhee Mountains to the south and grassy foothills rising to distant peaks to the north. Tree-lined reservoirs and rivers shade the settlements of Boise, Idaho's capital city, and the smaller clusters of Nampa and Caldwell, just west. A half-dozen high-rises climb into the sky before the Capitol dome on one end of a broad boulevard and the train depot, perched on a hill, on the other end. The parks of the Greenbelt hug the Boise River as it meanders through the center of town. Brick St. Luke's Hospital and white St. Al's Hospital to the west stand out. Golf courses, cemeteries and Boise Towne Square, the city's mall, cover large chunks of land. The most dramatic rise is the jut of Table Rock, with its lighted cross, on the valley's eastern flank. The most dramatic color is the blue artificial turf of the Boise State University football stadium that gleams like a giant swimming pool on a long and narrow riverside campus. Interstate 84 and its downtown connector, Business 84 or I-184, join like a slingshot that catapults commuter traffic west in the direction of most noticeable valley growth.

Boise's Comprehensive Plan divides the city into six planning and zoning areas, each with distinct characteristics. We'll look at each of those and Garden City, stitched as incongruously as a fish into its middle, before mov-ing west to the fast-growing satellite towns of Meridian, Eagle, Star and Kuna, and farther west on the I-84 corridor to Nampa and Caldwell.

Neighborhoods

Boise

Northeast

Boise's two grandest streets are in its oldest areas, the East End and North End, and above those, very much like southern California, are ridges populated with expensive view houses that are destined to multiply and demand traffic corridors through the fine, old, beloved neighborhoods below. Will the automobile rule Boise, or will the older parts of the city keep their leafy, laid-back charm? That question is debated at the planning commission, city council and public hearings by neighborhood associations and developers and on editorial pages and TV.

Meanwhile life goes on along and around the majestic mansions and spacious lawns of Warm Springs Avenue on the East End, where Oregon Trail pioneers entered Boise, and in the North End divided by Harrison Boulevard, where the big shots and merely well-to-do enjoy a long tree island in the middle of the road that buds beautifully in spring and streaks the fall with luscious color. Historic old houses, towering hardwoods, sidewalks filled with dogs, families and kids, the active contours of Camelback Park and pocket-sized serenity of

Elm Grove Park please the 23,800 residents of these old "Ends" of town. It's a quick rise into the foothills and ski area, downtown and shopping are close, and every house has at least one bicycle, cat and hound.

Houses come in all sizes, shapes and colors but are generally wood, tasteful and well-kept. Green, flowery yards, porches and fireplace chimneys are common. Shabby areas are vanishing as young families and retired people move in, bringing the life of hammer-and-nail, fresh paint and additions to structures that sometimes go back into the last century. Residential densities are much greater than in other parts of town because of small lots and tightly gridded streets — six to eight units per acre compared to three for the rest of the city. About 40 percent of the homes in the Northeast are rented, the highest percentage in town except for the area around Boise State University. Renters are attracted to the tree-clad, New England atmosphere of the area, and many end up purchasing property here. Northeasters can't imagine living anywhere else.

With the discovery of Boise by companies and people looking for a better quality of life, home prices in the last seven years have risen more rapidly in the Northeast than in the rest of Ada County. The median price (half the homes above, half below) for a single family Ada County home went from $64,500 in 1989 to $110,500 in 1996. It is difficult to find a house in the North and East ends for less than $100,000 today. Rentals, however, run from $700 to $1,200 a month depending on size and location.

Northwest

Open areas grazed by horses and cows and long tree-covered avenues with large lots and subdivisions wedged between characterize Northwest Boise. It's a patch-quilt area of old and new that bristles with development beside sleepy age and may be reconfigured with the widening of two of its major roads, Hill Road and 36th Street, to accommodate more traffic.

Waterways, quail, deer, raccoon and wild turkeys punctuate the quiet farmland and rolling hills adjacent to the perspiration and noise of building sites. New rooftops span the horizon beside old family fields that won't be passed on to junior because of advancing dozers. However, there is space here for the horse people and for those who grow corn and large gardens that should last and become more valuable in its retreat and solitude as things fill in elsewhere.

Northwest Boise began in the 1880s, a generation after Boise was founded at its present downtown location and the North End. Collister Road goes back to Dr. George Collister who, like other pioneers, planted orchards and established a rural character that has endured for more than a century. Pierce Park Road goes back to Walter Pierce, who built a park for picnicking and boating that was connected by railroad in the 1890s that is now Plantation Golf Course, which sits beside busy State Street. Today Northwest Boise is home to 15,500 people.

Foothills above Northwest Boise contain some of Boise's most expensive homes. At Quail Ridge, a Foothills development with nature trails and man-made waterfalls, the average price of a home is $337,000.

Real estate agents and others consider high-end Riverside Village, set along the north shore of the Boise River, and the Plantation subdivisions part of Northwest Boise, though they are officially in Garden City. Including those areas and the Foothills, the cost of a two-bedroom house averages $93,000; a three-bedroom, $136,000; and a five-or-more bedroom, $365,000.

Garden City

Visitors and residents alike wonder at the oddity of Garden City, which slices into the northwest shoulder of Boise. It is the legacy of slot machine operators who in 1949 were outlawed in Boise and incorporated an adjacent village for their one-armed bandits. They named their enclave Garden City after earlier Chinese gardens in the area. They were only able to continue their casino play until 1954 when the state legislature banned gambling statewide.

Garden City, with busy Chinden Boulevard flanked by hundreds of businesses running through, is thought of mostly as commercial, sports and entertainment territory. It is home to the Western Idaho Fairgrounds, the baseball stadium of the minor league Boise Hawks, Les Bois Racetrack, Plantation Golf Course, Westy's Garden Lanes for bowling and a huge Fred Meyer store. But 8,000 people live between Chinden and the Boise River, which cuts lengthwise through the northern half of Garden City.

Much of this area has been populated by mobile homes, shacks and manufactured housing, but that is changing with the construction of upscale river's-edge residences and the city's River Front Urban Renewal Plan. The plan is intended to clean up rundown areas near the river, lower crime and increase civic pride. However, low-income residents are afraid they will be moved out with no alternative living choices in the Boise area.

Garden City's recent growth is credited to lower water rates and city taxes, a more efficient City Hall, the city's stretch of river and greenbelt, and small-town atmosphere. With residential developments such as Riverside Village, Plantation Place, Willow Brook, Silver Wood, Meadow Creek and River's Edge, families are moving in, even though Garden City has no schools within its boundaries. Children are bused to outside schools, which is a problem for students who want to participate in extracurricular activities. The construction of an elementary school and more parks are among the city's goals.

Houses run from $70,000 for a two-bedroom house to $130,000 for a three-bedroom and $220,000 for a five-bedroom.

West Bench

Bluffs opposite the Boise River slice northwest through the city, creating a plateau above downtown, Garden City and timbered northern districts that reach out to the Foothills. It's called the "Bench" and is divided into two parts, West Bench and Central Bench.

Piecemeal building over the years on eas-

ily developed, flat, inexpensive land made the West Bench Boise's largest area, with 56,300 residents and 28,000 jobs.

Hewlett-Packard Co., Boise's second largest employer, TCI Cablevision and the Boise Research Center are located here as is the largest shopping area in the state, Boise Towne Square and the scores of stores that surround it. Heavily-trafficked Fairview Avenue, Boise's biggest commercial strip and gateway to the west, runs through.

This is a big family area, and 90 percent of the houses are owned by their inhabitants. Although most farms have been rubbed out, small pastures with horses and other animals remain.

It's a comfortable and convenient territory with panoramic views on the rim, spruce neighborhoods free of cut-through traffic and new subdivisions that could be anywhere in America. Residents like the greater feeling of space here than in older city neighborhoods. Shopping centers are strategically placed at intersections, providing nearby shops and meeting places. A lack of parks has been ameliorated by construction of a beautiful new YMCA and city pool at McMillan and Cloverdale roads and a nearby 20-acre community park at Hobble Creek subdivision. A 40-acre park at McMillan and Eagle roads and a 7-acre neighborhood park behind Pioneer Elementary School are being added to the fold.

A two-bedroom house runs $70,000; a three-bedroom, $105,000; and a five-or-more-bedroom, $175,000.

Central Bench

This is a mixed area developed in the '40s and '50s that is home to 40,000 people. Commercial strips are set off from dwellings, chiefly along Orchard Street, Overland Road and Vista Avenue, which is the main corridor into the city from Boise Municipal Airport.

People of many income levels live in Central Bench. Homes of different sizes are adjacent to each other, and small apartment buildings share streets with single-family houses. Many homes still get irrigated water that flows in canals that crisscross neighborhoods. Pastures and old wooded patches can still be

Photo: Courtesy of Peter Rose

Newcomers who enjoy cycling, walking or in-line skating may want to consider a home's proximity to the Greenbelt. It's the city's best venue for these activities.

found here. Young families who want a safe neighborhood that is near downtown and parks are moving in.

Grid-style streets allow people on foot or bike to cross easily between neighborhoods and commercial streets. However, cut-through traffic is a problem, and more speed humps, meant to slow down cars, are being installed by the Ada County Highway District.

A two-bedroom house averages $77,000; a three-bedroom, $110,000; and a five-or-more-bedroom, $215,000.

Southeast

Southeast Boise, a far-flung territory of ledges, flats and slopes rising above the Boise River, is the fastest growing part of town. Since the '70s, agricultural land and older homes have given way to planned developments, apartment complexes and business centers.

Micron Technology Inc., the area's largest employer, is located here in sleek, white buildings beside I-84. Headquartered at fashionable ParkCenter is Albertsons Inc., the fourth largest and most profitable supermarket chain in the country; Truss Joist MacMillan, the country's largest wood-engineering firm; Ore-Ida Foods Inc., known for its frozen foods;

and Diamond Sports, which owns professional baseball, ice hockey and tennis franchises and is part-owner of the Bank of America Centre. J.R. Simplot's handsome food processing headquarters is situated on a hill with a grand view. In the downtown portion of the area is Idaho's largest university, Boise State — a grassy, brick campus stretched along the river, with circular dorms on one end and the towering, diagonal concrete slabs of the football stadium on the other.

Farmers began settling the Southeast near the Boise River in 1865, and by 1880 the entire area was irrigated. The area's first subdivisions were mapped in 1890. Garfield School was built at the turn of the century. A village of South Boise was founded in 1902 and incorporated into Boise a decade later. Streetcars traveled Broadway Avenue from 1905 until 1928, when the road was paved for automobiles.

Retail areas that serve Southeast Boise include the Southshore Center at Apple Street and Park Center Boulevard, the nearby Eastgate Shopping Center at Apple Street and E. Boise Avenue and the Factory Outlet Mall on I-84. Broadway Avenue has a long string of shops, stores and restaurants. The area has six elementary schools and Les Bois Junior High School.

More than 30,000 people live here. Identical homes sell for 5 to 10 percent more than in the Northwest. Columbia Village, a large, modern subdivision, is located here. The swank River Run condos and some of the area's most expensive houses are built along the river. The last lot, just under an acre, on The Island at River Run was recently sold for $350,000 to Micron Vice President Kipp Bedard who is building a $1.2 million house on the property.

There is concern about overpopulation and too much traffic. The biggest single development proposal in Boise history is planned for Harris Ranch on land stretching from the Boise River to the Foothills. Developers want to build 3,300 homes and 1.5 million square feet of office and commercial space on 1,740 acres. Opponents to the proposal, major parts of which have been approved by the city Planning and Zoning Commission, say the development will put too much traffic onto Warm Springs Avenue, one of Boise's two grand streets, flanked by mansions, broad lawns and majestic hardwoods; that it will degrade wildlife habitat in the Foothills; and that it will put homes too close to the river for safety.

The average two-bedroom house costs $85,000; three-bedroom, $140,000; and five-or-more-bedroom, $210,000.

Southwest

Out past the airport it is wide open and quiet, the place to own a sizable piece of land not far from the city. The sign on earth-covered Amity School says, "Keep horses off the grass." These 17 square miles of sage and grassland grew only 13 percent in population, to an estimated 21,413 people, from 1980 to 1996.

A moratorium clamped on building for much of the 1980s because of lack of sewers kept the population down, making this the area of slowest growth. But sewers are heading out as Boise extends its tentacles into this semirural territory of widely spaced homes and horse pastures. Annexation by the city is in the picture, which would raise property taxes now lower than those in Boise.

Under a new comprehensive plan, no more than three houses can be built on an acre, and rural features such as creeks and open

space are to be protected. The plan proposes an urban village around the Lake Hazel shopping center that now consists of the Wooden Nickel Saloon, a bowling alley, the $1-per-ticket Frontier Cinema and a small supermarket.

The Southwest has little retail, except on its northern edge where a new Wal-Mart has been built. Golfers play at Indian Lakes and Boise Ranch. A mile-long, 163-acre park filled with ball fields, tennis courts and perhaps a pool will be built by the city in 1998 along the New York Canal to become Boise's biggest park.

Lot prices at a subdivision near Amity School run $59,000 to $72,000.

A two-bedroom house averages $115,000; a three-bedroom, $120,000; a four-bedroom, $165,000; and a five-or-more-bedroom, $180,000.

Meridian

This has become the chief bedroom community for Boise, where young families buy subdivision starter houses and take I-84 or one of the large avenues that run through town to work. About 30,000 people live in Meridian, and it is growing by 3,000 a year. By 2015 the population is expected to reach 80,000.

Overcrowded schools are a big issue here. Bond elections for new construction are constantly coming up as the district struggles to keep up with its new families.

The average two-bedroom house costs $90,000. Three-bedroom homes average $120,000; a four-bedroom, $160,000; and a five-or-more-bedroom, $190,000.

Eagle and Star

The small town of Eagle recently got a bypass on Idaho Highway 44, but that's not preventing big spenders and others in search of space with a rural character from pouring in. New developments along the river and pricy estate-type properties have led to the construction of new high, middle and elementary schools that have an excellent reputation.

Albertsons, McDonald's and First Security Bank are among the businesses that have moved in to serve Eagle's 7,000 citizens.

Star, just west of Eagle, has about 1,000

people who are deciding if they want to incorporate. It has three new subdivisions, a new trailer park and a branch of the Ada County Community Library.

A two-bedroom home runs $100,000; a three-bedroom, $140,000; and a five-or-more-bedroom, $380,000.

Kuna

Kuna is agricultural and horse country that is being filled in with subdivisions. Its 4,000 residents enjoy Ada County's lowest tax rate and help themselves by planting trees and cleaning up the community. The town has prepared for growth by expanding its sewer and water systems to accommodate 6,000 people.

The town has a new mall, large supermarkets, banks and other services. A greenbelt has been partially built and will expand as the budget allows.

A two-bedroom house costs $80,000; a three-bedroom, $105,000; a four-bedroom, $160,000; and a five-or-more-bedroom, $185,000.

Nampa

Nampa courts population and business as avidly as any community in the state. Its sewer and water systems are built ahead for great expansion, and 700 houses are going up per year. The city prides itself on being friendly and helping newcomers find housing and job opportunities. The population number of the green Nampa highway sign reads 35,333, although the actual figure is closer to 43,000, which shows how fast things are moving here.

Micron Electronics, a subsidiary of Boise chip maker Micron Technology, has been a boon for the community. The computer maker employs 3,500 people, has jobs for 400 to 500 more and has breathed new life into the northeast section of town that only a few years ago was considered to be industrial, run-down and a place to avoid.

Job diversity has also been provided by J.R. Simplot processed food operations, chip maker Zilog, Mercy Medical Center and Pacific Publishers, a Seventh Day Adventist religious group that moved from California.

Northwest Nazarene College, a small, highly rated liberal arts school, is also in Nampa. Nampa residents built their own golf course, Centennial, and recently the go-go town constructed a new city hall, civic center and recreation center.

Realtors divide Nampa into three areas: the Northeast, which is north of the railroad tracks, the West and the South.

The Northeast, with Micron's arrival, has seen new developments and subdivisions. Older, fixer-up houses can be had for $50,000 to $70,000; new homes cost $75,000 to $125,000.

The middle-class West, with slow, steady growth, has been the stable part of Nampa over the years. It has many subdivisions and is known for its good schools and shopping at Karcher Mall. Houses range from $60,000 to $150,000.

The upper-end South has Mercy Medical Center, new parks, a new shopping center and much of the new town growth. Houses run $90,000 to $250,000. Lots in the Bay Hill subdivision, which have views of Lake Lowell, run $53,000.

Caldwell

Caldwell, a town of 20,000, is sleepier and slower than its big brother, Nampa, which is just east and connected by the busy Nampa-Caldwell Boulevard. But Caldwell seems to like it that way. Only 110 new houses are built each year compared to Nampa's 700, and they generally cost 5 to 10 percent less. There is a need to pass a major sewer bond up the line to sustain growth.

Caldwell is proud of its school systems and takes special delight in Albertson College of Idaho, one of the top liberal arts colleges in

INSIDERS' TIP

Check the school districts closely before you choose a place to buy or rent. Some schools operate year-round; others follow a nine-month schedule.

the West. It has a stately campus that could have been bottled and shipped from New England into the midst of this high-desert, agricultural panorama.

Its heart remains, however, that of a farmer. Local businesses include creameries, dairies and poultry plants as well as cattle, fruit, grain and seed dealers. It is the seat of Canyon County, which is rated 47th out of approximately 3,000 counties in the country in agricultural production.

Unlike many other western towns, Caldwell has no freeway connector and the teeming franchise businesses that typically line such appendages. The town insisted that the freeway run through its middle, and access is better and more aesthetic because of that. However, most recent growth has occurred on the broad, fertile southern incline, stretching the town in that direction. Farmers can sell their rich farmland for $3,000 to $3,500 for crop use or $8,000 to a developer. Most farmers are choosing the latter, naturally.

Some of the nicest houses in Caldwell are located in an old, leafy neighborhood adjacent and northwest of Albertson College of Idaho and in Rio Vista, just east of the freeway, overlooking the Boise River.

Caldwell has six elementary schools, a grade school, a junior high and a high school built three years ago. The generosity of land, landscaping and construction of these schools make some of them look like college campuses.

Of the new and existing homes sold in Canyon County in the first half of 1997, 317 out of 791, or about 40 percent, fell into the $70,000 to $89,999 price range; 101, or 12 percent, were priced between $90,000 and $99,999; 100, or 12 percent, cost $100,000 to $119,999; and 62, or 8 percent, cost $120,000 to $159,999.

Real Estate

Scores of Treasure Valley real estate agencies have offices in Boise and surrounding towns. With the tremendous population growth of the '90s, new agencies and franchise affiliates have heated up the competition.

Independence as a Key to Success

The King of the Lone Wolf Realtors in the Treasure Valley is Mike Eddy, known for his Hawaiian shirts, laid-back manner and classic '64 Sedan De Ville black Caddy that along with his cellular phone pretty much serves as his office.

Of his casual appearance — brown beard, mustache, ponytail, shades, island shirts

and typically a baseball cap and sneakers — he says, with a dimpled smile and tongue-in-cheek, "If they realize you know what you're talking about, I figure they don't care what you look like."

Eddy has sold 400 to 500 properties since 1980 and fervently declares, "Every good economist should be in real estate, whether you work on your own investments or someone else's. Otherwise you pay an unnecessary 3 percent on every project you're involved with."

Realtors come in all stripes, colors and shapes and with every kind of past, but few studied physics cosmology, the big-bang theory and atom-smasher philosophy, like Eddy did back in Cal Poly Pomona before the Army drafted him and changed his priorities.

"After two years in the Army, I wanted to find out about political/economic power," he says. "I thought they were more important than gravity and electricity. I already knew about those."

Eddy studied economics and mathematics while earning a master's degree from California State University in Los Angeles. After coming to Boise in the late '70s, Eddy

— continued on next page

Photo: Courtesy of Mike Eddy

Mike Eddy has been part of the Boise realty scene since 1980.

worked for the state and privately as a public utilities economist, which he found boring and repetitious. His escape was going solo as a Realtor and small business consultant.

He was able to acquire repossessed $35,000 Housing and Urban Development houses for $100 down in the mid- and late '80s and rent them until the local recession ended at the turn of the decade, before selling for juicy profits. He put his earnings into a 5.5-acre Arapaho Cove subdivision along a waterway in blue-chip Riverside Village, which coupled with other real estate sales made him a millionaire and allowed him to move his family from a hillside town house into a spacious custom-built luxury house on his Arapaho property, where his fishing line perpetually dangles from his deck into a ducky trout stream.

In 1992 Eddy and a business colleague, Dave Kent, renovated an old, solidly made pizza parlor at the foot of Bogus Basin Road, which leads to the ski area, and turned it into one of Boise's first two microbrewery/restaurants, Harrison Hollow. That successful venture has since led to their building another restaurant in Bend, Oregon, and a microbrewery in Maui, Hawaii, where they brew, sell and export Hulaberry beer.

Instead of expanding with a real estate office and agents, Eddy remains a one-man gang at Michael J. Eddy Realty, (208) 853-8300, answering his own calls, wearing Hawaiian shirts and taking around clients in his black Caddy. "I'd rather work with peoples' opportunities than with peoples' problems, which is what would happen if I had a bunch of employees," he quips.

Eddy enjoys his perks — playing poker with the same group for 15 years; playing rhythm guitar in a rock 'n' roll and blues band that meets at his house each week; going with friends each year to the Oregon coast during the World Series; serving as Northwest Boise Kiwanis Club president; attending Boise Hawks professional baseball games; getting away to his cabin near Cascade Lake; golfing and fishing; and helping charity groups.

Agencies

The Brandt Agency Real Estate
203 11 Ave. S., Nampa • (208) 466-7821

John Brandt, 93, started the agency in 1937 and still comes into the office to oversee operations. His son, Don Brandt, is now the manager. The company has nine agents and works mainly in Nampa and Caldwell.

Bullock & Company Realtors
304 12th Ave., Nampa • (208) 466-1010

Agent Sue Thompson and her husband, Bill, ran a Nampa realty company for 20 years until Bill decided to join the professional golf senior mini-tour in Florida, Arizona and California. Now Sue has joined Greg and Scott Bullock and another agent, Dave Humphries, at Bullock & Company, a new office with 60 combined years of real estate experience.

Coldwell Banker Aspen Realty Inc.
6933 W. Emerald St., Boise
• (208) 377-2310
Boise Towne Square Mall, 350 N.
Milwaukee St., Boise • (208) 376-5551
99 E. State St., Eagle • (208) 939-4430
900 N. Linder Rd., Meridian
• (208) 884-1300
521 12 Ave. S., Nampa • (208) 467-5272

This is the largest real estate agency in Idaho with 160 agents working out of its five Treasure Valley offices, including 85 in its largest office on W. Emerald Street. It markets 40 subdivisions in the Treasure Valley. The company's Idaho branch is part of an international network that includes 2,700 offices and 60,000 real estate agents. Coldwell Banker was a pioneer in the use of videos to sell real estate and is often featured in national publications such as *Dupont* and *Unique Homes* magazines.

Holland Realty
4720 W. Emerald St., Boise
• (208) 336-3393

Holland is one of three local companies that works with customers on picking out land, constructing a house and doing everything necessary through closing. The company works with 60 builders on houses in all price ranges throughout the Treasure Valley. It also works, as other companies do, on lot and residential re-sale. John Holland founded the company in 1979. It has eight agents.

Homeland Realty
1919 W. State St., Boise
• (208) 342-2700, (800) 535-0743

This locally owned agency in the North End has been in business since 1983. Its agents average seven years in experience and $3 million in annual sales. Homeland Realty is known for its relocation department, which started eight years ago, and has a full-time, salaried person who works on introducing newcomers to the Treasure Valley.

Jensen Real Estate
1420 W. Washington, Boise
• (208) 344-0200
360 E. State St., Eagle • (208) 939-4364
7th Ave. and Blaine St., Caldwell
• (208) 459-0736

Stanton Jensen started the company in 1946 and is succeeded by his sons Jeffrey, Gregory and Stephen at three different locations. Jeffrey runs the Caldwell office and knows the territory well. The company is home-owned, not a franchise like many agencies in the Treasure Valley.

McLeod Realty
1403 W. Franklin St., Boise
• (208) 343-4240
597 E. State St., Eagle • (208) 939-3777, (800) 995-4240

In 1973 Adelaide McLeod, a native of Boise, started the company in a beautiful old Victorian house in downtown Boise that was built in the early 1900s for the state treasurer. McLeod, a broker as well as company president, is known for her knowledge of the area and the real estate industry. The Boise office has more than 40 agents, and the Eagle office has seven. McLeod was one of the first Boise agencies to offer a video about Boise and the state.

Parke Pointe
6223 Discovery Wy., Ste. 100, Boise
• (208) 323-4000, (800) 524-4663
312 3 Ave. S., Nampa • (208) 463-0000

One of the largest nonfranchise agencies in the Treasure Valley, Parke Pointe employees 76 Boise and 16 Nampa agents. The company is especially noted for residential subdivision development and works with many builders and developers. It also has a separate relocation company that offers language services and helps trailing spouses. Hewlett-Packard is a frequent client.

Premier Properties, Inc.
2869 Autumn Way, Meridian
• (208) 345-3600

This locally owned agency handles residential, commercial and investment properties as well as new construction. President Ken Reed and secretary/treasurer Susan Broadie have more than 25 years of experience in the real estate industry. Lori B. Keller specializes in helping clients with relocation.

Richard B. Smith Realty
2417 Bogus Basin Rd., Boise
• (208) 343-5412, (800) 343-5412

Richard B. Smith's grandfather started the agency in the 1800s, which makes it one of the oldest surviving Boise companies. The company developed the Crane Creek area in the Highlands, a hilly residential area above the North End, in the 1970s and does a lot of work in the North End and Highlands. It's staffed by 20 agents.

Rentals

Hammack Management Inc.
3775 Cassia St., Boise • (208) 342-7368

This is the largest locally owned real estate management company in Boise. It has 1,200 multiple-family and 250 single-family listings. About a quarter of its listings are new properties that didn't sell; about three-quarters are owned by investors.

The company says that a two-bedroom apartment in Ada County will typically rent for $550 a month; a three-bedroom, from $600 to $1,200. For houses, expect to pay around $600 range for two bedrooms, $800 for three bedrooms and $1,000 to $1,200 for four bedrooms.

There are a few rentals available in the downtown Washington Mutual Capitol Plaza, a soaring, modern building with condos that are mostly in the hands of homeowners. A two-bedroom rental runs $1,600, and there is

one three-bedroom with an office penthouse that goes for $5,000.

Homefinders Rental Service
3302 Overland Rd., Boise
• (208) 345-2900

Brad and Traci Nishitani have been finding homes for people in the Treasure Valley for 15 years. A great amount of their work is with out-of-staters who are not familiar with the area. They have a rental listing service for prospective renters and a service for house owners looking for tenants. They try to carry at least 90 percent of the active rental properties in the area, which they get from newspaper ads, from exploring the territory themselves and from management companies. They charge $25 for a one-time list and $45 to search the market for people looking for a certain kind of rental.

Rentmasters
13340 Horseshoe Bend Rd., Boise
• (208) 939-0667

Debbie Langer and an assistant manage about 200 rental houses and apartments in the Treasure Valley, something Langer has been doing for 10 years. According to Langer, a two-bedroom apartment will typically rent for $450 to $550; a two-bedroom house, $600 to $750; a three-bedroom house, $700 to $850; and a four-bedroom house, $850 to $1,000.

Resources

Harmon Homes Magazine
5018 W. Emerald St., Boise
• (208) 375-3028

Harmon Homes free magazine, which has real estate agency advertisements for homes and properties in Boise, Nampa, Meridian and Caldwell and real estate classifieds, is available at stores and public boxes throughout the Treasure Valley.

The Idaho Statesman
1200 N. Curtis Rd., Boise
• (208) 377-6200

The Idaho Statesman, the Boise daily newspaper, prints a Treasure Valley real estate magazine each Saturday that is filled with real estate agency advertisements on homes and properties for sale. *The Statesman's* daily rental classifieds are closely followed by prospective renters and a good place to check for the latest listings.

Property by Owner
For Sale by Owner, 1390 N. Cole, Ste. A, Boise • (208) 322-1100, (800) 733-0343

Property by Owner, now in its 15th year, has black-and-white photos and information about properties for sale by owner. It's published monthly by For Sale by Owner and is available for free at public locations throughout the Treasure Valley. For a charge, the company provides advice, seminars, signs, videos and optional professional services for people who want to sell their property without an agent, which saves sellers the typical seven percent agent's fee.

Rent It Magazine
2905 N. 28th St., Boise • (208) 343-7368

This free monthly magazine is available at supermarkets and public racks throughout the Treasure Valley. It's filled with advertisements for apartments, condos, town houses and homes in Boise, Meridian, Nampa and Caldwell. It also has an apartment amenities guide and area map.

The largest school district in Idaho, Boise has more than 27,000 students enrolled at 34 elementary, eight junior high and four high schools.

Child Care
and Education

Boise's recent population growth has resulted in an increasing need for child care. Fortunately, day-care centers, services and programs have multiplied in response to these numbers. The Treasure Valley offers child-care centers, babysitting services and nannies as well as home day-care operators. In this chapter we provide clearinghouse numbers and agencies that can help you find just the right person or center to take care of your child.

The second half of the chapter deals with the education scene in the area, including the public school systems and some of the private schools. Higher education and continuing education options are at the end of the chapter and include Boise State University, the largest university in Idaho.

Child Care

Information Centers

Child Care Connections
Mountain States Group, 1607 W.
Jefferson St., Boise • (208) 342-4453
Nearly 500 licensed child-care providers in the greater Boise area have registered

with this resource and referral agency, which pairs parents with day-care homes and centers based upon mutual considerations. (A nominal fee is charged for this service, based upon parents' salary, but not more than $35 annually.) Parents are advised on what to look for in a child-care provider, and what questions are important to ask. CCC also recruits and trains providers, maintains a toy and book-lending library, coordinates the federal food program and lobbies in the state Legislature on behalf of children's issues. Office hours are 8 AM to 5:30 PM Monday through Friday.

Great Beginnings
913 S. Latah St., Boise • (208) 344-7255
This resource and referral service provides parents with the Boise-area list of child-care providers licensed by the state, broken out by zip code, at no charge. It requests only that parents pick it up from the office themselves, or send a stamped, self-addressed envelope to Great Beginnings, 913 S. Latah Street, Boise, ID 83705. The same list can be obtained from the state Department of Health & Welfare but at a substantial cost. The office is open from 8 AM to 5 PM Monday through Friday.

Idaho CareLine

State Department of Health & Welfare, 1790 Westgate Dr., Boise

• **(800) 926-2588**

The CareLine assists families with referrals for child care and medical services. These referrals provide information on family-planning and crisis-intervention services as well as recommend doctors, dentists, counselors and other providers who accept Medicaid payments. CareLine is available from 8 AM to 6 PM Monday through Friday. An answering machine accepts messages during off hours.

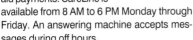

www.insiders.com
See this and many other
Insiders' Guide® destinations
online — in their entirety.
Visit us today!

Western Idaho Community Action Program

521 S. Kit Ave., Caldwell

• **(208) 454-0675**

A nonprofit, government-funded agency, WICAP performs a variety of functions for lower-income families throughout the Nampa-Caldwell area (Canyon County). In addition to recruiting child-care providers and making referrals, it offers family counseling and budgeting assistance, dispenses emergency food and clothing (and toys at Christmas) and handles applications for winter heating assistance. The agency is open 8 AM to 5 PM Monday through Friday.

Finding a Sitter

The folks at Child Care Connections, (208) 342-4453, suggest talking to local high-school family and consumer science (formerly home economics) departments for recommendations of students who may live in your neighborhood. If you'd prefer someone older, contact the **Boise State University** student employment office, 1910 University Drive, Boise, (208) 385-1745. You decide how much you want to pay a sitter from BSU, but it must be at least minimum wage.

Babysitting classes are regularly offered by each of the following agencies, which may be good places for recommendations of competent and qualified babysitters: **American Red Cross**, 254 S. Cole Road, Boise, (208) 375-0314; **St. Alphonsus Regional Medical Center**, 1055 N. Curtis Road, Boise, (208) 367-2097; **St. Luke's Birth & Parenting Education**, 325 W. Idaho Street, Boise, (208) 381-1200; and **Mercy Medical Center**, 1512 12th Avenue Road, Nampa, (208) 467-1171.

Nannies

A nanny cares for your children in your home, either under a part-time or full-time arrangement. One local agency that specializes in nanny placements is **There's No Place Like Home Nannies, Inc.**, (208) 388-0552. The agency performs all background checks, including fingerprinting, and assures that all nannies are certified in first aid and CPR. The agency has been in business since 1987 and is a member of the International Nanny Association. It places 24 to 30 nannies a year on a permanent basis and many others on a part-time basis. A live-in nanny runs $200 to $300 a week; part-time, $6 to $10 an hour. The company also provides babysitters for hotel or home sitting. There's a $10 fee for this service, and sitters are paid $7 to $8 an hour.

Day-Care Homes and Centers

Full-time child care in the Boise area averages around $100 per week, but cost depends on neighborhood, facilities, a child's age and other factors. Care provided in Nampa/Caldwell, for instance, tends to be less expensive than in Boise. Check with the **Idaho**

CareLine, (800) 926-2588, or **Child Care Connections**, (208) 342-4453, if you need information about sliding scale fees.

What follows is a handful of licensed day-care centers. Most day-care centers accept children full-time or part-time. Some will take them from infancy, others from toddler age only. Transportation is sometimes available, and a few day-care options are open Saturdays as well as weekdays.

The largest locally owned network of day-care centers is **New Horizon Child Care**, 1551 Bloom Street, Boise, (208) 853-9638. Although based at the Lakeharbor development in northwest Boise, it has 10 other locations in the capital, two more in Meridian and one in Eagle. Its primary preschool program (for children infant-age to school-age) is at 2112 Gekeler Lane, (208) 345-0073, in southeast Boise. There's also an extensive after-school program for kids 6 and older, including a summer program, based at 155 E. Boise Avenue, Boise, (208) 386-9108. New Horizon also has a school in Caldwell at 1717 Arlington Avenue, (208) 455-3777.

Other day-cares that say "yes" to infants include **ABC Preschool & Daycare**, 1819 N. 18th Street, Boise, (208) 336-7228; **Candyland Daycare**, 1131 W. Cherry Lane, Meridian, (208) 887-3699; and **For Kids Sake**, 1720 S. Curtis Road, Boise, (208) 377-4649.

Additionally, there are excellent programs at **A Tot's World**, 1714 Highland Street, Boise, (208) 342-2335; **All of Me Preschool and Kindergarten**, 2995 N. 38th Street, Boise, (208) 387-0917; and the **Boise Bears Child Care Center**, 3900 Hill Road, Boise, (208) 343-8919, and 1803 N. 9th Street, Boise, (208) 343-3817.

Gymboree, based at the WCA (formerly the YWCA), 720 W. Washington Street, Boise, (208) 343-4647, emphasizes play for newborns through age 5 as the best means for developing early-childhood motor and social skills.

A more distinct academic learning emphasis is placed on preschool at numerous schools, including 10 Montessori schools in the Boise area that take children beginning at 2½ years. The **Boise Montessori Center**, 2999 Moore Street, Boise, (208) 343-1481, can tell you all about their program as well as those at schools in the North End, the Bench, west Boise and Meridian. Each school is independently operated, so if you're interested in Montessori, it's

important to shop around. Reading, writing, arithmetic, geography, foreign languages and less cerebral pursuits, such as music and art, cooking and gardening, are spooned forth at these internationally renowned private schools.

Other preschools with limited enrollments and strong learning emphases include the **Bright Beginnings Learning Center**, 510 E. Watertower Lane, Meridian, (208) 884-0383 (it has six computer stations); **Parkside Preschool**, 1938 Parkside Drive, Boise, (208) 343-3344; **Pierce Park Academy for Child Care & Development**, 5008 Pierce Park Lane, Boise, (208) 853-5412; and **Prime Time Daycare & Learning Centers**, Fairwood Plaza, Fairview and Milwaukee streets, Boise, (208) 377-5200.

Often parents look for preschools that reinforce Christian values through their children's play and social interaction. Among these are the **Eagle Adventist Christian Preschool**, 538 W. State Street, Eagle, (208) 939-5544, and **Trinity Treasures**, 2626 S. Gekeler St., Boise, (208) 343-3486.

Recommended preschools in Canyon County include **Centennial Children's Center**, 3626 E. Ustick Road, Caldwell, (208) 454-8993; **The Creative Child**, 150 Delaware Avenue, Nampa, (208) 467-3652, and 1502 Main Street, Nampa, (208) 459-1854; and **Myla's Preschool & Daycare**, 1115 Dearborn Street, Nampa, (208) 459-8414.

Family and Extended Care Issues

The following listing enumerates agencies that deal with issues of children's physical development and psychological growth. In most cases, they willingly provide referrals to a wide range of other programs.

Adult and Child Development Center
State Department of Health & Welfare, 1790 Westgate Dr., Boise
• **(208) 334-0900**

Infants and toddlers receive in-house therapy for developmental delays and possible mental or physical disabilities. At the age of 3, local school districts take the lead, according to terms of the national Individuals

BSU proudly occupies 110 acres on the south bank of the Boise River.

with Disabilities Education Act (IDEA). Services are provided at no cost to families.

Big Brothers/Big Sisters of Southwestern Idaho
9696 Overland Rd., Boise
• (208) 336-2552

Community volunteers are paired with at-risk children — as referred by parents, teachers or school counselors — for one-on-one mentoring. Program options are site-based, in which volunteers and children meet at a specific location, or traditional, in which volunteers and children share activities in the community.

Community Youth Connection
Fort Boise Recreation Center, 110 Scout Ln., Boise • (208) 384-4177

Crisis and counseling centers, job information, activities and events and much more are readily accessible, here. The CYC also networks with schools and other social-service agencies and provides a forum where youth can voice their opinions and have their achievements promoted.

Family Wellness Center
420 W. Bannock St., Boise
• (208) 344-0094

Lutheran Social Services provides counseling for families and individual children, including pre- and post-adoption counseling.

Idaho Parents Unlimited and Parent Education & Resource Center
4696 Overland Rd., Ste. 478, Boise
• (208) 342-5884, (800) 242-IPUL

The families of children with disabilities get assistance from this federally funded, nonprofit organization. Besides agency referrals and training workshops, the center provides information on specific disabilities and support groups and tells parents what can be expected from schools and what rights are afforded to the disabled.

Idaho Youth Ranch
7025 W. Emerald St., Boise
• (208) 377-2613

Originally set up to provide long-term residence for youth with behavioral problems, the IYR has evolved into much more.

It still has a large working farm, which is on desert land north of Rupert, 175 miles east of Boise, where 50-some teenagers live, work and play. In addition, the Hays Shelter Home in Boise offers assistance to homeless, runaway and abused youth, while the Nampa Boys Home and Boise's Emancipation Home provide residential facilities closer to home. IYR has a family-services program for in-home assistance, as well as pregnancy and adoption services.

Just for Kicks 4-H Adventure Program
Boise School District, 1207 W. Fort St., Boise • (208) 338-3400

Latchkey kids are targeted by this program offered at 13 Boise elementary schools. Rather than leaving school-age children on their own for several hours before and after school, working parents can enroll them in this program of supervised activities during nonschool hours from 7 AM to 6 PM weekdays at the school. Kids who attend kindergarten through 6th grade may attend. A summer program also has been launched.

Mountain States Group
1607 W. Jefferson St., Boise • (208) 336-5533

This downtown Boise social-services collective is the home of Child Care Connections (see Information Centers in this chapter). Its other programs include Kids Count, for the prevention of child abuse and neglect; the Foster Grandparents Program; and the Idaho Head Start-Public School Transition Project that demonstrates and evaluates the support of families as their children move from Head Start to the third grade.

Warm Springs Counseling Center
740 Warm Springs Ave., Boise • (208) 343-7797

Operated by The Children's Home Society of Idaho, this handsome building, occupying a former orphanage, contains the offices of numerous mental-health practitioners who provide counseling services for children and families. Counseling is available to anyone, regardless of financial situation, on a sliding fee basis.

Youth Employment Service
219 W. Main St., Boise • (208) 334-6217

The job-service office takes youth registration from 3 to 4:30 PM Tuesdays, Wednesdays and Thursdays. Kids as young as 12 have been placed in part-time jobs, but most who apply are at least 15. There's another employment office in Meridian, (208) 895-6602.

Youth United
Treasure Valley United Way, 5420 W. Franklin Rd., Boise • (208) 336-1070

Two students from each Boise-area high school and one from each junior high comprise a core group represented on the United Way board of directors. In their own schools, they raise funds through dances, contests or car washes to go into a common Youth United fund. The core group then apportions the funds to needy groups in the health and human-services fields — not necessarily United Way agencies. Some youth also have become involved with agencies on a service-project basis.

Education

Public Schools

According to Idaho state law, all children between the ages of 7 and 16 must attend either a public or private school or be formally enrolled in home schooling. Children who turn 6 by September 1 of any given school year may attend first grade. Kindergarten, which is typically a half-day program is not mandatory.

Normally students attend the school nearest their home. But local school boards have adopted policies that restrict student enrollments (to prevent overcrowding) and occasionally may cause a previously unenrolled child to attend a school outside of his or her home district. Unless your child is preregistered, you'll need to go to your neighborhood school sometime during the last two weeks of August for registration. New students must provide a certified birth certificate, proof of immunization and the name and address of their previous school. It is also helpful for them to bring a copy of their school transcript.

This is especially true for high school students. Junior high and high school students who are new to the area are advised to call the school office ahead of time to find out when they should register, which is normally based upon the first letter of their last names, and to see if they need to schedule an appointment with a school counselor.

Boise School District
1207 W. Fort St., Boise • (208) 338-3400

The largest school district in Idaho, Boise schools have more than 27,000 students enrolled at 34 elementary schools, eight junior high schools and four high schools, with a new junior high and high school set to open in fall 1998. You can find out which school's attendance area your home falls into by calling the district transportation office at (208) 338-3661.

Boise schools place a strong basic emphasis on mathematics, science, literature and writing, developing student skills in verbal and written communication and collaborative team processes. Scholastic achievement tests indicate that Boise students rank in the top third of those in the nation; the 69 to 72 percentile for junior high and high school students is notably better than the 57 to 66 percentile for Idaho as a whole. ACTs — college admission tests for high school seniors — reflect similar success.

Computers, CD-ROMs and laser disks have augmented more traditional classroom tools like textbooks and films, and every school library now offers Internet access.

Boise schools offer occupational education programs for high school students that range from computer technology and electronics to fish and wildlife studies. Students attending advanced placement courses in high schools earn college credits. Special programs at earlier grade levels include special education (for physically or mentally challenged), a gifted and talented program, Boise Language Academy for foreign students, Chapter I to provide tutorial assistance where needed, and alternative schools for students who might otherwise not succeed in a regular school setting.

Numerous parent and community programs are offered by the district as well. They include a Parent Education Center that features courses in discipline and support groups for parents of attention deficit disorder children.

Meridian School District
911 N. Meridian Rd., Meridian
• (208) 888-6701

Meridian School District has more than 20,000 students in grades K-12. It includes the communities of Meridian, Star and Eagle, part of Garden City, west Boise, southwest Boise and rural areas between those communities. It is the second largest and fastest growing school system in Idaho. Over the past 25 years, student enrollment has increased sixfold. Planning for and managing that growth is a top priority.

Elementary schools are strategically located throughout the 384-square-mile district. They range in size from 250 students to more than 800 students.

Middle schools serve as a bridge for pre-adolescent students as they move from elementary school to high school. A team approach is used in core classes during grade 6 to ease the transition from the elementary classroom. Academic emphasis is placed on traditional subjects such as language arts, social sciences, mathematics and science.

The district's three high schools offer a full academic program with courses in basic skills and college-preparatory courses. These schools are in Idaho's A-1 athletic competition and have other competitive programs such as music, drama and debate.

Nampa School District
619 S. Canyon St., Nampa
• (208) 465-2700

Until recently, it was an easy walk from one school to another in Nampa. However, with town growth of 35 percent since 1990, the district now has 15 schools in an area of 70 square miles. Nampa has two high schools: Nampa High School, which has 1,191 students and 71 teachers, and Skyview, which has 1,150 students and 63 teachers. Four elementary schools are experimenting with year-round schedules in the 1998-99 school year. In general, students are in class for 45-day sessions and out for 15 days in the program. First, second, third and fourth grades, with 898, 807, 813 and 796 students, make up the largest class groups in the district.

Caldwell School District
1101 E. Cleveland Blvd., Caldwell
• (208) 455-3300

Established in 1884, Caldwell School District has a tradition of excellence. It typically does well in National Merit competition, and its graduates often earn more than $1 million in scholarships and awards.

The district has 577 teachers and support staff at eight schools. It has 5,000 students in preschool through grade 12. The student-teacher ratio is 24-to-1 in elementary schools and 16-to-1 in secondary schools.

College credit opportunities are available to high school students through a cooperative attendance program with Albertson College of Idaho. Enrichment classes for younger students are offered at the district-operated Technology Enrichment and Children Center.

Vallivue School District
2423 S. Georgia Ave., Caldwell
• (208) 454-0445

Vallivue School District is the largest geographical district in Canyon County. The dropout rate of the senior class is typically below 3 percent, and ACT scores are often above state and national averages. There are waiting lists of out-of-district students requesting admittance to Vallivue.

More than 3,000 students attend three elementary schools, a junior high and a beautiful new high school. Student-teacher ratios are 19-to-1 at the elementary level and 18-to-1 at the junior high and high school levels.

Small school districts and their main numbers include Emmett, 601 E. 3rd St., Emmett, (208) 365-6301; Kuna, 610 N. School Ave., Kuna, (208) 922-1000; Melba, 520 Broadway Ave., Melba, (208) 495-1141; and Middleton, 5 S. 3rd Ave. W., Middleton, (208) 585-3027.

Private Schools

Most Idahoans have a strong Christian ethic, so it's no surprise that many of them eschew public schools for their children and send them instead to church-related educational institutions. These represent a wide range of denominations, from Roman Catholic to fundamentalist Protestant, from Lutheran

to Seventh-day Adventist. If this is the sort of education you seek for your child, your best reference perhaps will come from your pastor.

Apart from schools with a religious orientation, there's not a lot of choice in the greater Boise area for parents who want to give their children a nontraditional, nonsectarian education at the elementary-school level and above.

Boise

Bishop Kelly High School
7009 W. Franklin Rd. • (208) 375-6010

Bishop Kelly, the only Catholic high school in Idaho, has 730 students in grade 9 through 12. Forty-five teachers are on staff. The school has strong sports teams and puts on two theatrical productions each year. Anywhere from 89 to 92 percent of students go on to higher education in a given class.

Boise Christian School
219 N. Roosevelt St. • (208) 342-4529

Although a Protestant school, Boise Christian is independently directed by a board of directors. It has 115 students and six teachers. The school has recently expanded from elementary education to offering classes for students K-12. The first senior class graduates in 1999. Academic excellence and Christian values are emphasized. No sports programs or extracurricular activities are offered.

Casa de Montessori
1004 Shoshone St. • (208) 344-1709

Teachers at this kindergarten-through-6th-grade facility emphasize personal interaction with their students, who typically number between 50 and 65. Different age groups are blended in each classroom, with a teacher-student ratio of about 1 to 10. This is a certified Montessori school; instructors all have teaching degrees as well as Montessori training. Children are encouraged to guide their own learning directions.

Foothills School of Arts & Sciences
618 S. 8th St. • (208) 331-9260

Seventy-eight students attend kindergarten through 9th grade at this private school, whose focus is "experiential education." Each grade level (there are five classes, with a three-grade middle school and 9th grade on its own) follows a thematic curriculum. Every subject taught is related to a concept with real-life importance: community, for instance, or for older students perhaps economics. There's no letter grading before 6th grade. The Foothills School is in Boise's old warehouse district across the street from the public library and adjacent to Julia Davis Park, the art and history museums and the Log Cabin Literary Center.

Hidden Springs Community School
5201 Drycreek Rd. • (208) 939-3000

Isolated in an evolving, self-contained community development just north of Boise, this school currently takes students from kindergarten through 8th grade but plans eventually to expand through high school. It is notable for its small class size and innovative teaching techniques. Traditional subjects provide the school's academic foundation, but individual students are challenged to explore themes not covered in typical curricula.

Maranatha Christian School
12000 Fairview Ave. • (208) 377-0423

Established in 1976, Maranatha Christian School encourages academic excellence and Christian values in its 300 students in grades K-12. There's also a preschool with 87 students who are as young as 3. A recent class saw 19 out of its 20 graduates go on to college. The school has two buildings, a gym and spacious grounds. Students participate in the major sports and in two theatrical performances each year.

Rose Hill Montessori School
4603 Albion St. • (208) 385-7674

With only 20 elementary students and another two dozen preschoolers, this small Bench school is able to provide personalized instruction not possible at larger facilities. The owner was trained by the Association for Montessori International; she is assisted by specialists in computers and art, foreign languages and physical education. Hands-on student involvement is encouraged.

Valley Christian High School
4950 Bradley St., Garden City
• (208) 375-6225

This school was established in 1989 and is operated in rented church space. About 130 students in grades 6 through 12 are taught by 12 teachers. The school offers programs in major sports, has a drama club and choir and encourages students to engage in academic challenges such as Math Counts.

Nampa

Nampa Christian School
439 Orchard Ave. • (208) 466-8451

This interdenominational religious school was established in the early 1960s. About 700 students beginning as young as 4 up through grade 12 are taught by 50 teachers. The school has teams for major sports as well as drama and music programs. Six buildings on 30 acres make up the campus.

Caldwell

Gem State Academy
1615 Montana Ave. • (208) 459-1627

Gem State, established in 1918, is a Seventh-Day Adventist school. Ten teachers offer instruction to 130 students in grades 9 through 12. Half of the student body lives on campus. Most of the students work at the school as teacher aides, receptionists and janitors or at the school's frozen dough plant or at the school's farm, which is part of the campus' 280 acres. The school has high academic standards: It averages one National Merit Scholarship finalist every two years.

Home-Schooling

Many parents choose to educate their children at home rather than sending them to a public or private school. For some, it's a distrust of educational systems that have strayed from traditional curricula and placed greater emphasis on socialization skills. For others, it's a desire to incorporate spiritual values in teaching without paying the price of a parochial education. Still others don't want their youngsters to face the temptations of drugs and gang-related pressure in the upper grades.

Home-schooling requires a serious commitment by parents to delegate sufficient time, energy and resources to their child's education. One local business that's doing its part to assist in the process is **Curriculum Cottage**, 2210 N. Meridian Road, Meridian, (208) 887-9292. Full teaching materials, including teachers' guides, are available on all traditional subjects including science, mathematics, grammar, phonics, social studies, history, geography, foreign languages, art and music. Other subject materials can be special-ordered.

Curriculum Cottage also has a science lab that welcomes students to perform experiments they may have read about in their homes. And it provides links with other home schoolers for group activities such as sports and recreation. Two such networks are **Treasure Valley Homeschoolers**, (208) 323-2741, and the **Family Unschooling Network**, (208) 345-2703.

Idaho does not require the testing of home-school students, although it is recommended that parents test their children at least yearly to assure they are keeping pace with others. Home-school students must pass standard college-admission tests to be accepted for higher education.

Home-school does not require any registration with authorities or government agencies.

Extra Help

Some students need help with study skills; others have disabilities that inhibit them from learning in a traditional environment. Still others have particular interests that may not be addressed in the everyday school system. The following is a handful of options that may be helpful.

PCS Edventures Learning Center
2675 W. Main St., Boise • (208) 345-8606

A science-based after-school program, PCS encourages children ages 6 to 18 (the mean age is 10 to 12) to learn through hands-on experience. Its most popular facility is a highly sophisticated Lego construction lab, but there's also a computer lab, a music-and-sound lab, a life-sciences lab and an electricity lab. Kids come once a week for three-month terms. The student-teacher ratio is just 4-to-1.

Sheridan Academy Learning Center
1273 Shoreline Dr., Boise
• (208) 331-2044

Students suffering from attention deficit disorder, dyslexia and various other learning disabilities attend this nonprofit private school. Most of the 20 youngsters attending in 1998 were referred by school districts. Individualized, therapeutic programs, including small classes based upon ability rather than age, and academic tutoring are the principal tools employed. A teacher-student ratio of 1-to-6 is supplemented by parent volunteers.

Sylvan Learning Center
355 N. Orchard St., Ste. 101, Boise
• (208) 322-3555

One of 700 franchised centers in the United States and Canada, Sylvan tests new students to assess their relative academic strengths and weaknesses. It then designs a tutorial program in reading, writing, math or study skills suited to an individual's personality and learning style. Most students who attend are between the ages of 9 and 14; they come twice a week for hourlong sessions.

Colleges and Universities

Albertson College of Idaho
2112 E. Cleveland Blvd., Caldwell
• (208) 459-5011

One of the West's most highly esteemed private, four-year, liberal-arts colleges, Albertson was founded by a Presbyterian minister, William Judson Boone, but is today a nonsectarian institution. The name of alumnus Joe Albertson, the late supermarket magnate, was conferred upon the former College of Idaho when he bequeathed millions of dollars of his fortune upon its 1991 centennial.

Spread across 40 acres near downtown Caldwell, Albertson College has an annual student enrollment of about 750 and a faculty-student ratio of 12-to-1. *U.S. News & World Report* in 1992 named it the fourth-best regional liberal-arts college in the American West. More than 95 percent of its prelaw and pre-med students are accepted by professional schools.

Boone Hall, the original campus building on the central quadrangle, is well-known for its collection of small museums (see Attractions). The campus also has a handsome new performing arts center and has invested more than $20 million in three new college facilities.

Boise Bible College
8695 Marigold St., Garden City
• (208) 376-7731

Nearly 150 students study for church leadership roles worldwide at this four-year nondenominational Christian college. Degrees are offered in the ministry, Biblical studies, Christian education and music. The five campus buildings are located on 11 acres off Glenwood Street north of the Western Idaho Fairgrounds.

Boise State University
1910 University Dr., Boise
• (208) 385-1011, (800) 632-6586

Idaho's largest institution of higher learning occupies a 110-acre campus on the south bank of the Boise River, between Capitol Boulevard and Broadway Avenue. Founded in 1932 as a private community college, it was granted four-year status upon entering the state system of higher education in 1965. In 1974 it was renamed Boise State University. Today it has 15,000 students who study on the semester system: fall (August to December) and spring (January to May).

BSU offers degrees in dozens of disciplines through its colleges of Arts and Sciences, Business and Economics, Education, Health Science, Social Sciences and Public Affairs, and Technology (including schools of Applied Technology and Engineering Technology). Its Graduate College confers degrees as high as a doctorate in education.

Perhaps the best-known campus building is the Morrison Center for the Performing Arts, renowned for its marvelous acoustics: The center had the same designer as the Lincoln Center in New York City. The 12,000-seat BSU Pavilion is used for basketball and concerts alike, while 30,000-seat Bronco Stadium is home to the university's football team.

Boise State University — Canyon County Center
2407 Caldwell Blvd., Nampa
• (208) 467-5707

This BSU extension has 5,000 students enrolled in more than 70 night classes and 60 short-term training and noncredit courses. The School of Applied Technology programs highlight the curriculum. The technology school has 36 different programs that include computer programming and computer repair, electronics broadcasting technology, refrigeration and heat, and welding. This institution has plans to relocate to east Nampa, just north of The Idaho Center.

Northwest Nazarene College
623 Holly St., Nampa • (208) 467-8011

A four-year Christian liberal-arts college with an enrollment of about 1,200 students, Northwest Nazarene was established in 1913. It offers bachelor's degrees in 50 arts-and-sciences disciplines, and master's degrees in business, education and ministry. The campus opened its new John Brandt Fine Arts Center in late 1997.

Continuing Education

Keep your eyes peeled in coffee shops and bookstores for bulletins announcing classes in such subjects as cookery (occasionally staged by local chefs) and alternative medicine (see our chapter on Healthcare). In general, though, these are some of the best places to find adult classes.

INSIDERS' TIP

An estimated 3,000 students are enrolled in church-affiliated schools in the Boise area that include Bishop Kelly High School, Marantha Christian School and Valley Christian Junior and Senior High schools. They make up about 5 percent of the student population.

Boise Schools
Community Education
301½ N. 29th St., Boise • (208) 338-3525

Fifteen hundred classes, 15,000 students and 800 instructors, at 20 schools and 37 local businesses: This community education program is a massive operation. A year-round schedule of activities and classes range from academic (computer programming, foreign languages) to mechanical (auto repair, home refurbishment), from physical (aerobics, yoga) to cultural (art, music, dance), and from practical (gardening, financial planning) to just-plain fun (fly fishing, travel).

Boise State University Continuing Education Program
1910 University Dr., Boise
• (208) 385-1709

A broad-based agency whose responsibilities include BSU summer school and international programs, Continuing Ed also offers outreach classes in Canyon County, McCall and the Mountain Home Air Force Base. It is in charge of state programs for professional certification and has developed additional programs for dispute resolution and child development. A pilot project launched in fall 1997 enables community members to register for noncredit classes, especially as referred by employers anxious to expand their skills and knowledge in particular areas.

Learning Lab
Boise Public Library, 715 S. Capitol
Blvd., Ste. 403, Boise • (208) 344-1335

Idaho's largest community-based literacy program, Learning Lab's focus is providing functionally illiterate adults and families with basic education in reading, writing and mathematics so that they may become self-supporting and contributing members of the community. Classes include two programs that address preschoolers' needs and English as a Second Language instruction for refugees from non-English-speaking countries.

Log Cabin Literary Center
801 S. Capitol Blvd., Boise
• (208) 331-8000

A variety of classes for those with special interests in poetry, fiction and nonfiction writing are offered evenings and weekends throughout the year. There also are regular readings by local and visiting authors, and a one-week summer camp program to spark a literary fever in youth.

If you've had an
accident, go to St. Al's;
if you're having a baby,
go to St. Luke's.

Healthcare

If you've had an accident, go to St. Al's; if you're having a baby, go to St. Luke's.

In a nutshell, that's the medical story in the Treasure Valley.

Although the scene has broadened and deepened over the years as Saint Alphonsus and St. Luke's Regional Medical Centers have grown like venerable trees with many branches of service pointing in numerous directions, they are still the giants that hold sway. Their performances have ranked them both in the top-100 hospital category in the country, and they are still the most likely places where accident victims and expecting mothers wind up.

Though St. Al's and St. Luke's come immediately to mind, Boise is also medically notable for its Veterans Affairs hospital and nursing home located on spacious and attractive historical grounds, for its continually expanding Idaho Elks Rehabilitation Hospital and for its two psychiatric hospitals. West of the capital city, Mercy Medical Center in Nampa and Columbia West Valley Medical Center in Caldwell are growing in size and stature with the rapid population growth of Canyon County.

Boise is by no means Boston when it comes to innovation, sophistication, range and capacity of its medical environment, but its cancer research, heart procedures, surgical and mending prowess and its Life Flight rescue helicopters present a picture of a smaller, more remote, high-desert version.

Hospitals

Boise

Saint Alphonsus Regional Medical Center
1055 N. Curtis Rd. • (208) 367-2121
Two days after Christmas in 1894 the Sisters of the Holy Cross opened the doors of Saint Alphonsus Hospital. In 1900 the hospital was proud to introduce the first x-ray machine to Idaho. In 1972 the hospital moved from downtown to a 75-acre site beside Interstate 84 where as a 269-bed regional medical center it serves the more than half-million people in southwestern Idaho, eastern Oregon and northern Nevada.

The hospital's programs and specialties include the following:

• Emergency/Trauma Services — The hospital is the designated trauma center for the region. It is also the home base for the Life Flight helicopter and the Life Flight XT airplane. Operating within a 150-mile basis, the Life Flight helicopter ensures that critically ill and injured patients receive immediate life support and transportation to the most appropriate hospital for treatment. Extended patient transfers are provided by the XT airplane.

• Orthopaedic Institute — The institute provides an integrated program of care for patients with musculoskeletal disease and those recovering from accidents. The hospital's team includes orthopaedic surgeons, radiologists, rheumatologists, rehabilitation physicians, nurse specialists, therapists, patient care coordinators and specialized patient care staff.

• Idaho Neurological Institute — A team of specialists diagnoses spinal cord injuries, tumors of the brain and spine, spine deformities, aneurysms, stroke, hemorrhages and other neurologic disorders.

• Nephrology Center — The center's kidney dialysis by an artificial kidney saves the lives of patients whose kidneys no longer function. St. Al's provides the largest dialysis service in the state. Treatment is also available at satellite facilities in Nampa and Ontario, Oregon.

• Eye Bank and Eye Institute — The Idaho Lions Eye Bank located here is the only tissue recovery center in the state. It obtains, medically evaluates and distributes donated eye tissue for use in corneal transplantation, research and education. The hospital's eye surgery center is equipped with the latest technology and a team of ophthalmologists that can perform virtually any eye procedure and treat patients of all ages.

• Humphrey's Diabetes Center — Jointly operated by St. Al's and St. Luke's, this is the only resource center in the region that provides tools necessary for diabetes self-management. The latest information on diet, exercise, drugs and self-monitoring are available as are free library services and continuing education for health professionals.

• Cancer Treatment Center — Diagnostic and treatment technologies are implemented by a team of specialists that works with each patient to determine an individual plan of care that meets physical, emotional and spiritual needs.

www.insiders.com

See this and many other **Insiders' Guide®** destinations online — in their entirety.

Visit us today!

• Heart Center — A full-service provider of cardiac care, the center has state-of-the-art open heart surgery suites, cardiac catheterization labs and cardiac diagnostic services including ECHO, EKG and vascular lab, a coronary care/telemetry unit, cardiac and pulmonary rehabilitation, cardiac disease prevention and wellness education.

St. Luke's Regional Medical Center
190 E. Bannock St. • (208) 381-2222

In 1902 the Rt. Reverend James B. Funsten observed with some concern that Boise, the capital city in his Episcopal Diocese of Idaho, "lacked sufficient proper facilities for the care of the sick." In April of that year he purchased the Charles Paynton home at First and Bannock streets for approximately $5,000. From this six-bed cottage grew a tall brick building with 300 patient beds that has become a regional center for cancer, cardiac, women's and children's services.

With an average profit of $12.2 million per year between 1990 and 1997, St. Luke's expanded its operations by opening a new urgent care and outpatient medical facility beside Interstate 84 in Meridian. It has partnerships with Mercy Medical Center in Nampa, Wood River Medical Center in Sun Valley and the Veterans Administration Center and Elks Rehabilitation Hospital in Boise.

Here's a rundown of their services:

• Children's Care — 25 percent, or more than 20,000 St. Luke's hospital patients in 1997, were kids. St. Luke's has the only Level III (highest level of care) neonatal intensive care unit in Idaho, which has 29 beds. It also has the largest pediatric unit in Idaho, with 23 beds, and the only pediatric intensive care unit in the state, with six beds.

• Heart Institute — The first open heart surgery in Idaho was performed here in 1969. Today, the institute annually performs more than 20,000 diagnostic heart procedures and 1,600 therapeutic procedures that include more than 800 open heart surgeries. A team of specially trained physicians, nurses, technicians, pharmacists and respiratory therapists works with patients in specialized care units and four cardiac catheterization labs.

• Mountain States Tumor Institute — In 1969 St. Luke's established the institute as a multidisciplinary, comprehensive cancer referral center for the region. Each year the institute performs more than 72,000 cancer care procedures at facilities in Boise and Nampa. Its Breast Cancer Detection Centers in the Treasure Valley provide 17,000 mammograms annually.

• Maternal/Women's Services — St. Luke's has been delivering babies for nearly a century. Prenatal care and education, nurseries and postpartum instruction are offered. The hospital has a new 32-bed mother/baby care unit. It offers patients specialized gynecology, oncology and cardiac services.

• Center for Medical/Surgical Services — A wide range of services are offered that include orthopaedics; general and special surgery; ears, nose and throat treatment; vascular surgery; diabetic care; endoscopy; neurology/neurosurgery; urology; and emergency care.

Idaho Elks Rehabilitation Hospital
204 Fort Pl. • (208) 343-2583

In response to a widespread polio epidemic in 1947, the Idaho State Elks Association con-

Photo: Saint Alphonsus Regional Medical Center

Saint Alphonsus is the designated trauma center for the region.

verted a spacious former residence of a local physician into the Idaho State Elks Convalescent Center for Children. Although children remain central to services provided by this hospital, people of all ages are assisted in improving or restoring their independence following illness, injury or developmental disability.

A team approach to recovery includes a rehabilitation physician; physical, occupational and recreational therapists; speech pathologists; social workers; nursing case managers; and the patient's family.

Programs include:

• Stroke Program — Physical, medical and cognitive services are offered to people who have had strokes. The goal of therapists, rehabilitation nurses, social workers and physicians is to return the patient home with increased independence. Also, many stroke services are offered to outpatients.

• Brain Injury Program — This program serves children, adolescents and adults through inpatient, day treatment and pediatric teams. Special emphasis is placed on life skills training, behavior management, cognitive training and vocational assessment and training.

• WorkFit — A comprehensive outpatient program focuses on physical and psychological rehabilitation for the injured worker.

• LifeFit — This program offers assistance to patients who experience chronic pain related to injury, disease or illness.

• Orthopaedics — A range of rehabilitation needs are addressed that extend from recovery following joint replacement surgery to the restoration of strength and mobility following traumatic skeletal injury.

• Comprehensive Rehabilitation Evaluation Clinics — Problems are identified and addressed that are associated with post-polio syndrome, amputations, stroke, spinal cord and brain injury, rheumatoid arthritis, spina bifida, muscular dystrophy and cerebral palsy, among others.

Healthwise Taps a Self-Care Gusher

Home remedies and horse sense used to cure the public of simple injuries and ailments before the automobile, TV and computers took over. Now for a beepered, faxed and e-mailed society, it's a rush to the doctor's office or hospital for anything that goes wrong.

A nonprofit Boise company, Healthwise, is trying to restore and improve upon the concept of self-care by embarking upon a three-year, $4 million medical experiment that involves three major factors:

• Sending out a 329-page medical book to all 126,000 households in the four-county region around Boise.

• Providing workshops for doctors, consumers and employers on use of the book.

• Establishing a dial-a-nurse phoneline and Internet system, Knowledgebase, that provides information on 450 health problems and 135-symptom-based topics and answers 520 consumer questions to be available at 20 different locations in the area, including the Boise Public Library, and online.

The goals of the project are to cut the costs and improve the quality of medical treatment. The reasoning is elemental: a more medically educated public should save money by treating itself whenever possible and by reviewing a problem before receiving professional care.

Don Kemper founded Healthwise in 1975. That year it published its first handbook with a grant from the W.W. Kellog Foundation. However, Kemper's idea about educating consumers to better manage their health problems met with little enthusiasm. But after 15 years of howling in the woods, Healthwise appears to have struck a gusher fueled by skyrocketing medical costs, demands for medical reform, an aging public and the information age. Clients ranging from Fortune 500 companies to managed-care organizations are now clamoring for Healthwise's services.

— continued on next page

Photo: Healthwise

Healthwise Handbook provides information on 180 common medical ailments.

In 1997 Healthwise moved into a new 29,000-square-foot office building above Bogus Basin Road that incorporates the surrounding sagebrush hills and Old West colors and textures into its clean, airy design. Its staff of 100 includes health educators, physicians, nurses and trainers.

More than 1,000 bookstores sell the company's *Healthwise Handbook*, which offers advice on 180 common medical problems ranging from chest pain and backache to how to remove a fishhook. At $16.95 a copy the book generates about $12 million in yearly revenue. Research shows that organizations that purchase the manual for their employees get a 3-to-1 return on their investment the first year in reduced medical costs.

The company expects its Internet Knowledgebase, which it calls a "100-year-project," to become its future core. Healthwise has spent about $10 million to develop Knowledgebase software over the last five years and is working to make it more user-friendly so that it can actually illustrate subjects, such as back exercises, instead of just describing them.

Kemper envisions five to 10 health-information sources in the country in 2005. He expects Healthwise to be among them and wants to reach a tenth of the U.S. population with Healthwise handbooks and Knowledgebase by the year 2015.

• Learning Abilities Clinic — Case management and treatment is offered to people with severe learning problems associated with Attention Deficit Disorder.

• Therapeutic Riding Program — This is a unique form of physical therapy that uses a horse for treatment. Balance, trunk control and equilibrium are enhanced through riding.

Veterans Affairs Medical Center
500 W. Fort St. • (208) 422-1000

The center is on the site of the 1863 army post known as Fort Boise and after 1879 as Boise Barracks that through the protection they offered early settlers influenced the establishment and growth of the city of Boise. Initial medical attention here was given to World War I veterans. Since 1930 the Veterans Administration has operated the hospital.

Today a 65-bed facility with an adjacent 32-bed nursing home care unit specializes in the rehabilitation of veterans.

The center has been a national leader in the development of Primary Care Teams. Each patient is assigned a primary care provider who along with other members of a multidisciplinary team coordinates and provides a full range of care. The center works with many private practice specialists throughout the Treasure Valley who provide much of the specialty care its patients require.

The center is also involved with:

• Education — Through its affiliation with the University of Washington School of Medicine, the Boise State School of Nursing and the Idaho State University School of Pharmacy, the center provides a wide range of educational opportunities for residents in primary care and family practice medicine as well as medical students, nurses, pharmacists, respiratory therapists, occupational therapists, social workers and other health professionals.

• Research — The center's research service includes more than a dozen investigators, six post-doctoral research fellows, and many graduate and medical students involved in biomedical and clinical science projects. Examples of those projects include studies of infectious disease, pharmaceuticals, pulmonary physiology, aging and drug metabolism and breast cancer.

Intermountain Hospital of Boise
303 N. Allumbaugh St. • (208) 377-8400

Established in 1980, this full-service psychiatric hospital offers programs for children, adolescents and adults who are experiencing biological, emotional, behavioral and/or substance abuse problems. Individuals are provided with personalized treatment plans based upon a medical and intensive therapeutic approach. Treatment allows for the least restrictive setting.

Short-term and long-term residential and educational programs are available for students up to age 18. A day school program funded by Boise and Meridian school districts is also available.

Northview Hospital
8050 Northview St. • (208) 327-0504

This 22-bed psychiatric hospital was established in 1993. It serves patients from throughout Idaho and eastern Oregon and specializes in geriatric psychiatry.

Northview offers treatment and advice in many other areas that include substance abuse of alcohol, stimulants, opiates, barbiturates and prescription drugs; compulsive behavior; eating disorders; manic depressive behavior; depression; suicide; schizophrenia; paranoia; organic psychosis; nervous breakdowns; anxiety disorders; dementia; and Alzheimer's disease.

Nampa

Mercy Medical Center
1512 12th Avenue Rd. • (208) 467-1171

This modern, full-service 152-bed hospital prides itself on its friendly atmosphere. The nonprofit acute care facility averages 5,600 admissions and 136,000 outpatient visits each year. Its 600 employees include a medical staff of 115 physicians, dentists and medical associates.

Hospital programs, services and departments include adult and adolescent chemical dependency units; emergency/outpatient services; home-care services; a 24-hour laboratory; medical and surgical units; radiology; rehabilitation; and a child development center that is managed by the YWCA.

Caldwell

Columbia West Valley Medical Center
1717 Arlington Ave. • (208) 459-4641

This recently renovated, 150-bed hospital takes an active community role as Caldwell moves from a small rural outpost to an integral part of the Treasure Valley. Its

Kaley Center is a gathering place for service groups, and the hospital is involved with the Chamber of Commerce and planning for the future. A quarter-century ago, the hospital's future was in doubt before the Hospital Corporation of America came in to rescue it. Today, it has some of the most modern medical equipment in the Treasure Valley, including a Bennett Contour Plus mammogram machine that adjusts to a woman's body.

This primary care center offers emergency care and delivers babies. It also has a new pediatrics unit, radiology, physical therapy, a sleep disorder lab and cardiac rehabilitation.

Emergency Services

Emergency help; ambulance; Life Flight dispatch • 911
Emergency Room (24 hours) St. Al's • (208) 367-3221
Emergency Room (24 hours) St. Luke's • (208) 381-2344
Mental Health/Mobile Crisis unit • (208) 334-0808
Suicide Hot Line • (800) 564-2120
Child Abuse Center Ada County • (208) 334-0808
Child Abuse Center Canyon County • (208) 454-0421
Alcohol Abuse Hotline • (800) 234-0420
YWCA Battered Women's and Abused Children's Center • (208) 343-7025
YWCA Rape Crisis Alliance • (208) 345-7273
Poison Control Center • (800) 632-8000
Sexual Abuse Hotline • (800) 234-0038

Walk-in Clinics

"Doc in the Box" is the slang for these immediate care locations that serve people with minor illnesses and injuries. An admitting nurse determines the level of assistance needed, and then patients are seen by a nurse practitioner and/or a doctor. X-rays and lab work are available, and all of these locations accept major credit cards and medical insurance.

Boise

St. Alphonsus Regional Medical Center Complete Care Offices
1526 S. Owyhee St. • (208) 367-6910
1625 W. State St. • (208) 367-6990
10255 Overland Rd. • (208) 367-6950
12273 McMillan Rd. • (208) 367-6970
These clinics are open from 8 AM to 8 PM daily.

St. Luke's Regional Medical Center Urgent Care Center
520 S. Eagle Rd., Meridian
• (208) 893-5000
This urgent care center is open from 8 AM to 10 PM daily.

Nampa

Primary Health
1418 Caldwell Blvd. • (208) 466-6567
Primary Health is open from 8 AM to 8 PM Monday through Saturday and 9 AM to 5 PM on Sunday.

Medical Center Physicians Quick Care Center
215 E. Hawaii St. • (208) 463-3309
This clinic is open from noon to 8 PM daily.

Terry Reilly Health Services
223 16th Ave. N. • (208) 466-7869
The clinic is open from 10 AM to 7:30 PM Monday through Friday.

Caldwell

Caldwell Convenience Clinic
222 E. Logan St. • (208) 454-0506
This clinic is open from 8 AM to 7:30 PM Monday through Friday; 8 AM to 5:30 PM Saturday; and noon to 5:30 PM Sunday.

Referrals and Questions
Ask-A-Nurse, St. Al's • (208) 367-3454
Ask-A-Nurse, St. Luke's
• (208) 381-1200
Cancer Helplink, St. Luke's
• (208) 381-3140, (800) 335-3143
Dental Access, Senior Programs
• (208) 345-7783
Dental Health, Central District Health Department • (208) 327-8547
Eye Care Helpline • (800) 222-3937
Physician Referral, St. Luke's
• (208) 381-3080, (800) 843-8703
Physician Referral, St. Al's
• (208) 367-3454
Alzheimer's Association
• (208) 384-1788
American Cancer Society
• (208) 343-4607
American Diabetes Association, Idaho
• (208) 342-2774
Muscular Dystrophy Association
• (208) 384-5886
Parkinson's Disease Information and Referral • (208) 367-6570
Epilepsy League of Idaho
• (208) 344-4340
Resources for the Blind of Idaho
• (208) 343-5066

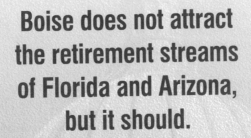

Boise does not attract the retirement streams of Florida and Arizona, but it should.

Retirement and Senior Services

Boise does not attract the retirement streams of Florida and Arizona, but it should.

Unless you are one of those people who never wants to see another snowflake, you should check it out as an older age option. Boise does get snow and is actually a ski town, with one of the finest nonprofit, community-run ski resorts, Bogus Basin, located a mile in altitude above the capital. But snow tends to be just a smattering in the city. Snow tires and shovels are recommended but infrequently needed in the high-desert Treasure Valley, where annual precipitation measures just 12 inches, and 20 inches of yearly white stuff dusts the contours.

The key word when it comes to weather and climate — a chief concern particularly to seniors and retirees because of health concerns and their greater time to play — is *dry*. The calendar strength of the 2,842-foot-high valley floor is a distinct, comfortable, highly-visual four seasons. Autumn is cool, clear and inflamed with color; spring bursts out all over the place; fireplace-winter gets plenty of sunny days; and summer demands air conditioners but has low humidity and can be caressing at night.

A river runs through the entire city, graced by long, green, leafy parks. Any visitor or resident points out the generous Greenbelt parks named after women — Kathryn Albertson, Ann Morrison, Julia Davis — and the miles-long stretches of the hooded and wide-open pathways. Greenbelt paths stretch more than 20 miles over 163 acres, and 1,500 acres of city parks offer tennis courts, a golf course, walking, jogging, bicycling, a zoo, museums and an art gallery. Altogether, the area has 69 parks covering 2,131 acres, in addition to two state parks within 12 miles of the city and a national forest 8 miles away.

Above, to the north, are foothills for picnics, views and various other vigorous and gentle pursuits that may require skis, wheels or binoculars. Of 15 Treasure Valley golf courses, 11 are public and high caliber (see our Recreation chapter for more information).

On the creative front, the arts are hot. Ballet, orchestra, opera, Shakespeare, the Boise Master Chorale, Jazz at the Winery — yours can be a full schedule of openings and outings. Professional sports, which include baseball, basketball, ice hockey and tennis, are minor-league spiffy, close and easy — more fun than the remote and commercial product that you find in the big city.

Centrally located Boise State University, a community-oriented drive-in that has climbed to the second tier of higher academic circles is awash with cultural and sports activities. And

INSIDERS' TIP

The Idaho Senior Games are held in Boise each August. They are open to people 50 and older and serve as a qualifier for the biennial National Senior Games. Events include golf, tennis, swimming, horseshoes, race/walking, track and field, pool and carpet bowling. For information, call (208) 345-7777 or (208) 334-3833.

at the university and high schools, educational opportunities for the part-time student of any age abound. The city's superbly renovated Fort Boise Community Center, which flanks the Boise Senior Center, offers a broad slate of recreational activities, from aerobics and dancing to a 4,500-square-feet art studio area where 80 to 85 separate art classes are held including painting, sculpting, drawing, ceramics, photography and audiovisuals.

So, for you senior troopers and retired lazybones, the insides and outsides of Boise provide plenty of physical action year round.

Senior Services and Agencies

There are two main offices in the Treasure Valley where information about senior organizations, programs, activities, assistance — the gamut from "A" through "Z" — is available:

Senior Programs Boise City/Ada County, is located at 3010 W. State Street, Suite 120, Boise, ID, (208) 345-7777. State Street is a main Boise artery, and this location is on the edge of the North End.

Canyon County Organization on Aging Inc., 304 N. Kimball, Caldwell, ID, (208) 459-0063. This is a short distance south from the 10th Avenue exit of I-84. Turn west on Belmont and drive to its intersection with Kimball, where the building is located.

Senior Programs Boise City/Ada County
3010 W. State St., Ste. 120, Boise
• (208) 345-7777

In addition to several other activities and services, Senior Programs coordinates a number of transportation programs for seniors. These include transportation for people unable to ride the bus; discount bus passes; transportation to medical appointments and meals; handicap vans; and subsidized taxi service. Boise City Scrip are coupons for the city bus system. A packet that costs $6 is good for $15 in rides, with a monthly maximum of $30 good for $75 in rides. Rural Scrip is used like

cash with local taxi cab companies and is available to people who live outside the Boise city limits but in Ada County. Each packet costs $5 and is worth $15 in rides. The monthly maximum is $60 for $180 worth of rides.

AARP (American Association of Retired Persons)
500 W. Washington St., Boise
• (208) 344-5700

This information center for 130,000 AARP members statewide will assist anyone on senior matters. AARP membership is available to anyone ages 50 and older. The AARP state legislative committee meets in this office to determine its lobbying course. The office organizes a 55 Alive driving course that garners insurance discounts and provides tax help. Golden Afternoons has presentations on topics such as Social Security, managed healthcare and medical fraud.

RSVP Treasure Valley Retired and Senior Volunteer Program
5420 W. Franklin Rd., Boise
• (208) 345-4357
411 E. Hawaii St., Nampa
• (208) 466-8982

Part of a national program, RSVP recruits and matches volunteers age 55 and older for service in nonprofit organizations, particularly in the areas of education, health and human needs, the environment and public safety.

Volunteers choose what they want to do, create their own schedules and provide skills, knowledge and friendship. RSVP holds an annual volunteer recognition event, and volunteers receive a newsletter that keeps them informed of new volunteer opportunities as well as items of general interest.

Idaho Office on Aging

The Idaho Office on Aging, Capitol building, between 6th and 8th streets on Jefferson Street, Room 108, Boise, (208) 334-3833, administers federally funded senior programs through offices in six state regions. Its Area Three Agency on Aging, listed below, offers programs in the southwest region, an area that includes Boise, Nampa and Caldwell. Its office is located in Weiser, 71 miles northwest of Boise, and can be reached via I-84 W. and U.S. Highway 95.

Area Three Agency on Aging
25 W. Idaho St., Weiser
• (208) 549-2411, (800) 859-0324

Programs provided by this agency aim to aid or protect seniors. It offers transportation to doctors, meal sites, shopping and recreational activities. Legal aid services include advice and counseling for problems such as consumer issues and tenant rights. The Ombudsman program investigates and settles complaints about care or treatment in nursing homes and helps resolve issues involving entitlement programs in the community. The agency also arranges the meal programs at senior centers and oversees Meals-on-Wheels delivery for people unable to leave their homes. It offers job training and placement or can find someone to help with tasks around the home for seniors who are unable to perform them. Adult Daycare provides a variety of health, social and related support services in a protective setting, and Respite Care provides relief caregivers to people 60 and older who are constantly helping others. A daily telephone service, ECHO, makes calls to at-risk and home-bound elderly to make sure they are okay. And finally, through Informational and Referral Assistance, senior have a reference to the appropriate agency or person that meets their needs.

Inquiries by mail should be addressed Area Three Agency on Aging, P.O. Box 311, Weiser, ID 83672-0311.

Senior Centers

These senior centers in the Boise area provide meals and a number of different activities, classes, services and events.

Boise

Boise Senior Center
690 Robbins Rd. • (208) 345-9921

A noon meal, provided by the Central District Health Department, is served here Monday through Friday for those age 60 and older. There is no charge, but donations are requested.

Seniors can participate in games such as bridge, cribbage, bingo, pool, carpet bowling and Mah Jongg. More educational pursuits include Spanish classes, discussions, senior driver training, a library and watercolor painting. And for those who like to keep moving, the center has Tai Chi, a Stretch & Glo exercise program and Happy Hoofers walks on the schedule. Dancing, health education and screening, and legal, income tax and insurance services are also offered.

A number of organizations, including AARP, the Ft. Boise Optimists and the Civilian Conservation Corps, meet at the center.

Eagle Senior Center
312 E. State St., Eagle • (208) 939-0475

The Eagle Senior Center serves a noon meal every Tuesday and Thursday. Anyone 60 or older is welcome, but a $2.50 donation is requested.

Services and activities include cards, exercise, foot clinics, blood pressure checks and potluck dinner with pinochle nights. Transportation is available to meals, grocery shopping, medical appointments and tours.

Garden City Senior Center
3858 Reed St., Garden City
• (208) 336-8122

Noon meals are served Wednesdays and Fridays for persons age 60 and older. A $2.50 donation is requested.

Activities at the center include pinochle, bingo, foot clinics, potluck dinners, guest speakers, special events and trips to casinos in Jackpot, Nevada. Transportation is available to the center for meals, and out-of-town trips are a highlight each month.

Kuna Senior Center
299 Avenue B, Kuna • (208) 922-9714

Noon meals are served Mondays, Wednesdays and Fridays for persons age 60 and older, with a $2.50 donation requested.

The center looks after the body with blood pressure checks and foot clinics; the mind, with art and quilting and sewing classes; and the soul with the music group

Old Time Fiddlers and evening dinners with bingo. Transportation is available to meals and to run errands in Kuna, Nampa, Meridian and Boise.

Meridian Senior Center
133 W. Broadway Ave., Meridian
• (208) 888-5555

Meridian serves a noon meal Monday through Friday for persons age 60 and older, with a $2.50 donation requested.

Card games, crafts, parties, quilting, billiards, exercise classes, bazaars and potlucks are among the center's roster of events. A van is available to transport seniors to the center, medical appointments and grocery shopping. Special trips are made to shopping malls, concerts, plays and other area events.

Star Senior Center
102 Main St., Star • (208) 286-7943

Noon meals are served Wednesdays and Fridays for age 60 and older, with a $2.50 donation requested.

Bingo, pinochle, potluck dinners, blood pressure checks, fairs, speakers, bake and yard sales and a weekly hot dog lunch keep seniors and the staff very busy. A van provides transportation to malls, grocery shopping, to visit other senior centers and for sightseeing trips. It also goes to Middleton once a month.

Nampa

Nampa Senior Center
207 Competition Way • (208) 467-7266

Noon meals are served Monday through Friday, with a suggested donation of $2.50.

Dances are held here every Thursday night, and the center's senior choir performs in the community. Foot clinics and blood pressure checks are provided. Games include bingo, cribbage and pinochle. Aerobics get the heart and body pumping. A van provides transportation for shopping, medical and hair appointments and brings seniors to the center for meals.

Caldwell

Caldwell Senior Center
1009 Everett St. • (208) 459-0132

If you're hungry around noontime, head over to this center to satiate your appetite. A $2.50 donation is requested. Transportation is available to meals and anywhere in Caldwell. Bingo is the popular pastime.

Photo: William H. Mullins

Fly-fishing is one of many outdoor activities available in the area.

Senior Housing

Thirty-five retirement and life care communities and homes exist in the Boise area. What follows is just a sampling of what's available.

Boise

Bee Hive Homes of Idaho
Meridian locations • (208) 888-5045

Five homes in Meridian, each with eight beds, offer seniors family-style living in a residential setting. Home-cooked meals, 24-hour supervision and private rooms with half-baths add to the comfort and peace of mind of residents and their families. Housekeeping and laundry services are provided. Rental fees range from $1,400 to $2,000 monthly.

Camlu Retirement Residence
5277 Kootenai St. • (208) 345 -2150

Forty-nine studio, 56 one-bedroom and six two-bedroom apartments are housed in this retirement community. The apartments come with a bath and a kitchenette, and residents have access to transportation services, an exercise room, a nine-hole putting green and a shopping mall next door. Rentals start at $875 monthly and include three meals daily and housekeeping services.

Hillcrest Retirement Center
1093 S. Hilton St. • (208) 345-4460

Hillcrest offers 19 studio, 87 one-bedroom and nine two-bedroom apartments, which have kitchenettes and emergency call systems. Residents enjoy transportation services and a 24-hour security monitoring system. Housekeeping and two meals daily are included in the rent, which ranges from $1,150 to $2,900 monthly.

Leisure Villa
3003 Overlook Rd. • (208) 345-1390

Residents of the eight one-bedroom and 28 two-bedroom apartments at Leisure Villa enjoy access to a clubhouse and laundry service or washer/dryer hookups. Lawns and flower gardens decorate the property. Clubhouse activities include card and table games and carpet bowling. Leisure Villa offers one free month's rent with a 12-month lease. Rental fees range from $495 to $650 monthly.

River Place & River Place Estates
739 E. Parkcenter Blvd. • (208) 338-5600

You'll find independent and assisted living services at this beautiful campus setting located next to St. Luke's Care Point. Restaurant-style dining, transportation and social activities are just a few of the perks for residents here. Rental fees run from $995 to $1,695 monthly.

Nampa

Clearwater House
715 W. Comstock Ave. • (208) 463-1732

Clearwater House, with its 33 studio and six one-bedroom apartments, seeks to provide affordable, quality housing and services that reflect and support independence, choice and privacy in a home-like environment that emphasizes privacy and individual choice and taste. Rental fees range from $1,595 to $2,475 a month.

Karcher Estates
1127 Caldwell Blvd. • (208) 465-4935

This retirement community with 11 studio, 20 one-bedroom and 24 two-bedroom apartments has three levels of residential living: independent apartments, residential care and health care/rehabilitation. Apartments have patios, balconies and appliances. Rental fees run from $1,222 to $1,998 monthly and include maid service, utilities (except phone) and three meals a day.

Senior Publications

Idaho Senior News
800 La Cassia Dr., Boise
• (208) 336-6707, (800) 657-6470

This monthly tabloid, which has been published for 18 years, generally runs 20 to 24 pages and emphasizes health matters and finances. It also has local and syndicated news, "You and the Law" and "It's Your Money" columns, and display and classified advertising. The monthly print run of 20,000 is available for free at businesses and public locations or for $12.95 by subscription.

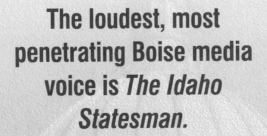

The loudest, most penetrating Boise media voice is *The Idaho Statesman.*

Media

With a metro population of 372,210, Boise is a medium-sized market — 127 out of 250 nationally. But its top media players wield more clout than organizations of the same size elsewhere because of the isolation of the Treasure Valley. Hundreds of miles separate Boise from the communications influence of big cities such as Portland, Oregon, and Salt Lake City. You don't see a clutch of news racks with hotly competing daily newspapers on a city corner, or TV beamed in from nearby cities. Like anywhere, there is cable TV and the PBS network. Regional, national and international newspapers and a broad range of magazines are available at Coffee-News Coffee-News, 801 W. Main Street, Boise, a pleasant stop that serves up food and drink with its reading matter. The Sunday *New York Times* is available at Albertsons Food & Drug Store at 1650 W. State Street, Boise, and home delivery of the daily and Sunday *Times* and *Wall Street Journal* are available from National News Services, (208) 343-1727.

The loudest, most penetrating media voices are the daily newspaper, The Idaho Statesman, and television station KTVB Channel 7 (NBC). For most people in the area, they are it when it comes to news.

What follows is a round up of the Treasure Valley's daily and weekly newspapers as well as its television and radio stations.

Newspapers

Dailies

The Idaho Statesman
1200 N. Curtis Rd., Boise
• (208) 377-6200

Accompanying population expansion in west Boise, the *Statesman* has placed greater emphasis on neighborhood, small-town coverage in that area. Its Friday "Scene" tab, which looks at movies, music, performing and fine arts, personalities, activities and events, is its most popular section. On Thursdays it publishes an Idaho recreation tab that has columns and features on recreational sports as well as local and regional travel getaways. The paper has closely covered the computer and Internet revolution.

Most notable among its editorial staff are columnist and feature writer Tim Woodward, who scores highest with his Boise nostalgia; Marianne Flagg, an intelligent, organized and articulate news and feature writer; the knowledgeable "Answer Man" and versatile reporter, Charles Etlinger; the bright and dedicated photo chief, Tom Shanahan; Camille Cooper, an imaginative and energetic city editor; and enigmatic, until it comes to writing rock music, Michael Deeds.

With a monopoly in a growing and prosperous area, the paper will undoubtedly continue to pile up a fortune. The *Statesman's* 66,000 daily and 88,000 Sunday circulation and its large bank of advertisers are significant contributors to Gannett Company Inc.'s pot of gold. Gannett stock has doubled as it has become the sixth largest media company in the United States. *The Statesman* is one of the most successful in this 92-newspaper group. Insiders say it ships more than $20 million each year to group headquarters in Arlington, Virginia.

The Idaho Press Tribune
1618 N. Midland Blvd., Nampa
• (208) 467-9251 (800) 561-5902

The newspaper prides itself on its Nampa and Caldwell reporting and its expanded news sections, which devote eight pages to subjects such as the juvenile justice system and understanding the area's Hispanic population. Its Thursday "More" entertainment section, which carries movie reviews, personality profiles and fine and performing arts feature stories, is very popular. Circulation has climbed from 18,500 to 21,000 in the last three years.

Weeklies

Boise Weekly
280 N. 8th St., Boise • (208) 344-2055

This alternative publication, which comes out on Thursdays, emphasizes entertainment, the arts and investigative stories. Allied with a local advertising agency, after six years of publication, it has made that glorious leap into the black. It has beat *The Statesman* to the punch on some big topics, such as claims of unpaid overtime and extra hours by employees of locally headquartered Albertsons supermarkets.

Copy can be illuminating and thorough. The best-known regular is columnist Bill Cope, who is outrageously imaginative or totally out-to-lunch, depending on your perspective.

A weekly circulation of 18,000 is available at 500 Treasure Valley locations, which include news racks, shops, motels and other public places.

The Idaho Business Review
4301 W. Franklin Rd., Boise
• (208) 336-3768

Boise has hundreds of ex-*Idaho Statesman* employees who leave the daily newspaper but don't want to leave town. One is Carl Miller, co-publisher and editor of *The Idaho Business Review*. In the early '80s, he was asked to revive an ailing business paper, and among the staff he hired was Kitty Fleischmann, who had journalism experience in Alaska. When the publisher who hired Miller reneged on promises, Miller and Fleischmann walked. As co-publishers of the new *Idaho Business Review*, with Miller handling news and Fleischmann handling advertising, they competed against their former publication. A loophole that allowed them to print legal notices was instrumental to their success. They drove the other publication out of business and have been able to survive against the mighty *States-*

man with a total staff the size of *The Statesman's* editorial business staff.

The *Business Review* has only two reporters, who also take photos and dig like crazy for fresh news through phone calls, leads clubs, where information about new business opportunities is exchanged and announced, and incoming tips. It is not uncommon for a *Business Review* story to become "big news" two weeks later when the *Statesman* and TV stations finally notice it.

The *Review* is filled with local stories about construction, expansion and new companies coming to town. It also has legal and advice columns, display and classified advertising and a records section. Published on Friday, it averages 42 tabloid pages, can be purchased at newsstands and has 3,000 subscribers.

Television

KBCI Channel 2 (CBS)
140 N. 16th St., Boise • (208) 336-5222

This station has a reputation for integrity that goes back to a prison riot in the '80s — it would not hand over footage to law enforcement agencies. It has gone to 24-hour news broadcasts to try to rebuild its image as a news station. It puts its field people out front, confident that their intelligence and enterprise, presented in an immediate and direct way, will hold viewer attention.

KAID Channel 4 (PBS)
1455 N. Orchard St., Boise
• (208) 373-7220

Among its programs, KAID produces 11 half-hour *Outdoor Idaho* shows each year that air on 20 public broadcasting systems nationally and on foreign stations, a legislative report during the three-month legislative session that has been cut back from a nightly to a once-a-week broadcast because of federal funding cuts, and a Dialogue interview show that has give and take on local issues, insights on community concerns and experts on matters that affect the Treasure Valley.

Separated from the influence of big cities, Boise residents rely
heavily on local media outlets for their news.

Reflecting its capital location, the presence of the largest state university and two liberal arts colleges in the Treasure Valley, the presence of 10 large companies, six of which are headquartered here, and the thousands of professional people who live in and around Boise, the station is well-supported by subscribers and its fund drives. Viewer donations average $63.

KIVI Channel 6 (ABC)
1866 E. Chisholm Dr., Nampa
• **(208) 381-6600**

Through station turmoil and turnover, pert TV anchorwoman Claudia Weathermon pulls a rare trick: Her energy and zeal can make life seem worthwhile despite all the bad news she doles out. Her husband, sports director Dave Tester, is a big friendly guy who flashes photos of kids who will some day make the Olympic team.

KTVB Channel 7 (NBC)
5407 Fairview Ave., Boise
• **(208) 375-7277**

Approximately 62,000 people watch Channel 7's 10 o'clock news, almost double the total of network competitors Channel 6 and Channel 2. Robert Krueger, who spent 40 years at Channel 7 before retiring in 1996, is credited with putting the station in the driver's seat by emphasizing local, live coverage.

Channel 7 has a slicker, more thorough and broader dimension and a more professional tone than the other stations. It heavily promotes its anchors and is ahead of other local stations in regards to technology. Krueger was first to use helicopters for aerial shots, and recently Channel 7 has gone to digital videotape editing — similar to the jump from producing a linear typewriter story to computer flexibility. In 1992 Channel 7 was the 14th station in the country to start weekend morning news.

The station offers 12 hours of news and 27 hours of local programming a week.

KNIN Channel 9
816 W. Bannock St., Boise
• **(208) 331-0909**

Noting that other Treasure Valley TV stations were selling all their prime-time advertising, Tim Bever, formerly of Fox, turned this VHF shopping network and movie station into a full-time broadcaster. With no news and syndicated shows like *Real Stories of the Highway Patrol*, *MASH* and *Star Trek*, its audience share is just behind Fox's Channel 12.

KTRV Channel 12 (FOX)
679 6th St. N., Nampa • (208) 888-1200

Before Fox, money-maker Channel 12 climbed as high as the No. 1 independent station in the country when it attracted an 18 market share. With Fox, it heavily promotes its nationally syndicated shows and sports events.

Cable Companies

TCI Cablevision of Treasure Valley
8400 Westpark St., Boise
• **(208) 375-8288**
5921 Timbre Dr., Caldwell
• **(208) 454-3061**

TCI offers more than 40 programming choices. Sega Channel has more than 50 games. Movie packages include HBO, Cinemax and Showtime. It also offers pay-per-view movies and events. DMX has 30 channels of digital music. TCI's basic cable rate is around $25 per month. With the inclusion of movie channels, the cost is around $7 more.

WBS Cable TV
3131 E. Lanark St., Meridian
• **(208) 888-1950, (800) 896-3113**

Service is available to residents who can see the lights of Bogus Basin Ski Area at night. More than 30 channels include the History Channel, ESPN2, Cartoon Network, Sci-Fi, Country Music Television, Univision and movie packages.

INSIDERS' TIP

Although Boise takes pride in its new-found sophistication, it still has a strong rural rodeo fiber and likes its country music, as evidenced by the country music format of two of its top-four radio stations, KIZN 92.3 FM and KQFC 97.9 FM.

Media Vet Rod Gramer Would
Never Live Elsewhere

Rod Gramer's knowledge of *The Idaho Statesman* and Channel 7 comes from working in the belly of both beasts, a crossover that no one else in Boise has accomplished. Gramer eyes the two Boise media giants like this:

"*The Idaho Statesman* is always controversial and in some circles unpopular. It's a real institution that has tremendous clout and always will."

Gramer points out that Boise's isolation makes *The Statesman* more important than other Gannett Company Inc. capital city daily newspapers in Salem, Oregon, and Olympia, Washington, which have larger dailies from Portland and Seattle, and more TV and radio stations to compete with.

"Because of *The Statesman's* influence, it attracts editors who want to work here," Gramer says.

If *The Statesman* is a brisk, well-read monopoly, Channel 7 has five scrambling competitors and a different image. "It's a very beloved station," Gramer says. "It is the preferred news source for 59 percent of the people in Boise and 64 percent in Ada County. Those are unheard of numbers in the industry. The closest to it that I know of anywhere is a station with a 42 percent rating."

Strangers who visit Boise say Channel 7 comes over much bigger than what would be expected in the 127th market in the nation. "They say it could fit easily into the top 70 markets," Gramer states.

Some of the things that set Channel 7 apart from other Boise stations are its integrated design, its graphics, look, polish and style. A viewer knows immediately what station it is. "Some of that is my background as a newspaper person who has worked with a style book — where consistency and familiarity are developed," Gramer says.

He worked for 13 years for *The Statesman* as city editor, editorial page editor, political reporter and special assignments writer, and for the last nine years has been news director at Channel 7.

At *The Statesman* he covered national stories such as the Teton Dam collapse in 1976, nuclear waste issues at the Idaho National Engineering Laboratory in the late '70s and Frank Church's Senate race in 1980. *Fighting the Odds*, a book he coauthored about the life of Sen. Frank Church, won the national Evans Biography Prize for the best biography of a western figure.

As news editor at Channel 7, he has made coverage decisions on stories ranging from the Ruby Ridge sniper killing and trial that involved the FBI and the state's first execution to natural disasters such as droughts, fires and floods.

Photo: Idaho's Newschannel 7

Rod Gramer rules the news at Channel 7.

— continued on next page

Gramer was born in Boise, grew up here, attended the University of Idaho in Moscow and will never go anywhere else. While in newspapers, he had a chance to go to *The San Diego Union*, a much larger daily than *The Statesman*, but turned it down. "Boise is a great place to live," he says. "I've often heard others say it's the kind of place they want to move to. It kind of gets into your blood."

The roots Gramer has sunk here are especially important to him. "What I love most is the sense of place," he explains. "My friends go back to childhood and contacts I've made through school and work. I think that's lacking in society, especially in journalism.

"Your friends rally around you here. Sure, it's possible to make more money and work for a company with more resources in a larger city. But you can't buy the outdoors. My family and I are close to the environment. It makes me comfortable to know that we can drive a couple of hours to the largest single wilderness area in the Lower 48 (The Frank Church River of No Return Wilderness Area)."

Attending school and staying to work in Idaho "is a great advantage" Gramer says, because lifelong relationships and knowledge of the territory builds over the years. His longevity first at *The Statesman* and now at Channel 7, and that of anchorwomen Carolyn Holly and Dee Sarton and weatherman Rick Lance at Channel 7, is seen by Gramer as a plus in an industry that typically has rapid turnover. "People want a personal relationship with their journalists," he explains. "Newspapers are moving away from that. I think it's something that should be developed."

WBS's basic cable rate is $23 a month. Various movie packages add to this price.

Radio

Christian
KTSY 89.5 FM
KBXL 94.1 FM
KAWS 106.7 FM (Christian talk radio)
KSPD 790 AM (Christian talk radio)
KBGN 1060 AM

Classical
KBSU 90.3 FM (some news)

Country
KIZN 92.3 FM
KSRV 96.1 FM (simulcast with KSRV-AM)
KQFC 97.9 FM
KLVJ 99.1 FM
KKIC 950 AM (classic country music; talk radio 9 AM to noon, Monday through Friday)
KSRV 1380 AM (simulcast with KSRV-FM)

Contemporary
KZMG 93.1 FM
KMCL 101.1 FM
KCID 107.1 FM
KXLT 107.9 FM
KCID 1490 AM

Jazz
KBSU 730 AM

Oldies
KLTB 104.3 FM ('50s to '60s classic oldies)
KGEM 1140 AM (hits from the '40s to '60s)

Rock
KFXD 94.9 FM (alternative)
KKGL 96.9 FM (classic rock)
KQXR 100.3 FM (modern rock)
KARO 103.3 FM ('70s rock 'n' roll)
KJOT 105.1 FM (classic and contemporary rock)
KCIX 105.9 FM (soft rock of the '70s to '90s)

Spanish-Speaking
KWEI 99.5 FM
KJHY 101.9 FM
KWEI 1260 AM

Talk and News
KBSX 91.5 FM
KFXD 580 AM (24-hour talk, news and sports)

KIDO 630 AM
KBOI 670 AM (music, news and information)
KTIK 1340 AM (sports talk)
KIOV 1450 AM (24-hour talk, news and sports)

If religion is statistically not as big here as elsewhere, the Mormons have always been well-represented, and their numbers are growing rapidly.

Worship

Like its Northwest neighbors, Oregon and Washington, Idaho is more "unchurched" than other areas of the country. Perhaps that's a legacy of the Oregon Trail that brought pioneers in search of gold and bountiful farmland who were also escaping, possibly to an even larger degree, from the decrees, restraints and responsibilities of civilization. Independence was a virtue unless a helping hand from the feds was needed for protection against Indians, irrigating farmland, damming rivers for hydroelectric power, building roadways, fighting fires and other dire necessities. A distrust of churches, their money, politics, narrowness and negative, forbidding outlook are reasons given by Idaho residents today for not taking part in religion. Figures provided by the Glenmary Research Center, a Catholic organization that surveys church population every 10 years, show that only 43 percent of Treasure Valley residents are affiliated with a church compared to 55 percent nationally.

But that same Oregon Trail was the corridor of escape for Mormons, traveling with wagons and handcarts, who were fleeing persecution in Illinois. When Joseph Smith, founder of the Church of Jesus Christ of Latter-Day Saints and translator of *The Book of Mormon, Another Testament of Jesus Christ*, was killed by a mob in Carthage, Illinois, church members gathered under the direction of Brigham Young and began their historic trek west to Salt Lake City, Utah, 434 miles southeast of Boise. The first group arrived in Salt Lake in 1847. During the next few years, thousands more completed the perilous journey, and by 1855 Brigham Young began colonizing Idaho and other surrounding territory so that the church would be self-sufficient through geographic and economic diversity.

If religion is statistically not as big here as elsewhere, the Mormons have always been well-represented, and their numbers are growing rapidly with increased population. They make up about 340,000, or 28 percent, of Idaho's 1.2 million population, with a high prevalence in southeast Idaho, close to Salt Lake City. An estimated 23 to 25 percent of the Treasure Valley is LDS. Catholics are about 10 percent, compared with 20 percent nationally, and Protestants about 7 percent. Because of the Mormon influence, a closer look at the LDS Church is tantamount to understanding a territory that is opening wider in new directions as well as taking on Mormon converts. We'll also look at formidable religious structures, both in history and in architecture, and briefly survey the religious spectrum, exploring a state initiative that matched conservative and liberal religious viewpoints and pointed to religious innovation in the Treasure Valley.

The Mormon Church in Idaho

Some historians suggest that without the Mormon population in the late 19th century, Idaho's land would have been annexed by adjoining states and Idaho would have never come into existence.

In 1855, 26 men were called by Brigham Young to locate a settlement among the Bannock and Shoshone Indian tribes on the Salmon River. They arrived and established Fort Lemni that same year, but problems with the Indians led to the settlement's abandonment in 1858.

In 1860 a party of colonizers arrived at what is now Franklin, in northern Cache Valley. Preston Thomas became the first bishop in the ward created there. Franklin is Idaho's as well as the Mormon Church's oldest permanent settlement. The settlers battled deep snows and extreme winter cold but were able to dig canals for crop irrigation in summer. In the next 18 years 16 settlements were founded in this region. Another colonization effort began over the mountains to the east where Apostle Charles C. Rich explored Bear Valley and established the settlement of Paris in 1863. In 1875 a third colonization movement came when LDS families settled in Oakley, Dayton, Elba and Almo in south-central Idaho.

In the late 1870s the Utah Northern Railroad line from Utah to Montana was completed. Many LDS members were employed in the construction of the rail line, which led to the colonization of the Upper Snake River Valley in 1879 and Rexburg in 1883. Basic to their success was their expertise in irrigation. By 1910 more than 100 canals had been dug in the Snake River Valley.

Church leaders encouraged members to continue to settle Idaho. Many migrated to the Boise and Payette rivers and farmed the land. By 1890, when Idaho was given statehood, about one-fifth of the state — somewhat less than today — was LDS. But anti-Mormon sentiment fueled by the LDS practice of polygamy — actually engaged in by a small percentage of usually powerful church members and long since banned — flared at the turn of the century. Mormon women showed their spirit and drive by leading a statewide effort for women's suffrage that was attained in 1896.

Following World War II, many LDS members migrated to the Boise area, where the first Boise stake had been created in 1913. Ezra Taft Benson was the stake's first president in 1938 and became one of three Idaho natives to serve as LDS President, which is equivalent to the Pope in the Catholic religion. Harold B. Lee and Howard W. Hunter were the others.

A religion that started with six members in 1830 now has 10 million members throughout the United States and 161 foreign countries where more LDS speak Spanish than English. Today in Idaho, 150 missionaries go out from missions in Boise and Pocatello in a continual effort to convert state residents to the LDS Church.

Emphasis on Family and Community

The Treasure Valley has 40 to 50 wards, 14 stakes and one of the two LDS temples that exist in Idaho. Wards are the basic units of a congregation, or stake, and consist of 280 to 680 people. Wards are led by a bishop and two counselors. Through religious study and church and community involvement, young men become deacons at 12, teachers at 14, enter the priesthood at 16 and are ordained to the higher priesthood at 18 or 19. After two years of serving on a mission that could be in this country or in places around the world, the men become elders. Young women join a Relief Society that with 5 million members may be the largest single women's organization in the world.

On Sundays Mormons meet for three-hour blocks of meetings at their congregations. There's a sacrament of the Lord's Supper, typically youth and adult speakers and music provided by soloists and choirs. The Old and New Testament, the Book of Mormon and Gospel Covenants are studied in sequence in Boise and around the world, so that the same subject, page and lines are considered in Rio, Stockholm and the Treasure Valley on the same day, week and year everywhere in the LDS realm. At Sunday School, groups are separated by age, sex and rank. During the week women meet to learn homemaking skills about health and other subjects beneficial to the family and home. Young men and women share activities and community service projects. Scout-

---

INSIDERS' TIP

You'll find information about churches and church services in the Yellow Pages and in the Saturday edition of *The Idaho Statesman*.

The Boise Idaho Temple is one of two LDS temples in Idaho.

ing is popular — nine out of 10 Eagle Scouts in the Treasure Valley are Mormons.

The temple is a place for the performance of sacred ordinances. Mormons believe that all their members must be baptized by immersion for the omission of sins and entering the Kingdom of God. This is done by proxy in the temple on behalf of dead LDS members. Also, marriages are performed in the temple as well as marriages by proxy of dead LDS couples who were unwed. The Mormons feel an obligation to take care of themselves and their ancestors and operate the most extensive genealogy center in the world at their temple square in Salt Lake City, which is accessible by computer in the Treasure Valley and elsewhere.

The LDS Church is well-known for taking care of its own and is also active with service-oriented, community outreach programs. It donated $25,000 and 110 mattresses to Boise's Community House, a center for homeless people that helps them get back on their feet. The church runs a large cannery in Garden City that receives beef and poultry from around the country that is destined for the Bishop's Storehouse, where it is available for needy LDS and non-church members. It also runs Deseret Industries, similar to Goodwill, where clothing, appliances and other goods are donated for repair and resale, which provides jobs and low-cost merchandise for the community at its Boise location, 10740 Fairview Avenue.

Catholic Expansion

The Catholic Church in Idaho has 72 parishes and 125,000 members, or about a tenth of the state population. It sees itself as a multicultural ministry that meets the religious needs of 90 percent of the state's Hispanic population and the many Asians who have moved here. It places a heavy emphasis on its kindergarten-to-college youth ministry, providing religious education for different student age groups. The church operates a dozen grade schools around the state, including four in Boise, and one high school, Bishop Kelly, in Boise.

Growing with the expanding community, the Catholics recently opened a new church in south Boise that serves 1,150 people. St. Marks, 7503 Northview Street, is the largest Catholic church in the city. It seats 500 people, and its six Sunday masses typically attract 2,200 people.

Episcopalians and Methodists

Episcopalians and Methodists were among the early Boise settlers. Their first churches are two of the finest of the cities structures today.

St. Michael's opened as the Episcopal Church of Boise City in 1866. It was the first church in Boise and the first Episcopal Church in Idaho, Wyoming, Montana and Utah. (See our Attractions chapter for more information about St. Michael's.) In 1892 the church established St. Margaret's School for Girls, which became Boise Junior College in 1932 and later Boise State University, which with 15,000 students is the largest university in Idaho.

The present St. Michael's Cathedral, located across the street from the Capitol at 8th and State streets, was dedicated in 1902. Today it serves about 600 households.

The Treasure Valley has seven Episcopalian churches and more than 6,000 members statewide. A new Episcopalian bishop, Harry B. Bainbridge, took office in the summer of 1998.

In 1873, 15 pioneers became the first Methodists to worship in Boise, when Idaho was still a territory. Today, about 2,400 Methodists and 12 church choirs occupy the handsome Cathedral of the Rockies, which takes up an entire downtown block at 1100 W. Franklin Street. (See our Attractions chapter for more information about the Cathedral.)

The Gay and Lesbian Initiative

State Proposition 1 in 1994 would have banned Idaho state laws giving gays and lesbians minority status. It was crafted by conservative Christians who held that the Biblical injunctions against homosexuality were clear and literal. Initial drafts were written in the office of Dennis Mansfield, Idaho Family Forum executive director. Mansfield said the initiative was intended "as a way to honor people we disagree with while making them accountable for their lifestyle." Conservative Christians such as Bryan Fisher, Community Church of the Valley pastor, climbed to the top of Table Rock to stand under Boise's signature cross, which is seen from the floor of the Treasure Valley, where he declared his love for gay people but his rejection of their behavior.

Voices of Faith, a coalition of mostly liberal Christian denominations and Jews, opposed the initiative by staging Holocaust vigils and human rights demonstrations. In a state known for conservative and even extremist views, Proposition 1 suffered a narrow defeat, by 3,098 out of 408,300 votes.

The First Congregational Church of Boise, 2201 Woodlawn Avenue, is among the churches in the Treasure Valley that welcomes diversity and accepts gay and lesbian worshippers. It has about 500 members and 100 "active friends," emphasizes personal moral-

ity and social ethics, and is a staunch supporter of public education. Its worship teams composed of clergy and laity work together equally to preach and lead worship services.

Religious Diversity

In addition to places of worship for Mormons, Catholics, Episcopalians and Methodists, you'll also find churches for Baptists as well as Assemblies of God, Nazarene and Christian Churches and Churches of Christ.

Jews congregate in Boise at a beautiful little synagogue, Ahavath Beth Israel, located at 1102 W. State Street, which serves about 300 families and is affiliated with the Reform branch of Judaism.

An unlisted Buddhist Temple located inside a house in a residential area of Boise hosts about 40 Vietnamese Buddhists each Sunday; the Tibetan Buddhists who live here worship privately. The Islamic Center of Boise, which has about 50 members, exists at 328 N. Orchard Street, Boise.

Wood River Valley

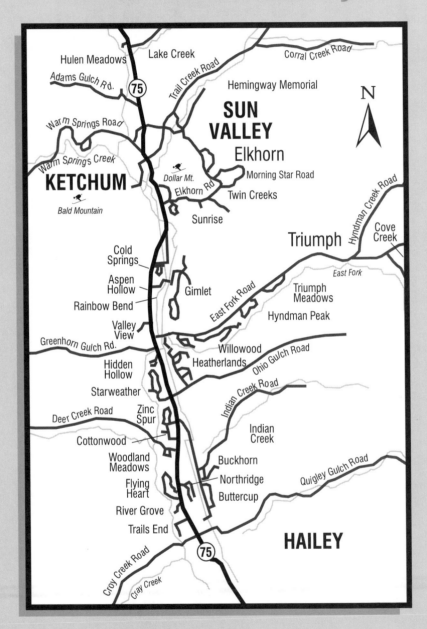

Sun Valley

When we think of Sun Valley the lyric from a classic old tune comes to mind: "You're much too much, much too very very, to ever be, in Webster's dictionary." In attitude, Sun Valley is in a separate country from Boise; in geography, they inhabit the same state. Sun Valley is as different from Boise as France from Germany, the South Pacific from the East Coast. It is a celebrity enclave wallpapered with money where well-heeled residents pause to appreciate the history of an ore wagon procession between the high-fashion bicycle workout and gourmet restaurant. It is a place of immense community zeal where legions of well-educated and classy volunteers produce exquisite winetastings, music, exhibits and outdoor challenges for good causes and where the person selling you a playsuit or waiting on you in a restaurant may have a doctorate in Chinese Mandarin, be the wife of a high-tech pioneer or be a youngster with Olympic talent who you will recognize on a TV screen four years hence and wish you had left a bigger tip. For the visitor seeking an immediate, well-equipped and beautifully maintained paradise of snow, trails, fishing, restaurants, lodging, golf and hiking in a sublime climate with spectacular views, Steven Spielberg couldn't come up with a better vision and Bill Gates couldn't manage it with more dash and precision. And visitors couldn't be in better company as Clint Eastwood, Demi Moore, Arnold Schwarzenegger, Janet Leigh and many other stars choose to hide out and occasionally shine in Sun Valley.

Visiting the Valley and its environs is a marvelous trip to yesterday today because of its preserved heritage within a modern capsule placed in the middle of nowhere. Anyone living in or visiting the Treasure Valley should make the effort to get there, just as anyone visiting Sun Valley should not neglect the magnificence of Boise now that it has so fully come into its own. The locations are only 150 miles

from each other, which in the West is just around the corner, and yet so far from each other in size, mentality, appearance and approach — except in this book, where we hope their back-to-back, dual inclusion serves you well.

In this chapter we look at the geography and history of the area before moving on to transportation, accommodations, restaurants and nightlife. Later sections explore the shopping, attractions and events. And then we wrap it all up with the arts organizations in the area and a look at both winter weather and warm weather recreations.

Area Overview

What confuses most people about Sun Valley is the neighboring town of Ketchum. Ketchum is downtown, where most of the restaurants and businesses are, and next to Bald Mountain. It's much more visible than adjacent, tucked-away, world-famous Sun Valley. The latest census figures show Ketchum with 2,685 residents and Sun Valley with 997. But Sun Valley includes the large Sun Valley and Elkhorn resorts, where many visitors make their home away from home.

Lay of the Land

If you think of Sun Valley/Ketchum as one geographic area and refer to it generally as Sun Valley (calling it the Sun Valley metropolitan area would be scandalous, since there are only three traffic lights and usually more skiers, bikers, joggers, walkers and dogs than cars in sight), you can go on to more important reckoning, such as deciding which of 6,276 resort, hotel, motel, condo, cottage and apartment pillows to sleep on; which of 70 restaurants to make your taste buds dance; which of 65 Bald Mountain or 15 Dollar Mountain ski runs to descend; and, if you are of such a notion, which of 264 real estate companies to consult with.

But to backtrack a moment, let's more thoroughly consider the geographic location. Sun Valley is in the south-central portion of Idaho, the 13th largest state, with a population of only 1.1 million. It is located at the north end of the Wood River Valley, which stretches about 15 miles south to the towns of Hailey and Bellevue and is about a mile above sea level. Sun Valley is three hours from Boise, five hours from Yellowstone National Park and 5½ hours from Salt Lake City. In other words, it's pretty isolated, which has helped maintain its character, texture and outdoor wealth.

Between sagebrush and lava drylands to the south and forested mountain ranges to the north, the valley has a mountain desert climate. With an average humidity of only 30 percent and 15 inches of precipitation a year, the northern latitude creates long summer and short winter days. Dry sunny summers and mild sunny winters give the resort community its well-deserved name. The average summer temperature is 78 degrees and average winter temperature is 23 degrees, with an annual snowfall of 150 inches. Ski season typically runs from Thanksgiving to Easter, but there are plenty of other pursuits that fill the calendar the rest of the year. See the Recreation section for details.

From Lead Mines to Ski Lodges

Sun Valley's first visitors weren't looking for rest, relaxation or recreation. In the 1880s, ore miners and smelters came from around the world lured by the opportunity for employment and adventure. These men traveled from mine to mine in search of the ever elusive fortune. The Philadelphia Smelter off Warm Springs Road, known as the most advanced smelter in the West, processed more than $1.5 million of lead and silver in 1881 and operated until the early 1890s. When the U.S. Post Of-

fice turned down the name "Leadville" for the new town because too many other Leadvilles peppered the West, a tall, slim, wiry man with long whiskers and a kindly disposition — but not someone to take liberties with — had the place named for him. A mountaineer, experienced pack train man and transient, David Ketchum was long gone when his namesake boomed.

During mining years, the new Guyer Hot Springs Resort on Warm Springs Creek, whose mineral waters, tennis, croquet, dancing and swimming attracted the likes of multimillionaire financier Jay Gould in a special train of luxurious "palace cars," was a glimpse of the future. The silver market collapse of 1894 resulted in a rapid mining collapse throughout the West. Because of its railway service, Ketchum survived but at a loss of 90 percent of its population.

After World War I sheep ranching caught on big, making Ketchum the second-largest sheep center after Sydney, Australia. Nevertheless, Ketchum's population stood at just 270 when Austrian Count Felix Schaffgotsch showed up in 1936, searching for a destination ski resort site that would match St. Moritz and others in Europe. He had turned down Aspen, Alta, Jackson Hole, Yosemite, Mount Rainier and Mount Hood. Within three days of arrival, he wired Union Pacific Railroad Chairman Averell Harriman: "Among the many attractive spots I have visited, this combines more delightful features of any place I have seen in the United States, Switzerland or Austria for a winter sports resort."

Harriman authorized the purchase of the Brass Ranch, east of Ketchum. Engineers and construction crews flocked to the area, and Sun Valley Resort, with an invitation list of Eastern millionaire socialites and Hollywood stars, opened to international publicity on December 21, 1936, just 11 months and five days after the arrival of Count Schaffgotsch. Ketchum's economic future was restored by tourism, but it retained its pioneer charm, as seen by many of its original buildings that look back on its colorful past.

Sun Valley's greatest ski numbers were in the early 1980s. The highest visitation was during the 1981-82 season, when 475,500 skier visits were recorded. In following years, newer, more modern resorts in Utah, Colorado and California began to rob Sun Valley of its exclusive appeal. Aspen, Vail, Steamboat Springs, Snowbird and Deer Valley began grabbing the limelight as well as the big bucks. Earl Holding, the owner of Little America, purchased Sun Valley Resort in 1976 and has spent $125 million to restore it to its earlier glory. He refurbished Sun Valley Lodge and Sun Valley Inn, built three princely glass, wood and stone day lodges at Bald Mountain, gave Baldy rapid transit with the installation of seven quad lifts and weatherproofed downhills with one of the world's top snowmaking systems that can cover nearly one-third of the mountain. In 1995 readers of *Ski Magazine* voted Sun Valley the best ski resort in the United States, and in 1996 readers of *Condé Nast Traveler* said it was the best in North America.

Residing in the Valley

In the last decade Sun Valley's major emphasis has changed from a vacation to a lifestyle market. Good schools, great recreation, spectacular surroundings and a wholesome environment have attracted people who could live anywhere. The lone eagles who built businesses in highly populated areas and can now carry on through fax, phone and computer transmission have rushed in, exorbitantly driving up property values while injecting energy, enthusiasm and knowledge into a broad range of community activities and business endeavors. You hear of Clint Eastwood, Michael Keaton, Arnold Schwarzenegger, Brooke Shields, Jamie Lee Curtis and especially about Bruce Willis and Demi Moore moving in. More important are the money managers, venture capitalists, bio-tech CEOs, lawyers, medical experts and other top professionals who have flooded the valley with wealth and IQ. High-tech and other companies have sprung up. Power Engineers Inc., in Hailey, an employee-owned engineering consulting firm, has 400 employees working out of offices in five states. By some estimates, less than 30 percent of community revenues now come from tourism.

If you're not rich, Sun Valley is a tough place to nest. A nice piece of land in River Woods, Beaver Springs, Flower Mill or Adam's Gulch will nick you $3 million, $4 million or even $5 million, and you'll probably want to put up a $10 million or $11 million mansion. Things are cheaper at Big Wood, North Wood and Lane Ranch, where you can get a large lot for as little as $300,000 to $600,000, and get away with a shack in the $900,000 to $1 million or $1.5 million range. In 1996 the average price of a single-family home in the town of Sun Valley was $712,500. In Ketchum, that dropped to $549,000, and in Hailey and Bellevue, to the south in the Wood River Valley, the average was a considerably lower $165,800. By 1998 the price of a three-bedroom house in Hailey was $200,000 to $225,000.

Needless to say, affordable housing is a big issue in the Wood River Valley, where someone must do the daily work at the hotels, restaurants, ski lifts and shops, while all the people with money are out skiing, golfing, fishing, biking, swimming, hiking and generally recreating. This is a problem in resort towns throughout the West. Sun Valley is ahead of Aspen, Vail, Telluride and other blue-chip resorts in its number of full-time residents relative to number of visitors. It doesn't empty out between peak seasons. There is a vital, year-round continuity to the place. And Sun Valley's property values are about 30 percent less than Aspen's and Vail's, 15 to 20 percent less than Telluride's and 10 to 15 percent less than Park City's.

The other big local issue is traffic. Twelve thousand vehicles travel the 12 miles between Sun Valley/Ketchum and Hailey on Idaho Highway 75 each day, which can make it a crowded, edgy and sometimes dangerous corridor. A wider, four-lane road is envisioned for the near future.

For the visitor in search of a paradoxical paradise, Sun Valley will do. At Sun Valley Village, the architecture is Tyrolean, as in the Austrian Alps; in Ketchum, the Old West pervades. The ski slopes are grand, the hiking awesome, and the fishing holes divine. The restaurants will fatten you like a Christmas goose, and the lodging will make you linger. Who could ask for anything more?

Getting Here

Back in 1936 Averell Harriman opened Sun Valley as the nation's first destination winter resort for the customers it would attract on his Union Pacific Railroad. With a blizzard of publicity and prestige that was unmatched by any vacation spot in the West, millionaire socialites and Hollywood stars rolled into a territory

that greatly reminded Harriman's advisor, Count Felix Schaffgotsch, of Austria. Today, the tracks have been transformed into a 30-mile recreation trail, so that visitors drive in by two-lane road, often coming from Friedman Memorial Airport in Hailey, 12 miles south of Sun Valley, or from Boise Air Terminal, 150 miles to the west and a 2½- to three-hour drive away.

One of the gripes of group travel planners and jet-setters who are hooked on long weekend getaways is that you don't pop in on Sun Valley. Its air transfers and shuttles make it more difficult to reach than Utah resorts that are within 45 minutes of the many direct flights into the Salt Lake City airport, or the Lake Tahoe resorts in California, or Colorado resorts up the Rocky Mountain incline from Denver.

But it's a sweet, water-laced ride to Sun Valley through immense valleys and forbidding lava fields back into the isolation of high round hills, jagged peaks, wondrous meadows and trout streams that do really seem cut off from the rest of the world. That isolation is part of the reason why people are so attracted to the place and so often return.

By Car

Interstate 84 runs from Salt Lake City, southeast of Sun Valley, all the way to Portland, Oregon, near the West Coast. Most vehicles going to Sun Valley will use I-84 for at least part of the way. It's well-built and well-maintained; speed limits reach 75 mph. Interstate 84 passes through Twin Falls, 82 miles south and 1½ hours by car from Sun Valley, and Boise, 150 miles west and 2½ to three hours by car.

From Twin Falls, it's a simple matter of following U.S. Highway 93 north through Shoshone, where it changes to Idaho Highway 75 and continues through Bellevue, Hailey and on to Ketchum and Sun Valley. The two-lane road passes through sagebrush, lava, ranchlands and, north of Shoshone, the Shoshone Ice Caves, a tourist attraction. There is a climb in elevation from 3,746 feet at Twin Falls to 5,750 feet in the Wood River Valley, where Ketchum and Sun Valley are located. During winter the road can be icy, snowy and

Photo: Kevin Syms

Sun Valley is circled by more than 12 miles of wildflower-lined bike trails.

foggy — in one stretch headlights are required around the clock. Tire chains or four-wheel drive may be required during or after storms, but snow plows are dispatched quickly. A scarcity of traffic below Bellevue makes this a passable stretch, even in bad weather, for the judicious driver.

From Boise, a driver has three route choices.

In the storms of winter, which generally clear up fast on the high-desert plain that covers much of the southern portion of the state, the safest choice is driving south on I-84 to Twin Falls and north on U.S. 93 and Idaho 75, as described previously. For a daily updated state report on road conditions, call (208) 336-6600.

A prettier, more scenic route, when weather conditions allow, is to drive from Boise to Mountain Home on I-84 and take U.S. Highway 20 north through the vast Camas Valley and past Fairfield and Soldier Mountain, where Bruce Willis and Demi Moore operate Soldier Mountain Ski Resort. Fairfield has grocery stores and a gas station and is a good leg-stretcher. This is wide-open western country

that will remind you of shoot-em-ups and galloping horses. Cattle are still moved by cowboys along this road. Turn from Idaho 20 north onto Idaho 75 and continue to Bellevue, Hailey, Ketchum and Sun Valley.

For a vehicle visitor to Sun Valley who is starting from and returning to Boise, it is possible to make a loop, with Sun Valley in the middle, that presents one of the most gorgeous driving experiences in America. Half the loop is the Camas Valley passage on U.S. 20, described previously. The other half, which is recommended only during nonwinter months because snow and ice can make the climb dangerous and even close down the road, is to take Idaho 75 north of Ketchum over 8,210-foot Galena Summit to Stanley, one of the most picturesque locations in the state and draped by soaring Sawtooth Mountain peaks. At Stanley, take Idaho Highway 21 west over 7,056-foot Banner Summit and along the South Fork of the Payette River, which has some of the most ferocious kayaking whitewater in the country. Turn on Idaho 21 at Lowman for the climb up to the old mining town of Idaho City, which is a good sightseeing stop that also has a number of restaurants and gas stations. Idaho 21 continues back into Boise. Figure about a half-hour longer taking this route than when returning to Boise via Twin Falls and I-84 or on U.S. 20 through Fairfield and the Camas Valley. (See our Daytrips chapter for more information about cities and attractions along these roadways.)

By Plane

Boise Air Terminal
3201 Airport Way, Boise
• (208) 383-3110

Six airlines serve Boise Air Terminal, which is 150 miles west of Sun Valley and a 2½-hour drive away. The airport averages 75 flights a day and is the 85th busiest airport in the world. The following airlines serve the airport: Delta Airlines, (800) 221-1212; Horizon Airlines, (800) 547-9308; Northwest Airlines, (800) 225-2525; SkyWest Airlines, (800) 453-9417; Southwest Airlines, (800) 435-9792; and United Airlines, (800) 241-6522. Car rental agencies include Avis Rent A Car, (800) 452-1506; Budget Rent A Car, (800) 527-0700; Dollar Rent-A-Car, (800) 800-4000; Hertz Rent A Car, (800) 654-3131; and National Car Rental Interrent, (800) 227-7368.

Sun Valley Express, (800) 634-6539, provides six daily trips between Boise Air Terminal and Sun Valley via custom vans that deliver passengers to their specific destinations. The one-way cost is $49; round-trip is $89.

(For more information about Boise Air Terminal, see the Getting Here, Getting Around chapter.)

Friedman Memorial Airport
4 Airport Way, Hailey • (208) 788-4956

Friedman Memorial Airport is beside Idaho Highway 75 and about 12 miles south of Sun Valley. Although a small airport that only recently put in a snack bar and gift shop for its passengers, it is, after the Boise Air Terminal, one of the busiest airports in the state because of the popularity of Sun Valley.

SkyWest Airlines, (800) 453-9417, which has a flight agreement with larger Delta Airlines, and Horizon Air, (800) 547-9308, which

works with larger Alaska Airlines, are the two commercial companies that fly into Friedman Memorial Airport. SkyWest has seven daily nonstop flights (eight on Saturday) from Salt Lake City to Hailey, which connect with Delta flights from around the country and the world. Horizon Air has 18 flights a week from Seattle with connections from throughout California and the Pacific Northwest.

If you have a private plane, you may fly into Friedman Memorial Airport, which is at an elevation of 5,315 feet. In winter, flying performance is not affected by the location or altitude, but summer heat can be a problem for the takeoff of some small planes. The airport has a good neighbor flying program that requires landings and takeoffs from the south and no operations between 11 PM and 6 AM. For information, call the airport manager at (208) 788-4956.

Daily airport fees for privately owned planes are $5 for a single-engine plane, $10 for a twin-engine, $15 for a jet and $25 for a large jet such as a Gulfstream or Challenger. Sun Valley Aviation, (208) 788-9511, provides fuel for private planes and offers free car parking to its customers.

If you are staying at a hotel or resort, ask if shuttle service is included for the 12 miles between Hailey and Sun Valley. If not, two taxi companies, **A-1 Taxi**, (208) 726-9351, and **Bald Mountain Taxi & Limousine Service**, (208) 726-2650, will provide transportation at a cost of $15 for one person, $25 for two people, $30 for three people, then $10 for each extra person.

Two rental car companies serve the airport. **Avis Rent A Car**, (208) 788-2382, is at the airport, and **Hertz Rent A Car**, (208) 788-4548, is at 1220B Airport Way.

Twin Falls City-County Airport
North end of Skyline Dr., Twin Falls
• (800) 782-4554

Every Saturday in January and February, Daman-Nelson Travel Inc. offers nonstop 140-passenger jet service via Alaska Airlines from San Francisco and Los Angeles into Twin Falls, 82 miles south of Sun Valley, along with charter bus transportation from Twin Falls to passenger destinations in Sun Valley. Private planes may also fly into this airport.

Getting Around

Parking

If you drive to Sun Valley to ski, you can park free at large lots on the River Run, on the southeast side of Bald Mountain. From Idaho Highway 75 just south of downtown Ketchum, turning west on Serenade Drive will take you directly into the lots. From downtown, drive west from Main Street at Rivers Street, First Street, Second Street or Sun Valley Road to Third Avenue, take a left and continue to the lots. Also from Main Street, drive west at Fourth, Fifth or Sixth streets to Second Avenue, take a left, and veer right at Third Avenue, then continue to the lots.

There is very little public parking on the Warm Springs side of the mountain to the north, so it is best to park at the Park and Ride lot at Warm Springs and Saddle roads. Coming from the south on Main Street, which is also Idaho 75, bear left at Warm Springs Road, and you'll see signs for the lot. Coming from the north on Idaho 75, take a right on 10th Street and another right on Warm Springs Road, and you'll see signs for the lot. A free Ketchum Area Rapid Transit (KART) bus transports skiers between the lot and Warm Springs lifts every 20 minutes. (See Riding the Bus in this chapter.)

Many people leave their vehicles in parking lots where they are staying and either walk to nearby locations or use the bus. Those without their vehicles won't miss having them unless they want to drive outside the Ketchum/Sun Valley area. When staying in or near downtown Ketchum, restaurants, shops, movies, museums, the library, community activities, bookstores, the athletic club and nightlife are close by. When staying farther out at Sun Valley Resort, which has its own Alpine village with restaurants, bars, shops and a movie house, at Sun Valley's Elkhorn Resort or at other lodging — most of which are within a mile of downtown Ketchum and Bald Moun-tain — it is easy to use the free KART bus system for transportation.

Riding the Bus

The **KART** buses, which are paid for by local option tax dollars collected by businesses in Ketchum and Sun Valley, run daily from 7:30 AM to midnight and provide free transportation not only to the Bald Mountain and Dollar Mountain lifts, but also to many downtown and area locations. For information call (208) 726-7140. A KART bus schedule and map may be picked up at the Sun Valley/Ketchum Chamber of Commerce, Main and Fourth streets, (208) 726-3423, at other public locations throughout the area and at many restaurants, resorts, hotels and motels.

Taxis, Limos and Shuttles

Bald Mountain Taxi & Limousine Service
(208) 726-2650

Bald Mountain Taxi & Limousine Service is available for private rides. A cab ride between the Sun Valley Resort and Ketchum costs $3 for one person, with $1 charged for each additional passenger; between Warm Springs and Ketchum it's $5, with $1 charged for each additional passenger; and to the town of Hailey, 12 miles south, it's $10 a person. The company owns two stretch limos that can be rented for $60 an hour.

Wild Country Shuttle
(208) 720-1566

Wild Country provides shuttle service to recreational areas throughout the Wood River Valley and Stanley, 61 miles north on Idaho 75. Trips require a four-person minimum, and there is an 11-person maximum. Round-trip rides cost $15 a person to Galena Lodge, $16 to Smiley Creek Lodge and $20 to the Stanley area.

INSIDERS' TIP

Pick up a copy of *The Idaho Mountain Express* or *The Wood River Journal* for up-to-the-minute information about what you must see and where you must be seen.

Accommodations

People don't just drop in on Sun Valley, unless, perhaps, they are summer visitors driving through to the 756,000-acre Sawtooth National Recreation Area 7 miles to the north, or are day skiers, golfers or anglers driving over from Boise, three hours west. The Wood River Valley is out of the way, which contributes to its allure after you get there: It is not overrun and maintains its strong identity. An estimated 91,000 people visit in winter and stay an average of six nights. The estimated 130,000 summer guests stay an average of five nights.

Visitors, especially in winter because of Sun Valley's reputation as a premier downhill ski location, come from all over. The winter breakdown for visitor origin is California, 22 percent; Idaho, 20 percent; Washington, 16 percent; international, 12 percent; central United States, 13 percent; and Northeast, 13 percent. The hiking and biking trails and other summer activities beckon to people closer by — 48 percent from Idaho and 33 percent from California and other western states.

In general, Sun Valley draws an educated, middle-aged, married and well-traveled crowd. The average visitor age for summer is 47; for winter, 42. The average household income for summer visitors is $75,000; for winter, $110,00. Ninety-two percent of the visitors have some college or higher education. In summer, 84 percent of the visitors are married; in winter, 70 percent.

The peak periods of winter visitation are Christmas week and Washington's birthday week; in summer, it's the Fourth of July and Labor Day weekends. Lodging occupancy rates are highest in February and March, July and August. November, April and May, when less than one-third of the area's 1,706 lodging units and 6,276 "pillows" are occupied, play to bargain visits. A standard room for two at historic and elegant Sun Valley Lodge drops from $139 in high season to $79 in low season, and similar drops can be found throughout the Wood River Valley.

If you are a skier and are concerned about expenses, you might want to consider ski packages and winter theme weeks that combine skiing and lodging at considerably reduced rates and can include welcome parties and live entertainment. Skiing that is very good but also expensive — $52 for a daily lift ticket at Bald Mountain — becomes a steal when combined with two-night, three-night, four-night or weeklong packages, which are offered, naturally, during quieter calendar periods. Having enough snow is always a consideration for skiers but not as much so at relatively low Sun Valley (the top of Bald Mountain is 9,000 feet above sea level, compared to many Utah and Colorado ski summits that are above 10,000 and 11,000 feet) because of its snowmaking capacity that can cover almost one-third of the mountain. That means there's usually machine-made snow and good runs to descend in November and December, the start of the ski season, when skiers pray to the snow gods for big dumps, and during dry spells that make natural snow scarce or nonexistent and can occur at any time.

The area's two big resorts, Sun Valley and Elkhorn, have about 1,000 lodging units and 3,500 pillows between them: That's well more than half the available space. Both are villages that offer many on-site amenities — restaurants, after-ski lounges, shops, golf, tennis, nightlife, swimming pools, ice-skating rinks — that could keep a couple, family or group constantly occupied.

The city of Ketchum has the next largest number of lodging units, 544, and pillows, 1,916. This is downtown, where the rhythmic thumps of the bars and dancing places keep the more youthful crowd swinging, and where most of the restaurants, shops, movies, museums and stages are located. Warm Springs Village, which is in Ketchum and tucked into a river valley near the Warm Springs ski lift, is another concentrated lodging area with 197 units and 871 pillows.

INSIDERS' TIP

You don't have to spend a lot of money to ski in Sun Valley. Special ski packages and theme weeks can make for an inexpensive stay.

Wherever you stay in Sun Valley or Ketchum, you're close to everything in a compact area that is surrounded by wilderness. Figure on five or 10 minutes by car with parking available on-site or close by — if you can't get there on foot. Walking in scenic, diverse, friendly Sun Valley is a joy. Many visitors forget their cars and use the excellent free public transportation: A bus leaves every 20 minutes from stops throughout the area.

Smoking is generally not allowed inside lodging properties, so ask when booking a room if this is a concern. Pets are allowed at a number of places: We've mentioned this perk in our entries about the following accommodations where appropriate.

We'll begin with lodging at Sun Valley and Elkhorn resorts, continue with a section on Ketchum and Warm Springs, list a few bed and breakfasts and then address the condo and home rental scene in the area. Towards the end of this section we'll look at the ski packages in the area, suggest a few places and services for entertaining or caring for chil-dren and give you the lowdown on the area veterinary hospital in case your four-legged friend develops the flu.

Price-Code Key

Our price-code key is based on average winter (February and March) and summer (July and August) peak rates for a one-night stay in a standard room for two adults. Prices are considerably lower during value seasons, which run from early April to the end of May and mid-October to mid-December. Many places have rooms, condos and cottages at various price levels. Some properties offer ski packages that include lodging and ski lift tickets.

$	Less than $75
$$	$75 to $125
$$$	$125 to $175
$$$$	$175 and more

Hotels and Resorts

Sun Valley

Sun Valley Resort
$$$ • Sun Valley and Dollar Rds.
• (208) 622-2151, (800) 786-8259

"This combines more delightful features than any place I have seen in the United States, Switzerland or Austria," Count Felix Schaffgotsch told Averell Harriman in 1935. Within days Harriman purchased the first 4,300 acres of what became America's first destination resort. "Roughing it in luxury" was Harriman's design, and this continues today at the resort's Lodge, Inn, condos and cottages, at its two heated, glass-enclosed swimming pools and year-round ice skating rink, and on evergreen walkways through its Tyrolean village. There is a splendid sweep to the well-kept grounds here — a feeling that you are sealed off in a wonderland. There are 18 tennis courts with ball machines and videotape equipment and an 18-hole, Robert Trent Jones Jr. golf course that winds 6565 yards along the waters of Trail Creek. Movies are shown at the historic Opera House. The Lodge, built in 1936, is still the center of attention, with large suites, a six-lane bowling alley, game room, beauty salon, massage center and four-star Lodge Dining Room (see Restaurants in this chapter). Lodge rooms are traditional and elegant. They have TVs, VCRs and coffee and room service. The Inn is a simpler, pleasant building that is more like a Gasthaus, or guesthouse, in the Alps. It is aproned by a lovely pond. If you are visiting as a family or group, you may want to check out the condos or cottages, which afford privacy and lower per-person rates. These accommodations are well-appointed, attractive and within walking distance of everything in the village.

Sun Valley's Elkhorn Resort
$$$ • Dollar and Elkhorn Rds.
• (208) 622-4511, (800) 737-0209

Situated just down the road and over a ridge from Sun Valley Resort, 120-acre Elkhorn Resort is nestled in the Elkhorn Valley at the base of Dollar Mountain, which is a whole ski mountain for beginners. Accommodations at the contemporary, full-service resort are in a modern Alpine-chalet style and feature a 132-room lodge and village. Of the 122 lodge rooms, seven are spacious suites with kitchenettes, separate living and dining areas, fireplaces and whirlpool tubs; 28 are deluxe guest rooms with mountain views and refrigerators; 30 are superior rooms with cable TV and refrigerators; and 66 are standard rooms with cable TV and refrigerators. Elkhorn also has condos with full kitchens and washer/dryers in sizes ranging from studios to four bedrooms in 10 different complexes within Elkhorn Valley. Many have their own pools/hot tubs and fireplaces, and all are close to the free bus line. Pets are allowed at Elkhorn.

Summertime recreation includes Elkhorn's 7100-yard Robert Trent Jones Jr. championship golf course, which is rated the 25th-best resort golf course by *Golf Illustrated*, and a tennis center with 18 hard-surface courts. An Olympic-size outdoor swimming pool has a whirlpool spa. The property has access to miles of paved bicycle and running trails.

Ketchum

Bald Mountain Lodge
$ • 151 S. Main St. • (208) 726-9663, (800) 892-7407

The rustic cabin lodge is on the National Register of Historic Places. Accommodations vary from spacious family units with two bedrooms, a dining area and complete kitchen to standard motel units with one or two beds.

The lodge is also the new home of Headwaters, home of Wood River Outfitters, which offers fly-fishing supplies, guided fly-fishing adventures, clothing, fine wines and gourmet foods along with beer and soft drinks.

Best Western Christiania Lodge
$$ • 651 Sun Valley Rd.
• (208) 726-3351, (800) 535-3241

The lodge's 38 rooms vary in type and size. They have microwaves and refrigerators; some have fireplaces. Roomside parking and cable TV are offered. An outdoor hot tub is open year-round; an outdoor heated pool is open in the summer. Pets are allowed. A complimentary continental breakfast is served in a sunny coffee area. The location is several blocks from restaurants, shops and nightlife.

Best Western Tyrolean Lodge
$$ • 260 Cottonwood St.
• (208) 726-5336, (800) 333-7912

This lodge, which looks like it was plucked out of the Austrian Alps, is 400 yards across from the River Run Plaza and ski lifts and is a four-block walk from nightlife, restaurants and shopping. It has the long balconies and A-shape roof of a typical Austrian Gasthaus and the cabinets, woodwork, furniture, lighting fixtures and paintings common in that cozy and beautiful part of the world. The 56 rooms offer large beds, down comforters and cable TV; some rooms have mountain views. Suites are equipped with a wet bar, microwave oven and refrigerator. Luxury suites offer spa baths. A complimentary continental breakfast of cereal, muffins, pastries, coffee, tea and juice is offered. The lodge hosts an Octoberfest and Shakespeare Festival each fall (see Events and Activities in this chapter).

Clarion Inn of Sun Valley
$$ • 600 N. Main St. • (208) 726-5900, (800) 262-4833

The 59 cleanly designed rooms in this inn have balconies, fireplaces, TVs with HBO and ESPN, and mountain views. The inn also has conference quarters with a capacity for 100 people and an on-site restaurant. The inn is near restaurants, shops and nightlife. Pets are allowed.

Heidelberg Inn
$$ • 1908 Warm Springs Rd.
• (208) 726-5361, (800) 284-4863

Heidelberg Inn is in a quiet, residential area midway between Ketchum and the Warm Springs lifts. It is set off by itself in a parklike area with Warm Springs Golf Course and tennis courts right across the street and restaurants, shops and nightlife minutes away by free shuttle bus. The inn's spacious rooms have recently been remodeled. Each offers large beds with down comforters, a microwave oven and refrigerator. Many rooms have fully

Ernest Hemingway in Idaho

Ernest Hemingway was a world adventurer who especially enjoyed Key West and Cuba, but for the last 20 years of his life, Sun Valley was his favorite.

Martha Gellhorn accompanied Hemingway on his first visit to Idaho in 1939, when they were guests at Averell Harriman's new Sun Valley Lodge. On their drive back east, they were married in Cheyenne, Wyoming. Hemingway would return often to the area's remote, rugged valleys and mountains to hunt, write and relax, and his three sons joined him for fall vacations in Sun Valley.

Close-up

During his initial visit, he stayed in Room 206 at the lodge, where a special bar and bookshelves had been installed as a courtesy of the resort. His mornings were reserved for writing *For Whom the Bell Tolls*; he spent his afternoons swimming, shooting, hunting, canoeing, fishing, horseback riding and playing tennis. He wrote the first 20 chapters of *For Whom the Bell Tolls*, corrected the proofs, received the reviews and sold the movie rights during his stay in Idaho in 1940.

During early visits with Martha, the Hemingways had parties at Trail Creek Cabin and picnics in the snow. The quantity and quality of their friendships was high: Hollywood personalities and the not-so-famous joined the Hemingways for drinks and conversation at restaurants or for roast game at home. Photographs of Hemingway from those days line the hallways off the lobby of the Sun Valley Lodge, and the Community Library's Regional History Collection contains more photos and memorabilia from the famous writer.

While in Idaho during the '50s, Hemingway worked on the manuscripts of his posthumously published books, *A Moveable Feast* and *Garden of Eden*. He wrote very little about his life in Idaho. "The Shot," an article about an antelope hunt in the Pahsimeroi Valley, appeared in *True* magazine in 1951.

Ernest brought his fourth wife, Mary Welsh, out in 1946. They stayed in Cabin 38 at what is now the Ketchum Korral just south of town. The writer's Ketchum haunts were many: He played slot machines (then legal) at the Casino Club still on Main Street, dined at the Christiana Restaurant on Sun Valley Road, ate steak at the Alpine (now Whiskey Jacques on Main Street) and drank at the Sawtooth Club on Main Street. He took his children to the St. Charles Catholic Church in Hailey.

In 1959 he and Mary bought a home in Ketchum on Big Wood River. That house is now the offices of the Nature Conservancy. Hemingway died July 2, 1961, in his home in Ketchum, at 61. He left the world three universally acclaimed novels, *The Sun Also Rises*, *A Farewell to Arms* and *For Whom the Bell Tolls*. His novels and short stories have

— continued on next page

Photo: Bruce Kendall

Hemingway wrote *For Whom the Bell Tolls* during a visit to Sun Valley.

significantly influenced writers and readers as well as altered literature and lives. He lies buried in Ketchum Cemetery. In 1967, friends built the Hemingway Memorial on Trail Creek Road, 1.5 miles above the Sun Valley Lodge before reaching Trail Creek Cabin, to commemorate his life.

Just off the bike path, a short walk leads to a bust by Robert Berks set in a grove of aspens and willows. At the base is the text of a memorial Hemingway wrote for a friend killed in a 1939 hunting accident, but which surely serves as Hemingway's own memorial as well:

Best of all he loved the fall
The leaves yellow on the cottonwoods
Leaves floating on the trout streams
And above the hills
The high blue windless sky
Now he will be part of them forever

equipped kitchenettes. Four-poster bed suites include an entertainment center and fireplace. Complimentary continental breakfasts and after-ski hot spiced wine are offered. An indoor spa and sauna are open year-round, and the outdoor pool is open in summer. The inn has a picnic area with outdoor barbecues and a guest laundry. Pets are allowed.

Kentwood Lodge
$$ • 180 S. Main St. • (208) 726-4114, (800) 805-1001

The high stone columns and imposing woodwork of this building make it a miniature version of the three immense, magnificent lodges at Bald Mountain. It's a modern well-designed building with 55 rooms that have solid textures and strong Western colors. It has an indoor heated swimming pool and spa, a microwave and refrigerator in each unit. Some rooms have balconies and fireplaces, and some suites have spas and kitchens. It also has a conference room, game room and covered parking. Located in downtown Ketchum, it's close to eateries, bars and shops.

Ketchum Korral Motor Lodge
$$ • 310 S. Main St. • (208) 726-3510, (800) 657-2657

The Korral has eight cabins and nine studio rooms that are screened from the road by towering pines. The cabins are individually furnished in early Western Americana. A private porch entrance leads to a living room with fireplace. A well-equipped kitchenette and separate bathroom and bedroom complete the layout. Studio rooms also have kitchens.

Gardens, a barbecue and picnic tables as well as a hot tub provide outdoor enjoyment. There is an unobstructed view of Bald Mountain. Pets are allowed. Summer rates are considerably less than winter ones, and value season rates are considerably less than those in the summer. Parking is available beside the cabins.

Ernest and Mary Hemingway, their family and guests often stayed at the Korral in the 1940s. They liked the casual atmosphere that offered a base camp for hunting and fishing. Today's visitors enjoy the lodge's proximity to downtown Ketchum's dining, shopping and nightlife options.

Knob Hill Inn
$$$$ • 960 N. Main St. • (208) 726-8010

Knob Hill Inn has 24 graciously appointed rooms with wet bars and fireplaces. Careful attention to detail enriches a distinctive decor that ranges from Southwestern to country designs. All accommodations have dressing rooms and marble bathrooms with a tub and separate shower, and each room has a balcony with views of the Sawtooth or Boulder mountain ranges. An indoor pool area has a Jacuzzi and patio. The Inn's European-style Konditorei is open mornings for breakfast and afternoons for espresso and pastries.

Felix at the Knob Hill Inn is the on-site restaurant (see Restaurants in this chapter).

Lift Tower Lodge
$$ • 703 S. Main St. • (208) 726-5163, (800) 462-8646

A section of an old ski lift with chairs hanging from it before the lodge serves as a landmark and provides the name for this accommodation. All rooms have two beds, a refrigerator, TV and phone. The front rooms are a little noisy in summer when the windows are open to let in air — there is no air-conditioning. However, at a mile high in elevation, excessive heat is generally not a problem. This lodge has two rooms set aside for smokers and a Jacuzzi outside in back. Complimentary breakfasts include bagels, coffee and orange juice. The free bus stops in front. During value season the price of a room can be halved.

The River Run ski lift is just around the corner; downtown Ketchum is just up the hill.

Pinnacle Inn
$$$ • At the base of the Warm Springs lifts • (208) 726-5700, (800) 255-3391

This is an attractive, slopeside building with rooftop flags, umbrellas above outside tables and an awning set before a high entranceway. Its rooms are warmly decorated and it has a cozy lounge. All rooms have a refrigerator and VCR; suites include a kitchen, fireplace, separate bedrooms and an extra bath; and some rooms have a Jacuzzi. A restaurant is on-site, and the eateries, bars and shopping of Warm Springs Village are nearby.

Ski View Lodge
$ • 409 S. Main St. • (208) 726-3441

These eight rustic individual cabins with open space before them and woodland and Bald Mountain views behind are near downtown Ketchum. The cabins have kitchens and phones, pets are welcome, and there is a senior citizen discount. Rates drop 40 percent during slow seasons.

Tamarack Lodge
$$ • 291 Walnut Ave. N. • (208) 726-3344, (800) 521-5379

All 26 rooms of this European-style lodge have balconies, direct-dial phones and cable TV with HBO. Open-beam ceilings and fireplaces add to the comfort of the rooms, which also have wet bars, refrigerators, microwaves and coffee makers. An indoor heated pool has a framed wooden ceiling with sky panels, and there is an outdoor Jacuzzi and deck. The lodge is close to Ketchum's restaurants, nightlife and shops.

Hailey

The Wood River Inn
$$ • 601 N. Main St. • (208) 578-0600

The use of dry stack rock-ledge stone at this new three-story motel harkens back to Hailey's mining days. The Inn has 57 rooms appointed for both the vacation and business traveler, including standard rooms with a king-size bed or two queen-size beds. There are suites with Jacuzzi tubs, executive suites with fireplaces and suites with full kitchen facilities. Conference facilities include a 1,000-foot meeting room and an executive board room. Rooms are equipped with a refrigerator, microwave and in-room coffee maker with complimentary coffee. Guests are treated to a complimentary continental breakfast every morning. An indoor heated pool and Jacuzzi are open year-round.

Bed and Breakfasts

The Idaho Country Inn
$$$ • 134 Latigo Ln., Sun Valley • (208) 726-1019, (800) 250-8341

This bed and breakfast is in a quiet neighborhood a half-mile from Sun Valley Resort and a half-mile from Ketchum. Log beams accent its structure inside and out. A spacious living room features a river-rock fireplace and well-stocked library. A sunny patio is also convenient for relaxation, and an outdoor hot tub has mountain views. Each of the inn's 10 rooms has an individual theme and balcony with a panoramic view. Themes include the area's early mining history, Idaho's Indian heritage, Idaho's various species of birds, winter activities, wildlife and Idaho's cowboy heritage. Each room has a private bath, direct-dial phone and refrigerator. Six of the 10 rooms have air-conditioning. Fax and photocopy machines are available. Idaho-style breakfasts, which include Idaho's Famous Potatoes, Eggs Sun Valley and hot-out-of-the-oven muffins, served family-style in the Sun Room.

Povey Pensione
$ • 128 W. Bullion St., Hailey
• (208) 788-4682

Owners Sam and Terrie Davis restored their 108-year-old residence to maintain the original character and fine workmanship of its builder, John Povey, a carpenter from Liverpool, England. Povey, who built and lived in the house with his wife, Elizabeth, when Hailey was a mining town, opened a lumber dealership next to the home supplied that building materials for many of the mines and buildings constructed in Hailey. Pastel wall coverings and antique furnishings give the four spacious bedrooms and two full shared baths an Old West character. A parlor and dining room are available for relaxing and enjoying the continental breakfast. The Pensione is within walking distance of Hailey shops and restaurants and 13 miles south of Ketchum and Sun Valley. This bed and breakfast does not cater to children younger than 12.

The River Street Inn
$$$ • 100 Rivers St. W., Ketchum
• (208) 726-3611, (800) 954-8585

This was Sun Valley's first bed and breakfast. It is tucked away on a quiet street, where its innovative architecture weaves Victorian sensibilities with the open spaces of contemporary Western design. A spacious living room offers comfortable couches and a natural brick fireplace. French doors open onto a deck. Cottonwoods and aspens rustle above Trail Creek, which runs below. The deck is an ideal spot for early morning bird-watching, afternoon tea or late night stargazing. Six guest suites overlook Trail Creek, and the other three offer clear views of Bald Mountain. All accommodations have a queen-size bed, a private bath with walk-in shower and Japanese soaking tub, phone, cable TV and a small refrigerator. Breakfasts can include Belgian waffles, fresh-baked scones, crepes, pancakes and mushroom and green pepper frittatas. Pets are allowed.

Povey Pensione

A Traditional Bed & Breakfast

*Rates: $60⁰⁰ per night
includes a full breakfast*

Hosts: Sam & Terrie Davis

128 W. Bullion • P.O. Box 1134 • Hailey, ID 83333

(208) 788-4682

Condo and Home Rentals

The condo and home rental agencies that follow are property management companies. The companies contract with people who would like to make a little money off their second homes or condos in Sun Valley and Ketchum when they're not in town. Generally, there's a three- or four-day minimum on rentals, which can vary in cost from $80 a day for a small condo to thousands of dollars a day for a luxury home. If you'd like to spend Christmas or July 4th weekend in Sun Valley, you'll most likely have to make your plans a year in advance. Otherwise, renters can usually be accommodated if they make reservations 30 days or more in advance.

Sun Valley

High Country Property Rentals, (208) 726-1256 or (800) 726-7076, offers rentals of more than 200 Sun Valley condos and homes.

Property Management Services, 1334 New Villagers, (208) 622-3510, rents condos of all sizes in old Sun Valley.

INSIDERS' TIP

Baby's Away, Baby Supply Rentals, (208) 788-7582 or (800) 327-9030, delivers a number of baby rental items, including cribs, strollers, rollaway beds, frame backpacks, tubs of toys, play pens, VCRs/tapes, car seats, humidifiers, gates, joggers, highchairs, booster seats and rocking chairs.

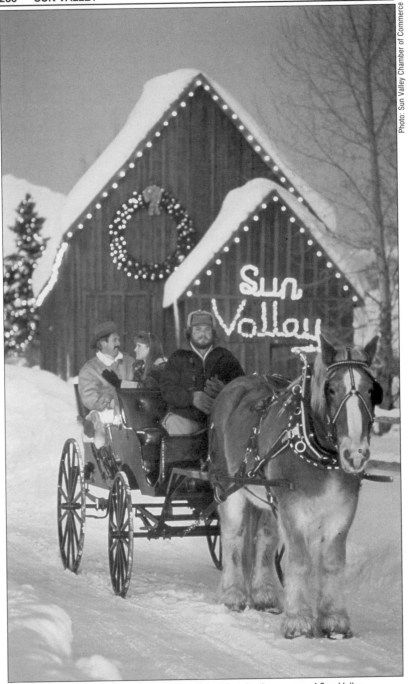

Photo: Sun Valley Chamber of Commerce

Sleigh rides are a popular way to take in the majestic scenery of Sun Valley.

Ketchum

Base Mountain Properties, 200 W. Rivers Street, (208) 726-5601 or (800) 521-2515, offers economy to luxury rentals throughout the area.

Distinctive Properties, 311 Sun Valley Road, (208) 726-7664, has luxurious homes and condos throughout the Wood River Valley.

Habitat 2000, 601 Leadville Avenue S., (208) 726-8584, offers two- and three-bedroom condos near downtown Ketchum.

Peak Investment Properties, 140 W. Second Street, (208) 726-2606, rents condos, homes and rustic cabins in the Sun Valley and Stanley areas.

Pennay's at River Run, next to the River Run lifts, (208) 726-9086 or (800) 736-7503, has one- and two-bedroom ski-out condos near the River Run lifts.

Premier Resorts at Sun Valley, 333 S. Main Street, (208) 727-4000 or (800) 635-4444, offers a wide range of accommodations throughout Sun Valley and Ketchum.

Private Idaho, 600 N. Main Street, (208) 726-7722 or (800) 249-7722, rents homes and condos with mountain views and provides 24-hour, personalized service.

Sun Valley Properties, 240 First Street N., (208) 726-1144 or (800) 622-7721, offers year-round rentals of one-, two-, three- and four-bedroom condos and homes near ski lifts, golf courses and the Wood River.

Sun Valley Vacations, 210 Sun Valley Road, Second Floor, (208) 725-0950 or (800) 626-1570, has rental properties at Warm Springs, Sun Valley's Elkhorn Resort and Ketchum.

Ski Packages

Lodging and ski lift tickets are included in two-, three- and four-night ski packages. There are also six different theme weeks that offer substantial savings over separate daily purchases of lodging and ski tickets. 2-Night Pre-Holiday Ski Packages begin at $118 a person; 3-Night Ski Packages begin at $238 a person; 4-Night Exclusive American Express Packages begin at $262 a person.

Theme week packages include seven nights of lodging and five days of skiing. Theme weeks include singles week, seniors week and ski club week. Per person prices vary from $315 to $457. Call (800) 634-3347 for information.

Child Care

Sun Valley Day Camp
Youth Center, Sun Valley Mall, east of Sun Valley and Dollar Rds. intersection, Sun Valley • (208) 622-2231

Sun Valley's Youth Program offers a variety of activities on a daily or weekly schedule for children ages 6 to 14 from early June to the beginning of September. Activities include bowling, crafts, field sports, boating, bike riding, hiking, ice skating, swimming, tennis, horseback riding, rock climbing and golf. Half-day is $40; full-day, $50; and five consecutive days, $210. Lunch is an additional $7 a day. All activities, except for horseback riding (which is an additional $12), are included in the rate. A Saturday barbecue and hayride is $10.

Sun Valley Play School
Just north of Sun Valley Mall behind the Gift Shop, Sun Valley • (208) 622-2288

Most children attending the Play School range in age from 2 to 6. The school's aim is to create a warm and loving atmosphere as well as a fun-filled vacation for children. In summer a well-equipped playground is available, and children enjoy supervised recreation, such as walks around picturesque Sun Valley Village, swimming, pony rides, picnics, hayrides and ice skating. In winter children may choose from many activities that include indoor/outdoor play, sledding and arts and crafts. Alpine skiing, cross-country skiing and ice skating are available at an additional cost. For infants 6 months to 1 year, the rate is $36 for three hours, $65 all day; for toddlers (1 year and older, not potty trained), the rate is $30 for three hours, $55 all day; and for those potty trained and older, it's $29 for three hours, $48 all day. Drop-ins are welcome, or you can make reservations.

Super Sitters
(208) 720-3836

Owner Sheila McLean has been a child-care provider in the Sun Valley area for 21 years. Her sitters are all young women who are older than 20 and know CPR and first-aid, are bonded and have certified background checks. They are available 24 hours a day and will go to a person's residence or rental location to care for a child. The cost is $14 an hour per child. Office hours are 7 to 8:30 AM and 4 to 7 PM. Phone messages will be returned during those office hours.

Pet Care

Sun Valley Animal Center
Idaho Hwy. 75, 2 miles south of Ketchum • (208) 726-7777

This full-service veterinary hospital offers 24-hour emergency care, a pet lodge and spa and doggie day care. There is a "cat house" that provides kitty condos and access to an indoor/outdoor lounging room that is decorated with scratching trees and multilevel perches. Indoor/outdoor dog facilities include heated kennel flooring that is covered with blankets and quilts; an outdoor area where dogs are taken at least four times a day; special diets and medications; and a playroom where dogs may play together, relax on couches and watch cartoon movies. Nightly rates for dogs run $12.75 for puppies in a cage and $15 to $20 for adult dogs. Nightly rates for cats run $8.50 to $10.

Restaurants

People go to Sun Valley to ski, ice-skate or take part in other vigorous winter activities during the cold months and to play golf, ride bicycles, hike or fish during warmer weather. But eating has to place way up on the scale of enjoyment for visitors and residents alike. Sun Valley and its environs are packed with first-rate restaurants that compete to please people from around the globe who know the culinary delights of Paris, San Francisco and Milan and are not going to settle for mediocrity. About 70 restaurants serve the 19,000 people who live in the Wood River Valley and hundreds of thousands of visitors who pour in each year.

Sushi, Italian, Chinese, Mexican, fresh Pacific and Atlantic seafood — never fear, you can find it here. And it is served in a great many ways at a wide variety of locations. World-class chefs and unusual dining experiences exist in the heart of town, on mountaintops and in the boondocks. Many simple places indulge in the little things — table settings, flowers, paintings, patios, music — that make a meal more than calories. Those at the head of the class spare nothing to make every moment count.

The bet here is that if you go to Sun Valley for a week's visit, you'll add 10 pounds because you can't say "no" in the restaurants. The locals have learned their lesson. They're all over the mountains, bike trails, swimming pools and skating rinks, afraid they'll turn round.

As with any resort location, there are high and low seasons, and you must plan accordingly when you go out to eat. By all means, make reservations early during the Christmas holidays and spring break. During quieter times you may be able to walk into someplace fancy at the last moment.

Meats — Cheeses
Espresso
COTTONWOOD
Desserts

Gourmet Deli café
Appetizers - Wine
Trattoria Style Italian Dinner

726-0606
The Atrium Building
5th and Leadville

Breads

Catering

Take - out — Beer/Wine

Price-Code Key

To help with planning, we've included a price guide, though remember it is only a guide. Menus change, and prices fluctuate. Prices are based on dinner for two, excluding cocktails and wine, appetizers and desserts, taxes and tip. Keep in mind a check total jumps considerably when you add extras. Restaurants mentioned here accept major credit cards.

$	Less than $25
$$	$25 to $50
$$$	$50 to $75
$$$$	$75 and more

At the Mountain

Baldy Base Club
$ • 106 Picabo St., at the base of the Warm Springs side of the mountain • (208) 726-3838

This traditional, relaxed, candlelit, after-ski location with big windows often attracts wall-to-wall crowds. Its decks are a big meeting and people-watching place during the summer. The tasty food includes pasta, pizza, steaks and salads. Daily seafood specials, pork medallions with apricot-hazelnut sauce and Portobello-stuffed wild chicken are also offered. At Downstairs/Below Baldy Base Club, package liquor, beer, wine, snacks, coffee and espresso are available. The Club is open daily for lunch and dinner.

Lookout Restaurant
$ • At the top of Lookout Express, Christmas and Challenger lifts on Bald Mountain • (208) 622-6261

A pleasant but modest eatery, Lookout Restaurant is what eateries used to be like on ski mountaintops before big money for amenities was poured into the equation. Table areas are divided by booths and etched-glass windows, mountain views are through "slits" compared to the new lodges, the ceiling is only about 8 feet high, and a serving line offers hamburgers, chili dogs, pizza, draft beer and a glass of Chardonnay or Cabernet wine. It's a nice stop and shelter from wind, fog and flakes with old two-quarter lockers that Jughead and Archie Andrews may have used. Lookout is open for breakfast and lunch daily during the ski season (Thanksgiving to Easter).

River Run Lodge
$ • River Run Plaza, at the base of the River Run side of Bald Mountain • (208) 622-6111

Built to gigantic scale like Seattle Ridge Day Lodge above it and Warm Springs Day Lodge on the other side of the mountain, River Run Lodge instantly increases the height of everyone who enters by 2 to 3 feet. Visitors expand because of an abundance of space, terrific mountain views, caressing furniture and fireplaces that could roast a dinosaur. Frank Lloyd Wright, the great architect known for fitting structure to natural terrain, would approve of the massive blond wood beams and windows that climb into the sky. Even if you are not a skier or mountain athlete, a visit to this lodge, because of its architectural wonder and wooded, riverside setting beneath majestic heights, is recommended. A huge terrace makes for great socializing and people-watching when temperatures do not nip the toes.

Breakfasts feature crepes and made-to-order omelettes, deli sandwiches are piled high, and stone-fired pizzas and stir-fry dishes at wok stations are included on an extensive menu. River Run serves breakfast, lunch and dinner daily.

Seattle Ridge Day Lodge
$ • At 8,600 feet on Bald Mountain above the Seattle Ridge quad lift
• (208) 622-6285

Panoramic views fill the eyes and stimulate the appetite at this excellent perch. Skiers are soothed by the magnificence of the $8 million, 17,000-square-foot log beauty. Non-skiers, too, are granted access by a chauffeur-driven, enclosed Sno-Cat that delivers them from the top of a high-speed quad lift after a 12-minute ride from the base to the mountaintop. The Sno-Cat takes passengers across a 1.5-mile ridge to the lodge and back for $15.

Wood-burning fireplaces set in giant rocks and views of the surrounding Sawtooth Rocky Mountains make concentration on the menu difficult. Specially heated outdoor plazas offer views of skiers and snowboarders below. Fleets of Sno-cats deliver fresh food before dawn every day. Prime rib, turkey breast, gourmet salads and wood-fired pizzas topped with basil pesto and sun-dried tomatoes tempt diners. Four kinds of made-to-order pasta and baked Idaho potatoes with delicacies like ratatouille Nicoise, shrimp and scallop Gruyère are also offered. Duck pot pie, grilled ahi, teriyaki shrimp kabobs, New York steak sandwiches, cheeseburgers and hot dogs are on the broad-ranging menu. Breakfast and lunch are offered daily during the ski season (Thanksgiving to Easter).

Warm Springs Day Lodge
$ • At the base of the Warm Springs side of Bald Mountain • (208) 622-6361

This was the first of the three new lodges built at Bald Mountain in the early '90s. Its dimensions are broad and high, and it has a large deck for after-ski music and socializing. Stone, wood and glass are joined together in a wonderful brawny creation at a lodge that is a little more basic than extravagant River Run and more seductive than Seattle Ridge.

Fresh pastas and pizza cooked in a wood-fired oven are two popular menu choices. Carved roast platters, soup, chili, breakfast omelettes and Caesar salad with grilled chicken are among the selections. Breakfast, lunch and dinner are served daily.

Sun Valley

Gretchen's
$$ • Sun Valley Lodge, Sun Valley and Dollar Rds. • (208) 622-2144

Located off the main lounge inside the lodge entranceway, Gretchen's has a light, airy atmosphere that is created by buttercup chandeliers, potted plants, wooden tables surrounded by stuffed chairs and a view outside to the terrace and ice-skating rink.

Breakfast offers waffles, pancakes, eggs, bacon and sausage and usually draws a good crowd of lodge guests. Rainbow trout and salmon are two of the lunch specialties. Salmon, duckling, quail and pasta are featured at dinner. Gretchen's is open daily for breakfast, lunch and dinner.

The Konditorei
$ • Sun Valley Mall, east of Sun Valley and Dollar Rds. intersection
• (208) 622-2235

The mall is designed as an Austrian village, and no such place is without a Konditorei, or pastry/coffee house, that teases your tongue and fattens your belly. This is an American version, with special coffees, sweets and a full menu of meals. You'll be surrounded by patterned tablecloths, glass-encased goodies, candle-like lighting fixtures and waitresses wearing dirndls.

Crepes Marseilles and the Austrian country breakfast are popular early day choices. The menu also includes bratwurst, chicken schnitzel and quiche.

The Ram
$$ • Sun Valley Mall, east of Sun Valley and Dollar Rds. intersection
• (208) 622-2225

Larry Harshbarger plays "As Time Goes By" and "If Ever I Would Leave You" on the piano, as he has been doing for nearly 20 years. The original light fixtures date back to 1939. The wooden tables bear carvings beneath the tablecloths of past visitors who wanted to leave their mark on this popular watering hole. Wooden booths provide privacy beneath chandeliers made of elk horns. Casual, European-style inn ambiance includes a comfortable bar in the next room and deck that is popular in summer.

Cheese fondue for two, pan-fried trout with citrus beurre blanc sauce, and pan-seared salmon with spinach, shallots and a white wine sauce are particularly good here. If you like prime rib, don't bother with the junior slab: Take the 16-ounce jumbo au jus with horseradish, which is as satisfying as you'll find anywhere.

Sun Valley Lodge Dining Room
$$$ • Sun Valley Lodge, Sun Valley and Dollar Rds. • (208) 622-2150

Do you have a birthday, anniversary or other special occasion to celebrate? Or would you just like to go back in time to the traditional elegance of chandeliers, tuxedo-clad waiters, beautiful table settings and a three-piece group playing dance music that doesn't taunt your ears? The Lodge Dining Room is on the second floor and overlooks the lodge swimming pool. It's a place to go for a leisurely night of excellent gourmet food, conversation, wine, dancing and perhaps some after-dinner treats. No need to hurry here. Soak up an atmosphere fit for kings, tycoons and others who are treated as such. Throw on your better clothes for a setting that will congratulate your finery.

Dishes include Chilean sea bass with crawfish butter and Sevruga caviar, grilled filet mignon stuffed with onions and Gruyère cheese, and other similarly prepared meals that feature guinea hen, salmon, elk and rack of lamb.

The Lodge is also known for its Sunday brunch that includes a wide variety of egg and meat dishes. The Lodge is open nightly for dinner.

Ketchum

Chandler's Restaurant
$$ • 200 S. Main St. • (208) 726-1776

Cozy and romantic, this restaurant is set among old evergreens with views of the mountains. In winter, visitors enjoy the fire in an antique-furnished dining room. During the long, summer days, dinner is served outdoors on a magnificent deck. Chef Michael Diem specializes in Pacific Northwest regional cooking.

There is a three-course, prix fixe American Dinner menu for $16.95 that features regional classics such as Yankee pot roast, roasted cornish game hen and Panzotti cheese ravioli. The à la carte menu features the likes of vegetable torte, Nova Scotia salmon, grilled Alaskan halibut and elk loin. Chandler's serves dinner nightly.

Christiana's
$$ • Sun Valley Rd. and Walnut Ave. • (208) 726-3388

Traditional French cuisine is offered on a patio and in the handsome Chamonix Room. The Olympic Bar offers light fare and full bar services. One of the best-known dishes is grilled fresh Atlantic salmon with roma tomatoes, wilted spinach and roasted shallot vinaigrette. The sauteed ruby Idaho trout with toasted hazelnuts and cream is another favorite. Chops, lamb, steak and veal liver also have special French preparations. The lightly smoked chicken breast comes with sun-dried tomatoes, artichoke hearts, spinach, olives and angel hair pasta. Daily fresh seafood and game specials are also available.

Christina's Restaurant
$ • 520 Second St. E. • (208) 726-4499

This one-level, L-shaped restaurant with tables placed close together is in a former house. Its soups, salads and bakery are well-known locally, and the restaurant is particularly well-frequented at lunch. Christina's is open daily for breakfast and lunch.

Cottonwood Café
$ • Atrium Building, 5th and Leadville Sts. • (208) 726-0606

The Cottonwood has deli meats, domestic and imported cheeses, specialty dry goods, desserts, espresso and beer. It's a gourmet deli cafe with take-out. Four antipasto dishes, including meats and cheeses with marinated vegetables, are served, and its primo platas include penne marinara, capellini di pesce al limme and pollo Parmesan.

Desperado's
$ • 211 Fourth St. • (208) 726-3068

This casual, one-room Mexican restaurant is decorated with sombreros and paintings of Mexican figures. Owner Jim Funk, who wanted to be in the restaurant business all his life, opened Desperado's nearly 15 years ago. It got its title from one of the carpenters who helped build the place.

The food is not the gluey melange sometimes found at "authentic" Mexican eateries. Pure canola oil, which has no cholesterol and is low in saturated fat, is used for frying. The black and refried beans are made with no added oils or fats, and the guacamole is made only with fresh avocados. The results are crisp and tasty burritos, tacos, enchiladas, tostadas and other typical Mexican dishes. A specialty is carnitas, which is roast pork, grilled chicken or charbroiled beef garnished with tomatoes, cilantro, guacamole, onions and lime, served with rice and beans and a choice of tortillas.

The restaurant has a small bar with a half-dozen stools and the open kitchen behind it. Mexican and American beer is available on tap. Diners sit at tiled tables. The wait staff wears T-shirts and sneakers, and customers are relaxed and animated in the simple and friendly atmosphere. Desperado's is open daily for lunch and dinner.

Esta
$ • 180 S. Main St. • (208) 726-1668

If you have a kid who impersonates Rembrandt, bring the artiste to Esta for breakfast, place a crayon in the little devil's hand, and let the scribbling on the tabletop begin. The management encourages this activity. Crayons are provided for childhood expressions of art on the brown butcher paper that

covers each table. A chalkboard and little wooden train set are also available for tyke use. Fox TV kid's programs play on TV. Over in the corner is an old cowboy easy chair set beside an eye-catching, woodcarved blonde cowgirl lamp that shows her with her saddle ready to ride the range.

An eclectic menu includes breakfast burritos, Mexican potatoes, a smoked salmon platter, Mafia salami and other meats, and The Cart — a carved selection of the day's roasted meats for a sandwich or platter with an Aioli side salad or grilled roasted vegetables. Breakfast, lunch and dinner are served daily.

Evergreen Restaurant
$$$ • Rivers St. and First Ave. • (208) 726-3888

Jazz floats through a two-story establishment that has glass breakfronts, tasseled windows and gilt-edged paintings.

The wine cellar features more than 400 labels from America, Italy and France and includes some vintage Bordeaux, such as Chateau Latour '53.

Starters include a delicious beet and endive salad tossed with nuggets of Roquefort; shrimp bisque swirled with herbed cream; and ahi tuna seared in cracked peppercorns and served with wasabi dipping sauce. Entrees include a rack of lamb with fresh mint; Thai bouillabaisse with shellfish and swordfish, redolent with lemongrass and poblano chiles; and a salmon fillet with a crackly sweet passion fruit glaze.

For dessert, melon-lime sorbet and mango-passion fruit sorbet are recommended. Chef Chris Kastner prepares the sorbets with a fruit-puree base that is purchased in France. A little vodka is added, which keeps the sorbets from freezing and gives them a creamy consistency.

Other desserts include mocha glace crunch, which is ice cream with toffee and caramel topping, and the Ultimate Chocolate Brownie, which is laced with peanuts and served with homemade vanilla ice cream and rich chocolate sauce.

Felix at the Knob Hill Inn
$$$ • 960 N. Main St. • (208) 726-8010

Chef Felix Gonzalez, a native of Madrid, learned to cook at the Sun Valley Resort and

Photo: Bruce Kendall

The immense day lodges on the mountain offer panoramic
views as well as a wide variety of cuisine.

Christiana's in Ketchum before becoming the
head chef at Felipe's in Snowmass, Colorado.
He later returned to the area and became chef
of the Knob Hill Inn kitchen. His menu offers
traditional dishes that are prepared with low-
fat ingredients such as garlic, fresh herbs and
olive oil. His specialties include roasted rack
of lamb au jus with fresh thyme, rosemary and
garlic; paella à la Valencia, which is chicken,
chorizo sausage, calamari and shellfish on a
bed of saffron rice; and tourneedo of beef ten-
derloin and light peppercorn crust.

In summer Gonzales typically prepares 20
to 30 different types of gazpacho. He has Spanish wines from Ribera del Duero, French wines
from 11 different wineries in Bordeaux, and a
wide selection of California reds and whites.

This small restaurant offers patio dining in
warm weather. It is tucked away in an inn that
also has a cafe with indoor dining and a sun-
dappled deck. It specializes in European past-

ries that include strudels, nussknackers, pies
and tortes and are served with espresso drinks.
Lunch and dinner are served daily.

(For more information about Knob Hill Inn,
see Accommodations in this chapter.)

The Ketchum Grill
$$ • Fifth St. and East Ave.
• (208) 726-4660

The restaurant is housed in an 1884 cabin
that belonged to the town's first postmaster.
White walls with green-trimmed windows, pol-
ished floors and tables set close together make
the place cozy. Scott and Anne Mason, who
previously worked in Santa Barbara and other
California kitchens, opened the restaurant five
years ago.

Appetizers include glazed beets with bal-
samic vinegar and honey served warm with a
sprinkling of goat cheese. Specialties cooked
on a wood-fired grill include farm-raised rabbit

with tomato-basil pistou, peppery duck breast with huckleberries and port, and homemade fennel sausage.

Pastry chef Anne Mason offers a delicious dried-cherry crisp with homemade cinnamon ice cream. The Grill serves dinner nightly.

The Kitchen
$ • 200 N. Main St. • (208) 726-3856

Keith Olander has been operating this popular breakfast and lunch restaurant, noted by an extensive and intriguing collection of celebrity wall pictures with messages, for nearly a quarter-century. "I'd jump over anything to eat with you," writes a hockey player who is leaping over a fallen opponent.

An open, easygoing ambiance filled with light is marked by the battered, red-and-blue sled used by Dawn Peterson of Ketchum in the 1988 Olympic Trials and World Cup races (it's so beat-up it could have careened over a volcanic rock field) as well as ski pictures, posters and an original Sun Valley Resort sign.

Breakfasts include peasant omelettes, with potatoes, bacon, green onions and cheddar, and the Sante Fe Special, which has scrambled eggs with onions and fresh cilantro wrapped in a flour tortilla, with melted cheddar cheese, salsa verde and sour cream, served with potatoes. A chicken diet plate, hot corned beef brisket on rye and a reuben sandwich with cheese, sauerkraut and Thousand Island dressing and soup are among the lunch choices. Breakfast and lunch are served daily.

Louie's Pizza and Italian Restaurant
$$ • 331 Leadville Ave. N.
• (208) 726-7775

Everyone knows Louie, "The only Italian you have to know," in Sun Valley — and in Boise, too, where he has another popular restaurant. According to the menu, this is his story:

"Louie's Restaurant was born of necessity in 1965. It was not so much that Ketchum-Sun Valley needed another restaurant. At the time, Louie Mallane, the founder and proprietor, was an accomplished ski bum seeking to support his ski habit. Relying on restaurant expertise gained in Utah and his Italian heritage, Louie opened Ketchum's first Italian restaurant, a venture that changed him from bum to businessman.

"With a bank loan of $150, he purchased flour, mushrooms, napkins and a few other necessary items. Then he rented the kitchen of Nedder's Bar and set up shop, making as many as 20 pizzas a day. Within six weeks, he had paid off his loan. Two-and-a-half years later he moved Louie's to its current location, a building that was the first church in Ketchum. With the acquisition of a pizza machine, Louie's pasta is made fresh every day. The pizzas are topped with all fresh ingredients, and the pizza dough is rolled as the customer orders. Louie opened a second restaurant in Boise in 1983 and a third in Idaho Falls in 1989."

A bell tower and quaint, tall church windows remain at Louie's, and other religious decor embellishes the booths and round tables. It's a casual, spacious place that draws a broad cross-section of people, including families with small kids. A pleasant bar is on the other side of the building.

In addition to pizza, Louie's serves veal Parmesan, scampi primavera, chicken cacciatore and manicotti. Louie's serves lunch and dinner Tuesday through Sunday. It's closed on Monday.

Ore House Restaurant
$$ • Sun Valley Rd. and Main St.
• (208) 726-2267

This is "The Seattle Connection" where Seafeasts for Two or More are served on candlelit hatch-cover tables. Restaurant owner Hal Griffith, who also has dining places in San Clemente, Newport Beach and Long Beach, California, as well as two in Seattle, flies in fresh fish from the West Coast every other day. According to the menu, the Seafeasts work like this: "We take a variety of fresh seafood, steamed and spiced, and put it on butcher paper on your table, and you get a mallet and bibs and go at it."

Combination plates include crabs, clams, shrimp and salmon. Mesquite-broiled trout, halibut and salmon are offered. Dungeness crabs, king crabs, brochettes and Maine lobster are also served. An extensive wine list includes Chardonnays, Cabernet Sauvignons and Merlots.

The dark, rugged, roomy enclosure is fronted by a large bar area and decorated by mounted game birds and paintings of Indians, trappers and cowboys. The cartoon menu jumps out at you with drawings of figures and food. Lunch and dinner are served daily.

Otter's Restaurant
$$$ • 180 Sixth St. • (208) 726-6837

Chefs and owners Keith Otter and Barbara Berry apply their French training to berries, game and other bounty of the Northwest at a hip and casual bistro that sports pewter-faced and etched-glass bars. A downstairs garden room features a mural of grapevines that matches the design on the handpainted appetizer plates. Decorated with plants and a fountain, the room looks out on Bald Mountain.

The food is arranged on oversized European china. Nightly specials might include Washington salmon encrusted with pepper and served with herb potato gnocchi that is sauced with shiitake mushrooms, roma tomatoes and sweet garlic. Seared sea bass comes in a pool of roasted shallots and garlic nage. The rock shrimp cakes with a red bell pepper sauce are strewn with crispy leeks. Game hen with Madeira and wild mushrooms and apricot-sour cream scones are also offered on a sophisticated and imaginative menu. Otter's is open daily for lunch and dinner.

Perry's Restaurant
$ • 131 W. Fourth St. • (208) 726-7703

At the counter, order Belgian waffles or the quiche of the day with an espresso drink, and read the paper at a booth or table. Many locals start their morning just that way at this casual, wide-open restaurant situated one block north of the post office. The garden salads — Caesar, dinner, chef, no-meat-please, albacore and Hawaiian — are well-known. Breads, including marbled rye, pumpernickel, natural grain, sourdough, baguettes, croissants and bagels, and other treats are baked daily. A wide range of sandwiches features the Cantonese turkey croissant, breast of turkey on a fresh-baked croissant with apple slices, raisins, sprouts and curry dressing, and the Black Forest, melted cheddar and Swiss cheese with bacon, lettuce, tomato and mayo on pumpernickel. Perry's serves breakfast, lunch and dinner daily.

The Pioneer Saloon
$$ • 520 N. Main St. • (208) 726-3139

"If you haven't been to the Pioneer, you haven't been to Ketchum," is the motto of this venerable wood-walled, stained-glass retreat that is liberally stocked with taxidermy trophies. Prime rib, the big item here, is as well-known as any dish served in the Wood River Valley. No reservations are accepted, and the place begins to overflow with the after-ski crowd at 5 PM. Drinks are nursed on couches and at the bar until a table opens in a large dark inner room and someone lucky gets to dig in. Arnold Schwarzenegger, one of numerous Hollywood stars with a house in the area, tried to big-shot his way in and was told to cool his heels. "Don't you know who I am?" he demanded. "Certainly, Mr. Schwarzenegger, and we'll let you know when your time comes, which should be about half an hour."

A place so well-frequented and targeted for one dish — where grandfathers, fathers and sons all seem to have devoured the same 2-pound slabs of prime rib — doesn't need a long menu. In addition to prime rib, the Pioneer offers steaks, seafood and a combination shrimp/teriyaki plate — that's it, four entrees, and people can't get enough. The Pioneer Saloon is open nightly for dinner.

The Roosevelt Tavern
$ • Sun Valley Rd. and Main St.
• (208) 726-0051

A small handsome bar stands beside an open, candlelit seating area and dance floor. The napkins are linen, and the metal ceiling tiles date back to the last century. Brick and wood-paneled walls frame an open kitchen in back. This place hops with live music, dancing and shows on Thursday, Friday and Saturday nights and after-ski presentations Wednesdays and Thursdays. In the summer a rooftop deck adds an outdoor dimension.

Appetizers include smoked salmon cakes and Asian baby back ribs. Turkey fajita and warm spinach are among the salads that are offered. Four kinds of 10-inch tavern pizzas are available. Main dishes include grilled salmon fillet, linguine, grilled rib-eye steak, and spinach and wild mushroom lasagna. Lunch and dinner are served daily.

The Sawtooth Club

$$ • 231 Main St. • (208) 726-5233

"Beware Pickpockets and Loose Women" reads a sign on the fireplace of this comfortable and pleasant establishment, which has a knotty-pine-paneled bar in front, game tables in back and dining upstairs. The Sawtooth Club is most known for its mesquite-grilled dishes — duck, T-bone, rack of lamb, trout and salmon. Many visitors socialize before or after dinner in the bar area, spending a good part of their night here. The after-ski crowd also enjoys this location. Lunch and dinner are served daily.

Sushi on Second

$ • 260 Second St. • (208) 726-5181

Owner and chef Travis Davis, formerly of the Seattle sushi scene, serves up squid, sea urchin and shrimp heads that are flown in every other day from San Francisco and delivered by taxi to the restaurant. Steaks and tempura are among the menu items, and a private Tatami Room is available for groups of up to 10. The atmosphere is urban. Sushi on Second is open nightly for dinner.

Western Cafe

$ • 115 N. Main St. • (208) 726-3396

A chuck wagon decorates the menu cover that reads, "Still Western after all these years." It's a spartan but clean and orderly place. A long counter with stools gives way to booths with Formica tabletops and wood chairs that surround plastic-covered tables. Country music plays on a radio. Traffic whizzes past the plate-glass windows. Local laborers, truck drivers and visitors seeking a plain-and-simple change-of-pace dig into the Lil' Buckeroo Breakfast, burgers and fries, rib-eye and top sirloin. A dinner special is less than $6. Visitors eye the old cow skeleton and horse harnesses on the wall; the menu quips: "Sweat is a waste of whiskey," and "Every jackass thinks he's got horse sense." Breakfast, lunch and dinner are served daily.

Whiskey Jacques

$ • 251 N. Main St. • (208) 726-3200

Log walls, a knotty-pine ceiling and three TVs carrying sports events greet the visitor to this locally well-known nightspot. Pool tables, Foosball and other board games are in the back. A pizza kitchen stands out beyond the bar in a broad and deep interior that has a well-used dance floor, which hosts many bands. Sandwiches and burgers and also available. Whiskey Jacques serves lunch and dinner daily. (See Nightlife in this chapter for more information.)

Hailey

Chapala Mexican Restaurant

$ • 502 N. Main St. • (208) 788-5065

The Chapala Mexican restaurants in Old Boise and Garden City are well-known and physically very different from each other, although they efficiently and quickly serve traditional Mexican dishes. The Hailey Chapala, too, is a different physical setup with the same favorites. Visitors order at a counter inside and sit at interior tables and booths or, in warm weather, at an outside deck. Dishes include beef and chicken fajitas, carne azada, pollo azada, pollo a la plancha and camarones almojo.

Clemente's

$ • Alturas Plaza, Main St.
• (208) 788-1557

Owner and chef Joe Clement was raised in his family's Italian restaurant, Russo's, in south New Jersey; His grandparents started Russo's in 1920, and it is still run by aunts, uncles and cousins. At Clemente's, family members pitch in at a quaint dining room and brass-top wine bar. You can stop for an appetizer and glass of wine, dessert and a cocktail or a full meal. Wednesday nights are for winetasting when Italian and West Coast wines take center stage.

Appetizers include polenta, which is traditional Italian cornmeal steamed with cheese and peppers, served with shiitake mushrooms and roasted tomato ragout; grilled smoked mozzarella and roasted peppers that are marinated in olive oil and herbs and served with black olives; and fettuccine Alfredo, which is imported fettucine tossed with butter, cream and Parmesan cheese.

Dinners include spaghetti with clam sauce and homemade lasagna. Also offered is chicken oreganata, which is a grilled boneless chicken breast topped with fresh lemon juice and herbed bread crumbs then lightly broiled and served with a side of pasta; and bombalotti al modo Giovanni — fennel sausage flamed with brandy and simmered with fresh fennel and tomato, chicken stock, white wine and cream and served over rigatoni pasta. Clemente's is open for dinner nightly.

The Splendid Boondocks

A Pacific or Mongolian Yurt
$$$$ • Off Warm Springs Rd., Sun Valley • (208) 788-7665

A Winter's Feast is a five-course gourmet meal served in a brand-new Pacific yurt or 100-year-old Mongolian yurt that is reached by an old-fashioned sleigh. Cross-country skiers and snowshoers may also make the trek. The cost is $60 a person for the meal and sleigh ride.

Four different dinners are served. The beef tenderloin dinner includes grilled chicken satay, spinach feta bisque, Idaho mashed potatoes, yogurt cheese and chocolate brownie pie drizzled with apricot syrup.

The fresh salmon dinner features grilled custom-made sausages, potato-leek soup, spinach salad, brown rice and a dessert of berry pinwheel cobbler with farm-fresh whipped cream.

The rack of lamb dinner starts with grilled sea scallops dressed with balsamic syrup and roasted red pepper rolls stuffed with capers, pine nuts and Pecorino Romano. The romaine salad has lemon-Caesar dressing. Dessert is rich bread pudding with a dried-cherry caramel sauce.

The fourth dinner, pork tenderloin, begins with a grilled whole shrimp with a peanut sauce and continues with roasted fennel and carrot soup. The pork is marinated and sauced with chipotle chile-orange sauce served on apple-quinoa couscous with grilled vegetables. Dessert is coconut rice pudding sprinkled with fresh fruit. The yurt serves dinner nightly during the winter.

Galena Lodge Full-Moon Dinners
$$ • Idaho Hwy. 75, 24 miles north of Ketchum • (208) 726-4010

On two days in December, January, Feb-

ruary, March and April, Galena Lodge offers a full-moon dinner at a renovated and remodeled lodge that goes back to mining days more than a century ago. Typically snow piled high outside twinkles in the moonlight, delicious smells pour out of the kitchen, and a crackling fire warms spirits and bodies that venture outdoors on cross-country skis and snowshoes.

A full-moon dinner costs $20 and is served family-style. The menu starts with tomato, fennel and white bean soup and continues with fresh spinach salad and curry vinaigrette. The choice of entrees includes beef medallions with mushrooms; rack of lamb with apple mint chutney; baked salmon with herb crust; curried Cornish game hens; and pumpkin ravioli with mushrooms. Side dishes include garlic mashed potatoes in phyllo, rice pilaf, fresh vegetables and fresh peppercorn bread. Dessert is mocha mouse.

The lodge also serves lunch daily year-round, offering soups, sandwiches, burgers, salads, hot drinks, microbrews and assorted wines.

Trail Creek Cabin
$$$ • 2 miles east of Sun Valley • (208) 622-2135

Constructed of logs and brick in 1937, the cabin, which stands alone in tall trees on Trail Creek, offers a warm and cozy rough-hewn atmosphere of early Ketchum mining and ranching days. It was popular with Clark Gable, Gary Cooper and Ava Gardner and was the place Ernest Hemingway and other personalities celebrated New Year's Eve. In winter the cabin may be reached by cross-country skis or sleigh. Horse-drawn sleighs that carry 20 people leave the Sun Valley Inn at 6, 7, 8 and 9 PM for a half-hour ride to the cabin. Blankets are provided on the sleighs, but dress warmly. A round-trip adult ticket costs $16; tickets for children younger than 12 are $12.

The specialty of the house is barbecued ribs. Other entrees include steaks, prime rib, roasted chicken and Idaho mountain trout. Dinner prices range from $16 to $24, and children's portions are available at reduced prices. A full bar and wine list are also available. Trail Creek Cabin serves dinner nightly.

Nightlife

Put dozens of exhaustive recreational activities and scores of top restaurants together, and what do you get at the end of the day? The Hot Tub Serenade. An orchestra of ZZZZs. Card games in condos, VCR cassettes, mellow conversation over a nightcap in a quiet lounge. But Sun Valley, if not a wild and crazy place, does have its share of nocturnal activity that ranges from a resort waltz to hot music and funky dancing downtown, several comedy acts and the Bruce Willis factor in Hailey. Residents and visitors alike avidly attend the latest cinema releases at Wood River Valley movie houses. Concerts, stage performances and arts events are presented each year at different times and locations (see Events and Activities and The Arts for more information).

The Sun Valley/Ketchum Chamber of Commerce, at the corner of Fourth and Main streets in Ketchum, (208) 726-3423, publishes a free, current events and activities calendar. The local weekly newspapers, *The Idaho Mountain Express* and *The Wood River Journal* are other good sources. These free newspapers come out on Wednesday and are available at public locations throughout the valley.

Sun Valley

The Boiler Room
Sun Valley Mall, east of Sun Valley and Dollar Rds. intersection • (208) 622-2223

Mike Murphy is a musical comedian who has been performing at Sun Valley for 20 years. His 5:30 to 7:30 PM winter shows at The Boiler Room have an $8 cover charge. Murphy is known for his song parodies and hilarious barbs on anyone and anything in current events as well as for establishing rapport with his audience. His most popular routine is his satire of John Ford's movie *Stagecoach*, complete with Sam Peckinpah slow motion, sound effects and a host of characters, including a cowboy whose horse has died. His Eaglesque "Hotel Radisson Elkhorn" and humor at John Denver's expense — "DWI Colorado" sung to the tune "Rocky Mountain High" — are also popular. The Boiler Room offers Friday and Saturday night music that features the Paul Tillotson Quartet and the Christi Bryant Band. The location is casual, with a large open room filled with tables and a bar.

Sun Valley Lodge
Sun Valley and Dollar Rds.
• (208) 622-2151

Dancing to live music is a Sun Valley tradition dating from 1935 when the resort first opened with the Eddie Duchin Band playing jazz nightly at the Sun Valley Lodge. These days, the lodge features dancing to music by the Joe Fos Trio every night during the winter season. Fos started his career as a teenager by winning a Liberace concert competition and has worked with Van Cliburn. The Fos trio plays in the Sun Valley Lodge Dining Room from 6:30 to 9 PM and then moves downstairs to the intimate Duchin Room from 9:30 to 11:30 PM. Ballroom dancing is the norm, not the exception. Even so, especially in the Duchin Room, dress is casual.

Sun Valley's Elkhorn Resort
Dollar and Elkhorn Rds. • (208) 622-4511

At various times during the year the Atrium Lounge, off the hotel lobby, features live entertainment, often offering the soothing music of a piano bar accompanied by a singer and a band. On occasion, the Elkhorn Saloon hosts a local theater company for a series of performances.

Free, outdoor jazz concerts are offered outdoors at the Elkhorn Plaza on Thursday evenings from 6:30 to 9 PM, June through August. The concerts feature The Steve Miller Band, Big Head Todd and other artists. (See Jazz on the Green under Events and Activities in this chapter.)

Ketchum

The Roosevelt Tavern
Sun Valley Rd. and Main St.
• (208) 726-0051

This restaurant has a small, handsome bar, candlelit tables, wood-paneled and brick walls that frame an open kitchen and metal ceiling tiles that date back to the last century. A dance floor hops with live music, dancing and shows on Thursday, Friday and Saturday nights. The Vaurnettes, a quartet of local women with cheeky takeoffs on popular songs, are the local rage. There's a comedy show here on Thursday nights; the cover price is $15. Other bands that perform are locally or regionally known, and the cover for their shows as well as for the Vaurnettes ranges from $3 to $20. (See Restaurants in this chapter for more information.)

Whiskey Jacques
251 N. Main St. • (208) 726-5297

This bar and restaurant has pool tables, Foosball, sports TV and a dance floor. Its regularly scheduled bands include a popular local group, the Bo-Bos, Tempo Times and Suns of Beach, which plays upbeat, rollicking '60s, '70s and '80s songs. Cover charges for the bands are $3 to $5. (See the Restaurants section of this chapter for more information about Whiskey Jacques.)

Movie Theaters

For its size, the Wood River Valley is loaded with movie houses. The historic Opera House at Sun Valley Mall, (208) 622-2244, shows ski films and first-run movies. In Ketchum the newest releases are shown at Magic Lantern Cinema, 207 Washington Avenue, (208) 726-4274; the Movie House, 207 Washington Avenue N., (208) 726-8239; and Ski Time 4 Cinemas, which has four theaters, 100 Second Street E., (208) 726-1039. Bruce Willis' renovated art deco theater, the Liberty Theatre, 110 N. Main Street, Hailey, (208) 788-3300, also shows current movies.

Shopping

Sun Valley is chic. It's got on the latest sunglasses, has the top horses under the hood, is clad in the finest, form-fitting fabrics and has mansions that rival modern castles anywhere. But it's also a compact, fun place with a lot of variety, where the average person with a few bucks to spend can have a good time nosing around the stores. There are top specialty shops, traditional mainstream favorites and quirky little stores that could only exist through nibbles from the jet streams of wealth.

Sun Valley is more of the world than of Idaho — a little stylish, recreational Paris, if you will. However, it maintains the easygoing good humor and rugged attitude of its actual location. Poke around through the shops and stores, and you may be amused and educated as well as well-served.

Sun Valley Mall is just east of the Sun Valley and Dollar roads intersection at Sun Valley Resort, an enclave of European style, trees, ponds and grass. In downtown Ketchum, Giacobbi Square, at Fourth Street and Leadville Avenue, is filled with shops.

Apparel and Jewelry

Barry Peterson Jewelers
511 Sun Valley Rd., Ketchum • (208) 726-5202

Barry Peterson has more than 25 years experience in jewelry-making and design. He also features well-known American jewelry designers such as Yurman, Hardy, Elizabeth Locke, Seiden Gang and Wendy Brigode. The shop has giftware, bridal jewelry and watches by Rolex, Breitling, Plaget and Tag-Heuer.

The Brass Ranch
Sun Valley Mall, east of Sun Valley and Dollar Rds. intersection, Sun Valley • (208) 622-2021

This fashionable, high-end shop has a celebrity following. It features Bogner skiwear in the winter and has a large selection of Ralph Lauren men's clothing. It is known for its Malo cashmere and after-ski boots for men and women. In the summer it carries golf sportswear and women's swim clothing, swimming suits and hats. A second Brass Ranch store at River Run Plaza, next to the ski lift, carries more sporty items — things that are needed at the mountain — such as Norwegian sweaters and Phoenix and Post Card brands, rather than high-end items.

I.M Woman
181 N. Main St., Ketchum • (208) 726-4692

If U.R Woman, consider stopping by this shop that sells oils and soaps, lingerie, aerobic and exercise wear, socks and some outer wear. It carries items that might be hard to find in a department store. The shop has washable linen and washable rayon products. Owner Claudia Greer tries to be a little different and a little more exclusive while carrying mainstream clothing at mainstream prices. She has 200 chiffon evening dresses on the rack as well as Relais sweaters.

Impressions in Gold
260 N. Main St., Ketchum
• (208) 726-5352

Mike and Rosemary Shefer design and cast half of the jewelry they sell, including Sun Valley sun faces. They do lots of custom work and repair jewelry. Earrings, watches, belts, necklaces and rings are among the items sold here.

Mercantile of Sun Valley
300 Main St., Ketchum • (208) 726-4126

This large, comfortable store in a brick building constructed in 1887, carries men's and women's clothing. It has sweaters, pants, leather jackets, hats and standard Western-style, rugged clothing. The shop is the only distributor of Donna Karan clothing in Idaho. It also carries men's and women's shoes, belts and accessories.

Ozzie's Shoes
407 Leadville Ave. N., Ketchum
• (208) 726-3604

Locally owned and operated since 1977, this large, smart-looking shop offers men's, women's, kid's, athletic and dress shoes. It has a good variety of winter boots that can be worn on the street, in the office and at home. The shop imports footwear from Austria, Germany, Italy and Canada. Lines featured include Cole Haan, Tecnica, Mephisto, Sorel, Nike and Reebok.

Purple Sage
211 N. Main St., Ketchum
• (208) 727-9002

In a brick building that dates back to Griffith's Grocery Store in 1887, a big *Ghost Riders in the Sky* movie poster catches visitors' eyes. The shop manufactures a lot of its own things for women, often reflecting styles of earlier eras. The store's philosophy is that because people are so stressed out they should have fun with their clothing. It's not like a department store, where someone comes in and finds something to wear. Sales associates get to know the customer and show her different looks. The shop has dresses, jackets, coats and clientele from New York, Dallas, Los Angeles and Seattle. Purple Sage also has antiques, estate jewelry and other estate items and tries to find new designers and manufacturers that have their own look and style.

Sheepskin Coat Factory
511 Sun Valley Rd., Sun Valley
• (208) 726-3588

Domestic and imported leathers, sheepskin and fur are offered in a shop that was founded in 1971. Gloves, hats, accessories and women's fine apparel by Le Painty are also for sale.

Silverado Western Wear
371 N. Main St., Ketchum
• (208) 726-2294

You see stagecoaches roll through sagebrush here. The roar of the rodeo is in your ears. The hero on the white horse is hot after the villain dressed in black, who has tied the beautiful girl on the railroad tracks as a locomotive puffs closer. That's the kind of imagination Silverado inspires. It has an entire wall filled with gleaming cowboy boots that is just a small part of the whole. John Wayne is slipping into jeans, and Hopalong Cassidy is trying on snap button shirts. Gary Cooper is modeling a smart Western jacket. You get the idea, pardner?

Sports Connection
The Galleria, Fourth St. and Leadville Ave., Ketchum • (208) 726-6090

Sports Connection has an eclectic mix of women's clothing and accessories. It carries workout clothes, casual clothes, trousers and sweaters for working women as well as evening wear. Among its brands are Basic Threads, Fitigues, Chava sweaters and Only in the U.S.A. It has lots of semiprecious jewelry, such as garnets and pearls, and sterling silver.

Photo: Sun Valley Chamber of Commerce

Hikers can enjoy everything from an easy afternoon stroll to a vigorous mountain climb along the numerous trails of Sun Valley.

Towne & Parke Fine Jewelry
Sun Valley Mall, east of Sun Valley and Dollar Rds. intersection, Sun Valley
• (208) 622-3522

This full-service jewelry store was founded in 1956. Custom design, manufacturing and repair are done on the premises. It has a large selection of fine jewelry and watches, including Sun Valley sun and snowflake charms in gold and silver.

Venzon Jewelry & Arts West
106 N. Main St., Hailey • (208) 788-1600

This custom jewelry shop offers handmade sterling, fine gold and platinum work by Don Venzon as well as jewelry and framed art made by artists from across the West. It also has diamonds and Citizen watches. Its Native American art includes carved animals, flutes and drums. Jewelry repair is also available.

Bookstores

Chapter One Bookstore
160 N. Main St., Ketchum
• (208) 726-5426

This is a well-organized, comfortable book shop in a long brick building that was a bank more than a century ago. Cheryl Welch has run the shop for a quarter-century; the two resident hounds probably haven't been around that long. This is a conversational meeting place where people pick up *The New York Times* and chat over a guidebook or bestseller that Ms. Welch is ringing up. The shop is particularly strong in women's literature, books about North America and metaphysical books. An organic juice bar is in the rear.

Ex Libris

Sun Valley Mall, east of Sun Valley and Dollar Rds. intersection, Sun Valley
• (208) 622-8174

Richard Bray has owned and managed this cozy little bookstore for 20 years. It's in the Sun Valley Village, between the Sun Valley Lodge and Sun Valley Inn. About half his clients are visitors and half town residents whom he advises on the latest selections. Contemporary fiction, books about the West and cookbooks are his strongest departments, although he also has a very good travel section.

Iconoclast Books

100 First Ave. N., Ketchum
• (208) 726-1564

Outside Iconoclast Books, a sculpted wolf sits on a bench reading a book with a crow looking over his shoulder. Sculptures of a cougar, horse and wolves prance around outside. A sign says, "Used, rare and out-of-print books. Buy, sell, trade. And video boutique." When Gary Hunt, the store owner, tried to find the classic movie *Citizen Kane*, it wasn't available in the Wood River Valley. That's when he started his large video rental collection, which includes films by Orson Welles, Ingmar Bergman, Andrzej Wazda, Andrei Tarkovosky, Satyajit Ray and Akira Kurosawa. The store sells new as well as used books, literary fiction and nonfiction. Rooms are filled with books of every kind, and painted footsteps lead to more in the cellar. The store has out-of-print Idaho and Sun Valley history books and out-of-print books by Ernest Hemingway.

Children's Stores

Chicken Lipps Toys & Clothing

Giacobbi Square, Fourth St. and Leadville Ave., Ketchum
• (208) 726-3199

Chicken Lipps has items for children up to 14 years of age. You'll find jackets, pajamas, hats, playsuits, games and sunglasses. It has an excellent collection of stuffed animals that includes gorillas, wolves and rabbits.

Sun Valley Kids and Toy Store

The Galleria, Fourth St. and Leadville Ave., Ketchum • (208) 726-9300

For more than a decade, Deborah Dunlop has owned this shop that specializes in educational toys, many of which are made of wood for infants to age 8. There are wooden barns, tractors, tool boxes and dump trucks. Some of the toys are interactive, so that parents and kids can play together. The store does a lot of custom work, such as fulfilling a bizarre request for a doll house painted in hockey club colors. Little hands find it hard to resist Noah's Ark, which comes with scores of fanciful wooden animals.

The Toy Store

102 Washington Ave., Ketchum
• (208) 726-5966

Encourage your child's penchant for fun and frolic at this large store. It's filled with children's books and coloring books, a wide variety of Playmobil toys, magnet kits, glow puzzles, dolls, board games for children and adults, toy railroads, wagons, bikes and sleds. The store also has a veritable zoo of stuffed animals.

Gifts

American West Gallery

520 Fourth St., Ketchum
• (208) 726-1333

This colorful shop is decorated with steer horns, pennants, an Indian totem, paintings and posters, a bronze sculpture of a cowboy on a rearing horse, and a finely woven Indian carpet. It offers 19th- and 20th-century American folk art, vintage West show posters, antique Beacon and Pendleton camp blankets and original Western movie posters from the 1920s through the '40s.

Angel Wings

320 Leadville Ave. N., Ketchum
• (208) 726-8708

Collectibles, antiques and a lot of Victorian silver are offered in this shop that has a different, dreamy atmosphere. Angels and cupids hang from the walls above a wood floor. Ceramic figures, candleholders, dishware and unusual picture frames catch visitors' eyes.

Idaho Country Store
531 N. Main St., Ketchum
• (208) 726-4949

This store lives up to its name with a wide variety of gifts for country living that include quilts, pottery, jewelry, candles, birdhouses, Christmas ornaments, handmade crafts, pet gifts, toys and penny candy.

Main Strip T's
240 Main St., Ketchum • (208) 726-9543

Owner Norma Hale stocks strictly T-shirts, sweatshirts and souvenirs. Hats, ski pins, patches, key chains and cups, many with Sun Valley emblems, are also for sale.

Sun Valley Gifts
Sun Valley Mall, east of Sun Valley and Dollar Rds. intersection, behind the post office, Sun Valley • (208) 622-2206

A wide range of specialty gifts are offered here including Sun Valley souvenirs, T-shirts, handpainted pottery, Western gifts, toys and jewelry.

Two Fishes
210 N. Main St., Ketchum
• (208) 726-7098

There is a Tooth Fairy Kit for sale. Whimsical cast-iron animals dance in a garden. Paintings, drawings, cabinets and furniture fill this unusual shop. Artists from around the world make fanciful objects that are on sale here. A dog with odd, crazy appeal and his tongue stuck out is in the window. The animal was created by Jim Lambert, whose pieces can be found in the American Folk Museum.

Home Decor and Necessities

Antiques and Country Pine
620 Sun Valley Rd., Sun Valley
• (208) 622-7551

This shop carries imported European antiques and pine reproductions. It also has accessories, lamps and gifts and offers an interior-design service.

Charles Stuhlberg Furniture
571 East Ave. N., Ketchum
• (208) 726-4568

A showroom display of 9,000 square feet features antiques, custom furniture, lamps, gifts and accessories. Interior-design services are also available.

Chateau Drug & Hardware
Giacobbi Square, Fourth St. and
Leadville Ave., Ketchum
• (208) 726-5696

This full-service pharmacy also has a huge selection of automotive items, toys, gifts, film, cards and hardware products as well as fishing, camping and sporting goods merchandise.

Ketchum Kitchens
Giacobbi Square, Fourth St. and
Leadville Ave., Ketchum
• (208) 726-1989

Ketchum Kitchens has a range of products that extends from simple and basic needs to gourmet cooking. It offers appliances, pottery, dinnerware, glassware, cutlery, flatware, textiles, cookbooks, gadgets, gifts and gourmet food products. If you are looking for ceramics or mugs with Sun Valley emblems, you've come to the right place.

Legacy Antiques and Imports
491 10th St., Ketchum • (208) 726-1655

This shop features sophisticated country and refined, rustic furniture. It has European architectural elements and imports from Europe, the Orient and Mexico. It also manufactures its own exclusive line of reproductions.

Salmon River Naturals
(208) 788-3252

Kim Crofts was born and raised in the Wood River Valley and has been involved in every aspect of designing and producing log furniture. He designs and builds custom furniture from trees selected from the floor of the Sawtooth National Forest. The designs can be small or large, tame or rugged, Scandinavian scribed or mortise and tenon. Beds, tables, chairs, benches and river-rock fireplaces accentuated by log mantels and hearths are some of the furniture that he makes.

The Great Outdoors

Packing Up

The Travel Smart Shoppe
**Giacobbi Square, Fourth St. and
Leadville Ave., Ketchum**
• **(208) 726-4884**

Tucked into the lower level of Giacobbi Square, this small shop has many handy travel items including luggage, duffel bags, packs, guidebooks, videos, maps, locks, money belts, loop wallets, leg carriers and bra packs.

Fly-Fishing Shops

For more information about fly-fishing in Sun Valley, including guides to the area and casting classes, see Fly-Fishing under Recreation later in this chapter.

Bill Mason Outfitters
**Sun Valley Mall, east of Sun Valley and
Dollar Rds. intersection, Sun Valley**
• **(208) 622-9305**

Bill Mason had one of the first stores in Henry's Fork, the famous eastern Idaho fly-fishing stream, and has run his Sun Valley shop for more than 25 years. He calls Sun Valley "one of the last great fly-fishing meccas." Mason has a broad selection of men's and women's outdoor apparel, fishing tackle and other equipment. He offers advice on weather and fishing conditions, hatching time tables and what equipment to use.

Lost River Outfitters
171 N. Main St., Ketchum
• **(208) 726-1706**

This shop has high-end and specialty rods, adventure travel clothing and rental equipment that includes graphite rods, waders and boots, float tubes and all the tackle necessary to fish local waters. It also has a good library, videotapes and a free casting clinic.

Silver Creek Outfitters
507 N. Main St., Ketchum
• **(208) 726-5282**

"NZ Trout" reads the license plate of the vehicle parked before this large and impressive log structure. A little sidewalk water basin is labeled "dog water." A canoe and giant fishing rod decorate the ceiling of the spacious interior. Paintings adorn the walls; there is a large, crackling fireplace that offers the relaxation of easy chairs and a spread of books, clothes, stuffed animals, videos and a separate hunting department.

Sports Shops

In an area that is mad for recreational sports, there are a number of sports shops in Sun Valley, Ketchum and at Bald Mountain that sell, rent, tune and repair winter and summer equipment as well as offer a broad range of clothes and accessories. Because Sun Valley is an uncrowded destination resort with many return visitors as opposed to a turnstile quick getaway for the masses, the shops tend to be friendly, the service good and prices reasonable.

Rentals are easy to manage, and terms from one shop to another do not vary much, if at all. For a rental package of skis, boots and poles, expect to pay $15 to $20 a day, and $10 to $12 a day when the package is rented for a week or longer. For a snowboard rental package of boots and board, figure $28 a day and $32 for high-end step-ins and pro models. For a mountain-bike rental, expect to pay $20 a day, unless it's a high-performance bike, which would run about $25. In-line skates rent for $20 a day, and one-speed bikes can be found for $10 a day.

The Board Bin
180 Fourth St., Ketchum
• **(208) 726-1222**

"Girls Kick Ass" says the placard in the shop window. Other window signs say "Girl Street." This snowboard shop has a special department for women's clothing, boots, bindings and other snowboard equipment that could be the only one of its kind in the country. The shop has snowboard magazines, videos and traditional and high-end pro step-ins and boards for sale and rent. The atmosphere is friendly and relaxed. In summer, The Board Bin becomes a skateboard and skateboard equipment shop.

Formula Sports
460 N. Main St., Ketchum
• **(208) 726-3194**

Fine European and American ski fashions and equipment are in stock here. The shop features custom boot fitting and has complete ski rental services and repair.

Kelly Sports
The Colonnade, 615 Sun Valley Rd., Ketchum • (208) 726-8503

High-performance skiwear and accessories are offered here. Ski pants, parkas, pants, fleece, gloves, neck gators, Sun Valley turtlenecks, long underwear, poles, goggles and sunglasses are available, as are 100 percent Canton Fleece cotton for casual and active wear.

Paul Kenny's Ski & Sports
At the base of the Warm Springs lift, Ketchum • (208) 726-7474

This shop offers rentals, ski and boot demos, repairs and nightly, weekly and season ski storage. It's a friendly shop with experienced employees and a good line of clothes and accessories.

Pete Lane's
Sun Valley Mall, east of Sun Valley and Dollar Rds. intersection, Sun Valley
• **(208) 622-4111**

Pete Lane's was the first sports shop in Sun Valley. It's an attractive store with a wide selection of men's and women's skiwear, vests, gloves, caps and other winter clothing. In the warm months, the focus is on golf, tennis and mountain attire. A busy back shop handles rentals and offers full-service tuning and repairs. The store features equipment from Volkl, Tecnica, Rossignol, Salomon, Scott, Marker and Volant.

Sturtevants
314 N. Main St., Ketchum
• **(208) 726-4501**

This is a large, 7,000-square-foot shop with upbeat sales associates. Bogner is the main clothing line, and Shoffel, North Face, Killy and Marker brands of equipment and clothing are also offered. Hats, jackets, helmets and pullovers fill the aisles. The shop has luggage and ice hockey departments. In the summer it offers bikes, tennis equipment and clothes, sportswear and hiking gear.

Sturtos
380 N. Main St., Ketchum
• **(208) 726-4512**

This snowboard shop is owned by the Sturtevants sports shop next door. It offers step-in bindings and boards for sale and rent as well as a selection of jackets and casual clothes for snowboarding and Alpine and freestyle skiing.

Thrift Stores

The Gold Mine
331 Walnut Ave. N., Ketchum
• **(208) 726-3465**

This thrift shop is run by the Community Library Association to raise funds for the town's excellent private library. It receives generous donations from the citizens of Sun Valley, who are known to keep up with the times with the latest in creature comforts and home trappings while jettisoning some very good stuff to the aptly named Gold Mine. At the upper end, a Land Rover was given to The Gold Mine to sell, and a precious silver setting was auctioned off. Where else do you find a ski shop within a thrift shop, where for a hundred bucks you can walk out with an entire ski or snowboard outfit — jacket, pants, cap, gloves, boots, skis, poles or bindings and board — that only leave you a few advertising campaigns behind the times? But this shop has much more than recreational items. It also has a broad assortment of clothes, books, appliances and furniture.

Attractions

Blaine County Native Arboretum
Wood River Trail, near Idaho Hwy. 75 and Fox Acres Rd., Hailey
• **(208) 788-2117**

This cooperative project of the Blaine County Recreation District and Sawtooth National Forest presents a sampling of Idaho plant communities from grassland to subalpine. A loop beside the Wood River Trail is planted with Aspen meadow, subalpine fir, Engelmann spruce, lodgepole pine, Douglas fir, ponderosa pine, grassland and sagebrush, limber pine, larch, juniper, and wildflowers. A free map and guide is available from the Blaine County Recreation District, 308 N. Main Street, Hailey, (208) 788-2117, or the Sawtooth National Forest, 121 N. River Street, Hailey, (208) 788-1850. There is no admission fee. The arboretum is open daily during daylight hours.

The Community Library
415 Spruce Ave., Ketchum
• **(208) 726-3493**

The Wood River Valley, strongly given to community involvement, waves a philanthropic banner at this unusual private library that receives no tax money from federal, state, county or city agencies. The Community Library Association was organized in 1955 by 17 local women who each contributed one dollar to a treasury and opened the Gold Mine Thrift Shop, whose proceeds were used to establish a library in 1957. (For more information about The Gold Mine, see Shopping in this chapter.)

The library moved from the thrift shop to its present site in 1976, doubled its size in 1986, added lecture and audiovisual rooms in 1989 and added a new Children's Library in 1996, when it also expanded its Regional History Department and Reference Room. In 1961, total expenses for operating the library and the Gold Mine were $4,435. In 1998 the projected cost is $1,109,015. This million-dollar volunteer organization is run by a 45-person board of directors, each of whom serves at least two volunteer hours a week. A staff of 14 paid employees handles the daily operation of the library.

The library has a broad circulation of hardcover books, cassettes, compact discs and videos; a reference library; an extensive Regional History Department; 175 periodicals and newspapers; paperback book trading; an audiovisual room; a twice-weekly story hour for preschoolers; library-science training for elementary-age schoolchildren during the school year; a summer reading program for children; and special programs in the Library Lecture Room.

The library is open 9 AM to 6 PM Monday and Saturday; noon to 9 PM Tuesday and Thursday; and 9 AM to 9 PM Wednesday. It's closed on Sunday.

Environmental Resource Center
411 E. Sixth St., Ketchum
• **(208) 726-4333**

Established in 1989, this nonprofit organization provides resources and educational programs about local, regional and global environmental issues. Its offices, library, conference room and gift shop receive more than 12,000 visitors each year. The staff includes an executive director, associate director, seasonal interns and a pool of more than 80 volunteers.

The center's Environmental Resource Library has computer catalogued books, magazines, videos, CD-Roms and extensive research files on local and global environmental issues. Its Work Center consists of desk space and computer terminals for organizing and researching environmental projects. A multipurpose Conference Room, which is available by reservation, is equipped with big-screen TV, a VCR and a slide projector and screen. The gift shop offers environmentally conscious products ranging from handcrafted jewelry to recycling bins. The center is open 10 AM to 5 PM Monday through Friday.

Ketchum-Sun Valley Heritage and Ski Museum
First and Washington Sts., Ketchum
• **(208) 726-8118**

This free museum is open seven days a week, except when it's closed in April and November. The simple little enclosure with stone tile floors and white walls is packed with nostalgia, memories and contemplative thoughts from the past. Exhibits rotate every six months. About 6,000 people visit annually for more background on Sun Valley. A History of the Olympics exhibit shows the participation of 50 people from the Wood River Valley in the Games. A 130-year-old piano that is without a scratch and has a beautiful tone was brought to the Wood River Valley in 1898 across the ocean from Denmark. Ski films are called up on a TV screen. A Hemingway exhibit explores the life of the great author in Idaho. Displays on mining, Basque sheep herding and wild-flowers are also presented. The museum is open from 1 to 5 PM daily.

Tour du Jour
(208) 788-3903

From April through the end of October, this company takes tours through wildlife refuges to view water birds, songbirds, raptors, big-game wildlife and an abundance of wildflowers. A four-hour tour of Silver Creek Preserve costs $50; a four-hour tour of the Carey Lake Wildlife Management Area is $50; and a six-hour tour of Centennial Marsh costs $65. Proprietor Poo Wright Pullman is licensed and bonded by the Idaho Outfitters and Guide Board and operates with a BLM special-use permit.

Events and Activities

The Wood River Valley has a tremendous physical, artistic and intellectual energy that is realized in events and activities throughout the year.

Sun Valley and Elkhorn Resorts organize many of the large events. There is also strong tradition and history in Ketchum and Hailey as well as widespread community zeal for sharing outings and holidays together. A short list of what the Wood River Valley has to offer follows.

The Sun Valley/Ketchum Chamber of Commerce, located at Fourth and Main streets in Ketchum, (208) 726-3423, has lists, fliers, schedules and pamphlets filled with current events and activities. The area's two well-read weekly newspapers, *The Idaho Mountain Express* in Ketchum and *The Wood River Journal* in Hailey, both of which come out on Wednesday and are available for free at many public locations, do a good job on advance reporting and covering of community activities.

January

Ski the Rails
Ketchum and Hailey • (208) 788-2117

This 20-mile cross-country ski tour sponsored by the Blaine County Recreation District promotes the Wood River Trail System, part of which follows the course of earlier railroad tracks. It's an easygoing event held the second week in January that is open to individuals of all ages, families and their dogs. Four refreshment stops along the way offer cold drinks, snacks, ski wax and extra poles. A free party is held after the tour. A hot, home-made lunch costs $8, and souvenir T-shirts, sweatshirts, fleece headbands and water bottles are on sale.

February

Gallery Walks
Ketchum and Sun Valley
• (208) 726-4174

For three hours on one evening in February, March, May, November and December some 25 galleries in Ketchum and Sun Valley open their doors to strollers. Wine is poured, hors d'oeuvres are offered, and artists are present to answer questions about their work. Most of the galleries are within walking distance of each other. Dress is casual, but this is a social event to see and be seen, so dressing up is not out of place.

Boulder Mountain Tour Annual Cross-Country Ski Race
Galena Lodge, Idaho Hwy. 75, 24 miles north of Ketchum • (208) 726-3423

This cross-country race attracts world-class skiers who complete the 30-kilometer course from Galena Lodge to the Sawtooth National Recreation Area in 75 minutes, novices who take five to six hours to get there, and those who fall in between. As many as 700 people take part. The race generally takes place on the first weekend of February. Participants must preregister during the month before the race.

March

Gallery Walks
Ketchum and Sun Valley
• (208) 726-4174

Galleries in Sun Valley and Ketchum treat passersby like royalty during this three-hour tour. Wine, refreshments and artists round out the evening. (See our entry under February for more information.)

Paw and Pole Cross-Country Race
Ketchum • (208) 788-4351

The Blaine County Animal Shelter sponsors this cross-country ski race in which owners compete with their dogs. Participants traditionally wear costumes, and a wide range of

awards are presented. This casual, fun family event raises money for the shelter.

May

Gallery Walks
Ketchum and Sun Valley
• (208) 726-4174

Art lovers should keep their eyes peeled

Photo: Sun Valley Chamber of Commerce

Golf is a popular summer pastime in Sun Valley.

for this one-night-only tour of Ketchum and Sun Valley's most popular galleries. For one evening in February, March, May, November and December, galleries offer their guests refreshments and the company of some of their most talented artists. (See our entry under February for more information.)

June

Jazz on the Green
Elkhorn Plaza at Sun Valley's Elkhorn Resort, Elkhorn Rd., Sun Valley • (208) 622-4511, (800) 737-0209

Bring a chair, blanket and picnic to this free jazz series on a grassy sweep of land beside a pond with three resident ducks. The Steve Miller Band, Big Head Todd and other local and nationally known musicians perform. The concerts attract thousands of spectators, and proceeds that are donated to charities or nonprofit organizations such as Women in Nordic Development, which developed a women's Olympic cross-country team. Jazz on the Green is held on Thursday evenings from June through August. Concerts begin around 6:30 and last until 9 PM.

The Sun Valley Ice Show
Sun Valley Resort, Sun Valley and Dollar Rds., Sun Valley • (208) 622-2231, (800) 786-8259

A live orchestra plays for individual presentations, skits and group numbers performed by champion ice skaters such as Oksana Baiul, Katarina Witt, Paul Wylie, Brian Boitano and Scott Hamilton. The outdoor rink is draped with evergreens and has a mountain backdrop. It's grand fun with humor, dash and elegance as well as a chance to see some of the world's best and most personable figure skaters close-up. Bleacher seats cost $27 to $47 for adults and $24 to $29 for children younger than 13. Seating in the Sun Valley Lodge's Sun Room Terrace costs $30 to $43. An excellent dinner buffet with the show costs $69 to $74 for adults and $51 to $56 for children younger than 13. Performances are staged on Saturday nights from the second week in June through mid-September.

July

Hailey Days of the Old West
Hailey • (208) 788-2700

The July 4th weekend in Hailey features a pancake breakfast, parade, barbecue, antique fair, rodeo and fireworks. The parade, which marches down the main road in Hailey, is notable for its Western authenticity that goes back to early days of settlement. The fireworks light up Hailey Saturday night.

Sun Valley Symphony Chamber Music Series
(208) 622-5607

Chamber music concerts are held throughout the Wood River Valley in late July. Nationally known musicians participate in these concerts.

Sun Valley Gallery Walking Tours
Meet at Ketchum Town Square, Fourth and Main Sts., Ketchum • (208) 726-4174

Take a guided tour through some 25 galleries to meet with artists and enjoy some tasty refreshments. The art ranges from blown glass to photography to abstract art. A large collection of landscapes and representational art that reflects the Sun Valley lifestyle are carried by the galleries. Works are fun, stimulating and keep with the lighthearted sophistication that characterizes the area. Tours are held Thursdays in July and August.

Jazz on the Green
Elkhorn Plaza at Sun Valley's Elkhorn Resort, Elkhorn Rd., Sun Valley • (208) 622-4511, (800) 737-0209

Thursday evenings in June, July and August come alive with the talent of area and visiting musicians. Thousands of people enjoy this free concert series that benefits nonprofit organizations in the Valley. (See our entry under June for more information.)

The Sun Valley Ice Show
Sun Valley Resort, Sun Valley and Dollar Rds., Sun Valley • (208) 622-2231, (800) 786-8259

Olympic hopefuls turned Olympic legends perform at this ice-skating extravaganza staged on Saturday nights from the second week in June until mid-September. An orchestra supplies the music, Sun Valley's natural wonders serve as the sets and your favorite ice-skaters provide the entertainment. (See our entry under June for more information.)

August

Sun Valley Writer's Conference
Community School, 181 Dollar Rd., Sun Valley • (208) 622-3955

Nationally known writers provide lectures, readings and Q&A sessions during a four-day conference in August. This is an "idea" rather than a "how-to" conference. Ideas, experiences and thoughts about writing are presented rather than cut-and-dried skills. The conference has featured top writers such as David Halberstam, Peter Mathiessen and William Stryon. Writers, prospective writers and readers are encouraged to attend.

Northern Rockies Folk Festival
Hop Pointer City Park, Bullion St., Hailey • (208) 788-0183

This three-day folk festival held in early August goes back more than 20 years and features performances by groups from throughout the United States and the Wood River Valley. Music workshops for children are also offered.

Sun Valley Center Arts & Crafts Festival
Grounds of the Sun Valley Resort, Sun Valley • (208) 726-9491

Anywhere from 120 to 140 artisans from throughout the country present their work at this annual festival that is rated in the top 20 nationally for this type of event. The event is held the second weekend in August.

Sun Valley Wine Auction
Sun Valley • (208) 726-9491

Local restaurants with superb vineyards roll out their top grape varietals for the Sun Valley Wine Auction. The four-day extravaganza in mid-August includes dozens of vintners and winery owners from California, Washington, Oregon and Idaho; live and silent auctions held at an annual dinner dance typically attended by 500 people; and a tent-covered tasting featuring 200 wines that is typically attended by 800 to 1,200 people. As much as $400,000 has been raised at this event to benefit the year-round programs of the Sun Valley Center for the Arts and Humanities.

Danny Thompson Memorial Golf Tournament
Sun Valley Resort and Sun Valley's Elkhorn Resort, Sun Valley • (208) 726-1049

This celebrity/charity tournament played in August at the area's two top golf courses raises money for leukemia and cancer research in the name of former Minnesota Twins' shortstop Danny Thompson. It's a chance to rub elbows with nationally known political and show people in the context of a tournament challenge. The tournament is generally held the third week in August/

Jazz on the Green
Elkhorn Plaza at Sun Valley's Elkhorn Resort, Elkhorn Rd., Sun Valley • (208) 622-4511, (800) 737-0209

Elkhorn Resort plays host to this outdoor concert series on Thursday evenings in June, July and August. Past performers have included The Steve Miller Band and Big Head Todd. (See our entry under June for more information.)

The Sun Valley Ice Show
Sun Valley Resort, Sun Valley and Dollar Rds., Sun Valley • (208) 622-2231, (800) 786-8259

Whether you sit in the bleachers or catch the show from Sun Valley Lodge's Sun Room Terrace, don't miss this production staged by champion ice-skaters. Former performers have included Oksana Baiul and Paul Wylie. (See our entry under June for more information.)

Sun Valley Symphony Chamber Music Series
Sun Valley Resort, Sun Valley and Dollar Rds., Sun Valley • (208) 622-5607

The Sun Valley Symphony performs a series of 12 open-air concerts at the Sun Valley Resort in early August.

Sun Valley Gallery Walking Tours
Meet at Ketchum Town Square, Fourth and Main Sts., Ketchum • (208) 726-4174

Ever wonder just what possessed an artist to use a particular color or create a particular piece? Well here's your chance to ask. Twenty-five galleries participate in these Thursday tours held in July and August. (See our entry under July for more information.)

September

Ketchum Wagon Days
Sun Valley and Ketchum
• (208) 726-3423

This carnival features antique fairs, a bull-riding contest, music festival and giant ore wagons. The Big Hitch Parade, believed to be the largest nonmotorized parade in the West, features wagons that are authentic remnants of the Wood River Valley's heritage. About 10,000 spectators line the parade route. A flap-jack breakfast, miner's lunch, fiddlers, Western humor, classic cars and a street dance are included in the fun. The event is held over Labor Day weekend.

The Sun Valley Ice Show
Sun Valley Resort, Sun Valley and Dollar Rds., Sun Valley • (208) 622-2231, (800) 786-8259

This is your last chance to catch former gold medalists jump, spin and glide in Sun Valley. Accompanied by an orchestra and the natural beauty of Sun Valley's environs, the ice-skating performances couldn't be any more magical. (See our entry under June for more information.)

Octoberfest
Best Western Tyrolean Lodge, 260 Cottonwood Dr., Ketchum
• (208) 726-5336

Arts and crafts booths, a German band and cloggers are part of this celebration of food and beer. It's held on grounds behind the Best Western Tyrolean Lodge, across the street from the River Run Plaza and lifts at Bald Mountain. Octoberfest is held the third week in September.

Shakespeare Festival
Best Western Tyrolean Lodge, 260 Cottonwood Dr., Ketchum
• (208) 726-5336

The Idaho Shakespeare Company, which performs throughout the summer in Boise, comes to Ketchum for several performances on the grounds outside the Best Western Tyrolean Lodge. This is an excellent theater group with a large Boise following that typically sells out its Ketchum engagements. Tickets cost $15 for these performances, which are staged the last week in September.

October

Swing 'n' Dixie Jazz Jamboree
Sun Valley Resort and Sun Valley's Elkhorn Resort, Sun Valley
• (208) 344-3768, (800) 484-9602

Ragtime, jazz and swing music played by 26 bands from the United States, Canada, Australia and Sweden are featured in this five-day event that is held at 12 resort and town locations. Dancing, Great Ladies of Song and Legends of Jazz presentations, and Afterglow Jazz Suppers are included in the activities. An all-events badge costs $60; one-day tickets are $15. The event takes place in mid-October.

November

Gallery Walks
Ketchum and Sun Valley
• (208) 726-4174

Wine, hors d'oeuvres, fine art. If this sounds like your kind of evening, keep your ear to the ground for details about this three-hour tour of Ketchum and Sun Valley art galleries. (See our entry under February for more information.)

Ski with a Snow Ranger
Lookout Restaurant, on the top of Bald Mountain at Sun Valley Ski Resort
• (208) 622-5371

Skiers meet with a Sawtooth National Forest ranger for a mountain tour. All ability levels are welcome. The subjects covered by the ranger include the early history of the area, future plans for the ski area, the towns of

Ketchum and Sun Valley and avalanche control. Tours are held Tuesdays and Thursdays during the ski season, which runs from Thanksgiving through Easter.

December

Gallery Walks
Ketchum and Sun Valley
• (208) 726-4174
Artists step out of their studios and into the area's most popular galleries during this tour offered in February, March, May, November and December. (See our entry under February for more information.)

Sun Valley Christmas Eve Torchlight Parade
Dollar Mountain, Sun Valley
• (208) 622-2135
Skiers, snowboarders and snow vehicles descend the mountain in a torchlight procession through the dark during this traditional holiday event. The grand illumination begins at 5:30 PM on December 24.

New Year's Eve Bonfire
Downtown Ketchum • (208) 726-3423
Hot cocoa and music accompany a warming blaze to create a casual, outdoor welcome to New Year's for families, friends and acquaintances.

The Arts

Year-round artistic activity in Sun Valley includes exhibits, stage performances, concerts, workshops and festivals. The Wood River Arts Alliance and the Sun Valley Center for the Arts & Humanities are the two major organizing groups. Sun Valley is loaded with artistic talent that has moved to the Wood River Valley to escape from the frantic commercial pace of other areas. Singers, dancers, musicians, painters, sculptors and actors who are widely known in their particular realms and sometimes by the public at large appear now and then, or on a whim, often in low-key or surprising fashion at nonprofit, holiday or summer events.

Organizations

Sun Valley Center for the Arts and Humanities
191 Fifth St., Ketchum • (208) 726-9491
The center mounts eight to 10 art exhibits a year that are free to the public. Some exhibits are museum-quality with no works for sale; others feature contemporary Northwest painters; and still others showcase artists that are internationally known. Most of the exhibits focus on the 20th century. Examples include the black-and-white documentary photography of Robert Frank in Paris and photographer Christina Patoski's *Front Yard Views of Christmas*, which shows Christmas as a commercial and spiritual blend that is not differentiated by some Americans.

Exhibits in the spacious, well-lighted gallery are sometimes augmented by music, such as a string quartet, lectures, classes or workshops. The center is involved in other community events such as an annual jazz festival held in October; a film festival that is held in April or May; a July wine auction that is its big fundraiser; and an arts-and-crafts festival held in August.

The center was started by Bill Janss, a former owner of Sun Valley Resort, in 1971 in order to establish an organization in the Wood River Valley that would focus on the arts and humanities. It now has more than 500 supporting members.

The Wood River Arts Alliance

The Wood River Arts Alliance, (208) 788-4244 or (208) 726-3576, brings various volunteer arts groups together so that they can coordinate schedules, exchange ideas and promote performances and activities.

The Ballet Foundation
(208) 726-1280
The Ballet Foundation is affiliated with Ballet Idaho in Boise and gives one annual performance in Sun Valley each spring. It offers dance classes and workshops for children 4 and older in spring and summer.

Boulder Mountain Clay Works
(208) 726-4484

Boulder Mountain Clay Works has a studio where people of all ages may learn ceramic art from local and guest instructors.

Company of Fools
(208) 788-6520

This Hailey company has Bruce Willis on its board of directors. It occasionally presents theater pieces such as *Our Town* and *Fool for Love*.

Footlight Dance
Sun Valley Athletic Club, 131 First Ave., Ketchum • (208) 726-3664

Classes are held in ballet, tap, jazz and modern dance for students age 4 to adult. The cost is $6 to $10 a class. Guest instructors have included flamenco and African dancers. Each February the group gives a performance.

Laughing Stock Theatre Company
(208) 726-3576

This theater company has presented family-orientated musicals and comedies for 20 years, including *Oklahoma*, *Annie* and Neil Simon plays. Professionals and semiprofessionals are in the casts. The company stages at least two performances a year and appears at various locations.

Mary Poppen Children's Choir
(208) 788-1474

This choir presents holiday concerts at churches or halls. The children are 7 to 16 years old.

The New Theatre Company
(208) 726-2271

The New Theatre Company stages modern, cutting-edge plays written by well-known playwrights. Performances are staged at different times of the year at various locations.

Pro Musica
(208) 788-9261

Pro Musica stages one opera each year that stars a well-known opera singer.

Sun Valley Repertory Company
(208) 726-0150

Sun Valley Repertory Company produces Christmas and midsummer shows at the Nex Stage Theatre, 120 S. Main Street, Ketchum.

Sun Valley Summer Symphony
(208) 622-5607

The symphony presents 12 summer concerts during a three-week period every August either in a picnic area or in a tent at Sun Valley Resort. It may be the largest free concert series in the West. (See Events and Activities in this chapter.)

Galleries

Sun Valley Gallery Association

The 12 member galleries of the Sun Valley Gallery Association, (208) 726-4950, feature a wide variety of fine art and crafts by internationally, nationally and regionally known artists. Collectively, the members of the association represent more than 500 artists. Free gallery walks, held once a month on Friday or Saturday evenings in February, March, May, July, August, November and December, offer an opportunity to view new exhibitions and visit with many of the artists. (See Events and Activities in this chapter for more information.)

African Fine Arts
601 Sun Valley Rd., Ketchum
• (208) 726-3144

This gallery specializes in museum-quality works of art from West, Central and Southern Africa. Featured are carvings by five of

Zimbabwe's world-renowned sculptors: John Chihowa, Nicholas Tandi, Richard Mteki, Marshall Sithole and Norbert Shamuyarira. Also on display are handwoven mohair rugs and tapestries, traditional and contemporary wood and stone carvings, baskets, ceremonial masks, beads, jewelry and music.

Anne Reed Gallery
620 Sun Valley Rd., Ketchum
• **(208) 726-3036**

This gallery features 20th-century painting, sculpture and photography by Jan Aronson, Lynda Benglis, Howard Ben Tre, Joel Brock, John Buck, Deborah Butterfield, Wendell Castle, Russell Chatham, Clarice Dreyer, Janet Fish and George Geyer. Charles Ginnever, Doug Granum, Gregory Grenon, Carol Hepper, Wade Hoefer, Kenro Izu, Jun Kaneko, Jesus Bautista Moroles, Manuel Neri, Gary Nisbet, Jim Palmersheim and Theodore Waddell are also represented.

Broschofsky Galleries
Sixth St. and Leadville Ave., Ketchum
• **(208) 726-4950**

Fine art from the 19th and 20th centuries are featured here. Displays include historic photographs by Edward S. Curtis, paintings by early artists of the West and contemporary Western paintings by William Matthews. Also featured are Native American imagery by Ted Villa, regional landscape paintings and modernistic and abstract works. The gallery offers a fine selection of historic Navajo weavings, pueblo pottery and artifacts.

Friesen Gallery • Fine Art
511 Building, Fifth St. and Leadville Ave., Ketchum • **(208) 726-4174**

The gallery exhibits paintings, sculpture and glass. Contemporary artists represented are Martin Blank, Patricia Davidson, Mark Dickson, Enrico Embroli, Steve Jensen, Sylvain Klaus and Tom Lieber. You'll also find the works of Dante Marioni, William Morris, Richard Royal, Darren Vigil Gray, Malei Young and Brandon Zebold.

Gail Severn Gallery
620 Sun Valley Rd., Ketchum
• **(208) 726-5079**

Contemporary painting, sculpture, photog-

raphy and fine craft are on display here. Artists include David Bates, Divit Cardoza, Dale Chihuly, James Cook, Edward Curtis, Dennis Evans, Michael Gregory, Morris Graves, Robert Helm and Richard Jolley. James Lavadour, Alden Mason, Nancy Mee, Gwynn Murrill, Don Nice, Joseph Raffael, Brad Rude, Italo Scanga, Julie Speidel, Mark Stasz, Therman Statom and David Wharton are also represented.

Kneeland Gallery
271 First Ave. N., Ketchum
• **(208) 726-5512**

The gallery exhibits paintings, sculpture and jewelry, with a focus on nationally known artists living in the West. An eclectic range of styles encompasses impressionism, realism and expressionism. Artists include Steven Lee Adams, Ovanes Berberian, George Carlson, John Horejs, Donna Howell Sickles, Linda Lillegraven, Jacqueline Rochester and Barbara Savage.

Pinson Fine Art
620 Sun Valley Rd., Ketchum
• **(208) 726-8461**

The surreal and floral paintings and sculpture of Sun Valley resident Joseph Kinnebrew are represented by Pinson Fine Art. Kinnebrew's work is found in prominent corporate collections and in permanent collections of more than 20 museums including the Guggenheim Museum and the Art Institute of Chicago. Studio visits can be arranged by the gallery.

River Run Gallery
291 First Ave. N., Ketchum
• **(208) 726-8878**

Exhibited artists at River Run Gallery include Cie Goulet, Jean Richardson, Doug West, Sari Staggs, Wendy Weldon and Selene Santucci. The gallery also displays fine crafts by nationally recognized artists in glass, jewelry, clay and metal, such as Ken Carlson, Craig Zweifel, Patrick Dragon and Bruce Anderson.

Sleeping Bear Gallery
601 Sun Valley Rd., Ketchum
• **(208) 726-3059**

Sleeping Bear Gallery features original

work by artists living in the West with a focus on representational and impressionistic paintings, ceramics and sculpture. Artists include Arlene Bowden, Peg Bodell, Gary Holland, Martha Saudek, Douglas Sievers, William Vincent, Bobbie West and Thomas Wezwick.

Stonington Gallery
220 East Ave., Ketchum • (208) 726-4826

An eclectic collection of fine arts and crafts by emerging and established artists is on display here. Local watercolors and limited-edition prints by Nancy Taylor Stonington, batiks and prints by Jennifer Bellinger, photographs by Ed Collins and bronzes by Robert Deurloo are exhibited.

Sun Valley Center for the Arts and Humanities
Fifth St. and Washington Ave., Ketchum
• (208) 726-9491

This nonprofit arts organization has been providing cultural and educational programming in the performing and visual arts for more than 25 years. Its gallery represents contemporary artists and provides a venue for educational and museum exhibits.

Toneri Art Gallery
620 Sun Valley Rd., Ketchum
• (208) 726-5639

Watercolorist Lynn Toneri, the gallery owner, creates strong, brilliant images that challenge the medium. Her diverse interests transform the gallery with constantly changing themes. She paints vast mountain scenes, glorified waterfowl and waterfowl on wing with an eye for detail that goes beyond realism. A wide range of contemporary artists working in a variety of styles and media are also represented.

Other Galleries

Art(x)Soul/Ochi Gallery
511 Building, Fifth St. and Leadville Ave.
• (208) 726-9123

The focus here is on art that is alive and drenched with the essence of culture. Small scale and editioned treasures by contemporary American masters as well as mid-career and emerging artists are on display, such as

Arnoldi, Francis, Berlant, Fischl, Hunt and Moses. Art books and gifts are also available.

Davies Reed Tribal Arts
140 Sun Valley Rd., Ketchum
• (208) 726-3453

Tribal rugs and Kelims and antique Oriental rugs are exhibited here. The gallery represents Woven Legends, Michaelian and Kohlberg, Tufenkian Carpets and Material Culture Furnishings. It also has textiles, artifacts and architectural finds from India, China and Pakistan.

Dream Catcher Southwest Gallery
Trail Creek Village, 200 S. Main St.,
Ketchum • (208) 726-1305

The gallery displays Native American pottery, jewelry, handicrafts and ceremonial pieces of museum quality. It has the largest Jemez Storyteller collection in the region, with pieces from Zuni, Acoma, Hopi, Navajo and Mohawk artists. It also has books for collectors and children.

Environmental Resource Center
Sixth St. and Leadville Ave.
• (208) 726-4333

This nonprofit educational organization has a fine art gallery where local artists exhibit works that address environmental themes. The gallery lighting is state-of-the-art, energy efficient, compact fluorescents. (See Attractions in this chapter for more information about the center.)

Hughes Jewel Gallery
Clarion Inn of Sun Valley, Sixth St. and
Leadville Ave., Ketchum
• (208) 726-3313

Fine jewelry by DeBeers Award-winning jeweler Vint Lee Hughes is on display here. Local jewelry and gem artists are also featured as well as fossil and gem specimens from around the world. Professional pearl knotting and jewelry repair and design are also offered.

Stoecklein Gallery
Tenth St., across from the Knob Hill Inn,
Ketchum • (208) 726-5191

The gallery represents the photography of David R. Stoecklein, including pieces from his exhibits at the Cowboy Hall of Fame and American Quarter Horse Museum. Stoecklein's photographic library houses a million Western, lifestyle and Sun Valley area images, all of which are available as signed original gallery prints and stock photography.

Sun Valley Art Gallery
Sun Valley Mall, east of Sun Valley and Dollar Rds. intersection, Sun Valley
• **(208) 622-2269**

The nationally acclaimed work of Jane Wooster Scott, including her original paintings, prints and cards that depict the magic of Sun Valley in all seasons, are featured here. You'll also find the scenic watercolors of Don "Bemco" Bennett and the local area photographs of Kevin Syms.

Turpen's Southwest Trading Company
The Colonnade, Sun Valley Rd. and Walnut Ave., Ketchum • (208) 726-4402

The Turpen family offers fine Indian and Southwestern arts and crafts as well as artifacts, Kachinas, drums, Navajo weavings and items for home decoration.

Recreation

Skiing was a new sport in 1936 when Union Pacific opened the Sun Valley Resort. Except for a few rope tows in New England, ski lifts were unknown in the United States. James Curran, a structural engineer, suggested applying the same cable tram that he had used for loading bananas onto fruit boats for transporting skiers. His idea led to Sun Valley's first ski lift and the great success of Sun Valley Resort and tourism throughout the Wood River Valley.

More than 60 years later, downhill skiing is still king here — the reason why most people visit. In 1996-97 ski season there were 436,700 skier visits to Bald and Dollar mountains. But the growth of the sport has been flat here as elsewhere with the great increase of snowboarding propping up lift ticket sales. Nordic, or cross-country, skier days have grown rapidly in Sun Valley, from 69,600 in 1991-92 to 96,500 in 1996-97.

As with downhill skiing, ice skating has always been popular at Sun Valley Resort and continues to be so year-round. The Wood River Valley and the mountainous, water-fed territory that cradles it are well-known for fly-fishing and hiking. A wonderful 12-mile bicycle path runs right through town. Two Robert Trent Jones Jr. golf courses, cloaked in rare scenic beauty, tempt duffers visiting Sun Valley. Tennis and swimming are also prevalent here.

There are recreational opportunities here that are not found in many other places. Heliskiing, being transported by helicopter to skiing terrain otherwise difficult or impossible to access, has been available here for more than 30 years, longer than anywhere else in the Lower 48. Dog sledding, hut-to-hut skiing, paragliding, soaring and snowmobiling are not commonly found together in one compact territory — Sun Valley is a rare and wonderful exception.

Several shops in the area rent and sell outdoors equipment such as skis and ski accessories, snowboards, bicycles and in-line skates. For a list of these stores and a general idea of rental costs, see Sports Shops under the Shopping section of this chapter.

Some Snow Required

Downhill Skiing and Snowboarding

Bald Mountain

Sun Valley's Bald Mountain is one of the finest downhill ski mountains in the country. It's actually a gigantic ski hill, without the rock peaks or spires that rise above many ski areas. It's smooth on top, which is how it got its name. The mountain is accessed from two sides that are more than a mile above sea level: at River Run in Ketchum and just north at Warm Springs, situated beside a valley creek. The highest mountain point is 9,154 feet, which allows for a very respectable 3,400-foot vertical drop.

Baldy, to her friends, has 78 ski runs and 2,054 skiable acres. The mountain's 14 chair lifts include seven high-speed quads that rapidly take skiers up the mountain. The Challenger lift at Warm Springs rises, from bottom to top, 3,142 feet in 10 minutes. A tremendous lift capacity means that lift lines are rare and skiers get all the downhill action they can handle.

Baldy is most distinguished by its long cruiser runs on continuous grades that are enjoyed by intermediate, advanced and expert skiers. There are outstanding mogul, or bump inclines, and a series of expert and advanced bowls with long, challenging, bump descents that test style and endurance. From above, there are staggering 360-degree panoramic views of mountains, valleys, towns, rivers and lakes. The construction of the Seattle Ridge Day Lodge on top of the mountain and the Warm Springs and River Run lodges at the two access points on the bottom brought stylish modern architecture and top dining and a relaxed atmosphere to the mountain. The snowmaking system is one of the best and most extensive in the world: It can cover almost a third of the mountain with machine-made flakes, making skiing and snowboarding not only possible, but also enjoyable when Mother Nature is uncooperative. (See our Close-up in this chapter for more information.)

The Warm Springs side of the mountain, shaped like an enormous half-pipe, is especially attractive to snowboarders. The mountain's cold morning temperatures and combination of natural and machine-made snow create a dense surface that is perfect for making radical arcs without losing an edge. River Run is also shaped like a half-pipe and is best ridden by snowboarders in early afternoon when the sun illuminates Baldy.

Full-day lift tickets are $52 for adults and $29 for children 11 and younger. Half-day tickets, good from after 1 PM to 4 PM when the lifts close, are $37 for adults and $21 for children 11 and younger. For more information about ski lift rates, call (208) 622-2231.

Like most ski areas, Sun Valley's season runs from Thanksgiving through Easter. However, Sun Valley has an unusual snowmaking capacity that can allow skiing earlier in November when below-freezing temperatures permit the making of snow. (See our Close-up in this chapter.)

Dollar Mountain

A second ski mountain at Sun Valley is Dollar Mountain, which has 13 runs, three double and one triple chair lifts and a vertical drop of 628 feet. This mountain, located five minutes from Baldy behind Sun Valley's Elkhorn Resort, is a seldom found learning and beginners slope all to itself. At most ski areas, beginners ski at the bottom of the regular mountain and can be intimidated by more advanced skiers whizzing through, by crowds of people going up the mountain and by the sight of "hairy" descents. Lump that with unfamiliar equipment, cold temperatures, high altitude and a need to master riding the lifts and it can be a dizzying experience. Dollar Mountain is the perfect option for the skittish skier.

Full-day lift tickets are $24 for adults and $17 for children 11 and younger. Half-day tickets run $16 for adults and $10 for children. For more information about ski lift rates in Sun Valley, call (208) 622-2231.

Ski and Snowboarding Instruction
(208) 622-2248

Sun Valley has 200 downhill and cross-country ski and snowboarding instructors. Friedl Pfeiffer and Otto Lang, well known in ski circles, have served as the school's directors, and this tradition of excellence has continued under the direction of Rainer Kolb since 1994. Aside from regular adult clinics and private lessons, there are women's intermediate to advanced clinics, snowboarding and cross-country classes and children's ski programs.

The fastest growing skier segments at Sun Valley are children and women. Children now start learning at ages 3 to 4 in Tiny Tracks programs, and Ski Wee clinics are tailored to the needs of ages 5 to 12. Women's intermediate-advanced clinics are taught by women, because it has been found that women respond better to female instructors. The primary focus of the clinics is balance, overcoming fear and working with equipment.

Groups sessions, running three hours, are $47 for one day, $90 for two days, $125 for three days and $180 for five days. (There's a two-person minimum for these classes.) A private lesson is $79 for one hour or $360 for the day.

The Women's Clinics are $170 for two days, $270 for three days or $380 for five days.

Children's Clinics, for ages 5 to 12, last for four hours. The charge is $65 for one day, $120 for two days, $170 for three days and $250 for five days. Tiny Track sessions for kids ages 3 to 4 are one hour and cost $22.

The Snowboard Clinic is $44 for two hours of instruction.

Cross-Country Skiing

Sun Valley Nordic and Snowshoe Center
Sun Valley Rd., Sun Valley
• (208) 622-2250, (800) 786-8259

The center is just above the Sun Valley Resort and Sun Valley Inn. Ski rentals, accessories, a wax room, a sunny deck and refreshments are available daily from 9 AM to 5 PM throughout the winter season. Forty kilometers, or about 25 miles, of marked trails begin at the Nordic Center. Gentle terrain at the trailhead progresses to challenging hills. Ten different loops that range in distance from 1 to 7 kilometers are available for use. A wide variety of skate skiing and ski touring is possible over glistening meadows at 6,000 feet. Telemark skiers get a lift on nearby Dollar Mountain, and telemark instruction continues from there to Bald Mountain. One of the most popular Sun Valley experiences is the 2-kilometer trip over gentle terrain to Trail Creek Cabin (see The Splendid Boondocks under Restaurants in this chapter). Spectacular views

of open meadows and meandering Trail Creek lead to a roaring fire at the cabin. Ski touring in the nearby Sawtooth Recreation Area may also be arranged at the center. Snowshoeing, the fastest growing outdoor winter activity, is also offered at the center on 6 kilometers of groomed and ungroomed trails. Snowshoes are available for rent: $13 for the whole day.

A daily maintenance fee is $11 for adults and $6 for children ages 6 to 12. No fee is charged for children younger than 6.

Ski instruction is offered at $18 for groups or $49 for a one-hour private lesson. Classical rental ski packages are $15 for the whole day; children's rental ski packages are $10.

Galena Lodge
Idaho Hwy. 75, 24 miles north of Ketchum • (208) 726-4010

Galena has a colorful history dating back to the late 1870s when the first mining claims were made in the area. The name "Galena" refers to basic ore, largely made of lead mixed with silver, that was found in the Senate and Gladiator mines. By 1879, Galena was a thriving community of 700 people making their living in the mines, mills and smelters. In 1890, Galena was a ghost town, and it lay fairly dormant for 100 years. The lodge was remodeled and renovated to its present state in 1987. The property was put up for sale in 1992. For two years the lodge remained closed and empty.

Facing a U.S. Forest Service deadline to remove the buildings, a volunteer committee formed to "help save Galena." Community support was overwhelming. Not long after the fundraising effort started, Teresa Heinz offered a $325,000 donation in memory of her husband, Senator John Heinz. In just three months, more than 1,000 people donated the additional $200,000 needed to establish an endowment fund for Galena's future.

Now Galena is an exciting cross-country skiing, bicycling and hiking destination for the people of the Wood River Valley who preserved its history and recreational opportunities as well as visitors to the area who are smart enough to realize a good thing when they see one.

The lodge is at 7,300 feet of elevation. *Snow Country* magazine has rated the lodge and its North Valley Trails as "arguably the best cross-country trail system in the country." There are more than 50 kilometers of ski trails in the immediate Galena area and miles of snowshoe and doggie trails where dogs accompany their owners. Overnight ski-in huts, a historic day lodge with a roaring fire that serves lunch daily, and a complete ski shop that offers ski rentals and lessons, complete the picture. In winter the lodge is open daily from Thanksgiving to Easter; the summer season is mid-June to mid-September.

A daily trail pass is $11 for adults and $2 for children 16 and younger. Season passes are available: $60 for singles, $110 for couples, $120 for a family of up to four people and $10 for dogs.

Full-day ski rental packages are $15 for adults, $9 for children 16 and younger. Snowshoe rental costs $10 for adults and $6 for children for the full day.

The lodge also offers ski lessons for $20 a person. There's also a package that includes

Snowmaking on Baldy
Assures a White Christmas

Five hundred and fifty-two yellow-hooded hydrants with guns sticking out line the Bald Mountain ski slopes. A master computer commands mist from these slaves that freezes snow onto 630 of the mountain's 2,000 skiable acres. It's not a cheap or easy system at a daily cost of $3,000 and the labor of 12 people each day necessary to operate. But it's very effective. Christmas 1997 was sold out at Sun Valley because of this artificial cover, when it otherwise would have been a bleak holiday season of cancellations and skier disgust because of an inadequate natural topping.

Close-up

Earl Holding, the owner of Sun Valley Resort, spent $2.6 million in 1989, $10.2 million in 1990 and a total of $16 million by 1998 on a system that has contributed to Sun Valley's No. 1 U.S. winter resort status and has assured a dollar flow even on dry winter months.

— continued on next page

Photo: Kevin Syms

Machine-made flakes at Sun Valley satisfy even the most finicky skier.

Traditionally, resorts pray for November and December snows that make them skiable during the critical Thanksgiving and Christmas holidays, when downhillers are hungry for action and have time and money to spend. Now Earl Holding and Sun Valley have those precious time slots in the bank as long as air temperature is cold enough — freezing — to turn spray into dense, white cover.

At Sun Valley, water for its illusion of natural-born flakes is drawn from two sources. On the Warm Springs, or north side, of the mountain, 46-degree creek water is drawn into the system and on the River Run, or eastern, side, 48-degree well water is tapped. The captured pools are cooled and mixed like a cocktail at an 11-to-1 air-to-water ratio as they waft onto the slopes. That's about as lean and loose as the man-made stuff gets. In climates with more moisture, the ratio can plunge to 3-to-1, making the snow a thick cement that is not fun to carve.

As far as Holding is concerned, he's spent so much on the system, he'd like to see it go full blast around the clock, 24 hours a day, so he'd always have enough, no matter what the weather does. He'd like to pile it up for a dry day, so to speak. But natural snow is the preferable, more aesthetic and softer skiing surface, so if that's there, it doesn't make sense to damage it with a coarse blanket. Night and day "bartenders" under the tutelage of snowmaking manager Peter Stearns shore up what's already there, making sure to cover areas with high skier traffic and excessive wind and sun exposure. There are about six areas around the mountain that they concentrate on, and they'll put down about 3 inches of cover before moving on to the next spot via handy computers in mountain offices where they study network diagrams on color screens.

The York Automatic Snow, Inc. system is a spin-off of York Refrigeration, out of York, Pennsylvania. Sun Valley snowmaking begins on November 1, when it takes about three weeks to lay white carpets to the top of the mountain. The manufacture of the tiny-as-possible particles continues to the end of March.

---

lessons, rentals and a trail pass: $35 for adults and $25 for children.

Three ski-in huts on the property sleep six people and have fireplaces, wood-burning stoves and propane gas stoves. They rent for $100 a weekend night or $75 a weekday night.

Other Skiing Options

Sun Valley Heli-Ski
(208) 726-6850, (800) 872-3108

For more than 30 years, Sun Valley Heli-Ski has flown skiers into the dramatic backcountry that surrounds Sun Valley. The company's U.S. Forest Service permit has grown to approximately 750 square miles — one of the largest in the continental United States. The company offers a guide/guest ratio of 1 to 4 for skiing or snowboarders on three mountain ranges and tailors adventures to the abilities and desires of its clients, who can be powder newcomers or seasoned veterans. Prices start at $300 for a half-day and $500 for a full day of skiing 6,000 vertical feet. Seven nights of lodging and 30,000 vertical feet of skiing costs $1,784.

Backcountry Ski Adventures
Sun Valley Trekking Co., 1660 2 Avenue N., Hailey • (208) 788-9585

Hut-to-hut skiing, one-day tours, Telemark instruction and multiday treks in remote wilderness are the specialties of this outfitter and guide service that was founded in 1982. The company owns five backcountry huts, at elevations ranging from 6,200 to 7,400 feet, that are equipped with wood stoves, pre-cut firewood, propane cooking units, kitchens, bunk beds and wood-fired hot tubs. Food and other suppliers must be carried in by skiers. Hut tours cost $125 to $150 a person a day; hut rentals cost $25 a night a person and $10 a person for day use; guide service and instruction costs $125 to $200 a day; and porter service costs $100 a porter a day.

Sawtooth Hut Skiing
Stanley • (208) 774-3324

Sawtooth Mountain Guides in Stanley, 61 miles north of Ketchum/Sun Valley, offers guided trips through the Sawtooth Mountains for $150 a day. Three huts in the Sawtooths rent for $30 a person a night. The huts have kitchenware, a wood stove and bunks — food and other supplies must be carried in by skiers. This is some of the most scenic country in Idaho, where granite spires rise above 10,000 feet.

Dogsledding

Sled Dog Adventures
(208) 788-3522

Brian Camilli of Hailey has five years of mushing experience, a staff that has backcountry skills and veterinary knowledge, and Alaskan huskies who train all year. They take people by sled over snowpacked trails through Idaho backcountry. One-and-a-half-hour trips cost $85; half-day trips over Muldoon summit to a rustic warming hut, where hot drinks and snacks are served, along with spectacular views of the Pioneer Mountains, cost $125; full-day trips that include a gourmet lunch cost $200; and an overnight trip to an 1870s cabin with wood stove that includes an evening meal, breakfast, snowshoeing or cross-country skiing costs $350.

Snowmobiling

Smiley Creek Lodge
Idaho Hwy. 75, 37 miles north of Ketchum • (208) 774-3547

The lodge is just north of Galena Summit on the valley floor, near the headwaters of the Salmon River. Groomed trails, which traverse the beautiful Stanley Basin, link Smiley Creek to Stanley and Lowman. They offer breathtaking views of the Sawtooth Mountains. There are also many ungroomed trails up major drainages in the adjacent, 760,000-acre Sawtooth National Recreation Area. Snowmobile daily rentals cost $99 for a single rider on

a machine; $149 for two riders on a machine; $15 for a snowmobile suit; and $5 for boots. Smiley Creek Lodge has rooms and cabins for rent that cost $40 to $70. It also has a restaurant, convenience store, RV Park and Laundromat.

Sawtooth Rentals Inc.
Idaho Hwy. 75, Stanley • (208) 774-3409, (800) 284-3185

Sawtooth Rentals Inc. is in Stanley, 61 miles north of Ketchum and Sun Valley. The Stanley Basin has 160 miles of groomed terrain for all levels of snowmobile riding experience. Guides are available for trips to Dagger Falls, Stanley Lake, Elk Meadows, Red Fish Lake and the headwaters of the Salmon River. Snowmobile daily rentals cost $100 for a single rider on a standard machine; $149 for two riders on a machine; $159 for a single rider on a high-performance machine; $150 for a guide with snowmobile; $15 for snowmobile suits; and $5 for boots. The company has a log motel with 16-foot decks that overlooks the Salmon River as well as log cabins and upstairs apartments. Rooms cost $55 or $75 a night.

No Snow Required

Bicycling

Sun Valley is circled by more than 12 miles of newly constructed or newly paved trails that provide practical transportation as well as good exercise and wonderful views. The 10-foot-wide path is lined with wildflowers and landscaping that reflects the Wood River Valley, and tumbling brooks and surrounding mountains provide constantly changing, invigorating scenery. The path runs along Sun Valley Road, continues beside the Big Wood River in Ketchum and circles around on Elkhorn Road through Sun Valley's Elkhorn Resort before passing near Sun Valley Lodge on Dollar Road. One good place to park is at River Run Day Lodge at the base of Bald Mountain, where the trail passes by and there is plenty of space for cars.

Sun Valley also has two of the best-known mountain-biking stretches in Idaho.

Adams Gulch is a beginner-to-intermediate trail network of long and short loops. To reach it, drive north from Ketchum on Idaho Highway 75 for 1.5 miles to Adams Gulch Road, turn left and drive .75 mile to the trailhead, making sure to veer right after crossing the bridge.

Trail Creek-Corral Creek is a gentle ride through aspens near Sun Valley. Riders feel like they are slalom skiing through the quaking trees. To reach this trail, drive east from Ketchum for 3 miles on Sun Valley Road, turn right and park at Trail Creek. Bike shops have more specifics on these and other bike rides in the area. The Sun Valley Chamber of Commerce, at the corner of Fourth and Main streets in Ketchum, (208) 726-3423, also has trail maps for the area.

Fly-Fishing

The area's most popular fly-fishing water are the Big Wood River, which runs through the length of the valley where Sun Valley and Ketchum are located; Silver Creek, to the south near Picabo; and the Salmon River, which runs north from the far side of Galena Summit. The Big Wood River is easily accessible and abundant with trout. The Salmon River, among the scenic splendors of the Sawtooth Mountains, is the home of steelhead and cutthroat. Silver Creek is one of the most famous streams in the angling world, where the trout are abundant and large. Copper Basin, 35 miles east of Sun Valley, has fish of exceptional size. The Little Wood River has big brown and rainbow trout. There are also many smaller streams and mountain lakes that may be fished. September and October are the best fishing months. June marks the start of the season. Although the general fishing season is closed locally in winter, the Big Wood River remains open for catch-and-release fishing. On warm winter days from December to March, consider an afternoon of fly-fishing a welcome change from the ski slopes.

There are seven fishing guides and outfitters in the area: Bill Mason Outfitters, Sun Valley Mall, (208) 622-9305; Lost River Outfitters, 171 N. Main Street, Ketchum, (208) 726-1706; Far and Away Adventures/Middle Fork River Co., (208) 726-8888; Middle Fork River Tours,

(208) 788-6545; Silver Creek Outfitters, 500 N. Main Street, Ketchum, (208) 726-5282; Two-M River Outfitters, (208) 726-8844; and Wild Horse Creek Ranch, 4387 Wild Horse Creek Road, Mackay, (208) 588-2575.

(Fore information about renting and buying equipment, see Fly-Fishing Shops under Shopping in this chapter.)

Bill Mason Outfitters
Sun Valley Mall, east of Sun Valley and Dollar Rds. intersection, Sun Valley
• **(208) 622-9305**

Bill Mason Outfitters has a fishing guide service and offers fly-fishing classes for adults and kids, bike and day hunting tours and winter as well as summer and fall fly-fishing outings. His winter fly-fishing half-day guided trip for one or two people, which includes transportation and rental equipment, costs $165. His full-day spring steelhead fishing trip, which includes guiding, transportation, lunch and refreshments, costs $250 for one or two people.

Lost River Outfitters
171 N. Main St., Ketchum
• **(208) 726-1706**

The shop offers guide service to the Big Lost, Silver Creek, Big Wood, Little Wood and Salmon rivers and also to Yellowstone National Park. It is not unusual for it to have 10 to 12 guides out with customers on the same day. Lost River is an authorized agent for Frontiers, a sporting adventure travel agent. Its guides have been bonefishing in Turks and Caicos, brown trout fishing in New Zealand, sea trout fishing in Tierra del Fuego and tarpon fishing in Belize, and they would be happy to guide you in these places. The shop prides itself on teaching beginners fly-fishing etiquette, which it says is the new approach. Before, numbers and size of fish that were caught, rather than why and how to catch fish, were most important. The shop charges $235 for a five- to six-hour guided trip, $285 for a full day with lunch, $185 for winter trips and $285 for steelhead trips in March and April.

Silver Creek Outfitters
507 N. Main St., Ketchum
• **(208) 726-5282**

Silver Creek's guides are prepared to take

anyone from a first-time beginner to experienced expert to Silver Creek, the Big Wood River, Big Lost River and other waters. Free casting clinics, which include the use of fly rods, are offered on Monday evenings during the summer. The shop prides itself on the quality of its rental gear, which includes graphite fly-rods, hip waders, chest waders, neoprene waders and float tubes. The shop charges $235 for a five- to six-hour Big Wood River Valley and Silver Creek guided fly-fishing trip for two people; and $295 for an all-day trip outside the Big Wood River Valley for two people, with lunch included. Silver Creek Outfitters also offers a winter fishing package, good from December 1 to the end of March, for two people that costs $195.

Golf

Visitors to Sun Valley Resort and Sun Valley's Elkhorn Resort have priority on reservations at the 18-hole golf courses at each location. They are top, popular courses, so if golf is important to your visit, you may want to stay at either resort, and reserve your tee time well ahead of time.

Sun Valley Course
Sun Valley Resort, Sun Valley and Dollar Rds., Sun Valley • (208) 622-2251

This course has been rated by *Golf Digest* as one of the best 100 golf courses in the United States. Designed by Robert Trent Jones Jr., it's a pretty 6565-yard layout with lots of streams and ponds that winds up and down Trail Creek. It has hills, good views, trees and plenty of challenge. Guest green fees for 18 holes cost $73; for a nonguest, $83. An electric cart rental is $11 a person for nine holes and $15 a person for 18 holes.

Elkhorn Golf Course
Sun Valley's Elkhorn Resort, Dollar and Elkhorn Rds., Sun Valley • (208) 622-4511

Like Sun Valley's course, this one was designed by Robert Trent Jones Jr. It's longer, more wide open and more forgiving than Sun Valley's. It also has a split personality — the front nine is mountainous, the back nine flat. The signature hole is No. 5, a 644-yard par 5.

Standing at the tee, ready to take a swing, the golfer is awarded with an awe-inspiring vista of the rugged Boulder Mountains rising out of the town of Sun Valley below. The length of the hole and its persistent downhill slope makes it a challenge even for the best golfers. *Golf Illustrated* has rated Elkhorn one of the top 25 resort courses in the country. A golf cart must be used when playing the course. Green fees, which include the use of a cart and bucket of range balls, are $74 for resort guests and $96 for nonguests.

Warm Springs Golf Course
One mile out on Warm Springs Rd., Ketchum • (208) 726-3715

This small, comfortable, nine-hole course has giant pine trees and is beside Warm Springs Creek. It's a good course for families and beginners. Green fees cost $18 for nine holes and $26 for 18 holes. Cart fees run $9 for nine holes.

Bigwood Golf Course
Saddle Rd., Ketchum • (208) 726-4024

This nine-hole, par 36 course is kept in very good shape. It stays open into mid-November, so it gets a lot of late season play. Green fees are $24 for nine holes and $35 for 18 holes. An electric cart rental costs $11 for nine holes and $15 for 18 holes.

Hiking

More than 40 miles of trails are within a 5-mile radius of Sun Valley/Ketchum. Many are used as exercise trails by Ketchum area residents, who often run or bike the trails. For quick recreation, these trails are unparalleled — from panoramic views atop Bald Mountain to golden aspen groves in Corral Creek. Due to the tremendous recreation pressure these trails receive, they are closed to use each spring during runoff months. The Sun Valley Chamber of Commerce at Fourth and Main streets in Ketchum, (208) 726-3423, has trail maps for the area. Here are four trails to get your feet moving.

Fox Creek Area Trails: These four loops of 3 to 5 miles have stunning views of the Boulder Mountains. To reach the Lake Creek Trailhead, drive north from Ketchum on Idaho

Highway 75 for 4 miles and turn left at Lake Creek Trailhead. To reach the Oregon Gulch Trailhead, drive north from Ketchum on Idaho Highway 75 for 7 miles and turn left just beyond North Fork Store onto Forest Road 143 to the start of the trail.

Adams Gulch Area Trails: This sunny canyon offers cool easy walks along Shadyside Trail, striking views on Adams Gulch Loop and Lane's Trails, and long rewarding hikes on Adams Gulch and Eve's Gulch Trails. Trail distances vary from 1.5 to 14 miles. To get there, drive north from Ketchum on Idaho Highway 75 for 1.5 miles, turn left at Adams Gulch Road, and follow this road for .75 mile to the trailhead, making sure to veer right after crossing the bridge.

Sun Valley Ski Area Trail: This is an invigorating 5-mile climb to the fire lookout on top of Bald Mountain. Be sure to climb to the viewing deck approximately 1.5 miles into the trail, where you can pick up a bit of Ketchum history. Approximately halfway up the mountain you can cool off in the shade of giant fir trees and get a drink at Louis Stur Memorial. Once on top, you will be treated to views of the nearby Boulder, Smoky and Pioneer mountains and the distant Jar Bridge Mountains of Nevada. To get there, drive west on Sun Valley Road through Ketchum. The road curves to the left onto Third Avenue. Follow this road to the River Run parking lot. Cross the bridge on foot and look for the trailhead on your right.

Trail Creek Area Trails: Four loops vary is distance from 1.5 to 3.5 miles. Proctor Mountain Trail offers a fine view of Bald Mountain and Sun Valley. Aspen Loop and Corral Creek Trails are rolling walks through aspen and mixed conifer forests. Trail Creek Trail is accessible for the disabled and features views of Trail Creek and Bald Mountain. To get there, drive east on Sun Valley Road for 3 miles, turn right and park at Trail Creek.

Horseback Riding

Horsemen's Center
Sun Valley Rd., Sun Valley
• **(208) 622-2387**
Spring and fall guided trail rides on Dollar Mountain are available, weather and trails permitting. One-hour rides cost $25 per person, and 1½-hour rides cost $36 per person. The minimum riding age is 8.

Ice Skating

Sun Valley Resort
Sun Valley and Dollar Rds., Sun Valley
• **(208) 622-2194**
The resort has indoor and outdoor skating rinks where the public may skate year-round. Admission costs $7.50 for an adult and $6 a child. Skate rental is $3. Private lessons are offered for $20, and group lessons can be arranged.

Sun Valley runs a well-known ice-skating school from early June to late August on its outdoor rink. It has more than 30 sessions a day to choose from and 10 different clinics. Its international staff includes more than 30 top professionals, many of whom are former champions. Six different plans that range from one session a day and six a week to six sessions a day and 36 a week are offered at a cost of $47 to $255.

Sun Valley's Elkhorn Resort
Elkhorn and Dollar Rds., Sun Valley
• **(208) 622-4511**
Elkhorn Plaza has a pond that freezes over in winter and may be skated on for free. Skate rentals cost $5.

Paragliding

Sun Valley Paragliding
260 First Ave. N., Ketchum
• **(208) 726-3332**
With no prior experience, you can soar the skies over Ketchum with an experienced, certified tandem pilot from Sun Valley Paragliding. The cost is $125. The company also offers a private instruction program utilizing tandem flights to teach and perfect inflight skills. This course includes multiple tandem flights, intensive ground handling, classroom and video work and radio-assisted flight instruction for initial solo flights. This five-day course costs $825.

Soaring

Sun Valley Soaring
(208) 788-3054

This company offers soaring rides in a high-performance Schweizer 2-32 sailplane that accommodates one or two passengers plus the pilot. The rides last from 30 to 40 minutes. In winter, all glider rides go above skiers on Bald Mountain. In summer, there is a morning ride above Baldy and Sun Valley and a shorter afternoon ride near Hailey. Rides cost $120 for one person and $150 for two people. On Sundays and Mondays during ski season, there is a two-for-one special — two people may ride for $120. The company also offers full service for sailplane owners — aerotows, tie-downs, start-gate and water. It organizes an annual Sailplane Regatta in the first two weeks of August.

Sports Centers and Clubs

Blaine County Aquatic Center
Fox Acres Rd., Hailey • (208) 788-2144

This is an outdoor swimming center that has a 25-yard, six-lane pool and baby pool that is open to the public in summer. It's especially known for its children's programs. A two-week swimming pass costs $35 for children and $60 for adults age 17 and older. The summer youth program, which includes many recreational activities, is divided into two five-week sessions. The cost is $40 for four days and $25 for Friday field days. More than 400 children take part in the summer programs.

Sun Valley Athletic Club
131 First Ave., Ketchum • (208) 726-3664

This club has a well-equipped weight and exercise room, a large room for aerobics and dance classes, a swimming pool with lap lanes and a Jacuzzi, and locker rooms. It offers many exercise, dance, swimming and children's classes. It costs $15 a visit, $55 for a week's pass, $85 a month, $235 for three months and

$110 for 10 visits. Guest fees are $10 when accompanied by a member. Lifetime memberships cost $250 for an individual and $225 a family member, with monthly dues running $49 to $54. The club offers day care for children at $2 an hour for a lifetime member and $3 an hour for a nonmember.

Tennis

Sun Valley Resort
Sun Valley and Dollar Rds., Sun Valley
• (208) 622-2156

The resort's 18 tennis courts are open all summer. Clinics, ball machines and videotape equipment are available. A large staff of instructors is headed by pro Mickey White. The pro shop is open daily. Resort guest court fees, per person per hour, are $8 for singles and $7 for doubles. For nonguests the per-person per-hour fees are $10 for singles and $9 for doubles. For children 10 and younger, the fees are $6 per child per day.

Sun Valley's Elkhorn Resort
Dollar and Elkhorn Rds., Sun Valley
• (208) 622-4511

The resort's center has 17 hard, leykold surface courts with a tennis pro shop and resident teaching pro. The courts are open from May through October, subject to weather. The courts are free for resort guests.

Warm Springs Tennis Club
One mile out on Warm Springs Rd.,
Ketchum • (208) 726-3715

The club has four hard tennis courts that are open to the public. The court rental cost for 1½ hours of play is $20.

Atkinson Park
Second Ave. and Sixth St., Ketchum
• (208) 726-3348

There are four outdoor courts beside Ernest Hemingway Grade School that may be used by the public for free when not being used by the school.

Index of Advertisers

Index

Going Somewhere?

Insiders' Publishing presents 51 current and upcoming titles to popular destinations all over the country (including the titles below) — and we're planning on adding many more. To order a title, go to your local bookstore or call (800) 582-2665 and we'll direct you to one.

Adirondacks	Michigan's Traverse Bay Region
Atlanta, GA	Minneapolis/St. Paul, MN
Bermuda	Mississippi
Boca Raton and the Palm Beaches, FL	Monterey Peninsula
Boulder, CO, and Rocky Mountain National Park	Myrtle Beach, SC
Bradenton/Sarasota, FL	Nashville, TN
Branson, MO, and the Ozark Mountains	New Hampshire
California's Wine Country	North Carolina's Central Coast and New Bern
Cape Cod, Nantucket and Martha's Vineyard, MA	North Carolina's Mountains
Charleston, SC	Outer Banks of North Carolina
Cincinnati, OH	The Pocono Mountains
Civil War Sites in the Eastern Theater	Relocation
Colorado's Mountains	Richmond, VA
Denver, CO	Salt Lake City
Florida Keys and Key West	Santa Fe
Florida's Great Northwest	Savannah
Golf in the Carolinas	Southwestern Utah
Indianapolis, IN	Tampa/St. Petersburg, FL
The Lake Superior Region	Tucson
Las Vegas	Virginia's Blue Ridge
Lexington, KY	Virginia's Chesapeake Bay
Louisville, KY	Washington, D.C.
Madison, WI	Wichita, KS
Maine's Mid-Coast	Williamsburg, VA
Maine's Southern Coast	Wilmington, NC
	Yellowstone

THE INSIDERS' GUIDE®

Insiders' Publishing • P.O. Box 2057 • Manteo, NC 27954
Phone (252) 473-6100 • Fax (252) 473-5869 • www.insiders.com